Ethics
and Public Policy
an introduction to ethics

Tom L. Beauchamp and
Terry P. Pinkard, editors
Georgetown University

Prentice-Hall, Inc., Englewood Cliffs, New Jersey 07632

HM
216
.E767
1983

Library of Congress Cataloging in Publication Data

Main entry under title:
Ethics and Public policy.

Includes bibliographies.
1. Social ethics—Addresses, essays, lectures.
I. Beauchamp, Tom L. II. Pinkard, Terry P.
HM216.E767 1983   170   82-11285
ISBN   0-13-290957-X

Interior design and production
supervision by Chrys Chrzanowski
Cover design by Karolina Harris
Manufacturing buyer: Harry P. Baisley

Previous edition published under the
title of *Ethics and Public Policy.*

Printed in the United States of America

10 9 8 7 6 5 4 3 2 1

ISBN 0-13-290957-X

PRENTICE-HALL INTERNATIONAL, INC., *London*
PRENTICE-HALL OF AUSTRALIA PTY. LIMITED, *Sydney*
PRENTICE-HALL CANADA, INC., *Toronto*
PRENTICE-HALL OF INDIA PRIVATE LIMITED, *New Delhi*
PRENTICE-HALL OF JAPAN, INC., *Tokyo*
PRENTICE-HALL OF SOUTHEAST ASIA PTE. LTD., *Singapore*
WHITEHALL BOOKS LIMITED, *Wellington, New Zealand*

Contents

iii

Preface

Philosophy has undergone what may appear to be dramatic changes in the last few years. Topics are now routinely treated in courses and journals that several years ago would have been considered outside the proper domain of academic philosophy. Among these new areas of concern is an enterprise commonly called "applied ethics." Here, general ethical theories are presumably applied to social and professional problems that are fundamentally moral. That is, philosophers apply the rigorous standards of the more abstract regions of ethical theory to relatively more concrete problems of public policy, professional ethics, and new problems created by the growth of technology.

The label "applied ethics" is, however, something of a misnomer. Applied philosophers do not mechanically, or even very directly, apply some general theory to a particular problem. Rather, they tend to do what philosophers have always done since Plato: They analyze concepts, submit to critical scrutiny various strategies that people use to justify policies and actions, examine the hidden presuppositions of ethical views, and offer new (and they hope better) philosophical accounts of the moral phenomena in question.

The authors represented in this book conform to this general model. No special or esoteric form of philosophy is presented. Philosophical reasoning is simply being applied to some of the more pressing ethical and public policy problems of the day. There is no mechanical application of pat ethical principles at work, and no special "field" of applied ethics can be distinguished from ethical theory itself. As represented here, applied ethics is simply good philosophy, done as it has been done for centuries.

The essays by the authors included have been chosen on the basis of depth and clarity of conceptual and ethical reflection, teachability, and significance for current controversies. Whenever possible, the essays have been arranged in a debate-like format: Divergent viewpoints have been juxtaposed, so that the reader may explore the strengths and weaknesses of alternative positions. In each of the three major parts, the readings are preceded by a lengthy editors' introduction, which sets the essays in a more general background and surveys the major arguments on each chapter topic. At the end of each chapter we have listed recommended readings.

This volume is, in effect, the second edition of an anthology originally published in 1975 as *Ethics and Public Policy*. (It cannot technically be called a second edition because of the addition of one new editor and a new subtitle.) Significant parts of the introductions from the first edition are retained here, and a few selections remain. Many persons were helpful in improving the quality of the introductions in the first edition, and we are pleased to acknowledge again an indebtedness for criticisms of those introductions to Elizabeth and Monroe Beardsley, Martin Benjamin, Dan Brock, Baruch Brody, and John Troyer. In this edition we also must acknowledge some helpful advice given by Arnold Davidson and H. Tristram Engelhardt, Jr.

We owe a great debt of gratitude to several persons who assisted us in the day-to-day preparation of this edition. Susan Lang and Dorle Vawter made helpful suggestions regarding selections, including ways to shorten them without loss of content. Mary Ellen Timbol, assisted by Kyle Ward, typed the introductions and bibliographies and was responsible for preparing the manuscript copy of the entire work. Ms. Timbol and Tim Hodges proofread the pages of the volume. Without the dedicated efforts of these conscientious people, our book could not have been efficiently brought to completion. We also wish to thank Ray O'Connell and Chrys Chrzanowski of Prentice-Hall for expertly overseeing the review and production of this work. Finally, we acknowledge with gratitude the sustained support provided to the Kennedy Institute by the Joseph P. Kennedy, Jr. Foundation.

T. L. B.
T. P.

Washington, D.C.
May, 1982

part one
Freedom

INTRODUCTION

We all want to be free from control by others, and at the same time we want to have rights to be protected against invasions by others. One person's rights limit the freedom of others, and the more others are free to do what they wish, the narrower is the protection of rights. It is a well-known adage that one's right to shake one's fist ends at another person's nose. Similarly, if one has a right to engage in private homosexual relations, then the state is not at liberty to control those relations. The first four chapters in this book deal with such relationships between freedom and rights.

However, before we turn directly to such subjects as the nature of rights, personal autonomy, and social liberty, a background in ethical theory that includes certain basic and recurring distinctions, definitions, and forms of moral reasoning is required. We begin with a fundamental distinction between two forms of moral reasoning—a distinction that provides a foundation needed for reading and criticizing essays in all the ensuing chapters of this volume.

CONSEQUENTIALISM
AND NONCONSEQUENTIALISM

Philosophers have often analyzed ethical theories and moral debates into two radically different types of arguments. These arguments are called *consequentialist* and *nonconsequentialist*. Consequentialist arguments judge the moral worth of an action by the relative goodness or badness of its consequences (what happens as a result of the action); nonconsequentialist arguments judge the moral worth of an action with regard to some feature of the action other than its consequences, usually by some measure of the intrinsic worth of the action. A fuller examination of these two approaches to moral thinking will make these abstract points clearer.

(1) One influential form of consequentialist reasoning is called *utilitarianism*. It is generally associated with the nineteenth-century British philosophers Jeremy Bentham and John Stuart Mill. They argued that we can assess the goodness or badness of actions and policies by reference to what produces the greatest possible balance of good consequences or the least possible balance of bad consequences. In taking this perspective, utilitarians invite consideration of the overall point or function of morality as a social institution, where "morality" is understood to include both shared rules of justice and other principles of the moral life. The underlying purpose of the institution of morality, utilitarians insist, is to promote human welfare by minimizing harms and maximizing benefits.

2

Mill and Bentham construed good consequences in terms of human happiness. They take "utility" to mean "what produces happiness." Of two actions or policies, A and B, if it can be determined that A has greater utility than B and will produce overall more happiness than B, then A is therefore morally preferable to B. Consider an example: Is lying wrong on a consequentialist, utilitarian model? A utilitarian might argue that if everyone lies, then eventually no one will be trusted. If nobody trusts anybody, then not only will our social lives be strained, but civilized society might not even function. However, if it is generally forbidden to lie, then society will function with less unhappiness, and our social lives will be correlatively less strained.

Two essential features of utilitarianism may be extracted from this basic reasoning of Bentham, Mill, and other utilitarians. First, utilitarianism is committed to the maximization of the good, for it asserts that we ought always to produce the greatest possible balance of value for all persons affected. The obvious means to maximization is efficiency, and utilitarians urge us to produce the *best* outcomes, not simply *good* outcomes. There is more to utilitarianism than efficiency, however, and hence a second essential feature must be considered. This feature is the utilitarians' theory of intrinsic value: Efficiency itself is simply an instrumental good. That is, efficiency is valuable strictly as a means to something else that is intrinsically good. But what things are intrinsically "good" for the utilitarian? And what does it mean to assert that some things are good in themselves and not merely good as a means to something else?

We can begin to frame an answer to this question by considering, as an illustration, the working of the stock market: Daily activities on Wall Street are not considered by anyone to be intrinsically good. The whole point is to provide a set of activities that are extrinsically good as a means to another end, such as a sense of financial security and happiness. Utilitarians believe that what we really ought to seek in life are certain experiences and conditions that are good in themselves without reference to their further consequences, and that all values are ultimately to be gauged in terms of these intrinsic goods. Health, friendship, and freedom from pain would be included among such values. An intrinsic value, then, is a value in life that we wish to possess and enjoy just for its own sake and not for something else that it brings.

However, utilitarians are in disagreement as to what constitutes the complete range of things or states that are good. Bentham and Mill believe that pleasure or happiness (which are synonymous terms in this context) alone are intrinsically good. Everything besides pleasure is merely good as a means to the end of pleasure. Later utilitarian philosophers, however, have argued that other values besides pleasure possess intrinsic worth— for example, values such as friendship, knowledge, courage, health, and beauty—and one popular contemporary approach is to appeal to the language of individual preferences. The concept of utility is understood from this perspective not in terms of experiences or states of affairs, but rather in terms of the actual preferences of an individual as determined by his or her behavior. Accordingly, to maximize a person's utility is to provide that which the person has chosen or would choose from among the available alternatives that might be produced. On any one of these theories, to maximize the utility of all persons affected by an action or policy is to maximize the utility of the aggregate group.

This utilitarian argument is thus a working out of the idea that morally right acts are those that make the world a better place for everyone. One makes the world better if and only if one's actions maximize goodness. It is important, however, to note what the utilitarian is *not* doing. First of all, the utilitarian is not arguing the simplistic thesis that the ends always justify the means. The *ends* of human actions are different from their consequences. The ends are what we aim at; the consequences are what happen as a result of what we do. A utilitarian consequentialist will always take both ends *and* means into account, since aiming for certain things has typical consequences, and using one set of means over another also has typical consequences. The utilitarian also need not argue that the majority should rule. "Promoting the greatest happiness" is not the same as "promoting the happiness of the majority." In fact, the two may clash. Even if it pleased 51 percent of a society to enslave the other 49 percent, it seems plausible that the amount of pain suffered by the 49 percent would offset the extra pleasure that the 51 percent receive by having the rest enslaved.

(2) The second model of moral reasoning mentioned above is nonconsequentialist and is most often associated with the thought of the eighteenth-century German philosopher, Immanuel Kant. It is often said in contemporary moral theory that most prominent nonconsequential theories, including Kant's, are "deontological," a technical term meaning duty-based. A deontological theory maintains that the concept of duty is independent of the concept of good, and that right actions are thus not determined by the production of goodness. Other features besides good outcomes determine the rightness of actions—for example, personal commitment, an act's being illegal, or an act's being required by a religious directive.

Kant emphasizes performing one's duty for the sake of duty and not for any other reason—one indicator that he espouses a pure form of deontology. He insists that all persons must act not only *in accordance with duty* but *for the sake of duty*. That is, the person's motive for acting must reside in a recognition of an act as resting on duty. It is not good enough, in Kant's view, that one merely performs the morally correct action, for one could perform one's duty for self-interested reasons having nothing to do with morality. For example, if a physician discloses a risk of surgery to a patient only because the physician fears a law suit, and not because of the duty of truth-telling, then the physician acts rightly but deserves no moral credit for doing so.

Kant tries to establish the ultimate basis for the validity of moral rules of duty in pure (practical) reason, not in intuition, conscience, or the production of utility. Morality, he contends, provides a rational framework of principles and rules that constrain and guide everyone, independent of personal goals and preferences. He thought all considerations of utility and self-interest secondary, because the moral worth of an agent's action depends exclusively on the moral acceptability of the rule from which the person is acting—or, as Kant prefers to say, moral acceptability depends on the rule that determines the agent's *will*. An action, therefore, has moral worth only when performed by an agent who possesses what Kant calls a good will; and a person has a good will only if the sole motive for the action is moral duty based on a valid rule.

When a person behaves according to binding moral rules valid for everyone, Kant considers that person to have an *autonomous* will. The autonomous agent must "accept" a moral principle, but this does not mean either that the principle is merely subjective or that each individual must wholly create (author or originate) his or her own moral principles. Kant holds only that each individual must will that others would accept these moral principles as ones to be acted upon; individuals must focus on the kinds of rules about which people could come to an ideal agreement. A person's autonomy consists in the ability to govern himself or herself through these moral principles. Kant develops this notion into a fundamental moral law which he characterizes as a categorical imperative that persons be treated as ends in themselves and never solely as means to the ends of others. This Kantian principle insists that one must treat persons as having their own autonomously established goals, and that one must never treat them simply as the means to one's own personal goals.

Kant's dictum "never treat persons in ways to which rational persons could not consent" obviously places a great emphasis on personal autonomy, but does it assert categorically that we can never treat another as a means to our ends? This interpretation seems to misrepresent Kant's views. He argues only that we must not treat another *exclusively* as a means to our own ends. To treat persons *merely* as means, strictly speaking, is to disregard their personhood by exploiting or otherwise using them without regard to their interests, needs, and conscientious concerns. When employees are ordered to perform odious tasks, they are treated as a means to an employer's or supervisor's ends, but they are not exclusively used for others' purposes if they do not become mere servants or objects. Kant does not prohibit this qualified "use" of persons categorically and without qualification. His imperative demands only that such persons be treated with the respect and moral dignity to which every person is entitled at all times, including those times when they are used primarily as means to the ends of others.

The difference between consequentialist and nonconsequentialist theories can be further illustrated in an example taken from Kant. A shopkeeper might decide not to shortchange his customers on two grounds. On reflection, he might decide that eventually he would be caught and when his reputation as a shortchanging shopkeeper got established, he would lose business. This reasoning would of course assess the morality of the action on the basis of consequences. Alternatively, the shopkeeper might decide on Kantian grounds that he would be using other people merely as a means to his own enrichment, that no rational person could consent to being used merely as a means, and that it is wrong on those grounds—irrespective of the consequences.

We must now leave the subject of consequential and nonconsequential reasoning. However, one of the important theoretical issues to keep in mind (when contrasting utilitarian and deontological thinking in particular) concerns a criticism made by Mill against Kant. Mill claimed that rational agents would always agree to principles that maximized utility, and that Kant relied on this consequential view himself; therefore, Kantianism collapsed into utilitarianism after all. In our readings in Part Two, John Rawls argues that ideally all would not accept utilitarianism and that this criticism is therefore false.

RIGHTS

What do these two approaches to ethical theory have to say about the moral rights mentioned at the beginning of this chapter? Moral rights, we shall now see, are valid claims derivable from some basic moral principles. Utilitarians argue that people have all and only those rights that lead to the overall promotion of utility. Kantians, by contrast, argue that people have the moral right to be treated as ends, never solely as means (and all that such a principle entails). In our readings, we will repeatedly find not only disagreement as to what moral rights, if any, there are, but strong disagreements even as to the *grounds* for deciding what rights there are. However, let us first consider the nature and grounding of rights in moral theory.

Many public policy issues are said to be matters of justice in that they concern rights or attempts to "secure" rights. Indeed, our political tradition has itself developed from a conception of "natural rights." How we define "rights" has been a matter of traditional debate, but it has often been assumed that they differ from privileges or from, for example, acts of charity. Historically, the notion of "natural"—or "moral" and "human"—rights arose from a need to check the sovereign power of states.

In this sense, rights are stronger protections of vital human interests than mere "edicts of toleration."* To say that a person or persons have a *right* to X is to say more than that the sovereign power tolerates their having something or exercising some power; it says that it would be wrong for them not to have X. Similarly, rights may be seen to be protections from a lack of sympathy from others. To say that one has a right to something is to say that people's sympathy for one's having it is irrelevant to the justice of having it, for rights are valid claims independent of others' feelings. Moral rights do not depend, as it were, on our lovability by others. Therefore, rights enable us to make claims *against* other people or institutions, such as the government. A claim may be said to be *valid* if it is derivable from some general rules or principles. By "derivable" we mean that it is "based on" or "supported by" appeal to the rules. For example, a right to privacy may be derived from general principles about the necessity to protect some features of human autonomy. We shall return to this point later.

A plausible analysis of rights is that any right entails an obligation on the part of others either to provide something or not to interfere with one's liberty. Thus, if a state promises or otherwise incurs an obligation to provide such goods as food stamps or certain forms of consumer protection, then citizens can claim an entitlement—a *positive* right—to the stamps or the protections when they meet the relevant criteria of need. The right to die, the right to privacy, the right to a healthy environment, and at least all liberty rights whatever may be treated as entailing that someone is obligated to abstain from interfering with one's intended course in life. This analysis accords with the widely accepted idea that the language of rights is translatable into the language of obligations—that is, that rights and obligations are correlative.

Many philosophers have maintained that we have *fundamental* rights, irrespective of merit, just because we are human. This view gives rise to a view of equality that is closely tied to the classical idea that humanity is a quality possessed by all people. This humanity is said to confer rights to impartial treatment in matters of justice, freedom, equality of opportunity, and so on. Thus, when members of minority groups complain about discriminatory hiring practices that destroy their human dignity and self-respect, one plausible interpretation of these complaints is that those who register them believe that their fundamental moral rights are being violated.

Everyone agrees that legal and other institutional rights exist and are commonly violated, but the status of moral rights is more puzzling, and the language of moral rights is still greeted by some with skepticism. Legal, institutional, and moral rights should therefore be distinguished from one

---

*"edicts of toleration": an official legal pronouncement requiring the toleration of some form of human behavior.

another. An *institutional right* is a claim that is supportable by reference to the basic rules of an institution. For example, by joining a club, one may, according to the rules governing the club, acquire the right to use its tennis courts; one's claim to the use of the tennis courts is justified by reference to the rules. *Legal rights* are similar. One has a legal right to something if one can derive a claim to it from rules and principles of law. Typically, legal rights are controversial, but *moral rights* are even more controversial. They are valid claims that are not necessarily derivable from legal or institutional rules, but that are derived from basic moral rules and principles such as those we studied in the section on consequential and nonconsequential reasoning. From considerations of, for example, the moral importance of respecting individuals, one might derive general moral rights such as those to life, liberty, and the pursuit of happiness.

Legal rights and moral rights are conceptually distinguishable and are often distinguishable in fact—as, for example, when one has a legal right to do something patently immoral or one has a moral right to something when no legal rule confers a right. Moreover, it is often claimed that moral rights exist independently of and can form a basis for justifying or criticizing legal rights, even though the reverse relation does not hold. For example, United Nations statements are invariably assertions of moral rights ("human or natural rights") that are aimed at reforming deficiencies in legal rights in various countries. The United States Congress, by contrast, is generally concerned with legal rights, although arguments in congressional debates often have a strong moral character.

The analysis of rights thus far suggests that rights are grounded in obligations. If so, a theory of rights would require a theory of obligations for its justification. The issue of whether there are rights to privacy, equal employment opportunity, or whatever would thus turn on whether there are certain moral obligations to provide these benefits or to ensure these liberties. Many writers in this text appeal to both consequential and nonconsequential theories of obligation in order to assert that we have some right they wish to protect by a moral theory.

AUTONOMY

Among the most frequently mentioned moral principles from which assertions about rights are derived is that of personal autonomy. *Autonomy* is generally understood as a form of personal liberty of action where the individual determines his or her own course of action in accordance with a self-designed plan. The autonomous person is said to be one who not only deliberates about and chooses such plans but who is capable of acting on the basis of such deliberations. A person of diminished autonomy, by contrast, is highly dependent on others and is, in at least some respect, incapable of deliberating or acting on the basis of such deliberations. Institutionalized populations such as prisoners and the mentally retarded may have diminished autonomy in this sense, for a form of psychological incapacitation afflicts the retarded, while a severely restricted social environment curtails the autonomy of prisoners.

The most general idea of autonomy is that of being one's own person, without constraints either by another's action or by a psychological or physical limitation. Thus, a person is autonomous if and only if he or she is self-governing. It is both tempting and common to assimilate this notion of self-governance to that of the absence of constraint, or freedom from constraint. Isaiah Berlin has warned against this assimilation.[1] The question "How is the individual person governed?" Berlin suggests, is quite different from the question "Is the person free from some governing body or force?" For the autonomous person must not only be independent of external interference from some controlling factors, but must be in control so as to govern his or her own person.

Two different aspects of autonomy may be seen by looking further at the two figures in the history of philosophy who have significantly shaped our understanding of autonomy and moral theory: Kant and Mill. Kant contrasted "heteronomy" (rule by other persons or conditions) and "autonomy." To be autonomous, in Kant's view, is to govern oneself, to make one's own choices in accordance with moral principles that are one's own but can be willed to be universally valid for everyone. Under "heteronomy," Kant included both external and internal determinations of the will, but *not* moral principles. Because one's own self-imposed rule obliges one to act, one is only complying with a self-legislated rule. One of Kant's main contributions to a theory of autonomy was his discussion of self-legislation. For him, a person is self-legislating if the reasons for actions are his or her *own* reasons, and the reasons are principled rather than arbitrary. This notion of self-directed action based on a rational principle accepted by the agent is a central ingredient in the concept of autonomy.

While Kant was largely concerned about the autonomy of the *will*, Mill was more concerned about the autonomy of *action*. As Mill recognized, the latter is more difficult to justify than the former. He argues that social and political control over individual actions is legitimate only if it is necessary to prevent harm to other individuals. He sees society as benefiting proportionately as individuals develop their own natural talents and capacities for judgment. In his discussion of individuality, Mill holds that a person "without character" is uncritically controlled by his environment— church, state, parents, family, and so on—whereas a person with true character is one of genuine individuality who takes from the culture only what he finds valuable.

[1] Isaiah Berlin, *Four Essays on Liberty* (London: Oxford University Press, 1969), p. 130.

The moral notion of respecting the autonomy of other persons can be formulated as a *principle of autonomy* that should guide our judgments about how to treat self-determining moral agents. It follows from the views advanced by Mill that insofar as an autonomous agent's actions do not infringe on the autonomous actions of others, that person should be free to perform such actions—even if they are of a type that involves serious risk for the agent and even if others consider them to be foolish. (In our readings, this will come up particularly in considerations of *paternalism*, which is defined as the limitation of another person's liberty on grounds that he or she might otherwise harm himself or herself.) Mill's ideas comprise the first aspect of the principle of autonomy. The second aspect follows from Kant's position: In evaluating the self-regarding actions of others, we ought to respect them as persons with the same right to their judgments as we have. So far as our actions with regard to others are concerned, it may be that the approaches taken by Mill and Kant do not lead to significantly different courses of action. Mill's view leads to a moral demand of noninterference with the autonomy of others in society, while Kant's leads to a moral demand that certain attitudes of respect be framed about the personhood and beliefs of others.

The idea that on at least some occasions human agents are autonomous is hardly troublesome or controversial. However, there are important issues about the extent to which exercises of individual autonomy are compatible with moral objectivity or with the universality of moral principles. Many contend that autonomy entails the reign of arbitrary, self-willed principles and choices in all important moral matters. In order to understand this viewpoint, consider the moral problem of suicide. Several writers have urged that respect for autonomy sanctions the right to commit suicide, while others have thought the extraction of such a view from considerations of autonomy incredible. In the eighteenth century David Hume argued in support of the moral permissibility of suicide, appealing heavily to an account of the right of autonomous choices. He even argued that occasionally resignation of one's life from the community "must not only be innocent, but laudable."[2] Other moral philosophers—Kant among them—have thought, however, that this conception of moral autonomy leads to an overemphasis on freedom and individuality in morals—an emphasis that threatens not only Kantian morality but all moral objectivity as well.

The principle of autonomy is accepted in contemporary ethical theory as an important—and some would say basic—ethical principle. However, one must expect ethical debate to center around arguments concerning its appropriate limitations and its implications for social freedom.

---

[2]David Hume, "On Suicide," in *Of the Standard of Taste and Other Essays*, ed. John Lenz (Indianapolis, Ind.: Bobbs-Merrill, 1965), esp. p. 158.

One would expect that the burden of proof ought not to be on those who defend or accept the principle of autonomy, which entails a presumption in favor of liberty for individuals, but should instead be on those who would wish to deny or limit it in some way. But this point is less easily defended than one might at first suppose. This leads to a debate over what Joel Feinberg calls "liberty-limiting principles" (see the essay in Chapter 3, "A Critique of Paternalism"). Following Feinberg, we can distinguish several possible principles for limiting liberty: (1) *the harm principle:* one limits a person's liberty in order to prevent him or her from harming others, (2) *paternalism:* one limits a person's liberty in order to prevent harm to himself or herself, or in order to provide some benefit to him or her, (3) *moralism:* one limits a person's liberty on grounds that what he or she is doing is a moral wrong, a sin, independently of whether or not his or her actions actually harm himself or herself or others, (4) *welfare:* one limits a person's liberty in order to provide another with a benefit. (If, for example, welfare rights exist, then they might plausibly be asserted as grounds for this kind of limitation of liberty. One might, that is, justifiably limit a person's liberty because another has a *right* to something.), and (5) *offense:* one might limit a person's liberty in order to prevent offense to others. (For example, one might prohibit certain kinds of public nudity on grounds of its offensiveness).

We shall return to several of these principles shortly. Let us first turn to the topics directly addressed in the articles in the first four chapters of this volume: *privacy, moral enforcement, paternalism,* and *freedom of expression.*

PRIVACY

In 1890 two young lawyers, Samuel D. Warren and Louis D. Brandeis (later to go on to a distinguished career as a justice on the Supreme Court) coauthored an article in the *Harvard Law Review* called "The Right to Privacy."[3] In that article, they argued that there exists a constitutional right to *privacy* distinct from other rights, one which consists of the right of an individual to be free from unauthorized publicity of his or her personal affairs. The article allegedly grew out of Warren's anger at somewhat embarrassing newspaper coverage of the arrangements for his daughter's engagement parties and wedding. Whatever the background considerations, the notion of a right to privacy caught on and the litigations, law review articles, and philosophical treatments on it have been growing ever since.

---

[3]Samuel D. Warren and Louis D. Brandeis, "The Right To Privacy," *Harvard Law Review* **4** (1890).

Despite the growth of both philosophical and popular literature and legal cases relating to privacy, it remains unclear what the right is that is being claimed. Is it a special or fundamental right on its own, or is it merely a compilation of other rights from which it is derived? The growth of sophisticated eavesdropping devices, along with the increasing requests for and storage of information by private industry and the government, have only made the question more urgent. Many are now concerned that citizens confront substantial danger of losing their privacy. But if so, then what is it they might lose? Is it such that it should not be lost?

Justice Rehnquist of the U.S. Supreme Court has recently argued that such questions simply have no clear answer. The value of privacy, whatever it is, is a value that must be balanced with other values. He illustrates this with several examples, one of which is the following: If police were to record lists of the license plates of cars belonging to patrons of a certain bar between the hours of 5:30 and 7:30 P.M. each day, and everything else was in order (the bar had a license to sell drinks, and so on), many people would consider this an invasion of privacy, even though the act of driving a car into a parking lot is not a "private" affair. However, if one imaginatively varies the story such that on two successive evenings, a patron of the bar had been murdered shortly after leaving the bar, that this took place between 5:30 and 7:30 P.M., and that the evidence suggested that the murderer had been at the bar when the patron left it, then not so many people would feel that the list-making is necessarily an invasion of privacy. Instead, it becomes a routine and necessary part of law enforcement. Rehnquist draws from this the conclusion that one must balance the effectiveness of law enforcement with individual claims to be let alone. A dogmatic insistence on privacy would undermine effective law enforcement, and an overly zealous insistence on effective law enforcement would run the danger of destroying privacy.

Rehnquist's argument, which is typical of many arguments about privacy, assumes that privacy is one good among others that must be balanced in order to maximize goodness. This view of privacy may be said to be based essentially on a consequentialist or utilitarian argument of the type discussed previously. In order to see this more clearly, we may recast Rehnquist's argument in a more explicitly utilitarian form: The utility of privacy must be balanced with the utility of effective law enforcement. Suppose one measures utility by satisfaction obtained, so that the balance must be struck in favor of a maximization of satisfaction. At some point, so Rehnquist's argument would go, the increase in satisfaction gained by additional safeguards on privacy would be offset by the anxiety and cost imposed by ineffective law enforcement. A moral right to privacy in Rehnquist's utilitarian view would be derived from general considerations concerning what would most effectively maximize overall utility, and the limitations of that right would depend on the same kinds of considerations.

Consider an alternative, nonconsequentialist assessment of the claim to privacy. Privacy, it would say, is not simply one good among others; it is a necessary condition for moral personality, or, so the argument might go, of individual autonomy. In Chapter 1, Hyman Gross makes such an argument. No person can be truly moral unless he or she is autonomous, and since privacy concerns the autonomy of the individual, it is a prime value—not just one more good to be put into the scales for weighing. This view of privacy is typical of the Kantian idea that some human interests are beyond measure, and that each individual has a worth—his or her dignity—that is incalculable. If the basis of such incalculable worth is personal autonomy, as Kantians usually take it to be, then there must be some core element of privacy that escapes utilitarian calculation.

It would be misleading, however, to think that utilitarians and Kantians necessarily come to different conclusions on this issue. The issue is not quite so simple. Kantians are not alone in linking privacy and autonomy; utilitarians such as Mill have also done so. The basis for assessing the right, however, is different in each case. Rights, it is to be remembered, are valid claims—that is, claims derivable from basic rules and principles. Utilitarians and deontologists disagree on what these basic rules and principles are. For the utilitarian, the basic principle is "maximize utility"—for example, maximize aggregate satisfaction, or the greatest numbers of preferences. For the Kantian, it is "act so that the policies which inform one's actions will show respect for persons as autonomous agents, independently of whether doing so will maximize utility."

Unfortunately, explaining what privacy is by linking it with autonomy is valuable only to the extent that we have a clear idea of what autonomy itself is and of what its value consists. The concepts of privacy and autonomy are without doubt pivotal concepts for many contemporary issues of public policy. More and more, citizens are complaining both of overregulation of their lives and of invasions of privacy. The complaints are addressed not only to government—federal, state, and local—but also to business. The debate is often obscured, however, by a failure to elucidate the concepts themselves. In Chapter 1, these concepts surface again and again as the significant points of debate. The first set of readings in the chapter concerns general reflections on the concepts and what their importance is, but the concepts reappear frequently in the other topics throughout this volume.

MORALISM AND THE
LIMITATION OF LIBERTIES

We are all opposed to having a moral view alien to our own forced on us by an external authority. Hence, when we approach discussions of moralism, or the legal enforcement of morality as such, we are inclined to be skeptical that it can be justified. On the other hand, the justification of many laws in our society is based on some form of moral belief, and this fact indicates that there is moral content already in our laws. The harm (to others) principle itself is a moral principle that provides the primary basis for a massive number of laws. Certainly immoral conduct is no trivial matter, as we all know from our own reactions to the indiscretions of politicians. Is it, then, legitimate to enforce moral views as such *if* they are of overwhelming importance to moral stability in a society? And are what we call "moral offenses," or offenses against morality and human decency, in some cases rightly subject to legal sanctions, even though they do not actually produce physical or psychological *harm* to the individuals involved?

These questions ask about the *kinds* of moral content and the *degree* of moral content that should be allowed in our laws. The issue is whether, in a pluralistic society, deviant moral conduct of any sort, however serious and controversial, is sufficient justification for limiting freedom by making such behavior illegal. This issue is especially troublesome, for example, when some sexual acts are widely regarded in a society as sexual perversions, and yet are also purely private affairs involving only consenting adults.

In considering how laws should function with reference to moral questions, especially those focused on sexual conduct, it is useful to distinguish between (1) crimes in which there is no victim because no person is directly harmed and everyone involved voluntarily consents, and (2) crimes in which there is a victim. Prostitution, homosexuality, gambling, smoking marijuana, and sexual stimulation in "massage parlors" are now familiar examples of crimes without victims. Rape—whether heterosexual or homosexual—is clearly a crime that does have a victim. The ethical issue is whether crimes without victims should be considered crimes at all.[4] Perhaps legal restrictions on homosexuality, for example, constitute unwarranted restrictions of liberty. It may be that even if the citizens of a state consider homosexual acts perverse, society should nonetheless allow individuals the personal freedom to engage in homosexual relations—and perhaps even marriage—between consenting adults, in the same way it allows such relations between heterosexual partners.

It is not because they are thought to harm citizens that crimes without victims are usually made illegal, but rather because they are thought to be inherently degrading, evil, or perverse. For this reason, states that legislate against such acts seem to become straightforwardly involved in the enforcement of morals—that is, in ensuring the maintenance of a community's moral standards. All activities involving the following

[4]There may, of course, be *indirect* victims of crimes that themselves do not have victims. If gambling houses force families below the poverty level and to a shortage of nourishing food, the children are indirect victims. It is also arguable that some participants—for example, prostitutes—*are* direct victims in an ethically significant sense.

actions—which are not limited to matters of sexual morality—have been considered candidates for such moral legislation:

1. Private use of pornographic films
2. Private use of drugs
3. Voluntary euthanasia
4. Voluntary psychosurgery
5. Gambling
6. Suicide
7. Cruelty to and experimentation on animals

It is imperative in a society that espouses the fair and nonoppressive rule of law that anyone seeking prohibitions on free choices provide adequate justification for substantial restrictions of individual freedoms. One must be able to advance some justification for legislating against certain private acts and not against other private acts that are similarly private, even if not identical in nature.

Although many philosophers have been concerned with questions about the legal enforcement of morals, Mill's monograph *On Liberty* (1859) has occupied and continues to occupy an especially prominent position. Mill inquired after the nature and limits of social control over the individual. The following passage is Mill's own summary of his central theses:

> The object of this Essay is to assert one very simple principle....That principle is, that the sole end for which mankind are warranted, individually or collectively, in interfering with the liberty of action of any of their number, is self-protection. That the only purpose for which power can be rightfully exercised over any member of a civilized community, against his will, is to prevent harm to others. His own good, either physical or moral, is not a sufficient warrant. He cannot rightfully be compelled to do or forbear because it will be better for him to do so, because it will make him happier, because in the opinion of others, to do so would be wise, or even right. These are good reasons for remonstrating with him, or reasoning with him or persuading him, or entreating him, but not for compelling him, or visiting him with any evil in case he do otherwise. To justify that, the conduct from which it is desired to deter him must be calculated to produce evil to someone else. The only part of the conduct of anyone, for which he is amenable to society, is that which concerns others. In the part which merely concerns himself, his independence is, of right, absolute.

Mill supposed he had articulated a general ethical principle that properly restricted social control over private morality, regardless of whether such control is legal, religious, economic, or of some other type. Mill defended his views with the utilitarian argument that such a principle, however dangerous to prevailing social beliefs, would produce the best possible conditions both for social progress and for the development of individual talents. Though widely disputed, his views have been enormously influential.

Since Mill, many attempts either to enforce morals or to eliminate existing enforcements have been made, but one attempt has become the classic case. In 1957 a report was produced in England by the Wolfenden Committee. This committee had been established in 1954 in response to complaints that aspects of English law dealing with homosexuality and prostitution were ineffective and unjust. The committee recommended both that English criminal law be amended so that homosexuality not be a crime, if engaged in by consenting adults, and that there be no change in existing laws that did not hold acts of prostitution intrinsically illegal. Their recommendations at several points read as if they were an application of Mill's general political-social theory. The committee first argued that firm distinctions should be drawn between crime and sin and between public decency and private morality. They then maintained that while the law must govern matters of public decency, private morality is not a matter to be legislated since "the function of the criminal law" is "to preserve public order and decency, to protect the citizen from what is offensive or injurious, and to provide sufficient safeguards against exploitation and corruption of others." They further maintained that it should not be considered the purpose of the law "to intervene in the private lives of citizens, or to seek to enforce any pattern of behavior" unless the purposes of the law outlined above were shown relevant.

The clear intent of the committee was to say that unless it could be shown that public indecency or personal exploitation were involved, the law should not prohibit activities such as homosexuality and prostitution. Their justification for this recommendation, which is both legal and ethical in character, was simply that the state does not and should not have the right to restrict any private moral actions that affect only the consenting adults involved. The state should not have this right, they argued, because of the supreme importance both social ethics and the law place on "individual freedom of choice and action in matters of private morality ... which is, in brief and crude terms, not the law's business." As we shall see in some detail, Lord Patrick Devlin is the most prominent spokesman in opposition to both Mill and the Wolfenden Report. His article, reprinted in Chapter 2, is in many respects another historical landmark.

In their struggle to provide rationally acceptable justifications for regulating or not regulating certain areas of moral conduct, ethicists have taken different positions on several fundamental issues. Three positions have typically been defended on this issue, the first unfavorable to enforcement, the other two favorable.

1. Arguments from the Principle of Individual Liberty.   The first argument springs from Mill's principle that state coercion is never permissible unless an individual's actions produce harm to others (the principle of individual liberty). This principle requires tolerance of all ethical perspectives, it is argued, and is not in the slightest in conflict with principles that require legal protection from harmful acts. Although there are several forms of this argument, the thrust of the contentions may be represented as follows: Any attempt to make immoral conduct illegal (criminal), when the conduct is not harmful to others, is unacceptable because it directly violates the principle of individual liberty. But suppose the conduct is harmful. If one is to be justifiably punished under law it must be because one's action harms someone else, not because a particular moral practice is involved. That any particular moral belief or practice is involved should be an irrelevant factor, so far as the law is concerned.

    2. Arguments from the Principle of Democratic Rule.   Here the argument is made that if some practice is regarded as an outrageously immoral action by the vast majority of citizens in a community, this in itself is sufficient to justify making the behavior illegal. It is maintained that both the principle of democratic rule and the institution of morality must be protected even at the expense of a risk to individual liberties. In democracies it is the weight of community sentiment that makes the law, and laws provide the standards of justice. Lord Devlin pays tribute, if not full allegiance, to this view when he concludes that: (1) a society is partially constituted by a "community of ideas," including moral ideas "about the way its members *should* behave and govern their lives"; and (2) if homosexuality is "a vice so abominable that its mere presence is an offense ... I do not see how society can be denied the right to eradicate it."

    3. Arguments from the Social Necessity of Morality.   Some authors have argued that the legal enforcement of morals is justified whenever threats to moral rules challenge the very order of society itself. The argument is that just as law and order through government are necessary to a stable society, so moral conformity is essential to a society's very continuation. Individual liberties are said to be protectable when, but only when, they do *not* erode those standards essential to the life of society. Lord Devlin again pays allegiance to this view when he argues that "society may use the law to preserve morality in the same way as it uses it to safeguard *anything* else that is essential to its existence."

PATERNALISM

Among the more controversial liberty-limiting principles is that of paternalism. The word "paternalism" is loosely used to refer to practices of treating individuals in the way a parent treats his or her children, but in ethical theory the word has a more restricted meaning. "Paternalism" is used here to refer to practices restricting the liberty of individuals, without their consent, where the justification for such actions is either the prevention of some harm they might do to themselves or the production of some benefit for them which they might not otherwise secure. (Paternalism in this sense should be distinguished from paternalism in the sense of "taking care of someone," for example, those who cannot take care of themselves. This latter sense is more like what we called the *welfare principle*. The main ethical issue centers on whether paternalistic justifications are morally acceptable. The *paternalistic principle*, as it will be referred to here, says that limiting a person's liberty is justified if through *one's own actions* a serious harm would be produced *to oneself* or one would fail to secure an important benefit. Those who support this general principle argue that it is justified to use the principle under certain conditions. Those who oppose paternalism argue that the principle itself is not a valid moral principle under any conditions.

Many kinds of actions, rules, and laws are commonly justified by appeal to the paternalistic principle. Examples include laws that protect drivers by requiring seat belts and motorcycle helmets, rules that do not permit a subject of biomedical research voluntarily to assume a risk when it is too great, court orders for blood transfusions when it is known that patients do not wish them, various forms of involuntary commitment to mental hospitals, and intervention to stop "rational" suicides.

The Justification of Paternalism. Any supporter of a wide-reaching paternalistic principle will specify with care precisely which goods, needs, and interests warrant paternalistic protection. In most recent formulations, it has been said that the state is justified in interfering with a person's liberty if by its interference it protects the person against his or her own actions where those actions are extremely and unreasonably risky, such as waterfall-rafting; or where they are potentially dangerous and irreversible in effect, as some drugs are. Even among supporters of justified paternalism it is widely accepted that it takes a heavy burden of justification to limit free actions by competent persons, especially since there is never direct subject consent—even if there might be second-party consent or direct consent by a prior agreement to be placed under a paternalistic power. According to this position, paternalism could be justified only if the evils prevented are greater than the evils—if any—caused by interference with his or her liberty, and if it is universally justified under relevantly similar circumstances to always treat persons in this way.

This position is defended by Dworkin in Chapter 3. Dworkin believes that paternalism should be looked at as a kind of "social insurance policy" that fully rational persons would secure for their own protection. Such persons would know, for example, that they might be strongly tempted at times to make decisions that are far-reaching, potentially dangerous, and irreversible, while at other times they might suffer extreme psychological or social pressures to do something which they truly believe too risky to be worth performing—for example, where one's honor is put in question by being challenged to fight. In still other cases, there might be dangers which persons do not sufficiently understand or appreciate but which are relevant to their conduct—for example, one might not know the facts about research on smoking. Dworkin concludes that we all ought to agree to a limited grant of legislative power to enact paternalistic laws.

Antipaternalistic Individualism. Some believe that paternalism is never justified, whatever the conditions. This position was defended in perhaps its most radical form by Mill, who argued that only the harm (to others) principle is a proper basis for justified limitations of liberty. This position is defended by Beauchamp. Against Dworkin, he argues that Mill's standard of the harm principle is sufficient by itself to ensure adequate protection by the state against harms that might befall individuals. He argues that the principle of paternalism ought not to be recognized as a valid principle for restricting liberty, because it allows, in principle, too much restriction. It is the serious adverse consequences of giving such power to the state that motivates Beauchamp to reject Dworkin's view that the fully rational person would accept paternalism. In the end, their disagreement seems to turn on whether acceptance of the principle of paternalism as valid would create a situation where, as Dworkin puts it, the "ignorance, ill-will and stupidity" of those in power might be used to override legitimate, though risky, exercises of freedom. Dworkin believes the risk of such unwarranted interference is worth taking in order to gain a kind of personal and social insurance policy, and Beauchamp believes the stakes are too high to make it worth the risk.

The issue is again one of how we justify claims to and limits of personal *autonomy*. We might put the general issue of paternalism in the following way: Does the value of free choice reside in what is chosen (its consequences) or is free choice a value on its own? Gerald Dworkin argues, for example, that the kinds of consequentialist reasons that Mill and other utilitarians employ to justify their antipaternalistic position will not yield those conclusions; he argues, rather, that consequentialists would be required to be in favor of paternalism and that only a nonconsequentialist line of argument could justify an antipaternalist position (although Dworkin himself ends up arguing for limited paternalism). Beauchamp's position is the opposite of Dworkin's, namely a defense of antipaternalism on strictly consequentialist grounds.

JOURNALISTIC FREEDOM

Questions regarding the proper role of the press and the legitimate limitations (if any) to be placed on the freedom of the press are coming more and more into prominence. The power of the press, some argue, is at least as great as that of the judiciary or the executive. Sometimes called the "fourth estate," it has come under fire in recent years on charges of "irresponsibility." Many believe that the press has abused its liberty and violated the public trust. The press and its defenders, on the other hand, argue that it serves a useful role as a public watchdog, albeit an unappointed one, that often depends on advertising from large firms for its revenue. Some hold that mistrust of the press is growing into open hostility. "We are getting to the point," argues journalist Daniel Schorr, "where a politician will be able to run against the news media as he used to run against Communism, crime or corruption—issues no longer available to some of them."[5]

The Watergate affair demonstrated the power of a press determined to expose willful wrongdoing by government officials when two reporters for the *Washington Post* uncovered an apparent conspiracy to obstruct justice by President Nixon and his closest aides. The result was the first resignation in history by a U.S. President and a series of books and movies about the affair.

Such watchdog roles by the press are generally applauded, yet many believe that in its zeal to catch and prosecute wrongdoers, the press often oversteps the bounds of propriety and does more damage than good. A debate also recently erupted over the propriety of the book *The Brethren* by Robert Woodward and Scott Armstrong, which details the inner workings of the Supreme Court. Does the book harm society by revealing too much? Does it invade privacy? Does it actually hamper the Court's operations? Or does it simply expose to public light the workings of a powerful, but until now, secretive institution? An examination of the arguments advanced to justify freedom of the press is therefore in order.

The issue has become more controversial as a result of two recent court cases. In *Zurcher v. Stanford Daily* [436 U.S. 547 (1978)], four members of the Palo Alto police department used a search warrant to search the offices of the *Stanford Daily*, the university's newspaper, in order to see if there were any photographs or negatives of an April 9, 1971 violent demonstration at the university. The purpose was to see if available photographs would disclose the identities of persons in the demonstration who assaulted police officers. No charge or insinuation of wrongdoing was leveled against the newspaper; the police simply wanted potential evidence they believed the newspaper might have. As it turned out, they found nothing beyond photographs the newspaper had already published. The newspaper filed a suit to have such searches declared unconstitutional, but the Supreme Court ruled against it, holding that the interest in gaining evidence of crime outweighs the newspaper's interest in

[5]*New York Times.* January 16, 1979, sec. A, p. 15.

confidentiality of its materials. Since neither the newspaper nor its staff were suspected of criminal conduct, the major issue centered on whose interests are to be protected while searching for evidence of a crime.

In another recent case a reporter for the *New York Times*, Myron Farber, was jailed and the *Times* heavily fined for Farber's refusal to reveal confidential sources. Farber did an investigative report on some hospital deaths. The report led to the indictment of a doctor on charges of murder. The doctor's lawyer requested that the judge order Farber to turn over his materials on the case, in order to ensure that his client receive a fair trial. Farber refused and was jailed for contempt. His lawyers argued that this order violated Farber's First Amendment rights and also violated a New Jersey "Shield Law" that provides journalists a right to refuse to disclose sources in a legal proceeding. The doctor's lawyer, on the other hand, argued that his client was thereby being denied a fair trial.

These cases raise important questions about the permissible extent of journalistic freedom. In particular, various problems about *rights* are again involved, for many arguments about freedom of the press turn on competing conceptions of rights. One also cannot ignore the rights of other affected parties, such as the police and innocent victims of criminal acts.

Again, the debate over utilitarian or Kantian principles is crucial to understanding these issues. In utilitarian theories, it counts in favor of a right if individuals exercising that right advance or secure some social goal. The rights that the press would have by a utilitarian theory would then be relative to the extent to which their having these rights tends to promote general utility. For example, arguments that anchor the freedom of the press in the need to maintain an educated electorate or in the press serving a "watchdog" role tend to be utilitarian in character. In the *Zurcher* and the *Farber* cases, it has been argued that submitting journalists to unannounced searches for their notes on the premises or forcing reporters to divulge the names of confidential sources will, respectively, put a chilling effect on investigative journalism or discourage confidential sources, which are the backbone of investigative journalism. Others, though, have argued that, valuable as the confidentiality of sources may be, they are overridden by the values of effective law enforcement.

The most familiar utilitarian argument for a right to freedom of speech (and correlatively to a right to freedom of the press) is Mill's "marketplace-of-ideas" argument. Mill argued that we should see the social and political arena as a vast marketplace where various ideas compete with each other for acceptance. Although bad, even pernicious ideas will always enter the market, they will, like all inferior products, be driven out by good ideas. In the marketplace-of-ideas, truth will always, or at least generally, triumph over time. Moreover, truth is always of greater utility to a society. While restriction of speech would no doubt keep some bad ideas off the market, it would also inevitably prevent some good ideas from entering it. Since the good ideas drive out the bad ideas, restriction of speech cannot help but be harmful to society's good.

Kantian theories, on the other hand, see the justification of rights as resting on claims that certain fundamental values are protected, such as the protection of individual dignity, respect for autonomy, or the safeguarding of individual liberties. It is maintained that these should be protected even if the awarding and exercise of these rights do not tend to advance some social goal such as general utility. Such a conception sees rights as "trumps," in Ronald Dworkin's phrase. That is, rights are viewed as claims that almost always take precedence over government counterclaims that social goals, such as cost effectiveness, are not advanced by the exercise of these rights. Such a theory, unless it is held in an extreme form—"Though the heavens may fall, let justice be done"—typically sees rights as "trumping" social goals, except in events of catastrophe, such as published information tipping off an enemy in wartime. Of course, if the value protected by the right—for example, individual dignity—is not at stake, and some other value—for example, not damaging another's reputation—is, or most important, when *competing rights* clash, then the two "trumps" must be balanced to see which is weightier. Many recent arguments concerning freedom of the press are built on this conception of the problem. In the *Farber* case, it has been argued that Farber's right to keep his sources confidential conflicts with the doctor's right to a fair trial, and the only resolution can come by weighing the two rights.

One troublesome conflict arises over what may be called *society's rights* as opposed to an *individual's rights*. It is unclear how this conflict is to be understood. If it involves conflicts other than between individuals, how are we to understand "society"? Does this term simply refer to the majority? If so, then conflicts over society's rights would be analyzed as conflicts between various sets of individuals' rights. If not, then "society" as an entity must have rights of its own which are irreducible to the rights which its members have. Such views are typical of "organic" theories of the state, which see the state as an organism having an independent identity of its own and being also the subject of rights on its own.

The above considerations pertain to criteria used to decide whether someone has a right to something. We need to consider also the question, "Under what conditions would it be appropriate to limit someone's liberty?" Since the presumption is ordinarily in favor of journalistic liberty, the focus of the debate would shift to possible justifications for limitation of that liberty. Among liberty-limiting principles, only the harm principle enjoys a broadly secure status in contemporary moral theory, and it is therefore not surprising that most people turn to this principle when discussing possible liimitations of journalistic liberty. Even when material is felt to be offensive, the argument frequently turns on claims not that it should be prohibited because it is offensive, but because it is harmful to some group or social institution. Similarly, arguments from the principle of moralism often slide into arguments about harm to society, such as in the statement that attacks on the "common moral code" of a society are harmful to valuable social practices. Lord Devlin's arguments in Chapter 2 are a case in point.

It could be argued, then, that the harm principle is sufficient to prevent such harms as slander, character assault, and group libel. A more difficult harm to calculate, however, would be an invasion of privacy. Whether an intervention is a *harmful* invasion of privacy is difficult to determine in most hard cases. Does, for example, printing the names of rape victims when those names are taken from the public record constitute an unwarranted and harmful invasion of privacy? The Courts have ruled that it does not, but it is easy to see why opinion may be sharply divided on this issue.

Arguments about limitations on journalistic liberty that turn on the harm principle do, in many cases, employ "balancing arguments." One must ask whether the so-called "right to know" on the part of the public "balances" some other right. It is not clear, however, that use of the harm principle can decide *all* issues of journalistic freedom. Problems about confidentiality of sources, for example, may not be decided on the basis of a harm. Some would argue that journalists have a right to keep information about sources confidential, that this right cannot be overridden, and moreover, that they have an obligation to their sources to protect confidentiality. But what if failure to divulge sources may result in someone's being harmed, killed, or, more likely—having their right to a fair trial denied—as in the *Farber* case? Under these conditions one has a conflict of rights that can perhaps be adjudicated only by a "balancing" of either harms or rights. Which, then, would be the greater injustice, violating a journalist's right to keep his or her sources confidential, or violating a person's right to a fair trial? On the other hand, if there is no overriding right to confidentiality of sources, and only the harm principle is used, then the person's right to a fair trial apparently will win out over the journalist's claim to keep the confidentiality of his or her sources. The invasion of this person's right to a fair trial clearly constitutes a harm, while the invasion of the right to protect one's sources does not necessarily result in harm to the journalist or to his or her sources. Recent court decisions have, indeed, decided against the existence of a special right to confidentiality of sources. The court distinguishes between a right to *publish* the news and a right to *gather* the news; journalists have no *special* right to the latter function—that is, they have no more right to confidentiality of sources than do nonjournalists.

In this chapter, Ronald Dworkin and Thomas Scanlon discuss alternative strategies of justifying rights to journalistic liberty. Dworkin distinguishes between arguments that protect the speaker's autonomy (Kantian arguments) and arguments that protect the audience (consequentialist, utilitarian arguments). Scanlon also discusses how denial of a right to freedom of speech is incompatible with acceptance of personal autonomy as a value. Dworkin defends a Kantian conception of balancing journalistic rights to freedom of speech and society's claims to security and attacks what seems to him to be misguided utilitarian conceptions of this balancing.

CONCLUSION

In this introduction to Part I several diverse concepts and issues have been examined. The objective has been to explore major options and distinctions to promote critical reflection on the articles in the four chapters in this Part, as well as in subsequent chapters. Many authors whose writings are found in later chapters would not subscribe without further qualification to the synopses we have presented of theories such as utilitarianism or deontology. Nonetheless, many appeals found in these authors conform to these descriptions in some form, and in this respect the broad theories traced here should prove useful for understanding the orientation of these authors.

chapter one

Privacy

The Right To Privacy

Hyman Gross

Why is privacy desirable? When is its loss objectionable and when is it not? How much privacy is a person entitled to? These questions challenge at the threshold our concern about protection of privacy. Usually they are pursued by seeking agreement on the boundary between morbid and healthy reticence, and by attempting to determine when unwanted intrusion or notoriety is justified by something more important than privacy. Seldom is privacy considered as the condition under which there is *control* over acquaintance with one's personal affairs by the one enjoying it, and I wish here to show how consideration of privacy in this neglected aspect is helpful in answering the basic questions. First I shall attempt to make clear this part of the idea of privacy, next suggest why privacy in this aspect merits protection, then argue that some important dilemmas are less vexing when we do get clear about these things, and finally offer a cautionary remark regarding the relation of privacy and autonomy.

From Hyman Gross, "Privacy and Autonomy," *Privacy:* Nomos XIII, J. Roland Pennock and John W. Chapman, eds. Reprinted by permission of the Publishers, Lieber-Atherton, Inc. Copyright © 1971. All rights reserved.

What in general is it that makes certain conduct offensive to privacy? To distinguish obnoxious from innocent interference with privacy we must first see clearly what constitutes loss of privacy at all, and then determine why loss of privacy when it does occur is sometimes objectionable and sometimes not.

Loss of privacy occurs when the limits one has set on acquaintance with his personal affairs are not respected. Almost always we mean not respected by *others,* though in unusual cases we might speak of a person not respecting his own privacy—he is such a passionate gossip, say, that he gossips even about himself and later regrets it. Limits on acquaintance may be maintained by the physical insulation of a home, office, or other private place within which things that are to be private may be confined. Or such bounds may exist by virtue of exclusionary social conventions, for example, those governing a private conversation in a public place; or through restricting conventions which impose an obligation to observe such limits, as when disclosure is made in confidence.

Limits operate in two ways. There are restrictions on what is known, and restrictions on who may know it. Thus, a curriculum vitae furnished to or for a prospective employer is not normally an invitation to undertake a detective investigation using the items provided as clues. Nor is there normally license to communicate to others the information submitted. In both instances there would be disregard of limitations implied by considerations of privacy, unless the existence of such limitations is unreasonable under the circumstances (the prospective employer is the CIA, or the information is furnished to an employment agency). But there is no loss of privacy when such limits as do exist are respected, no matter how ample the disclosure or how extensive its circulation. If I submit a detailed account of my life while my friend presents only the barest resume of his, I am not giving up more of privacy than he. And if I give the information to a hundred employers, I lose no more in privacy than my friend who confides to only ten, provided those informed by each of us are equally restricted. More people know more about me, so my *risk* of losing privacy is greater and the threatened loss more serious. Because I am a less-private person than my friend, I am more willing to run that risk. But until there is loss of control over what is known, and by whom, my privacy is uncompromised—though much indeed may be lost in secrecy, mystery, obscurity, and anonymity.

Privacy is lost in either of two ways. It may be given up, or it may be taken away. Abandonment of privacy (though sometimes undesired) is an inoffensive loss, while deprivation by others is an offensive loss.

If one makes a public disclosure of personal matters or exposes himself under circumstances that do not contain elements of restriction on further communications, there is loss of control for which the person whose privacy is lost is himself responsible. Such abandonment may result from indifference, carelessness, or a positive desire to have others become acquainted. There are, however, instances in which privacy is abandoned though this was not intended. Consider indiscretions committed while drunk which are rued when sober. If the audience is not under some obligation (perhaps the duty of a confidant) to keep dark what was revealed, there has been a loss of privacy for which the one who suffers it is responsible. But to constitute an abandonment, the loss of privacy must result from voluntary conduct by the one losing it, and the loss must be an expectable result of such conduct. If these two conditions are not met, the person who suffers the loss cannot be said to be responsible for it. Accordingly, a forced revelation, such as an involuntary confession, is not an abandonment of privacy, because the person making it has not given up control, but has had it taken from him.

Regarding the requirement of expectability, we may see its significance by contrasting the case of a person whose conversation is overheard in Grand Central Station with the plight of someone made the victim of eavesdropping in his living room. In a public place loss of control is expectable by virtue of the circumstances of communication: Part of what we mean when we say a place is public is that there is not present the physical limitation upon which such control depends. But a place may be called private only when there is such limitation, so communication in it is expectably limited and the eavesdropping an offensive violation for which the victim is not himself responsible. And consider the intermediate case of eavesdropping on a conversation in a public place—a distant parabolic microphone focused on a street-corner conversation, or a bugging device planted in an airplane seat. The offensive character of such practices derives again from their disregard of expectable limitations, in this instance the force of an exclusionary social convention which applies to all except those whose immediate presence enables them to overhear.

So far there has been consideration of what constitutes loss of privacy, and when it is objectionable. But to assess claims for protection of privacy we must be clear also about *why* in general loss of privacy is objectionable. This becomes especially important when privacy and other things we value are in competition, one needing to be sacrificed to promote the other. It becomes important then to understand what good reasons there are for valuing privacy, and this is our next item of business.

II

There are two sorts of things we keep private, and with respect to each, privacy is desirable for somewhat different reasons. Concern for privacy is sometimes concern about what of us can become known, and to whom. This includes acquaintance with all those things which make up the person as he may become known—identity, appearance, traits of personality and character, talents, weaknesses, tastes, desires, habits, interests—in short, things which tell us who a person is and what he's like. The other kind of private matter is about our lives—what we've done, intend to do, are doing now, how we feel, what we have, what we need—and concern about privacy here is to restrict acquaintance with these matters. Together these two classes of personal matters comprise all those things which can be private. Certain items of information do indeed have aspects which fit them for either category. For example, a person's belief is something which pertains to him when viewed as characteristic of him, but pertains to the events of his life when viewed as something he has acquired, acts on, and endeavors to have others adopt.

Why is privacy of the person important? This calls mainly for consideration of what is necessary to maintain an integrated personality in a social setting. Although we are largely unaware of what influences us at the time, we are constantly concerned to control how we appear to others, and act to implement this concern in ways extremely subtle and multifarious. Models of image and behavior are noticed, imitated, adopted, so that nuances in speech, gesture, facial expression, *politesse*, and much more become a person as known on an occasion. The deep motive is to influence the reactions of others, and this is at the heart of human social accommodation. Constraints to imitation and disguise can become a pathological problem of serious proportions when concern with appearances interferes with normal functioning, but normal behavior allows, indeed requires, that we perform critically in presenting and withholding in order to effect certain appearances. If these editorial efforts are not to be wasted, we must have a large measure of control over what of us is seen and heard, when, where, and by whom. For this reason we see as offensive the candid camera which records casual behavior with the intention of later showing it as entertainment to a general audience. The victim is not at the time aware of who will see him and so does not have the opportunity to exercise appropriate critical restraint in what he says and does. Although subsequent approval for the showing eliminates grounds for objection to the publication as an offense to privacy, there remains the lingering objection to the prior disregard of limits of acquaintance which are normal to the situation and so presumably relied on by the victim at the time. The nature of the offense is further illuminated by considering its aggravation when the victim has been deliberately introduced unawares into the situation for the purpose of filming his behavior, or its still greater offensiveness if the setting is a place normally providing privacy and assumed to be private by the victim. What we have here are increasingly serious usurpations of a person's prerogative to determine how he shall appear, to whom, and on what occasion.

The same general objection applies regarding loss of privacy where there is information about our personal affairs which is obtained, accumulated, and transmitted by means beyond our control. It is, however, unlike privacy of personality in its untoward consequences. A data bank of personal information is considered objectionable, but not because it creates appearances over which we have no control. We are willing to concede that acquaintance with our reputation is in general not something we are privileged to control, and that we are not privileged to decide just what our reputation shall be. If the reputation is correct we cannot object because we do not appear as we would wish. What then are the grounds of objection to a data bank, an objection which indeed persists even if its information is correct and the inferences based on the information are sound? A good reason for objecting is that a data bank is an offense to self-determination. We are subject to being acted on by others because of conclusions about us which we do not know and whose effect we have no opportunity to counteract. There is a loss of control over reputation which is unacceptable because we no longer have the ability to try to change what is believed about us. We feel entitled to know what others believe—and why—so that we may try to change misleading impressions and on occasion show why a decision about us ought not to be based on reputation even if the reputation is justified. If our account in the data bank were made known to us and opportunity given to change its effect, we should drop most (though not all) of our objection to it. We might still fear the danger of abuse by public forces concerned more with the demands of administrative convenience than justice, but because we could make deposits and demand a statement reflecting them, we would at least no longer be in the position of having what is known and surmised about us lie beyond our control.

Two aspects of privacy have been considered separately, though situations in which privacy is violated sometimes involve both. Ordinary surveillance by shadowing, peeping, and bugging commonly consists of observation of personal behavior as well as accumulation of information. Each is objectionable for its own reasons, though in acting against the offensive practice we protect privacy in both aspects. Furthermore, privacy of personality and of personal affairs have some common ground in meriting protection, and this has to do with a person's role as a responsible moral agent.

In general we do not criticize a person for untoward occurrences which are a result of his conduct if (through no fault of his own) he lacked the ability to do otherwise. Such a person is similarly ineligible for applause for admirable things which would not have taken place but for his conduct. In both instances we claim that he is not responsible for what happened, and so should not be blamed or praised. The principle holds true regarding loss of privacy. If a person cannot control how he is made to appear (nor could he have prevented his loss of control), he is not responsible for how he appears or is thought of, and therefore cannot be criticized as displeasing or disreputable (nor extolled as the opposite). He can, of course, be condemned for conduct which is the basis of the belief about him, but that is a different matter from criticism directed solely to the fact that such a belief exists. Personal gossip (even when believed) is not treated by others as something for which the subject need answer, because its existence defies his control. Responsible appraisal of anyone whose image or reputation is a matter of concern requires that certain private items illicitly in the public domain be ignored in the assessment. A political figure may, with impunity, be known as someone who smokes, drinks, flirts, and tells dirty jokes, so long (but only so long) as this is not the public image *he* presents. The contrasting fortunes of two recent political leaders remind us that not being responsible for what is believed by others can be most important. If such a man is thought in his private life to engage in discreet though illicit liaisons he is not held accountable for rumors without more. However, once he has allowed himself to be publicly exposed in a situation which is in the slightest compromising, he must answer for mere appearances. And on this same point, we might consider why a woman is never held responsible for the way she appears in the privacy of her toilette.

To appreciate the importance of this sort of disclaimer of responsibility we need only imagine a community in which it is not recognized. Each person would be accountable for himself however he might be known, and regardless of any precautionary seclusion which was undertaken in the interest of shame, good taste, or from other motives of self-regard. In such a world modesty is sacrificed to the embarrassment of unwanted acclaim, and self-criticism is replaced by the condemnation of others. It is part of the vision of Orwell's *1984*, in which observation is so thorough that it forecloses the possibility of a private sector of life under a person's exclusionary control, and so makes him answerable for everything observed without limits of time or place. Because of this we feel such a condition of life far more objectionable than a community which makes the same oppressive social demands of loyalty and conformity but with the opportunity to be free of concern about appearances in private. In a community without privacy, furthermore, there can be no editorial privilege exercised in making oneself known to others. Consider, for example, the plight in which Montaigne would find himself. He observed that "No quality embraces us purely and universally. If it did not seem crazy to talk to oneself, there is not a day when I would not be heard growling at myself: 'Confounded fool!' And yet I do not intend that to be my definition." Respect for privacy is required to safeguard our changes of mood and mind, and to promote growth of the person through self-discovery and criticism. We want to run the risk of making fools of ourselves and be free to call ourselves fools, yet not be fools in the settled opinion of the world, convicted out of our own mouths.

III

Privacy is desirable, but rights to enjoy it are not absolute. In deciding what compromises must be made, some deep quandaries recur, and three of them at least seem more manageable in light of what has been said so far.

In the first place, insistence on privacy is often taken as implied admission that there is cause for shame. The assumption is that the only reason for keeping something from others is that one is ashamed of it (although it is conceded that sometimes there is in fact no cause for shame even though the person seeking privacy thinks there is). Those who seek information and wish to disregard interests in privacy often play on this notion by claiming that the decent and the innocent have no cause for shame and so no need for privacy; "Only those who have done or wish to do something shameful demand privacy." But it is unsound to assume that a claim for privacy implies such an admission. Pride, or at least wholesome self-regard, is the motive in many situations. The famous Warren and Brandeis article on privacy which appeared in the *Harvard Law Review* in 1890 was impelled in some measure, we are told, by Samuel Warren's chagrin. His daughter's wedding, a very social Boston affair, had been made available to the curious at every newsstand by the local press. Surely he was not ashamed of the wedding even though outraged by the publicity. Or consider Miss Roberson, the lovely lady whose picture was placed on a poster advertising the product of Franklin Mills with the eulogistic slogan "Flour of the family," thereby precipitating a lawsuit whose consequences included the first statutory protection of privacy in the United States. What was exploited was the lady's face, undoubtedly a source of pride.

Both these encroachments on privacy illustrate the same point. Things which people like about themselves are taken by them to belong to them in a particularly exclusive way, and so control over disclosure or publication is especially important to them. The things about himself which a person is most proud of he values most, and thus are things over which he is most interested to exercise control. It is true that shame is not infrequently the motive for privacy, for often we do seek to maintain conditions necessary to avoid criticism and punishment. But since it is not the only motive, the quest for privacy does not entail tacit confessions. Confusion arises here in part because an assault on privacy always does involve humiliation of the victim. But this is because he has been deprived of control over something personal which is given over to the control of others. In short, unwilling loss of privacy always results in the victim being shamed, not because of what others learn, but because they and not he may then determine who else shall know it and what use shall be made of it.

Defining the privilege to make public what is otherwise private is another source of persistent difficulty. There is a basic social interest in making available information about people, in exploring the personal aspects of human affairs, in stimulating and satisfying curiosity about others. The countervailing interest is in allowing people who have not offered themselves for public scrutiny to remain out of sight and out of mind. In much of the United States the law has strained with the problem of drawing a line of protection which accords respect to both interests. The result, broadly stated, has been recognition of a privilege to compromise privacy for news and other material whose primary purpose is to impart information, but to deny such privileged status to literary and other art, to entertainment, and generally to any appropriation for commercial purposes. Development of the law in New York after Miss Roberson's unsuccessful attempt to restrain public display of her picture serves as a good example. A statute was enacted prohibiting unauthorized use of the name, portrait, or picture of any living person for purposes of trade or advertising, and the legislation has been interpreted by the courts along the general lines indicated. But it is still open to speculation why a writer's portrayal of a real person as a character in a novel could qualify as violative, while the same account in a biographical or historical work would not. It has not been held that history represents a more important social interest than art and so is more deserving of a privileged position in making known personal matters, or, more generally, that edification is more important than entertainment. Nor is the question ever raised, as one might expect, whether an item of news is sufficiently newsworthy to enjoy a privilege in derogation of privacy. Further, it was not held that the implied statutory criterion of intended economic benefit from the use of a personality would warrant the fundamental distinctions. Indeed, the test of economic benefit would qualify both television's public affairs programs and its dramatic shows as within the statute, and the reportage of *Life* magazine would be as restricted as the films of De Mille or De Sica. But in each instance the former is in general free of the legal prohibition while the latter is not. What, then, is the basis of distinction? Though not articulated, a sound criterion does exist.

Unauthorized *use* of another person—whether for entertainment, artistic creation, or economic gain—is offensive. So long as we remain in charge of how we are used, we have no cause for complaint. In those cases in which a legal wrong is recognized, there has been use by others in disregard of this authority, but in those cases in which a privilege is found, there is not *use* of personality or personal affairs at all, at least not use in the sense of one person assuming control over another, which is the gist of the offense to autonomy. We do indeed suffer a loss of autonomy whenever the power to place us in free circulation is exercised by others, but we consider such loss offensive only when another person assumes the control of which we are deprived, when we are used and not merely exposed. Failure to make clear this criterion of offensiveness has misled those who wish to define the protectable area and they conceive the problem as one of striking an optimal balance between two valuable interests, when in fact it is a matter of deciding whether the acts complained of are offensive under a quite definite standard of offensiveness. The difficult cases here have not presented a dilemma of selecting the happy medium, but rather the slippery job of determining whether the defendant had used the plaintiff or whether he had merely caused things about him to become known, albeit to the defendant's profit. The difference is between managing another person as a means to one's own ends, which is offensive, and acting merely as a vehicle of presentation (though not gratuitously) to satisfy established social needs, which is not offensive. Cases dealing with an unauthorized biography that was heavily anecdotal and of questionable accuracy, or with an entertaining article that told the true story of a former child prodigy who became an obscure eccentric, are perplexing ones because they present elements of both offensive and inoffensive publication, and a decision turns on which is predominant.

There remains another balance-striking quandary to be dismantled. It is often said that privacy as an interest must be balanced against security. Each, we think, must sacrifice something of privacy to promote the security of all, though we are willing to risk some insecurity to preserve a measure of privacy. Pressure to reduce restrictions on wiretapping and searches by police seeks to push the balance toward greater security. But the picture we are given is seriously misleading. In the first place we must notice the doubtful assumption on which the argument rests. It may be stated this way: The greater the ability to watch what is going on, or obtain evidence of what has gone on, the greater the ability to prevent crime. It is a notion congenial to those who believe that more efficient law enforcement contributes significantly to a reduction in crime. We must, however, determine if such a proposition is in fact sound, and we must see what crimes are suppressible, even in principle, before any sacrifice of privacy can be justified. There is, at least *in limine,** much to be said for the conflicting proposition that once a generally efficient system of law enforcement exists an increase in its efficiency does not result in a corresponding reduction in crime, but only in an increase in punishments. Apart from that point, there is an objection relating more directly to what has been said here about privacy. Security and privacy are both desirable, but measures to promote each are on different moral footing. Men ought to be secure, we say, because only in that condition can they live a good life. Privacy, however, like peace and prosperity, is itself part of what we mean by a good life, a part having to do with self-respect and self-determination. Therefore, the appropriate attitudes when we are asked to sacrifice privacy for security are first a critical one which urges alternatives that minimize or do not at all require the sacrifice, and ultimately regret for loss of a cherished resource if the sacrifice proves necessary.

*_in limine:_ preliminarily

In speaking of privacy and autonomy there is some danger that privacy may be conceived as autonomy. Such confusion has been signaled in legal literature by early and repeated use of the phrase "right to be let alone" as a synonym for "right of privacy." The United States Supreme Court succumbed completely in 1965 in its opinion in *Griswold v. Connecticut,* and the ensuing intellectual disorder warrants comment.

In that case legislative prohibition of the use of contraceptives was said to be a violation of a constitutional right of privacy, at least when it affected married people. The court's opinion relied heavily on an elaborate *jeu de mots,** in which different senses of the word "privacy" were punned upon, and the legal concept generally mismanaged in ways too various to recount here. In the *Griswold* situation there had been an attempt by government to regulate personal affairs, not get acquainted with them, and so there was an issue regarding autonomy and not privacy. The opinion was not illuminating on the question of what are proper bounds for the exercise of legislative power, which was the crucial matter before the court. It is precisely the issue of what rights to autonomous determination of his affairs are enjoyed by a citizen. The *Griswold* opinion not only failed to take up that question in a forthright manner, but promoted confusion about privacy in the law by unsettling the intellectual focus on it which had been developed in torts and constitutional law. If the confusion in the court's argument was inadvertent, one may sympathize with the deep conceptual difficulties which produced it, and if it was deliberately contrived, admire its ingenuity. Whatever its origin, its effect is to muddle the separate issues, which must be analyzed and argued along radically different lines when protection is sought either for privacy or for autonomy. Hopefully, further developments will make clear that while an offense to privacy is an offense to autonomy, not every curtailment of autonomy is a compromise of privacy.

jeu de mots: play on words

The Right to Privacy

Judith Jarvis Thomson

I

Perhaps the most striking thing about the right to privacy is that nobody seems to have any very clear idea what it is. Consider, for example, the

Judith Jarvis Thomson, "The Right to Privacy," *Philosophy & Public Affairs,* vol. 4, no. 4 (Summer 1975). Copyright © 1975 by Princeton University Press. Reprinted by permission of Princeton University Press.

I am grateful to the members of the Society for Ethical and Legal Philosophy for criticisms of the first draft of the following paper. Alan Sparer made helpful criticisms of a later draft.

familiar proposal that the right to privacy is the right "to be let alone." On the one hand, this doesn't seem to take in enough. The police might say, "We grant we used a special X-ray device on Smith, so as to be able to watch him through the walls of his house; we grant we trained an amplifying device on him so as to be able to hear everything he said; but we let him strictly alone: we didn't touch him, we didn't even go near him—our devices operate at a distance." Anyone who believes there is a right to privacy would presumably believe that it has been violated in Smith's case; yet he would be hard put to explain precisely how, if the right to privacy is the right to be let alone. And on the other hand, this account of the right to privacy lets in far too much. If I hit Jones on the head with a brick, I have not let him alone. Yet, while hitting Jones on the head with a brick is surely violating some right of Jones', doing it should surely not turn out to violate his right to privacy. Else, where is this to end? Is *every* violation of a right a violation of the right to privacy?

It seems best to be less ambitious, to begin with at least. I suggest, then, that we look at some specific, imaginary cases in which people would say, "There, in that case, the right to privacy has been violated," and ask ourselves precisely why this would be said, and what, if anything, would justify saying it.

II

But there is a difficulty to be taken note of first. What I have in mind is that there may not be so much agreement on the cases as I implied. Suppose that my husband and I are having a fight, shouting at each other as loud as we can; and suppose that we have not thought to close the windows, so that we can easily be heard from the street outside. It seems to me that anyone who stops to listen violates no right of ours; stopping to listen is at worst bad, Not Nice, not done by the best people. But now suppose, by contrast, that we are having a quiet fight, behind closed windows, and cannot be heard by the normal person who passes by; and suppose that someone across the street trains an amplifier on our house, by means of which he can hear what we say; and suppose that he does this in order to hear what we say. It seems to me that anyone who does this does violate a right of ours, the right to privacy, I should have thought.

But there is room for disagreement. It might be said that in neither case is there a violation of a right, that both are cases of mere bad behavior—though no doubt worse behavior in the second case than in the first, it being very much naughtier to train amplifiers on people's houses than merely to stop in the street to listen. Or, alternatively, it might be said that in both cases there is a violation of a right, the right to privacy in fact, but that the violation is less serious in the first case than in the second.

I think that these would both be wrong. I think that we have in these two cases, not merely a difference in degree, but a difference in quality:

that the passerby who stops to listen in the first case may act badly, but violates no one's rights, whereas the neighbor who uses an amplifier in the second case does not merely act badly but violates a right, the right to privacy. But I have no argument for this. I take it rather as a datum in this sense: it seems to me there would be a mark against an account of the right to privacy if it did not yield the conclusion that these two cases do differ in the way I say they do, and moreover explain why they do.

But there is one thing perhaps worth drawing attention to here: doing so may perhaps diminish the inclination to think that a right is violated in both cases. What I mean is this: There is a familiar account of rights—I speak now of rights generally, and not just of the right to privacy—according to which a man's having a right that something shall not be done to him just itself consists in its being the case that anyone who does it to him acts badly or wrongly or does what he ought not do. Thus, for example, it is said that to have a right that you shall not be killed or imprisoned just itself consists in its being the case that if anyone does kill or imprison you, he acts badly, wrongly, does what he ought not do. If this account of rights were correct, then my husband and I would have a right that nobody shall stop in the street and listen to our loud fight, since anyone who does stop in the street and listen acts badly, wrongly, does what he ought not do. Just as we have a right that people shall not train amplifiers on the house to listen to our quiet fights.

But this account of rights is just plain wrong. There are many, many things we ought not do to people, things such that if we do them to a person, we act badly, but which are not such that to do them is to violate a right of his. It is bad behavior, for example to be ungenerous and unkind. Suppose that you dearly love chocolate ice cream but that, for my part, I find that a little of it goes a long way. I have been given some and have eaten a little, enough really, since I don't care for it very much. You then, looking on, ask, "May I have the rest of your ice cream?" It would be bad indeed if I were to reply, "No, I've decided to bury the rest of it in the garden." I ought not do that; I ought to give it to you. But you have no right that I give it to you, and I violate no right of yours if I do bury the stuff.

Indeed, it is possible that an act which is not a violation of a right should be a far worse act than an act which is. If you did not merely want that ice cream but needed it, for your health perhaps, then my burying it would be monstrous, indecent, though still, of course, no violation of a right. By contrast, if you snatch it away, steal it, before I can bury it, then while you violate a right (the ice cream is mine, after all), your act is neither monstrous nor indecent—if it's bad at all, it's anyway not very bad.

From the point of view of conduct, of course, this doesn't really matter: bad behavior is bad behavior, whether it is a violation of a right or not. But if we want to be clear about *why* this or that bit of bad behavior is bad, then these distinctions do have to get made and looked into.

III

To return, then, to the two cases I drew attention to, and which I suggest we take to differ in this way: in one of them a right is violated, in the other not. It isn't, I think, the fact that an amplifying device is used in the one case, and not in the other, that is responsible for this difference. On the one hand, consider someone who is deaf: if he passes by while my husband and I are having a loud fight at an open window and turns up his hearing-aid so as to be able to hear us, it seems to me he no more violates our right to privacy than does one who stops to listen and can hear well enough without a hearing-aid. And on the other hand, suppose that you and I have to talk over some personal matters. It is most convenient to meet in the park, and we do so, taking a bench far from the path since we don't want to be overheard. It strikes a man to want to know what we are saying to each other in that heated fashion, so he creeps around in the bushes behind us and crouches back of the bench to listen. He thereby violates the right to privacy—fully as much as if he had stayed a hundred yards away and used an amplifying device to listen to us.

IV

The cases I drew attention to are actually rather difficult to deal with, and I suggest we back away from them for a while and look at something simpler.

Consider a man who owns a pornographic picture. He wants that nobody but he shall ever see that picture—perhaps because he wants that nobody shall know that he owns it, perhaps because he feels that someone else's seeing it would drain it of power to please. So he keeps it locked in his wall-safe, and takes it out to look at only at night or after pulling down the shades and closing the curtains. We have heard about his picture, and we want to see it, so we train our X-ray device on the wall-safe and look in. To do this is, I think, to violate a right of his—the right to privacy, I should think.

No doubt people who worry about violations of the right to privacy are not worried about the possibility that others will look at their *possessions*. At any rate, this doesn't worry them very much. That it is not nothing, however, comes out when one thinks on the special source of discomfort there is if a burglar doesn't go straight for the TV set and the silver, and then leave, but if he stops for a while just to look at things—e.g. at your love letters or at the mound of torn socks on the floor of your closet. The trespass and the theft *might* swamp everything else; but they might not: the burglar's merely looking around in that way might make the episode feel worse than it otherwise would have done.

So I shall suppose that we do violate this man's right to privacy if we use an X-ray device to look at the picture in his wall-safe. And now let us ask how and why.

To own a picture is to have a cluster of rights in respect of it. The cluster includes, for example, the right to sell it to whomever you like, the right to give it away, the right to tear it, the right to look at it. These rights are all "positive rights": rights to do certain things to or in respect of the picture. To own a picture is also to have certain "negative rights" in respect of it, that is, rights that others shall not do certain things to it—thus, for example, the right that others shall not sell it or give it away or tear it.

Does owning a picture also include having the negative right that others shall not look at it? I think it does. If our man's picture is good pornography, it would be pretty mingy of him to keep it permanently hidden so that nobody but him shall ever see it—a nicer person would let his friends have a look at it too. But he is within his rights to hide it. If someone is about to tear his picture, he can snatch it away: it's his, so he has a right that nobody but him shall tear it. If someone is about to look at his picture, he can snatch it away or cover it up: it's his, so he has a right that nobody but him shall look at it.

It is important to stress that he has not merely the right to snatch the picture away in order that nobody shall tear it, he has not merely the right to do everything he can (within limits) to prevent people from tearing it, he has also the right that nobody *shall* tear it. What I have in mind is this. Suppose we desperately want to tear his picture. He locks it in his wall-safe to prevent us from doing so. And suppose we are so eager that we buy a penetrating long-distance picture-tearer: we sit quietly in our apartment across the street, train the device on the picture in the wall-safe, press the button—and lo! we have torn the picture. The fact that he couldn't protect his picture against the action of the device doesn't make it all right that we use it.

Again, suppose that there was a way in which he could have protected his picture against the action of the device: the rays won't pass through platinum, and he could have encased the picture in platinum. But he would have had to sell everything else he owns in order to pay for the platinum. The fact he didn't do this does not make it all right for us to have used the device.

We all have a right to do what we can (within limits) to secure our belongings against theft. I gather, however, that it's practically impossible to secure them against a determined burglar. Perhaps only hiring armed guards or sealing the house in solid steel will guarantee that our possessions cannot be stolen; and perhaps even these things won't work. The fact (if it's a fact) that we can't guarantee our belongings against theft; the fact (if it's a fact) that though we can, the cost of doing so is wildly out of proportion to the value of the things, and therefore we don't; neither of these makes it all right for the determined burglar to walk off with them.

Now I said that if a man owns a picture he can snatch it away or he can cover it up to prevent anyone else from *looking* at it. He can also hide it in his wall-safe. But I think he has a right, not merely to do what he can (within limits) to prevent it from being looked at: he has a right that it shall not be looked at—just as he has a right that it shall not be torn or taken away from him. That he has a right that it shall not be looked at comes out, I think, in this way: if he hides it in his wall-safe, and we train our X-ray device on the wall-safe and look in, we have violated a right of his in respect of it, and the right is surely the right that it shall not be looked at. The fact that he couldn't protect his picture against the action of an X-ray device which enables us to look at it doesn't make it all right that we use the X-ray device to look at it—just as the fact that he can't protect his picture against the action of a long-distance picture-tearing device which enables us to tear his picture doesn't make it all right that we use the device to tear it.

Compare, by contrast, a subway map. You have no right to take it off the wall or cover it up: you haven't a right to do whatever you can to prevent it from being looked at. And if you do cover it up, and if anyone looks through the covering with an X-ray device, he violates no right of yours: you do not have a right that nobody but you shall look at it—it's not *yours*, after all.

Looking at a picture doesn't harm it, of course, whereas tearing a picture does. But this doesn't matter. If I use your toothbrush I don't harm it; but you, all the same, have a right that I shall not use it.

However, to have a right isn't always to claim it. Thus, on any view to own a picture is to have (among other rights) the right that others shall not tear it. Yet you might want someone else to do this and therefore (1) invite him to, or (2) get him to whether he wants to or not—e.g. by carefully placing it where he'll put his foot through it when he gets out of bed in the morning. Or again, while not positively wanting anyone else to tear the picture, you might not care whether or not it is torn, and therefore you might simply (3) let someone tear it—e.g. when, out of laziness, you leave it where it fell amongst the things the children are in process of wrecking. Or again still, you might positively want that nobody shall tear the picture and yet in a fit of absent-mindedness (4) leave it in some place such that another person would have to go to some trouble if he is to avoid tearing it, or (5) leave it in some place such that another person could not reasonably be expected to know that it still belonged to anybody.

Similarly, you might want someone else to look at your picture and therefore (1) invite him to, or (2) get him to whether he wants to or not. Or again, while not positively wanting anyone else to look at the picture, you might not care whether or not it is looked at, and therefore you might simply (3) let it be looked at. Or again still, you might positively want that nobody shall look at the picture, and yet in a fit of absent-mindedness (4) leave it in some place such that another person would have to go to some trouble if he is to avoid looking at it (at least, avert his eyes) or (5) leave it in some place such that another person could not reasonably be expected to know that it still belonged to anybody.

In all of these cases, it is permissible for another person on the one hand to tear the picture, on the other to look at it: no right of the owner's is violated. I think it fair to describe them as cases in which, though the owner had a right that the things not be done, he *waived* the right: in cases (1), (2), and (3) intentionally, in cases (4) and (5) unintentionally. It is not at all easy to say under what conditions a man has waived a right—by what acts of commission or omission and in what circumstances. The conditions vary, according as the right is more or less important; and while custom and convention, on the one hand, and the cost of securing the right, on the other hand, play very important roles, it is not clear precisely what roles. Nevertheless there plainly is such a thing as waiving a right; and given a man has waived his right to a thing, we violate no right of his if we do not accord it to him.

There are other things which may bring about that although a man had a right to a thing, we violate no right of his if we do not accord it to him: he may have transferred the right to another or he may have forfeited the right or he may still have the right, though it is overridden by some other, more stringent right. (This is not meant to be an exhaustive list.) And there are also some circumstances in which it is not clear what should be said. Suppose someone steals your picture and invites some third party (who doesn't know it's yours) to tear it or look at it; or suppose someone takes your picture by mistake, thinking it's his, and invites some third party (who doesn't know it's yours) to tear it or look at it; does the *third* party violate a right of yours if he accepts the invitation? A general theory of rights should provide an account of all of these things.

It suffices here, however, to stress one thing about rights: a man may have had a right that we shall not do a thing, he may even still have a right that we shall not do it, consistently with its being the case that we violate no right of his if we go ahead.

If this is correct, we are on the way to what we want. I said earlier that when we trained our X-ray device on that man's wall-safe in order to have a look at his pornographic picture, we violated a right of his, the right to privacy, in fact. It now turns out (if I am right) that we violated a property right of his, specifically the negative right that others shall not look at the picture, this being one of the (many) rights which his owning the picture consists of. I shall come back a little later to the way in which these rights interconnect.

V

We do not, of course, care nearly as much about our possessions as we care about ourselves. We do not want people looking at our torn socks; but it would be much worse to have people watch us make faces at ourselves in the mirror when we thought no one was looking or listen to us while we fight with our families. So you might think I have spent far too much time on that pornographic picture.

But in fact, if what I said about pornographic pictures was correct, then the point about ourselves comes through easily enough. For if we have fairly stringent rights over our property, we have very much more stringent rights over our own persons. None of you came to possess your knee in exactly the way in which you came to possess your shoes or your pornographic pictures: I take it you neither bought nor inherited your left knee. And I suppose you could not very well sell your left knee. But that isn't because it isn't yours to sell—some women used to sell their hair, and some people nowadays sell their blood—but only because who'd buy a used left knee? For if anyone wanted to, you are the only one with a right to sell yours. Again, it's a nasty business to damage a knee; but you've a right to damage yours, and certainly nobody else has—its being your left knee includes your having the right that nobody else but you shall damage it. And, as I think, it also includes your having the right that nobody else shall touch it or look at it. Of course you might invite somebody to touch or look at your left knee; or you might let someone touch or look at it; or again still, you might in a fit of absent-mindedness leave it in some place such that another person would have to go to some trouble if he is to avoid touching or looking at it. In short, you might waive your right that your left knee not be touched or looked at. But that is what doing these things would be: waiving a right.

I suppose there are people who would be deeply distressed to learn that they had absent-mindedly left a knee uncovered, and that somebody was looking at it. Fewer people would be deeply distressed to learn that they had absent-mindedly left their faces uncovered. Most of us wouldn't, but Moslem women would; and so might a man whose face had been badly disfigured, in a fire, say. Suppose you woke up one morning and found that you had grown fangs or that you no longer had a nose; you might well want to claim a right which most of us so contentedly waive: the right that your face not be looked at. That we have such a right comes out when we notice that if a man comes for some reason or another to want his face not to be looked at, and if he therefore keeps it covered, and if we then use our X-ray device in order to be able to look at it through the covering, we violate a right of his in respect of it, and the right we violate is surely the right that his face shall not be looked at. Compare again, by contrast, a subway map. No matter how much you may want a subway map to not be looked at, if we use an X-ray device in order to be able to look at it through the covering you place over it, we violate no right of yours: you do not have a right that nobody but you shall look at it—it is not *yours*, after all.

Listening, I think, works in the same way as looking. Suppose you are an opera singer, a great one, so that lots of people want to listen to you. You might sell them the right to listen. Or you might invite them to listen or let them listen or absent-mindedly sing where they cannot help but listen. But if you have decided you are no longer willing to be listened to; if you now sing only quietly, behind closed windows and carefully sound-proofed walls; and if somebody trains an amplifier on your house so as to be able to listen, he violates a right, the right to not be listened to.

These rights—the right to not be looked at and the right to not be listened to[1]—are analogous to rights we have over our property. It sounds funny to say we have such rights. They are not mentioned when we give lists of rights. When we talk of rights, those that come to mind are the grand ones: the right to life, the right to liberty, the right to not be hurt or harmed, and property rights. Looking at and listening to a man do not harm him, but neither does stroking his left knee harm him, and yet he has a right that it shall not be stroked without permission. Cutting off all a man's hair while he's asleep will not harm him, nor will painting his elbows green; yet he plainly has a right that these things too shall not be done to him. These un-grand rights seem to be closely enough akin to be worth grouping together under one heading. For lack of a better term, I shall simply speak of "the right over the person," a right which I shall take to consist of the un-grand rights I mentioned, and others as well.

When I began, I said that if my husband and I are having a quiet fight behind closed windows and cannot be heard by the normal person who passes by, then if anyone trains an amplifier on us in order to listen he violates a right, the right to privacy, in fact. It now turns out (if I am right) that he violates our right to not be listened to, which is one of the rights included in the right over the person.

---

[1]In "A Definition of Privacy," *Rutgers Law Review,* (1974), p. 281, Richard B. Parker writes:

> The definition of privacy defended in this article is that *privacy is control over when and by whom the various parts of us can be sensed by others.* By "sensed," is meant simply seen, heard, touched, smelled, or tasted. By "parts of us," is meant the parts of our bodies, our voices, and the products of our bodies. "Parts of us" also includes objects very closely associated with us. By "closely associated" is meant primarily what is spatially associated. The objects which are "parts of us" are objects we usually keep with us or locked up in a place accessible only to us.

The right to privacy, then, is presumably the right to this control. But I find this puzzling, on a number of counts. First, why *control?* If my neighbor invents an X-ray device which enables him to look through walls, then I should imagine I thereby lose control over who can look at me: going home and closing the doors no longer suffices to prevent others from doing so. But my right to privacy is not violated until my neighbor actually does train the device on the wall of my house. It is the actual looking that violates it, not the acquisition of power to look. Second, there *are* other cases. Suppose a more efficient bugging device is invented: instead of tapes, it produces neatly typed transcripts (thereby eliminating the middlemen). One who reads those transcripts does not *hear* you, but your right to privacy is violated just as if he does.

On the other hand, this article is the first I have seen which may be taken to imply (correctly, as I think) that there are such rights as the right to not be looked at and the right to not be listened to. And in any case, Professor Parker's interest is legal rather than moral: he is concerned to find a definition which will be useful in legal contexts. (I am incompetent to estimate how successful he is in doing this.)

I am grateful to Charles Fried for drawing my attention to this article.

I had said earlier that if we use an X-ray device to look at the porno-graphic picture in a man's wall-safe, we violate his right to privacy. And it then turned out (if I was right) that we violated the right that others shall not look at the picture, which is one of the rights which his owning the pic-ture consists in.

It begins to suggest itself, then, as a simplifying hypothesis, that the right to privacy is itself a cluster of rights, and that it is not a distinct cluster of rights but itself intersects with the cluster of rights which the right over the person consists in and also with the cluster of rights which owning pro-perty consists in. That is, to use an X-ray device to look at the picture is to violate a right (the right that others shall not look at the picture) which is both one of the rights which the right to privacy consists in and also one of the rights which property-ownership consists in. Again, that to use an amplifying device to listen to us is to violate a right (the right to not be listened to) which is both one of the rights which the right to privacy consists in and also one of the rights which the right over the person consists in.

Some small confirmation for this hypothesis comes from the other listening case. I had said that if my husband and I are having a loud fight, behind open windows, so that we can easily be heard by the normal person who passes by, then if a passerby stops to listen, he violates no right of ours, and so in particular does not violate our right to privacy. Why doesn't he? I think it is because, though he listens to us, we have *let* him listen (whether intentionally or not), we have waived our right to not be listened to—for we took none of the conventional and easily available steps (such as closing the windows and lowering our voices) to prevent listening. But this would only be an explanation if waiving the right to not be listened to were waiving the right to privacy, or if it were at least waiving the only one among the rights which the right to privacy consists in which might plausibly be taken to have been violated by the passerby.

But for further confirmation, we shall have to examine some further violations of the right to privacy.

VI

The following cases are similar to the ones we have just been looking at. (a) A deaf spy trains on your house a bugging device which produces, not sounds on tape, but a typed transcript, which he then reads. (Cf. footnote 1.) (b) A blind spy trains on your house an X-ray device which produces, not views of you, but a series of bas-relief panels, which he then feels. The deaf spy doesn't listen to you, the blind spy doesn't look at you, but both violate your right to privacy just as if they did.

It seems to me that in both these cases there is a violation of that same right over the person which is violated by looking at or listening to a per-son. You have a right, not merely that you not be looked at or listened to but also that you not have your words transcribed, and that you not be modeled in bas-relief. These are rights that the spies violate, and it is these rights in virtue of the violation of which they violate your right to privacy. Of course, one may waive these rights: a teacher presumably waives the former when he enters the classroom, and a model waives the latter when he enters the studio. So these cases seem to present no new problem.

VII

A great many cases turn up in connection with information.

I should say straightaway that it seems to me none of us has a right over any fact to the effect that that fact shall not be known by others. You may violate a man's right to privacy by looking at him or listening to him; there is no such thing as violating a man's right to privacy by simply knowing something about him.

Where our rights in this area do lie is, I think, here: we have a right that certain steps shall not be taken to find out facts, and we have a right that certain uses shall not be made of facts. I shall briefly say a word about each of these.

If we use an X-ray device to look at a man in order to get personal information about him, then we violate his right to privacy. Indeed, we violate his right to privacy whether the information we want is personal or impersonal. We might be spying on him in order to find out what he does all alone in his kitchen at midnight; or we might be spying on him in order to find out how to make puff pastry, which we already know he does in the kitchen all alone at midnight; either way his right to privacy is violated. But in both cases, the simplifying hypothesis seems to hold: in both cases we violate a right (the right to not be looked at) which is both one of the rights which the right to privacy consists in and one of the rights which the right over the person consists in.

What about torturing a man in order to get information? I suppose that if we torture a man in order to find out how to make puff pastry, then though we violate his right to not be hurt or harmed, we do not violate his right to privacy. But what if we torture him to find out what he does in the kitchen all alone at midnight? Presumably in that case we violate both his right to not be hurt or harmed and his right to privacy—the latter, presumably, because it was personal information we tortured him to get. But here too we can maintain the simplifying hypothesis: we can take it that to torture a man in order to find out personal information is to violate a right (the right to not be tortured to get personal information) which is both one of the rights which the right to privacy consists in and one of the rights which the right to not be hurt or harmed consists in.

And so also for extorting information by threat: if the information is not personal, we violate only the victim's right to not be coerced by threat; if it is personal, we presumably also violate his right to privacy—in that we violate his right to not be coerced by threat to give personal information, which is both one of the rights which the right to privacy consists in and one of the rights which the right to not be coerced by threat consists in.

I think it is a plausible idea, in fact, that doing something to a man to get personal information from him is violating his right to privacy only if doing that to him is violating some right of his not identical with or included in the right to privacy. Thus writing a man a letter asking him where he was born is no violation of his right to privacy: writing a man a letter is no violation of any right of his. By contrast, spying on a man to get personal information is a violation of the right to privacy, and spying on a man for any reason is a violation of the right over the person, which is not identical with or included in (though it overlaps) the right to privacy. Again, torturing a man to get personal information is presumably a violation of the right to privacy, and torturing a man for any reason is a violation of the right to not be hurt or harmed, which is not identical with or included in (though it overlaps) the right to privacy. If the idea is right, the simplifying hypothesis is trivially true for this range of cases. If a man has a right that we shall not do such-and-such to him, then he has a right that we shall not do it to him in order to get personal information from him. And his right that we shall not do it to him in order to get personal information from him is included in both his right that we shall not do it to him, and (if doing it to him for this reason is violating his right to privacy) his right to privacy.

I suspect the situation is the same in respect of uses of information. If a man gives us information on the condition we shall not spread it, and we then spread it, we violate his right to confidentiality, whether the information is personal or impersonal. If the information is personal, I suppose we also violate his right to privacy—by virtue of violating a right (the right to confidentiality in respect of personal information) which is both one of the rights which the right to privacy consists in and one of the rights which the right to confidentiality consists in. The point holds whether our motive for spreading the information is malice or profit or anything else.

Again, suppose I find out by entirely legitimate means (e.g. from a third party who breaks no confidence in telling me) that you keep a pornographic picture in your wall-safe; and suppose that, though I know it will cause you distress, I print the information in a box on the front page of my newspaper, thinking it newsworthy: Professor Jones of State U. Keeps Pornographic Picture in Wall-Safe! Do I violate your right to privacy? I am, myself, inclined to think not. But if anyone thinks I do, he can still have the simplifying hypothesis: he need only take a stand on our having a right that others shall not cause us distress, and then add that what is violated here is the right to not be caused distress by the publication of personal information, which is one of the rights which the right to privacy consists in, and one of the rights which the right to not be caused distress consists in. Distress, after all, is the heart of the wrong (if there is a wrong in such a case): a man who positively wants personal information about himself printed in newspapers, and therefore makes plain he wants it printed, is plainly not wronged when newspapers cater to his want.

(My reluctance to go along with this is not due to a feeling that we have no such right as the right to not be caused distress: that we have such a right seems to me a plausible idea. So far as I can see, there is nothing special about physical hurts and harms; mental hurts and harms are hurts and harms too. Indeed, they may be more grave and long-lasting than the physical ones, and it is hard to see why we should be thought to have rights against the one and not against the other. My objection is, rather, that even if there is a right to not be caused distress by the publication of personal information, it is mostly, if not always, overridden by what seems to me a more stringent right, namely the public's right to a press which prints any and all information, personal or impersonal, which it deems newsworthy; and thus that in the case I mentioned no right is violated, and hence, a fortiori, the right to privacy is not violated.[2]

VIII

The question arises, then, whether or not there are *any* rights in the right to privacy cluster which aren't also in some other right cluster. I suspect there aren't any, and that the right to privacy is everywhere overlapped by other rights. But it's a difficult question. Part of the difficulty is due to its being (to put the best face on it) unclear just what is in this right to privacy cluster. I mentioned at the outset that there is disagreement on cases; and the disagreement becomes even more stark as we move away from the kinds of cases I've so far been drawing attention to which seem to me to be the central, core cases.

What should be said, for example, of the following?

(a) The neighbors make a terrible racket every night. Or they cook foul-smelling stews. Do they violate my right to privacy? Some think yes, I think not. But even if they do violate my right to privacy, perhaps all would be well for the simplifying hypothesis since their doing this is presumably a violation of another right of mine, roughly, the right to be free of annoyance in my house.

(b) The city, after a city-wide referendum favoring it, installs loudspeakers to play music in all the buses and subways. Do they violate my right to privacy? Some think yes, I think not. But again perhaps all is well: it is if those of us in the minority have a right to be free of what we (though not the majority) regard as an annoyance in public places.

---

[2] It was Warren and Brandeis, in their now classic article, "The Right to Privacy," *Harvard Law Review*, **4** (1890), who first argued that the law ought to recognize wrongs that are (they thought) committed in cases such as these. For a superb discussion of this article, see Harry Kalven, Jr., "Privacy in Tort Law—Were Warren and Brandeis Wrong?" *Law and Contemporary Problems* (Spring 1966).

(c) You are famous, and photographers follow you around, everywhere you go, taking pictures of you. Crowds collect and stare at you. Do they violate your right to privacy? Some think yes, I think not: it seems to me that if you do go out in public, you waive your right to not be photographed and looked at. But of course you, like the rest of us, have a right to be free of (what anyone would grant was) annoyance in public places; so in particular, you have a right that the photographers and crowds not press in too closely.

(d) A stranger stops you on the street and asks, "How much do you weigh?" Or an acquaintance, who has heard of the tragedy says, "How terrible you must have felt when your child was run over by that delivery truck!"[3] Or a cab driver turns around and announces, "My wife is having an affair with my psychoanalyst." Some think that your right to privacy is violated here; I think not. There is an element of coercion in such cases: The speaker is trying to force you into a relationship you do not want, the threat being your own embarrassment at having been impolite if you refuse. But I find it hard to see how we can be thought to have a right against such attempts. Of course the attempt may be an annoyance. Or a sustained series of such attempts may become an annoyance. (Consider, for example, an acquaintance who takes to stopping at your office *every morning* to ask if you slept well.) If so, I suppose a right *is* violated, namely, the right against annoyances.

(e) Some acquaintances of yours indulge in some very personal gossip about you.[4] Let us imagine that all of the information they share was arrived at without violation of any right of yours, and that none of the participants violates a confidence in telling what he tells. Do they violate a right of yours in sharing the information? If they do, there is trouble for the simplifying hypothesis, for it seems to me there is no right not identical with, or included in, the right to privacy cluster which they could be thought to violate. On the other hand, it seems to me they *don't* violate any right of yours. It seems to me we simply do not have rights against others that they shall not gossip about us.

(f) A state legislature makes it illegal to use contraceptives. Do they violate the right to privacy of the citizens of that state? No doubt certain techniques for enforcing the statute (e.g., peering into bedroom windows) would be obvious violations of the right to privacy; but is there a violation of the right to privacy in the mere enacting of the statute—in addition to the violations which may be involved in enforcing it? I think not. But it doesn't matter for the simplifying hypothesis if it is: making a kind of conduct illegal is infringing on a liberty, and we all of us have a right that our liberties not be infringed in the absence of compelling need to do so.

---

[3]Example from Thomas Nagel.
[4]Example from Gilbert Harman.

The fact, supposing it a fact, that every right in the right to privacy cluster is also in some other right cluster does not by itself show that the right to privacy is in any plausible sense a "derivative" right. A more important point seems to me to be this: The fact that we have a right to privacy does not explain our having any of the rights in the right to privacy cluster. What I have in mind is this. We have a right to not be tortured. Why? Because we have a right to not be hurt or harmed. I have a right that my pornographic picture shall not be torn. Why? Because it's mine, because I own it. I have a right to do a somersault now. Why? Because I have a right to liberty. I have a right to try to preserve my life. Why? Because I have a right to life. In these cases we explain the having of one right by appeal to the having of another which includes it. But I don't have a right to not be looked at because I have a right to privacy; I don't have a right that no one shall torture me in order to get personal information about me because I have a right to privacy; one is inclined, rather, to say that it is because I have *these* rights that I have a right to privacy.

This point, supposing it correct, connects with what I mentioned at the outset: that nobody seems to have any very clear idea what the right to privacy is. We are confronted with a cluster of rights—a cluster with disputed boundaries—such that most people think that to violate at least any of the rights in the core of the cluster is to violate the right to privacy; but what have they in common other than their being rights such that to violate them is to violate the right to privacy? To violate these rights is to not let someone alone? To violate these rights is to visit indignity on someone? There are too many acts in the course of which we do not let someone alone, in the course of which we give affront to dignity, but in the performing of which we do not violate anyone's right to privacy. That we feel the need to find something in common to all of the rights in the cluster and, moreover, feel we haven't yet got it in the very fact that they *are* all in the cluster, is a consequence of our feeling that one cannot explain our having any of the rights in the cluster in the words: "Because we have a right to privacy."

But then if, as I take it, every right in the right to privacy cluster is also in some other right cluster, there is no need to find the that-which-is-in-common to all rights in the right to privacy cluster and no need to settle disputes about its boundaries. For if I am right, the right to privacy is "derivative" in this sense: it is possible to explain in the case of each right in the cluster how come we have it without ever once mentioning the right to privacy. Indeed, the wrongness of every violation of the right to privacy can be explained without ever once mentioning it. Someone tortures you to get personal information from you? He violates your right to not be tortured to get personal information from you, and you have that right because you have the right to not be hurt or harmed—and it is because you have this right that what he does is wrong. Someone looks at your pornographic picture in your wall-safe? He violates your right that your belongings not be looked at, and you have that right because you have ownership rights—and it is because you have them that what he does is wrong. Someone uses an X-ray device to look at you through the walls of your house? He violates your right to not be looked at, and you have that right because you have rights over your person analogous to the rights you have over your property—and it is because you have these rights that what he does is wrong.

In any case, I suggest it is a useful heuristic device in the case of any purported violation of the right to privacy to ask whether or not the act is a violation of any other right, and if not whether the act *really* violates a right at all. We are still in such deep dark in respect of rights that any simplification at all would be well worth having.[5]

[5]Frederick Davis' article, "What Do We Mean by 'Right to Privacy'?" *South Dakota Law Review* (Spring 1959), concludes, in respect of tort law, that

If truly fundamental interests are accorded the protection they deserve, no need to champion a right to privacy arises. Invasion of privacy is, in reality, a complex of more fundamental wrongs. Similarly, the individual's interest in privacy itself, however real, is derivative and a state better vouchsafed by protecting more immediate rights [p. 20] ... Indeed, one can logically argue that the concept of a right to privacy was never required in the first place, and that its whole history is an illustration of how well-meaning but impatient academicians can upset the normal development of the law by pushing it too hard [p. 230].

I am incompetent to assess this article's claims about the law, but I take the liberty of warmly recommending it to philosophers who have an interest in looking further into the status and nature of the right to privacy.

SELECTED SUPPLEMENTARY READINGS

BARNES, JOHN ARUNDEL, *Who Should Know What? Social Science, Privacy, and Ethics.* New York: Cambridge University Press, 1980.

BRANDEIS, LOUIS D., AND CHARLES WARREN, "The Right to Privacy," *Harvard Law Review* 4 (1890).

CAPLAN, ARTHUR L., "On Privacy and Confidentiality in Social Science Research," in *Ethical Issues in Social Science Research,* eds. Tom L. Beauchamp, Ruth R. Faden, R. Jay Wallace, Jr., and LeRoy Walters. Baltimore: The Johns Hopkins University Press, 1982.

DAVIS, F., "What Do We Mean By 'Right' to Privacy?," *South Dakota Law Review* (Spring 1959).

DIONISOPOULOS, P. ALLAN, AND CRAIG R. DUCAT, *The Right to Privacy: Essays and Cases.* St. Paul, Minn.: West Publishing Co., 1976.

FRIED, CHARLES, "Privacy: A Rational Context," in *Today's Moral Problems* (2nd ed.), ed. Richard A. Wasserstrom. New York: Macmillan, 1979.

GARVISON, RUTH, "Privacy and the Limits of Law," *Yale Law Journal* 89 (January 1980).

GERSTEIN, ROBERT, "Privacy and Self-Incrimination," *Ethics* 80 (1970).

50   Freedom

GORDIS, LEON, AND ELLEN GOLD, "Privacy, Confidentiality, and the Use of Medical Records in Research," *Science* **207** (January 11, 1980).
GREENAWALT, KENT, "Privacy and Its Legal Protections," *Hastings Center Studies* (September 1974).
———"Privacy," in *The Encyclopedia of Bioethics*, vol. 3, ed. Warren T. Reich. New York: Macmillan, Free Press, 1978.
HUMPHREYS, LAUD, *Tearoom Trade: Impersonal Sex in Public Places*. Chicago: Aldine, 1975.
KALVEN, HARRY, JR., "Privacy in Tort Law—Were Warren and Brandeis Wrong?" *Law and Contemporary Problems* (Spring 1966).
KELMAN, HERBERT C., "Privacy and Research with Human Beings," *Journal of Social Issues* **33** (1977).
McCLOSKEY, H. J., "Privacy and the Right to Privacy," *Philosophy* **55** (1980).
PARKER, RICHARD B., "A Definition of Privacy," *Rutgers Law Review* (1974).
PENNOCK, J. ROLAND, AND JOHN W. CHAPMAN, eds., *Privacy, Nomos XIII*. New York: Lieber-Atherton, Inc., 1971.
PINKARD, TERRY, "Invasions of Privacy in Social Science Research," in *Ethical Issues in Social Science Research*, eds. Tom L. Beauchamp, Ruth R. Faden, R. Jay Wallace, Jr., and LeRoy Walters. Baltimore: The Johns Hopkins University Press, 1982.
PRIVACY PROTECTION STUDY COMMISSION, *Personal Privacy in an Information Society*. Washington, D.C.: U.S. Government Printing Office, 1977.
PROSSER, DEAN, "Privacy," *California Law Review* **48** (August 1960).
RACHELS, JAMES, "Why Privacy is Important," *Philosophy and Public Affairs* **4** (Fall 1975).
REHNQUIST, WILLIAM, "Is an Expanded Right of Privacy Consistent with Fair and Effective Law Enforcement?," *Kansas Law Review* **23** (1974).
REIMAN, J. H., "Privacy, Intimacy, and Personhood," *Philosophy and Public Affairs* **6** (Fall 1976).
RUEBHAUSEN, OSCAR M., AND ORVILLE G. BRIM, JR., "Privacy and Behavioral Research," *Columbia Law Review* **65** (1965), and *American Psychologist* **21** (1966).
SCANLON, THOMAS, "Thomson on Privacy," *Philosophy and Public Affairs* **4** (Fall 1975).
Survey Research and Privacy: Report of a Working Party. London: Social and Community Planning Research, 1973.
WASSERSTROM, RICHARD A., "Privacy," in his *Today's Moral Problems* (2nd ed.). New York: Macmillan, 1979.
WESTIN, ALAN, *Privacy and Freedom*. New York: Atheneum, 1967.
YOUNG, JOHN B., *Privacy*. New York: John Wiley, 1978.

chapter two

Moral Enforcement

Morals and the Criminal Law

Patrick Devlin

I think it is clear that the criminal law as we know it is based upon moral principle. In a number of crimes its function is simply to enforce a moral principle and nothing else. The law, both criminal and civil, claims to be able to speak about morality and immorality generally. Where does it get its authority to do this and how does it settle the moral principles which it enforces? Undoubtedly, as a matter of history, it derived both from Christian teaching. But I think that the strict logician is right when he says that the law can no longer rely on doctrines in which citizens are entitled to disbelieve. It is necessary therefore to look for some other source.

In jurisprudence ... everything is thrown open to discussion and, in the belief that they cover the whole field, I have framed three interrogatories addressed to myself to answer:

1. Has society the right to pass judgment at all on matters of morals? Ought there, in other words, to be a public morality, or are morals always a matter for private judgment?
2. If society has the right to pass judgment, has it also the right to use the weapon of the law to enforce it?
3. If so, ought it to use that weapon in all cases or only in some; and if only in some, on what principles should it distinguish?

1*

I shall begin with the first interrogatory and consider what is meant by the right of society to pass a moral judgment, that is, a judgment about what is good and what is evil. The fact that a majority of people may disapprove of a practice does not of itself make it a matter for society as a whole. Nine men out of ten may disapprove of what the tenth man is doing and still say that it is not their business. There is a case for a collective judgment (as distinct from a large number of individual opinions which sensible people may even refrain from pronouncing at all if it is upon somebody else's private affairs) only if society is affected. Without a collective judgment there can be no case at all for intervention. Let me take as an illustration the Englishman's attitude to religion as it is now and as it has been in the past. His attitude now is that a man's religion is his private affair; he may think of another man's religion that it is right or wrong, true or untrue, but not that it is good or bad. In earlier times that was not so; a man was denied the right to practice what was thought of as heresy, and heresy was thought of as destructive of society.

The language [in] . . . the Wolfenden Report suggests the view that there ought not to be a collective judgment about immorality per se. Is this what is meant by "private morality" and "individual freedom of choice and action"? Some people sincerely believe that homosexuality is neither immoral nor unnatural. Is the "freedom of choice and action" that is offered to the individual, freedom to decide for himself what is moral or immoral, society remaining neutral; or is it freedom to be immoral if he wants to be? The language of the Report may be open to question, but the conclusions at which the Committee arrive answer this question unambiguously. If society is not prepared to say that homosexuality is morally wrong, there would be no basis for a law protecting youth from "corruption" or punishing a man for living on the "immoral" earnings of a homosexual prostitute, as the Report recommends.[1] This attitude the Committee make even clearer when they come to deal with prostitution. In truth, the Report takes it for granted that there is in existence a public morality which condemns homosexuality and prostitution. What the Report seems to mean by private morality might perhaps be better described as private behaviour in matters of morals.

This view—that there is such a thing as public morality—can also be justified by *a priori* argument. What makes a society of any sort is community of ideas, not only political ideas but also ideas about the way its members should behave and govern their lives; these latter ideas are its morals. Every society has a moral structure as well as a political one: or

---

*Insertions in brackets are additions to the original text. (Ed.)

[1]Para. 76.

rather, since that might suggest two independent systems, I should say that the structure of every society is made up both of politics and morals. Take, for example, the institution of marriage. Whether a man should be allowed to take more than one wife is something about which every society has to make up its mind one way or the other. In England we believe in the Christian idea of marriage and therefore adopt monogamy as a moral principle. Consequently the Christian institution of marriage has become the basis of family life and so part of the structure of our society. It is there not because it is Christian. It has got there because it is Christian, but it remains there because it is built into the house in which we live and could not be removed without bringing it down. The great majority of those who live in this country accept it because it is the Christian idea of marriage and for them the only true one. But a non-Christian is bound by it, not because it is part of Christianity but because, rightly or wrongly, it has been adopted by the society in which he lives. It would be useless for him to stage a debate designed to prove that polygamy was theologically more correct and socially preferable; if he wants to live in the house, he must accept it as built in the way in which it is.

We see this more clearly if we think of ideas or institutions that are purely political. Society cannot tolerate rebellion; it will not allow argument about the rightness of the cause. Historians a century later may say that the rebels were right and the Government was wrong and a percipient and conscientious subject of the State may think so at the time. But it is not a matter which can be left to individual judgment.

The institution of marriage is a good example for my purpose because it bridges the division, if there is one, between politics and morals. Marriage is part of the structure of our society and it is also the basis of a moral code which condemns fornication and adultery. The institution of marriage would be gravely threatened if individual judgments were permitted about the morality of adultery; on these points there must be a public morality. But public morality is not to be confined to those moral principles which support institutions such as marriage. People do not think of monogamy as something which has to be supported because our society has chosen to organize itself upon it; they think of it as something that is good in itself and offering a good way of life and that it is for that reason that our society has adopted it. I return to the statement that I have already made, that society means a community of ideas; without shared ideas on politics, morals, and ethics no society can exist. Each one of us has ideas about what is good and what is evil; they cannot be kept private from the society in which we live. If men and women try to create a society in which there is no fundamental agreement about good and evil they will fail; if, having based it on common agreement, the agreement goes, the society will disintegrate. For society is not something that is kept together physically; it is held by the invisible bonds of common thought. If the bonds were too far relaxed the members would drift apart. A common morality is part of the bondage. The bondage is part of the price of society; and mankind, which needs society, must pay its price.

Common lawyers used to say that Christianity was part of the law of the land. That was never more than a piece of rhetoric as Lord Sumner said in *Bowman v. The Secular Society.*[2] What lay behind it was the notion which I have been seeking to expound, namely that morals—and up till a century or so ago no one thought it worth distinguishing between religion and morals—were necessary to the temporal order. In 1675 Chief Justice Hale said: "To say that religion is a cheat is to dissolve all those obligations whereby civil society is preserved."[3] In 1797 Mr. Justice Ashurst said of blasphemy that it was "not only an offence against God but against all law and government from its tendency to dissolve all the bonds and obligations of civil society."[4] By 1908 Mr. Justice Phillimore was able to say: "A man is free to think, to speak and to teach what he pleases as to religious matters, but not as to morals."[5]

2

You may think that I have taken far too long in contending that there is such a thing as public morality, a proposition which most people would readily accept, and may have left myself too little time to discuss the next question which to many minds may cause greater difficulty: to what extent should society use the law to enforce its moral judgments? But I believe that the the answer to the first question determines the way in which the second should be approached and may indeed very nearly dictate the answer to the second question. If society has no right to make judgments on morals, the law must find some special justification for entering the field of morality: if homosexuality and prostitution are not in themselves wrong, then the onus is very clearly on the lawgiver who wants to frame a law against certain aspects of them to justify the exceptional treatment. But if society has the right to make a judgment and has it on the basis that a recognized morality is as necessary to society as, say, a recognized government, then society may use the law to preserve morality in the same way as it uses it to safeguard anything else that is essential to its existence. If therefore the first proposition is securely established with all its implications, society has a prima facie right to legislate against immorality as such.

[2](1917), A.C. 406, at 457.
[3]*Taylor's Case,* 1 Vent. 293.
[4]*R. v. Williams,* 26 St. Tr. 653, at 715.
[5]*R. v. Boulter,* 72 J.P. 188.

The Wolfenden Report, notwithstanding that it seems to admit the right of society to condemn homosexuality and prostitution as immoral, requires special circumstances to be shown to justify the intervention of the law. I think that this is wrong in principle and that any attempt to approach my second interrogatory on these lines is bound to break down. I think that the attempt by the Committee does break down and that this is shown by the fact that it has to define or describe its special circumstances so widely that they can be supported only if it is accepted that the law is concerned with immorality as such.

The widest of the special circumstances are described as the provision of "sufficient safeguards against exploitation and corruption of others, particularly those who are specially vulnerable because they are young, weak in body or mind, inexperienced, or in a state of special physical, official or economic dependence." [6] The corruption of youth is a well-recognized ground for intervention by the State and for the purpose of any legislation the young can easily be defined. But if similar protection were to be extended to every other citizen, there would be no limit to the reach of the law. The "corruption and exploitation of others" is so wide that it could be used to cover any sort of immorality which involves, as most do, the cooperation of another person. Even if the phrase is taken as limited to the categories that are particularized as "specially vulnerable," it is so elastic as to be practically no restriction. This is not merely a matter of words. For if the words used are stretched almost beyond breaking-point, they still are not wide enough to cover the recommendations which the Committee make about prostitution.

Prostitution is not in itself illegal and the Committee do not think that it ought to be made so. [7] If prostitution is private immorality and not the law's business, what concern has the law with the ponce or the brothel-keeper or the householder who permits habitual prostitution? The Report recommends that the laws which make these activities criminal offences should be maintained or strengthened and brings them (so far as it goes into principle; with regard to brothels it says simply that the law rightly frowns on them) under the head of exploitation. [8] There may be cases of exploitation in this trade, as there are or used to be in many others, but in general a ponce exploits a prostitute no more than an impresario exploits an actress. The Report finds that "the great majority of prostitutes are women whose psychological makeup is such that they choose this life because they find in it a style of living which is to them easier, freer and more profitable than would be provided by any other occupation.... In

[6]Para. 13.

[7]Paras. 224, 285, and 318.

[8]Paras. 302 and 320.

the main the association between prostitute and ponce is voluntary and operates to mutual advantage."[9] The Committee would agree that this could not be called exploitation in the ordinary sense. They say: "It is in our view an oversimplification to think that those who live on the earnings of prostitution are exploiting the prostitute as such. What they are really exploiting is the whole complex of the relationship between prostitute and customer; they are, in effect, exploiting the human weaknesses which cause the customer to seek the prostitute and the prostitute to meet the demand."[10]

All sexual immorality involves the exploitation of human weaknesses. The prostitute exploits the lust of her customers and the customer the moral weakness of the prostitute. If the exploitation of human weaknesses is considered to create a special circumstance, there is virtually no field of morality which can be defined in such a way as to exclude the law.

I think, therefore, that it is not possible to set theoretical limits to the power of the State to legislate against immorality. It is not possible to settle in advance exceptions to the general rule or to define inflexibly areas of morality into which the law is in no circumstances to be allowed to enter. Society is entitled by means of its laws to protect itself from dangers, whether from within or without. Here again I think that the political parallel is legitimate. The law of treason is directed against aiding the king's enemies and against sedition from within. The justification for this is that established government is necessary for the existence of society and therefore its safety against violent overthrow must be secured. But an established morality is as necessary as good government to the welfare of society. Societies disintegrate from within more frequently than they are broken up by external pressures. There is disintegration when no common morality is observed and history shows that the loosening of moral bonds is often the first stage of disintegration, so that society is justified in taking the same steps to preserve its moral code as it does to preserve its government and other essential institutions.[11] The suppression of vice is as

[9]Para. 223.
[10]Para. 306.
[11]It is somewhere about this point in the argument that Professor Hart in *Law, Liberty and Morality* discerns a proposition which he describes as central to my thought. He states the proposition and his objection to it as follows (p. 51). "He appears to move from the acceptable proposition that *some* shared morality is essential to the existence of any society [this I take to be the proposition on p. 12] to the unacceptable proposition that a society is identical with its morality as that is at any given moment of its history, so that a change in its morality is tantamount to the destruction of a society. The former proposition might be even accepted as a necessary rather than an empirical truth depending on a quite plausible definition of society as a body of men who hold certain moral views in common. But the latter proposition is absurd. Taken strictly, it would prevent us saying that the morality of a given society had changed and would compel us instead to say that one society had disappeared and another

much the law's business as the suppression of subversive activities; it is no more possible to define a sphere of private morality than it is to define one of private subversive activity. It is wrong to talk of private morality or of the law not being concerned with immorality as such or to try to set rigid bounds to the part which the law may play in the suppression of vice. There are no theoretical limits to the power of the State to legislate against treason and sedition, and likewise I think there can be no theoretical limits to legislation against immorality. You may argue that if a man's sins affect only himself it cannot be the concern of society. If he chooses to get drunk every night in the privacy of his own home, is any one except himself the worse for it? But suppose a quarter or a half of the population got drunk every night, what sort of society would it be? You cannot set a theoretical limit to the number of people who can get drunk before society is entitled to legislate against drunkenness. The same may be said of gambling. The Royal Commission on Betting, Lotteries, and Gaming took as their test the character of the citizen as a member of society. They said: "Our concern with the ethical significance of gambling is confined to the effect which it may have on the character of the gambler as a member of society. If we

one taken its place. But it is only on this absurd criterion of what it is for the same society to continue to exist that it could be asserted without evidence than any deviation from a society's shared morality threatens its existence." In conclusion (p. 82) Professor Hart condemns the whole thesis in the lecture as based on "a confused definition of what a society is."

I do not assert that *any* deviation from a society's shared morality threatens its existence any more than I assert that *any* subversive activity threatens its existence. I assert that they are both activities which are capable in their nature of threatening the existence of society so that neither can be put beyond the law.

For the rest, the objection appears to me to be all a matter of words. I would venture to assert, for example, that you cannot have a game without rules and that if there were no rules there would be no game. If I am asked whether that means that the game is "identical" with the rules, I would be willing for the question to be answered either way in the belief that the answer would lead to nowhere. If I am asked whether a change in the rules means that one game has disappeared and another has taken its place, I would reply probably not, but that it would depend on the extent of the change.

Likewise I should venture to assert that there cannot be a contract without terms. Does this mean that an "amended" contract is a "new" contract in the eyes of the law? I once listened to an argument by an ingenious counsel that a contract, because of the substitution of one clause for another, had "ceased to have effect" within the meaning of a statutory provision. The judge did not accept the argument; but if most of the fundamental terms had been changed, I daresay he would have done.

The proposition that I make in the text is that if (as I understand Professor Hart to agree, at any rate for the purposes of the argument) you cannot have a society without morality, the law can be used to enforce morality as something that is essential to a society. I cannot see why this proposition (whether it is right or wrong) should mean that morality can never be changed without the destruction of society. If morality is changed, the law can be changed. Professor Hart refers (p. 72) to the proposition as "the use of legal punishment to freeze into immobility the morality dominant at a particular time in a society's existence." One might as well say that the inclusion of a penal section into a statute prohibiting certain acts freezes the whole statute into immobility and prevents the prohibitions from ever being modified.

These points are elaborated in the sixth lecture at pp. 15–16.

were convinced that whatever the degree of gambling this effect must be harmful we should be inclined to think that it was the duty of the state to restrict gambling to the greatest extent practicable."[12]

3

In what circumstances the State should exercise its power is the third of the interrogatories I have framed. But before I get to it I must raise a point which might have been brought up in any one of the three. How are the moral judgments of society to be ascertained? By leaving it until now, I can ask it in the more limited form that is now sufficient for my purpose. How is the law-maker to ascertain the moral judgments of society? It is surely not enough that they should be reached by the opinion of the majority; it would be too much to require the individual assent of every citizen. English law has evolved and regularly uses a standard which does not depend on the counting of heads. It is that of the reasonable man. He is not to be confused with the rational man. He is not expected to reason about anything and his judgment may be largely a matter of feeling. It is the viewpoint of the man in the street—or to use an archaism familiar to all lawyers—the man in the Clapham omnibus. He might also be called the right-minded man. For my purpose I should like to call him the man in the jury box, for the moral judgment of society must be something about which any twelve men or women drawn at random might after discussion be expected to be unanimous. This was the standard the judges applied in the days before Parliament was as active as it is now and when they laid down rules of public policy. They did not think of themselves as making law but simply as stating principles which every right-minded person would accept as valid. It is what Pollock called "practical morality," which is based not on theological or philosophical foundations but "in the mass of continuous experience half-consciously or unconsciously accumulated and embodied in the morality of common sense." He called it also "a certain way of thinking on questions of morality which we expect to find in a reasonable civilized man or a reasonable Englishman, taken at random."[13]

Immorality then, for the purpose of the law, is what every right-minded person is presumed to consider to be immoral. Any immorality is capable of affecting society injuriously and in effect to a greater or lesser extent it usually does; this is what gives the law its *locus standi.** It cannot be shut out. But—and this brings me to the third question—the individual has a *locus standi* too; he cannot be expected to surrender to the judgment

[12](1951) Cmd. 8190, para. 159.

[13]*Essays in Jurisprudence and Ethics* (1882). Macmillan, pp. 278 and 353.

*locus standi: a right of appearance in a court on a given question.

of society the whole conduct of his life. It is the old and familiar question of striking a balance between the rights and interests of society and those of the individual. This is something which the law is constantly doing in matters large and small. To take a very down-to-earth example, let me consider the right of the individual whose house adjoins the highway to have access to it; that means in these days the right to have vehicles stationary in the highway, sometimes for a considerable time if there is a lot of loading or unloading. There are many cases in which the courts have had to balance the private right of access against the public right to use the highway without obstruction. It cannot be done by carving up the highway into public and private areas. It is done by recognizing that each have rights over the whole; that if each were to exercise their rights to the full, they would come into conflict; and therefore that the rights of each must be curtailed so as to ensure as far as possible that the essential needs of each are safeguarded.

I do not think that one can talk sensibly of a public and private morality any more than one can of a public or private highway. Morality is a sphere in which there is a public interest and a private interest, often in conflict, and the problem is to reconcile the two. This does not mean that it is impossible to put forward any general statements about how in our society the balance ought to be struck. Such statements cannot of their nature be rigid or precise; they would not be designed to circumscribe the operation of the law-making power but to guide those who have to apply it. While every decision which a court of law makes when it balances the public against the private interest is an *ad hoc* decision, the cases contain statements of principle to which the court should have regard when it reaches its decision. In the same way it is possible to make general statements of principle which it may be thought the legislature should bear in mind when it is considering the enactment of laws enforcing morals.

I believe that most people would agree upon the chief of these elastic principles. There must be toleration of the maximum individual freedom that is consistent with the integrity of society. It cannot be said that this is a principle that runs all through the criminal law. Much of the criminal law that is regulatory in character—the part of it that deals with *malum prohibitum** rather than *malum in se*†—is based upon the opposite principle, that is, that the choice of the individual must give way to the convenience of the many. But in all matters of conscience the principle I have stated is generally held to prevail. It is not confined to thought and speech; it extends to action, as is shown by the recognition of the right to conscientious objection in wartime; this example shows also that conscience will be respected

---

*malum prohibitum: a thing which is wrong because it is prohibited and not because it is inherently immoral.

†*malum in se*: a wrong in itself by its very nature.

even in times of national danger. The principle appears to me to be peculiarly appropriate to all questions of morals. Nothing should be punished by the law that does not lie beyond the limits of tolerance. It is not nearly enough to say that a majority dislike a practice; there must be a real feeling of reprobation. Those who are dissatisfied with the present law on homosexuality often say that the opponents of reform are swayed simply by disgust. If that were so it would be wrong, but I do not think one can ignore disgust if it is deeply felt and not manufactured. Its presence is a good indication that the bounds of toleration are being reached. Not everything is to be tolerated. No society can do without intolerance, indignation, and disgust;[14] they are the forces behind the moral law, and indeed it can be argued that if they or something like them are not present, the feelings of society cannot be weighty enough to deprive the individuals of freedom of choice. I suppose that there is hardly anyone nowadays who would not be disgusted by the thought of deliberate cruelty to animals. No one proposes to relegate that or any other form of sadism to the realm of private morality or to allow it to be practised in public or in private. It would be possible no doubt to point out that until a comparatively short while ago nobody thought very much of cruelty to animals and also that pity and kindliness and the unwillingness to inflict pain are virtues more generally esteemed now than they have ever been in the past. But matters of this sort are not determined by rational argument. Every moral judgment, unless it claims a divine source, is simply a feeling that no right-minded man could behave in any other way without admitting that he was doing wrong. It is the power of a common sense and not the power of reason that is behind the judgments of society. But before a society can put a practice beyond the limits of tolerance there must be a deliberate judgment that the practice is injurious to society. There is, for example, a general abhorrence of homosexuality. We should ask ourselves in the first instance whether, looking at it calmly and dispassionately, we regard it as a vice so abominable that its mere presence is an offence. If that is the genuine feeling of the society in which we live, I do not see how society can be denied the right to eradicate it. Our feeling may not be so intense as that. We may feel about it that, if confined, it is tolerable, but that if it spread it might be gravely injurious; it is in this way that most societies look upon fornication, seeing it as a natural weakness which must be kept within bounds but which cannot be rooted out. It becomes then a question of balance, the danger to society in one scale and the extent of the restriction in the other. On this sort of point the value of an investigation by such a body as the Wolfenden Committee and of its conclusions is manifest.

---

[14]These words which have been much criticized, are considered again in the Preface at p. viii in *The Enforcement of Morals*.

The limits of tolerance shift. This is supplementary to what I have been saying but of sufficient importance in itself to deserve statement as a separate principle which law-makers have to bear in mind. I suppose that moral standards do not shift; so far as they come from divine revelation they do not, and I am willing to assume that the moral judgments made by a society always remain good for that society. But the extent to which society will tolerate—I mean tolerate, not approve—departures from moral standards varies from generation to generation. It may be that overall tolerance is always increasing. The pressure of the human mind, always seeking greater freedom of thought, is outwards against the bonds of society forcing their gradual relaxation. It may be that history is a tale of contraction and expansion and that all developed societies are on their way to dissolution. I must not speak of things I do not know; and anyway as a practical matter no society is willing to make provision for its own decay. I return therefore to the simple and observable fact that in matters of morals the limits of tolerance shift. Laws, especially those which are based on morals, are less easily moved. It follows as another good working principle that in any new matter of morals the law should be slow to act. By the next generation the swell of indignation may have abated and the law be left without the strong backing which it needs. But it is then difficult to alter the law without giving the impression that moral judgment is being weakened. This is now one of the factors that is strongly militating against any alteration to the law on homosexuality.

A third elastic principle must be advanced more tentatively. It is that as far as possible privacy should be respected. This is not an idea that has ever been made explicit in the criminal law. Acts or words done or said in public or in private are all brought within its scope without distinction in principle. But there goes with this a strong reluctance on the part of judges and legislators to sanction invasions of privacy in the detection of crime. The police have no more right to trespass than the ordinary citizen has; there is no general right of search; to this extent an Englishman's home is still his castle. The Government is extremely careful in the exercise even of those powers which it claims to be undisputed. Telephone tapping and interference with the mails afford a good illustration of this. A Committee of three Privy Councillors who recently inquired[15] into these activities found that the Home Secretary and his predecessors had already formulated strict rules governing the exercise of these powers and the Committee were able to recommend that they should be continued to be exercised substantially on the same terms. But they reported that the power was "regarded with general disfavour."

This indicates a general sentiment that the right to privacy is something to be put in the balance against the enforcement of the law. Ought

[15](1957) Cmd. 283.

the same sort of consideration to play any part in the formation of the law? Clearly only in a very limited number of cases. When the help of the law is invoked by an injured citizen, privacy must be irrelevant; the individual cannot ask that his right to privacy should be measured against injury criminally done to another. But when all who are involved in the deed are consenting parties and the injury is done to morals, the public interest in the moral order can be balanced against the claims of privacy. The restriction on police powers of investigation goes further than the affording of a parallel; it means that the detection of crime committed in private and when there is no complaint is bound to be rather haphazard and this is an additional reason for moderation. These considerations do not justify the exclusion of all private immorality from the scope of the law. I think that, as I have already suggested, the test of "private behaviour" should be substituted for "private morality" and the influence of the factor should be reduced from that of a definite limitation to that of a matter to be taken into account. Since the gravity of the crime is also a proper consideration, a distinction might well be made in the case of homosexuality between the lesser acts of indecency and the full offence, which on the principles of the Wolfenden Report it would be illogical to do.

Social Solidarity and the Enforcement of Morality

H. L. A. Hart

It is possible to extract from Plato's *Republic* and *Laws,* and perhaps from Aristotle's *Ethics* and *Politics,* the following thesis about the role of law in relation to the enforcement of morality: the law of the city-state exists not merely to secure that men have the opportunity to lead a morally good life, but to see that they do. According to this thesis not only may the law be used to punish men for doing what morally it is wrong for them to do, but it should be so used; for the promotion of moral virtue by these means and by others is one of the Ends or Purposes of a society complex enough to have developed a legal system. This theory is strongly associated with a specific conception of morality as a uniquely true or correct set of principles—not man-made, but either awaiting man's discovery by the use of his reason or (in a theological setting) awaiting its disclosure by revelation. I shall call this theory "the classical thesis" and not discuss it further.

From the classical thesis there is to be distinguished what I shall call

Reprinted by permission of the author and publisher, from 35 *U. Chi. L. Rev.* 1 (1967). Footnotes included.

"the disintegration thesis." This inverts the order of instrumentality between society on the one hand and morality on the other as it appears in the classical thesis; for in this thesis society is not the instrument of the moral life; rather morality is valued as the cement of society, the bond, or one of the bonds, without which men would not cohere in society. This thesis is associated strongly with a relativist conception of morality: according to it, morality may vary from society to society, and to merit enforcement by the criminal law, morality need have no rational or other specific content. It is not the quality of the morality but its cohesive power which matters. "What is important is not the quality of the creed but the strength of the belief in it. The enemy of society is not error but indifference."[1] The case for the enforcement of morality on this view is that its maintenance is necessary to prevent the disintegration of society.

The disintegration thesis, under pressure of the request for empirical evidence to substantiate the claim that the maintenance of morality is in fact necessary for the existence of society, often collapses into another thesis which I shall call "the conservative thesis." This is the claim that society has a right to enforce its morality by law because the majority have the right to follow their own moral convictions that their moral environment is a thing of value to be defended from change.[2]

The topic of this article is the disintegration thesis, but I shall discharge in relation to it only a very limited set of tasks. What I shall mainly do is attempt to discover what, when the ambiguities are stripped away, is the empirical claim which the thesis makes and in what directions is it conceivable that a search for evidence to substantiate this claim would be rewarding. But even these tasks I shall discharge only partially.

I

The disintegration thesis is a central part of the case presented by Lord Devlin[3] justifying the legal enforcement of morality at points where followers of John Stuart Mill and other latter-day liberals would consider this

---

[1] P. Devlin, *The Enforcement of Morals* (1965), p. 114 [hereinafter cited as Devlin]. *Cf. id.* at 94. "Unfortunately bad societies can live on bad morals just as well as good societies on good ones."

[2] This characterization of the conservative thesis is taken from Dworkin, "Lord Devlin and the Enforcement of Morals," 75 *Yale L.J.* 986 (1966). Professor Dworkin distinguishes the parts played in Lord Devlin's work by the disintegration thesis and the conservative thesis, and his essay is mainly concerned with the critical examination of Lord Devlin's version of the latter. The present essay, by contrast, is mainly concerned to determine what sort of evidence is required if the disintegration thesis is not to collapse into or to be abandoned for the conservative thesis.

[3] See principally the lecture by Lord Devlin entitled "The Enforcement of Morals" which he delivered as the Second Maccabaean Lecture in Jurisprudence of the British Academy and which is reproduced in Devlin, Chap. I, as "Morals and the Criminal Law."

an unjustifiable extension of the scope of the criminal law. The morality, the enforcement of which is justified according to Lord Devlin, is variously described as "the moral structure" of society, "a public morality," "a common morality," "shared ideas on politics, morals, and ethics," "fundamental agreement about good and evil," and "a recognized morality."[4] This is said to be part of the "invisible bonds of common thought" which hold society together; and "if the bonds were too far relaxed the members would drift apart."[5] It is part of "the bondage . . . of society" and is "as necessary to society as, say, a recognized government."[6] The justification for the enforcement of this recognized morality is simply that the law may be used to preserve anything essential to society's existence. "There is disintegration when no common morality is observed and history shows that the loosening of moral bonds is often the first stage of disintegration."[7] If we consider these formulations, they seem to constitute a highly ambitious empirical generalisation about a necessary condition for the existence or continued existence of a society and so give us a sufficient condition for the disintegration of society. Apart from the one general statement that "history shows that the loosening of moral bonds is often the first stage of disintegration," no evidence is given in support of the argument and no indication is given of the kind of evidence that would support it, nor is any sensitivity betrayed to the need for evidence.

In disputing with Lord Devlin,[8] I offered him the alternative of supplementing his contentions with evidence, or accepting that his statements about the necessity of a common morality for the existence of society were not empirical statements at all but were not disguised tautologies or necessary truths depending entirely on the meaning given to the expressions "society," "existence," or "continued existence" of society. If the continued existence of a society meant living according to some specific shared moral code, then the preservation of a moral code is logically and not causally or contingently necessary to the continued existence of society and this seems too unexciting a theme to be worth ventilating. Yet at points Lord Devlin adopts a definition of society ("a society *means* a community of ideas"[9]) which seems to suggest that he intended his statements about the necessity of a morality to society's existence as a definitional truth. Of course, very often the expressions "society," "existence of society," and "the same society" are used in this way: that is, they refer to a form or type of social

---

[4]Devlin, 9–11.

[5]Devlin, 10.

[6]Devlin, 10–11.

[7]Devlin, 13.

[8]See H.L.A. Hart, *Law, Liberty and Morality* (1963).

[9]Devlin, p. 10 (emphasis added). But *cf.* "What makes a society of any sort is community of ideas . . . ." (p. 9).

life individuated by a certain morality or moral code or by distinctive legal, political, or economic institutions. A society in the sense of a form or type of social life can change, disappear, or be succeeded by different forms of society without any phenomenon describable as "disintegration" or "members drifting apart." In this sense of "society," post-feudal England was a different society from feudal England. But if we express this simple fact by saying that *the same English society* was at one time a feudal society and at another time not, we make use of another sense of society with different criteria of individuation and continued identity. It is plain that if the threat of disintegration or "members drifting apart" is to have any reality, or if the claim that a common morality is "as necessary to society as, say, a recognised government" is taken to be part of an argument for the enforcement of morality, definitional truths dependent upon the identification of society with its shared morality are quite irrelevant. Just as it would be no reply to an anarchist who wished to preserve society to tell him that government is necessary to an organised society, if it turned out that by "organised society" we merely meant a society with a government, so it is empty to argue against one who considers that the preservation of society's code of morality is not the law's business, that the maintenance of the moral code is necessary to the existence of society, if it turns out that by society is meant a society living according to this moral code.

The short point is that if we *mean* by "society ceasing to exist" not "disintegration" nor "the drifting apart" of its members but a radical change in its common morality, then the case for using the law to preserve morality must rest not on any disintegration thesis but on some variant of the claim that when groups of men have developed a common form of life rich enough to include a common morality, this is something which ought to be preserved. One very obvious form of this claim is the conservative thesis that the majority have a right in these circumstances to defend their existing moral environment from change. But this is no longer an empirical claim.

II

Views not dissimilar from Lord Devlin's, and in some cases hovering in a similar way between the disintegration thesis and the conservative thesis, can be found in much contemporary sociological theory of the structural and functional prerequisites of society. It would, for example, be profitable, indeed necessary for a full appreciation of Talcott Parsons' work, to take formulations of what is apparently the disintegration thesis which can be found in almost every chapter of his book *The Social System,* and enquire (1) what precisely they amount to; (2) whether they are put forward as empirical claims; and (3) if so, by what evidence they are or could be supported. Consider, for example, such formulations as the following: "The sharing of such common value patterns...creates a solidarity among those mutually oriented to the common values.... [W]ithout attachment to the constitutive common values the collectivity tends to dissolve."[10] "This integration of a set of common value patterns with the internalised need-disposition structure of the constituent personalities is the core phenomenon of the dynamics of social systems. That the stability of any social system is dependent on a degree of such integration may be said to be the fundamental dynamic theorem of sociology."[11] The determination of the precise status and the role of these propositions in Parsons' complex works would be a task of some magnitude, so I shall select from the literature of sociology Durkheim's elaboration of a form of the disintegration theory, because his variant of the theory as expounded in his book, *The Division of Labour in Society,* is relatively clear and briefly expressed, and is also specifically connected with the topic of the enforcement of morality by the criminal law.

Durkheim distinguishes two forms of what he calls "solidarity" or factors tending to unify men or lead them to cohere in discriminable and enduring societies. The minimum meaning attached to society here is that of a group of men which we can distinguish from other similar groups and can recognise as being the same group persisting through a period of time though its constituent members have been replaced during that time by others. One of the forms of solidarity, "mechanical solidarity," springs from men's resemblances and the other, "organic solidarity," from their differences. Mechanical solidarity depends on, or perhaps indeed consists in, sharing of common beliefs about matters of fact and common standards of behaviour among which is a common morality. This blend of common belief and common standards constitutes the *"conscience collective,"* which draws upon all the ambiguities of the French word *conscience* as between consciousness or knowledge and conscience. The point of the use of this terminology of *conscience* is largely that the beliefs and subscription to the common standards become internalised as part of the personality or character of the members of society.

Organic solidarity by contrast depends on the dissimilarities of human beings and their mutual need to be complemented by association in various forms with others who are unlike themselves. The most prominent aspect of this interdependence of dissimilars is the division of labour, but Durkheim warns us that we must not think of the importance of this as a unifying element of society as residing simply in its economic payoff. "[T]he economic services that it [the division of labour] can render

[10] T. Parsons, *The Social System* (1951), p. 41.

[11] Parsons, p. 42.

are picayune compared to the moral effect that it produces, and its true function is to create in two or more persons a feeling of solidarity."[12] Generally, mechanical solidarity is the dominant form of solidarity in simple societies and diminishes in importance, though apparently it is never eliminated altogether as a unifying factor, as organic solidarity develops in more complex societies. According to Durkheim the law presents a faithful mirror of both forms of solidarity, and can be used as a gauge of the relative importance at any time of the two forms. The criminal law, with its repressive sanctions, reflects mechanical solidarity; the civil law reflects organic solidarity, since it upholds the typical instruments of interdependence, e.g., the institution of contract, and generally provides not for repressive sanctions, but for restitution and compensation.

Somewhat fantastically Durkheim thinks that the law can be used as a measuring instrument. We have merely to count the number of rules which at any time constitute the criminal law and the number of rules which constitute the civil law expressing the division of labour, and then we know what fraction to assign to the relative importance of the two forms of solidarity.[13] This fantasy opens formidable problems concerning the individuation and countability of legal rules which occupied Bentham a good deal[14] but perhaps need not detain us here. What is of great interest, however, is Durkheim's view of the role of the criminal law in relation to a shared morality. Durkheim is much concerned to show the hollowness of rationalistic and utilitarian accounts of the institution of criminal punishment. For him, as for his English judicial counterpart, utilitarian theory fails as an explanatory theory for it distorts the character of crime and punishment and considered as a normative theory would lead to disturbing results. Durkheim therefore provides fresh definitions of both crime and punishment. For him a crime is essentially (though in developed societies there are secondary senses of crime to which this definition does not apply directly) a serious offence against the collective conscience—the common morality which holds men together at points where its sentiments are both strong and precise. Such an act is not condemned by that morality because it is independently a crime or wrong, it is a crime or wrong because it is so condemned. Above all, to be wrong or a crime an act need not be, nor even be believed to be, harmful to anyone or to society in any sense other than that it runs counter to the common morality at points where its sentiments are strong and precise. These features of Durkheim's theory are striking

[12]E. Durkheim, *The Division of Labour in Society* (3d ed. Simpson transl. 1964), p. 56.

[13]Durkheim, p. 68.

[14]Bentham devoted a whole book to the questions: What is one law? What is part of a law? What is a complete law? See J. Bentham, *The Limits of Jurisprudence Defined* (C. Everett ed. 1945).

analogues of Lord Devlin's observation that it is not the quality of the morality that matters but the strength of the belief in it and its consequent cohesive power and his stipulation that the morality to be enforced must be up to what may be called concert pitch: it must be marked by "intolerance, indignation, and disgust."[15]

What, then, on this view, is punishment? Why punish? And how severely? Punishment for Durkheim is essentially the hostility excited by violations of the common morality which may be either diffused throughout society or administered by official action when it will usually have the form of specifically graduated measures. His definition, therefore, is that punishment is "a passionate reaction of graduated intensity" to offences against the collective conscience.[16] The hollowness of utilitarian theory as an explanation of criminal punishment is evident if we look at the way that, even in contemporary society, criminal punishments are graduated. They are adapted not to the utilitarian aim of preventing what would be ordinarily described as harmful conduct, but to the appropriate expression of the degree of feeling excited by the offence, on the footing that such appropriate expression of feeling is a means of sustaining the belief in the collective morality.[17] Many legal phenomena bear this out. We punish a robber, even if he is likely to offend again, less severely than a murderer whom we have every reason to think will not offend again. We adopt the principle that ignorance of the law is no excuse in criminal matters and, he might have added, we punish attempts less severely than completed offences thereby reflecting a difference in the resentment generated for the completed as compared with the uncompleted crime.

Hence, to the question "Why punish?" Durkheim's answer is that we do so primarily as a symbolic expression of the outraged common morality the maintenance of which is the condition of cohesion resulting from men's likenesses. Punishing the offender is required to maintain social cohesion because the common conscience, violated by the offence, "would necessarily lose its energy if an emotional reaction of the community [in the form of punishment] did not come to compensate its loss, and it would result in a breakdown of social solidarity."[18]

This thumbnail sketch of Durkheim's theory presents its essentials, but there are two complexities of importance, as there are also in Lord Devlin's case. Both have to do with the possibilities of change in the common morality. Both theorists seem to envisage a spontaneous or natural change and warn us in different ways that the enforcement of morality

[15]Devlin, pp. viii–ix, 17.

[16]Durkheim, p. 90.

[17]*Cf.* Devlin, p. 114: "When considering intangible injury to society it is moral belief that matters; immoral activity is relevant only insofar as it promotes disbelief."

[18]Durkheim, p.108.

must allow for this. Thus Lord Devlin issues prudential warnings to the legislator that "[t]he limits of tolerance shift"[19] and that we should not make criminal offences out of moral opinion which is likely soon to change and leave the law high, and, so to speak, morally dry. Durkheim similarly says that his theory does not mean that it is necessary to conserve a penal rule because it once corresponded to the collective sentiments, but only if the sentiment is still "living and energetic." If it has disappeared or enfeebled, nothing is worse than trying to keep it alive artificially by the law.[20] This means that we must distinguish a natural or nonmalignant change in the social morality or a natural "shift in its limits of tolerance" from a malignant form of change against which society is to be protected and which is the result of individual deviation from its morality. It is, however, a further complexity in these theories that the function of punishment, or rather the mechanism by which punishment operates in preserving a social morality from malignant change, differs as between Durkheim and Lord Devlin. For Lord Devlin punishment protects the existing morality by repressing or diminishing the number of immoral actions which in themselves are considered "to threaten" or weaken the common morality. For Durkheim, however, punishment sustains the common morality, not mainly by repressing the immoral conduct, but principally by giving satisfactory vent to a sense of outrage because if the vent were closed the common conscience would "lose its energy" and the cohesive morality would weaken.

III

If we ask in relation to theories such as Lord Devlin's and Durkheim's precisely what empirical claim they make concerning the connection between the maintenance of a common morality and the existence of society, some further disentangling of knots has to be done.

It seems a very natural objection to such theories that if they are to be taken seriously as variants of the disintegration thesis, the justification which they attempt to give for the enforcement of social morality is far too general. It is surely both possible and good sense to discriminate between those parts of a society's moral code (assuming it has a single moral code) which are essential for the existence of a society and those which are not. Prima facie, at least, the need for such a discrimination seems obvious even if we assume that the moral code is only to be enforced where it is supported by "sentiments which are strong and precise" (Durkheim) or by

---

[19]Devlin, p. 18. *Cf.* p. 114: "[T]here is nothing inherently objectionable about the change of an old morality for a new one . . . . [I]t is the interregnum of disbelief that is perilous."

[20]Durkheim, p. 107, n. 45.

"intolerance, indignation, and disgust" (Devlin). For the decay of all moral restraint or the free use of violence or deception would not only cause individual harm but would jeopardise the existence of a society since it would remove the main conditions which make it possible and worthwhile for men to live together in close proximity to each other. On the other hand the decay of moral restraint on, say, extramarital intercourse, or a general change of sexual morality in a permissive direction seems to be quite another matter and not obviously to entail any such consequences as "disintegration" or "men drifting apart."[21]

It seems, therefore, worthwhile pausing to consider two possible ways of discriminating within a social morality the parts which are to be considered essential.

(1) The first possibility is that the common morality which is essential to society, and which is to be preserved by legal enforcement, is that part of its social morality which contains only those restraints and prohibitions that are essential to the existence of any society of human beings whatever. Hobbes and Hume have supplied us with general characterisations of this moral minimum essential for social life: they include rules restraining the free use of violence and minimal forms of rules regarding honesty, promise keeping, fair dealing, and property. It is, however, quite clear that neither Devlin nor Durkheim means that only these elements, which are to be found in common morality, are to be enforced by law, since any utilitarian or supporter of the Wolfenden Report would agree to that. Quite clearly the argument of both Lord Devlin and Durkheim concerns moral rules which may differ from society to society. Durkheim actually insists that the

---

[21]Lord Devlin in a footnote concedes that not every *breach* of a society's moral code threatens its existence. His words are: "I do not assert that *any* deviation from a society's shared morality threatens its existence any more than I assert that *any* subversive activity threatens its existence. I assert that they are both activities which are capable in their nature of threatening the existence of society so that neither can be put beyond the law" (Devlin, p. 13, n. 1; emphasis in original). This passage does not mean or imply that there are any parts of a social morality which though supported by indignation, intolerance, and disgust can be regarded as not essential for society's existence: on this point Lord Devlin plainly inclines towards the conception of a social morality as a seamless web. (Devlin, p. 115.) But Professor Dworkin argues, convincingly in my opinion, that Lord Devlin uses the same criterion (in effect "passionate public disapproval") to determine both that a deviation from public morality *may* conceivably threaten its existence and that it in fact *does* so, so as to justify actual punishment. Dworkin, "Lord Devlin and the Enforcement of Morals," 75 *Yale L.J.* 986, 990–92 (1966). This leaves his version of the disintegration thesis without empirical support. Thus, according to Lord Devlin: "We should ask ourselves in the first instance whether, looking at homosexuality calmly and dispassionately, we regard it as a vice so abominable that its mere presence is an offence. If that is the genuine feeling of the society in which we live, I do not see how society can be denied the right to eradicate it." (Devlin, p. 17.) But he offers no evidence that in these circumstances the legal toleration of homosexuality would in fact endanger society's existence. Contrast the foregoing with the principles applied by Lord Devlin to fornication in relation to which "feeling may not be so intense." In *that* case: "It becomes *then* a question of balance, the danger to society in one scale and the extent of the restriction in the other." (Devlin, pp. 17–18; emphasis added.)

common morality, violations of which are to be punished by the criminal law, may have no relation to utility: "It was not at all useful for them [these prohibitions] to be born, but once they have endured, it becomes necessary that they persist in spite of their irrationality."[22] The morality to be punished includes much that relates "neither to vital interests of society nor to a minimum of justice."[23]

(2) The second possibility is this: The morality to be enforced, while not coextensive with every jot and tittle of an existent moral code, includes not only the restraints and prohibitions such as those relating to the use of violence or deception which are necessary to any society whatever, but also what is essential for a particular society. The guiding thought here is that for any society there is to be found, among the provisions of its code of morality, a central core of rules or principles which constitutes its pervasive and distinctive style of life. Lord Devlin frequently speaks in this way of what he calls monogamy adopted "as a moral principle,"[24] and of course this does deeply pervade our society in two principal ways. First, marriage is a *legal* institution and the recognition of monogamy as the sole legal form of marriage carries implications for the law related to wide areas of conduct: the custody and education of children, the rules relating to inheritance and distribution of property, etc. Second, the principle of monogamy is also morally pervasive: monogamous marriage is at the heart of our conception of family life, and with the aid of the law has become part of the structure of society. Its disappearance would carry with it vast changes throughout society so that without exaggeration we might say that it had changed its character.

On this view the morality which is necessary to the existence of society is neither the moral minimum required in all societies (Lord Devlin himself says that the polygamous marriage in a polygamous society may be an equally cohesive force as monogamy is in ours),[25] nor is it every jot and tittle of a society's moral code. What is essential and is to be preserved is the central core. On this footing it would be an open and empirical question whether any particular moral rule or veto, e.g., on homosexuality, adultery, or fornication, is so organically connected with the central core that its maintenance and preservation is required as a vital outwork or bastion. There are perhaps traces of some of these ideas in Lord Devlin but not in Durkheim. But even if we take this to be the position, we are still not really confronted with an empirical claim concerning the connection of the maintenance of a common morality and the prevention of disintegra-

[22]Durkheim, p. 107.
[23]Durkheim, p. 81.
[24]Devlin, p. 9.
[25]Devlin, p. 114.

tion or "drifting apart." Apart from the point about whether a particular rule is a vital outwork or bastion of the central core, we may still be confronted only with the unexciting tautology depending now on the identification of society, not with the whole of its morality but only with its central core or "character" and this is not the disintegration thesis.

IV

What is required to convert the last mentioned position into the disintegration thesis? It must be the theory that the maintenance of the core elements in a particular society's moral life is in fact necessary to prevent disintegration, because the withering or malignant decay of the central morality is a disintegrating factor. But even if we have got thus far in identifying an empirical claim, there would of course be very many questions to be settled before anything empirically testable could be formulated. What are the criteria in a complex society for determining the existence of a single recognised morality or its central core? What is "disintegration" and "drifting apart" under modern conditions? I shall not investigate these difficulties but I shall attempt to describe in outline the types of evidence that might conceivably be relevant to the issue if and when these difficulties are settled. They seem to be the following:

(a) Crude historical evidence in which societies—not individuals—are the units. The suggestion is that we should examine societies which have disintegrated and inquire whether their disintegration was preceded by a malignant change in their common morality. This done, we should then have to address ourselves to the possibility of a causal connection between decay of a common morality and disintegration. But of course all the familiar difficulties involved in macroscopic generalisations about society would meet us at this point, and anyone who has attempted to extract generalisations from what is called the decline and fall of the Roman Empire would know that they are formidable. To take only one such difficulty: suppose that all our evidence was drawn from simple tribal societies or closely-knit agrarian societies (which would seem to be the most favorable application of Durkheim's theory of mechanical solidarity). We should not, I take it, have much confidence in applying any conclusions drawn from these to modern industrial societies. Or, if we had, it would be because we had some well developed and well evidenced theory to show us that the differences between simple societies and our own were irrelevant to these issues as the differences in the size of a laboratory can safely be ignored as irrelevant to the scope of the generalisations tested by laboratory experiments. Durkheim, it may be said, is peculiarly obscure on just this point, since it is not really clear from his book whether he means that in advanced societies characterised by extensive division of labour the mechanical solidarity which would still be reflected in its criminal law would be disregarded or not.

(b) The alternative type of evidence must be drawn presumably from social psychology and must break down into at least two subforms according to the way in which we conceive the alternatives to the maintenance of a common morality. One alternative is general uniform *permissiveness* in the area of conduct previously covered by the common morality. The lapse, for example, of the conception that the choices between two wives or one, heterosexuality or homosexuality, are more than matters of personal taste. This (the alternative of permissiveness) is what Lord Devlin seems to envisage or to fear when he says: "The enemy of society is not error but indifference," and "Whether the new belief is better or worse than the old, it is the interregnum of disbelief that is perilous."[26] On the other hand the alternative may be not permissiveness but *moral pluralism* involving divergent submoralities in relation to the same area of conduct.

To get off the ground with the investigation of the questions that either of these two alternatives opens up, it would be reasonable to abandon any general criteria for the disintegration of society in favor of something sufficiently close to satisfy the general spirit of the disintegration thesis. It would be no doubt sufficient if our evidence were to show that malignant change in a common morality led to a general increase in such forms of antisocial behaviour as would infringe what seem the minimum essentials: the prohibitions and restraints of violence, disrespect for property, and dishonesty. We should then require some account of the conceivable psychological mechanisms supposed to connect the malignant decay of a social morality with the increase in such forms of behaviour. Here there would no doubt be signal differences between the alternatives of permissiveness and moral pluralism. On the permissiveness alternative, the theory to be tested would presumably be that in the "interregnum conditions," without the discipline involved in the submission of one area of life, e.g., the sexual, to the requirements of a common morality, there would necessarily be a weakening of the general capacity of individuals for self-control. So, with permissiveness in the area formally covered by restrictive sexual morality, there would come increases in violence and dishonesty and a general lapse of those restraints which are essential for any form of social life. This is the view that the morality of the individual constitutes a seamless web. There is a hint that this, in the last resort, is Lord Devlin's view of the way in which the "interregnum" constitutes a danger to the existence of society: for he replied to my charge that he had assumed without evidence that morality was a seamless web by saying that though "[s]eamlessness presses the simile rather hard," "most men take

[26]Devlin, p. 114.

their morality as a whole."[27] But surely this assumption cannot be regarded as obviously true. The contrary view seems at least equally plausible: permissiveness in certain areas of life (even if it has come about through the disregard of a previously firmly established social morality) might make it easier for men to submit to restraints on violence which are essential for social life.

If we conceive the successor to the "common morality" to be not permissiveness but moral pluralism in some area of conduct once covered by a sexual morality which has decayed through the flouting of its restrictions, the thesis to be tested would presumably be that where moral pluralism develops in this way quarrels over the differences generated by divergent moralities must eventually destroy the minimal forms of restraints necessary for social cohesion. The counter-thesis would be that plural moralities in the conditions of modern large scale societies might perfectly well be mutually tolerant. To many indeed it might seem that the counter-thesis is the more cogent of the two, and that over wide areas of modern life, sometimes hiding behind lip service to an older common morality, there actually are divergent moralities living in peace.

I have done no more than to sketch in outline the type of evidence required to substantiate the disintegration thesis. Till psychologists and sociologists provide such evidence, supporters of the enforcement of morality would do better to rest their case candidly on the conservative rather than on the disintegration thesis.

[27]Devlin, p. 115.

SELECTED SUPPLEMENTARY READINGS

BAYLES, MICHAEL, "Comments on Feinberg: Offensive Conduct and the Law," in *Issues in Law and Morality*, eds. N.S. Care and T.K. Trelogan. Cleveland, Ohio: Case Western Reserve Press, 1973.

BEAUCHAMP, TOM L., WILLIAM T. BLACKSTONE, AND JOEL FEINBERG, *Philosophy and the Human Condition*. Englewood Cliffs, N.J.: Prentice-Hall, 1980, chap. 8.

DEVLIN, LORD PATRICK, *The Enforcement of Morals*. Oxford, England: Oxford University Press, 1965.

———, "Law, Democracy, and Morality," *University of Pennsylvania Law Review* **110** (1962).

DWORKIN, RONALD, "Lord Devlin and the Enforcement of Morals," *Yale Law Journal* **75** (May 1966).

FEINBERG, JOEL, "Harmless Immoralities and Offensive Nuisances," in *Issues in Law and Morality*, eds. N.S. Care and T.K. Trelogan. Cleveland, Ohio: Case Western Reserve Press, 1973. (With a reply to Bayles.)

———, *Rights, Justice, and the Bounds of Liberty*. Princeton, N.J.: Princeton University Press, 1980.

GILBY, THOMAS, O.P "The Crimination of Sin," *Blackfriars* **41** (1960).

GINSBERG, MORRIS, "Law and Morals," *The British Journal of Criminology* (January 1964).

GUSSFIELD, J., "On Legislating Morals," *California Law Review* **56** (1968).

HART, H.L.A., "Immorality and Treason," *The Listener* (July 1959). Reprinted in *The Law as Literature,* ed. L.J. Blom-Cooper. Bodley Head, 1961.

——, *Law, Liberty, and Morality.* Stanford, Calif.: Stanford University Press, 1963.

——, *The Morality of the Criminal Law.* Jerusalem: Magnes Press, 1964, Lecture 2.

——, "The Use and Abuse of the Criminal Law," *Oxford Lawyer* **4** (1961).

HENKIN, LOUIS, "Morals and the Constitution: The Sin of Obscenity," *Columbia Law Review* **63** (1963).

HUGHES, GRAHAM, "Morals and the Criminal Law," *Yale Law Journal* **71** (1962).

JENKINS, IREDELL, *Social Order and the Limits of Law.* Princeton, N.J.: Princeton University Press, 1980, chap. 19.

MACPHERSON, C.B., "The Maximization of Democracy," in *Philosophy, Politics, and Society* (Third Series), eds. Peter Laslett and W.G. Runciman. Oxford, England: Basil Blackwell, 1967.

MEWETT, ALAN W., "Morality and the Criminal Law," *University of Toronto Law Journal* **14** (1962).

MILL, JOHN STUART, *On Liberty.* London, 1859. (Many editions.)

MITCHELL, B., *Law, Morality, and Religion in a Secular Society.* London: Oxford University Press, 1967.

"Private Consensual Adult Behavior: The Requirement of Harm to Others in the Enforcement of Morality," *U.C.L.A. Law Review* **14** (1967).

RADCLIFF, PETER, ed., *Limits of Liberty.* Belmont, Calif.: Wadsworth, 1966.

ROSTOW, EUGENE, "The Enforcement of Morals," *Cambridge Law Journal* (1960). Reprinted in E. ROSTOW, *The Sovereign Prerogative.* New Haven, Conn.: Yale University Press, 1962.

SCHUR, EDWIN M., *Crimes Without Victims.* Englewood Cliffs, N.J.: Prentice-Hall, 1965.

SKOLNICK, J., "Coercion to Virtue," *Southern California Law Review* **41** (1968).

WASSERSTROM, RICHARD, ed., *Morality and the Law.* Belmont, Calif.: Wadsworth, 1971.

WHITELEY, C.H., AND W.M. WHITELEY, *Sex and Morals.* New York: Basic Books, 1967.

WILLIAMS, GLANVILLE, *The Sanctity of Life and the Criminal Law.* New York: Alfred A. Knopf, 1957.

——, "Sex and Morals in the Criminal Law," *Criminal Law Review* (1964).

"Wolfenden Report." Report of the Committee on Homosexual Offences and Prostitution, 1957, Cmd. 247.

WOLLHEIM, RICHARD, "Crime, Sin, and Mr. Justice Devlin," *Encounter* **13** (November 1959).

WOOTTON, BARBARA, *Crime and the Criminal Law.* London: Stevens and Sons, 1963.

chapter three

Paternalism

Paternalism

Gerald Dworkin

I take as my starting point the "one very simple principle" proclaimed by Mill in *On Liberty*. ... I assume that no one with the possible exception of extreme pacifists or anarchists questions the correctness of the first half of the principle. This essay is an examination of the negative claim embodied in Mill's principle—the objection to paternalistic interferences with a man's liberty.

I

By paternalism I shall understand roughly the interference with a person's liberty of action justified by reasons referring exclusively to the welfare, good, happiness, needs, interests or values of the person being coerced. One is always well-advised to illustrate one's definitions by examples but it is not easy to find "pure" examples of paternalistic interferences. For almost any piece of legislation is justified by several different kinds of reasons and even if historically a piece of legislation can be shown to have been introduced for purely paternalistic motives, it may be that advocates

From Gerald Dworkin, "Paternalism," *The Monist* **56** (January 1972), pp. 64–84. Reprinted by permission of the author and the publisher.

of the legislation with an anti-paternalistic outlook can find sufficient reasons justifying the legislation without appealing to the reasons which were originally adduced to support it. Thus, for example, it may be that the original legislation requiring motorcyclists to wear safety helmets was introduced for purely paternalistic reasons. But the Rhode Island Supreme Court recently upheld such legislation on the grounds that it was "not persuaded that the legislature is powerless to prohibit individuals from pursuing a course of conduct which could conceivably result in their becoming public charges," thus clearly introducing reasons of a quite different kind. Now I regard this decision as being based on reasoning of a very dubious nature but it illustrates the kind of problem one has in finding examples. The following is a list of the kinds of interferences I have in mind as being paternalistic.

II

1. Laws requiring motorcyclists to wear safety helmets when operating their machines.
2. Laws forbidding persons from swimming at a public beach when lifeguards are not on duty.
3. Laws making suicide a criminal offense.
4. Laws making it illegal for women and children to work at certain types of jobs.
5. Laws regulating certain kinds of sexual conduct, e.g. homosexuality among consenting adults in private.
6. Laws regulating the use of certain drugs which may have harmful consequences to the user but do not lead to anti-social conduct.
7. Laws requiring a license to engage in certain professions with those not receiving a license subject to fine or jail sentence if they do engage in the practice.
8. Laws compelling people to spend a specified fraction of their income on the purchase of retirement annuities. (Social Security)
9. Laws forbidding various forms of gambling (often justified on the grounds that the poor are more likely to throw away their money on such activities than the rich who can afford to).
10. Laws regulating the maximum rates of interest for loans.
11. Laws against duelling.

In addition to laws which attach criminal or civil penalties to certain kinds of action there are laws, rules, regulations, decrees, which make it either difficult or impossible for people to carry out their plans and which are also justified on paternalistic grounds. Examples of this are ... civil commitment procedures when these are specifically justified on the basis of preventing the person being committed from harming himself ... [and] putting fluorides in the community water supply. ...

III

Bearing these examples in mind let me return to a characterization of paternalism....

...We may first divide paternalistic interferences into "pure" and "impure" cases. In "pure" paternalism the class of persons whose freedom is restricted is identical with the class of persons whose benefit is intended to be promoted by such restrictions. Examples: the making of suicide a crime, requiring passengers in automobiles to wear seat-belts, requiring a Christian Scientist to receive a blood transfusion. In the case of "impure" paternalism in trying to protect the welfare of a class of persons we find that the only way to do so will involve restricting the freedom of other persons besides those who are benefitted....

Paternalism then will always involve limitations on the liberty of some individuals in their own interest but it may also extend to interferences with the liberty of parties whose interests are not in question.

IV

Finally, by way of some more preliminary analysis, I want to distinguish paternalistic interferences with liberty from a related type with which it is often confused. Consider, for example, legislation which forbids employees to work more than, say, 40 hours per week. It is sometimes argued that such legislation is paternalistic for if employees desired such a restriction on their hours of work they could agree among themselves to impose it voluntarily. But because they do not the society imposes its own conception of their best interests upon them by the use of coercion. Hence this is paternalism.

Now it may be that some legislation of this nature is, in fact, paternalistically motivated. I am not denying that. All I want to point out is that there is another possible way of justifying such measures which is not paternalistic in nature. It is not paternalistic because as Mill puts it in a similar context such measures are "required not to overrule the judgment of individuals respecting their own interest, but to give effect to that judgment: they being unable to give effect to it except by concert, which concert again cannot be effectual unless it receives validity and sanction from the law."[1]...

...In these cases compulsion is not used to achieve some benefit which is not recognized to be a benefit by those concerned, but rather because it is the only feasible means of achieving some benefit which *is*

[1]J.S. Mill, *Principles of Political Economy* (New York: P.F. Collier and Sons, 1900), p. 442.

recognized as such by all concerned. This way of viewing matters provides us with another characterization of paternalism in general. Paternalism might be thought of as the use of coercion to achieve a good which is not recognized as such by those persons for whom the good is intended. Again while this formulation captures the heart of the matter—it is surely what Mill is objecting to in *On Liberty*—the matter is not always quite like that. For example when we force motorcyclists to wear helmets we are trying to promote a good—the protection of the person from injury—which is surely recognized by most of the individuals concerned. It is not that a cyclist doesn't value his bodily integrity; rather, as a supporter of such legislation would put it, he either places, perhaps irrationally, another value or good (freedom from wearing a helmet) above that of physical well-being or, perhaps, while recognizing the danger in the abstract, he either does not fully appreciate it or he underestimates the likelihood of its occurring. But now we are approaching the question of possible justifications of paternalistic measures and the rest of this essay will be devoted to that question.

V

I shall begin for dialectical purposes by discussing Mill's objections to paternalism and then go on to discuss more positive proposals.

An initial feature that strikes one is the absolute nature of Mill's prohibitions against paternalism. It is so unlike the carefully qualified admonitions of Mill and his fellow Utilitarians on other moral issues. . . .

Clearly the operative premise here is [that "We either cannot advance the interests of the individual by compulsion, or the attempt to do so involves evil which outweigh the good done;"] and it is bolstered by claims about the status of the individual as judge and appraiser of his welfare, interests, needs, etc. . . . These claims are used to support the following generalizations concerning the utility of compulsion for paternalistic purposes. . . .

> But the strongest of all the arguments against the interference of the public with purely personal conduct is that when it does interfere, the odds are that it interferes wrongly and in the wrong place.[2]

> All errors which the individual is likely to commit against advice and warning are far outweighed by the evil of allowing others to constrain him to what they deem his good.[3]

[2]J.S. Mill, *Utilitarianism* and *On Liberty*, ed. M. Warnock (London: Fontana Library, 1962), p. 214.
[3]Mill, p. 207.

Performing the utilitarian calculation by balancing the advantages and disadvantages we find that:

> Mankind are greater gainers by suffering each other to live as seems good to themselves, than by compelling each other to live as seems good to the rest. . . .[4]

. . . This is clearly the main channel of Mill's thought and it is one which has been subjected to vigorous attack from the moment it appeared—most often by fellow Utilitarians. The link that they have usually seized on is, as Fitzjames Stephen put it, the absence of proof that the "mass of adults are so well acquainted with their own interests and so much disposed to pursue them that no compulsion or restraint put upon them by any others for the purpose of promoting their interest can really promote them."[5] Even so sympathetic a critic as Hart is forced to [this] conclusion. . . . [Now] Mill does not declare that there should never be government interference with the economy but rather that

> . . . in every instance, the burden of making out a strong case should be thrown not on those who resist but on those who recommend government interference. Letting alone, in short, should be the general practice: every departure from it, unless required by some great good, is a certain evil.[6]

In short, we get a presumption not an absolute prohibition. The question is why doesn't the argument against paternalism go the same way?

I suggest that the answer lies in seeing that in addition to a purely utilitarian argument Mill uses another as well. As a Utilitarian Mill has to show, in Fitzjames Stephen's words, that

> Self-protection apart, no good object can be attained by any compulsion which is not in itself a greater evil than the absence of the object which the compulsion obtains.[7]

To show this is impossible; one reason being that it isn't true. Preventing a man from selling himself into slavery (a paternalistic measure which Mill himself accepts as legitimate), or from taking heroin, or from driving a car without wearing seat-belts may constitute a lesser evil than allowing him to do any of these things. A consistent Utilitarian can only argue against paternalism on the grounds that it (as a matter of fact) does not maximize the good. It is always a contingent question that may be refuted by the evi-

---

[4]Mill, p. 138.

[5]J.F. Stephen, *Liberty, Equality, Fraternity* (New York: Holt, Rinehart & Winston, n.d.), p. 24.

[6]Mill, p. 451.

[7]Stephen, p. 49.

dence. But there is also a non-contingent argument which runs through *On Liberty*. When Mill states that "there is a part of the life of every person who has come to years of discretion, within which the individuality of that person ought to reign uncontrolled either by any other person or by the public collectively" he is saying something about what it means to be a person, an autonomous agent. It is because coercing a person for his own good denies this status as an independent entity that Mill objects to it so strongly and in such absolute terms. To be able to choose is a good that is independent of the wisdom of what is chosen. . . .

. . . The main consideration for not allowing such a contract is the need to preserve the liberty of the person to make future choices. This gives us a principle—a very narrow one—by which to justify some paternalistic interferences. Paternalism is justified only to preserve a wider range of freedom for the individual in question. How far this principle could be extended, whether it can justify all the cases in which we are inclined upon reflection to think paternalistic measures justified remains to be discussed. What I have tried to show so far is that there are two strains of argument in Mill—one a straight-forward Utilitarian mode of reasoning and one which relies not on the goods which free choice leads to but on the absolute value of the choice itself. The first cannot establish any absolute prohibition but at most a presumption and indeed a fairly weak one given some fairly plausible assumptions about human psychology; the second while a stronger line of argument seems to me to allow on its own grounds a wider range of paternalism than might be suspected. I turn now to a consideration of these matters.

VI

We might begin looking for principles governing the acceptable use of paternalistic power in cases where it is generally agreed that it is legitimate. Even Mill intends his principles to be applicable only to mature individuals, not those in what he calls "non-age". What is it that justifies us in interfering with children? The fact [is] that they lack some of the emotional and cognitive capacities required in order to make fully rational decisions. . . . Extensions of paternalism are argued for by claiming that in various respects, chronologically mature individuals share the same deficiencies in knowledge, capacity to think rationally, and the ability to carry out decisions that children possess. Hence in interfering with such people we are in effect doing what they would do if they were fully rational. Hence we are not really opposing their will, hence we are not really interfering with their freedom. The dangers of this move have been sufficiently exposed by Berlin in his Two Concepts of Liberty. I see no gain in theoretical clarity nor in practical advantage in trying to pass over the real nature of the interferences with liberty that we impose on others. Still the basic notion of consent is important and seems to me the only acceptable way of trying to delimit an area of justified paternalism.

Let me start by considering a case where the consent is not hypothetical in nature. Under certain conditions it is rational for an individual to agree that others should force him to act in ways in which, at the time of action, the individual may not see as desirable. If, for example, a man knows that he is subject to breaking his resolves when temptation is present, he may ask a friend to refuse to entertain his requests at some later stage.

A classical example is given in the Odyssey when Odysseus commands the men to tie him to the mast and refuse all future orders to be set free, because he knows the power of the Sirens to enchant men with their songs. . . .

. . . However in . . . this case . . . the measure to be enforced is specifically requested by the party involved and at some point in time there is genuine consent and agreement on the part of those persons whose liberty is infringed. Such is not the case for the paternalistic measures we have been speaking about. What must be involved here is not consent to specific measures but rather consent to a system of government, run by elected representatives, with an understanding that they may act to safeguard our interests in certain limited ways.

I suggest that since we are all aware of our irrational propensities, deficiencies in cognitive and emotional capacities and avoidable and unavoidable ignorance it is rational and prudent for us to in effect take out "social insurance policies." We may argue for and against proposed paternalistic measures in terms of what fully rational individuals would accept as forms of protection. Now, clearly since the initial agreement is not about specific measures we are dealing with a more-or-lesss blank check and therefore there have to be carefully defined limits. What I am looking for are certain kinds of conditions which make it plausible to suppose that rational men could reach agreement to limit their liberty even when other men's interests are not affected.

Of course as in any kind of agreement schema there are great difficulties in deciding what rational individuals would or would not accept. Particularly in sensitive areas of personal liberty, there is always a danger of the dispute over agreement and rationality being a disguised version of evaluative and normative disagreement.

Let me suggest types of situations in which it seems plausible to suppose that fully rational individuals would agree to having paternalistic restrictions imposed upon them. It is reasonable to suppose that there are "goods" such as health which any person would want to have in order to pursue his own good—no matter how that good is conceived. This is an argument that is used in connection with compulsory education for children but it seems to me that it can be extended to other goods which have this character. Then one could agree that the attainment of such goods should be promoted even when not recognized to be such, at the moment, by the individuals concerned.

An immediate difficulty that arises stems from the fact that men are always faced with competing goods and that there may be reasons why even a value such as health—or indeed life—may be overridden by competing values. Thus the problem with the Jehovah's Witness and blood transfusions. It may be more important for him to reject "impure substances" than to go on living. The difficult problem that must be faced is whether one can give sense to the notion of a person irrationally attaching weights to competing values.

Consider a person who knows the statistical data on the probability of being injured when not wearing seat-belts in an automobile and knows the types and gravity of the various injuries. He also insists that the inconvenience attached to fastening the belt every time he gets in and out of the car outweighs for him the possible risks to himself. I am inclined in this case to think that such a weighing is irrational. Given his life-plans which we are assuming are those of the average person, his interests and commitments already undertaken, I think it is safe to predict that we can find inconsistencies in his calculations at some point. I am assuming that this is not a man who for some conscious or unconscious reasons is trying to injure himself nor is he a man who just likes to "live dangerously." I am assuming that he is like us in all the relevant respects but just puts an enormously high negative value on inconvenience—one which does not seem comprehensible or reasonable. . . .

. . . But why may we not extend our interference to what we might call evaluative delusions? After all in the case of cognitive delusions we are prepared, often, to act against the expressed will of the person involved. If a man believes that when he jumps out the window he will float upwards—Robert Nozick's example—would not we detain him, forcibly if necessary? The reply will be that this man doesn't wish to be injured and if we could convince him that he is mistaken as to the consequences of his action he would not wish to perform the action. But part of what is involved in claiming that a man who doesn't fasten his seat-belts is attaching an irrational weight to the inconvenience of fastening them is that if he were to be involved in an accident and severely injured, he would look back and admit that the inconvenience wasn't as bad as all that. So there is a sense in which if I could convince him of the consequences of his action he also would not wish to continue his present course of action. . . .

Some of the decisions we make are of such a character that they produce changes which are in one or another way irreversible. Situations are created in which it is difficult or impossible to return to anything like the initial stage at which the decision was made. In particular some of these changes will make it impossible to continue to make reasoned choices in the future. I am thinking specifically of decisions which involve taking drugs that are physically or psychologically addictive and those which are destructive of one's mental and physical capacities.

I suggest we think of the imposition of paternalistic interferences in situations of this kind as being a kind of insurance policy which we take out against making decisions which are far-reaching, potentially dangerous and irreversible. Each of these factors is important. Clearly there are many decisions we make that are relatively irreversible. In deciding to learn to play chess I could predict in view of my general interests in games that some portion of my free-time was going to be preempted and that it would not be easy to give up the game once I acquired a certain competence. But my whole life-style was not going to be jeopardized in an extreme manner. Further it might be argued that even with addictive drugs such as heroin one's normal life plans would not be seriously interfered with if an inexpensive and adequate supply were readily available. So this type of argument might have a much narrower scope than appears to be the case at first.

A second class of cases concerns decisions which are made under extreme psychological and sociological pressures. I am not thinking here of the making of the decision as being something one is pressured into— e.g. a good reason for making duelling illegal is that unless this is done many people might have to manifest their courage and integrity in ways in which they would rather not do so—but rather of decisions such as that to commit suicide which are usually made at a point where the individual is not thinking clearly and calmly about the nature of his decision. In addition, of course, this comes under the previous heading of all-too-irrevocable decision. Now there are practical steps which a society could take if it wanted to decrease the possibility of suicide—for example not paying social security benefits to the survivors or as religious institutions do, not allowing such persons to be buried with the same status as natural deaths. I think we may count these as interferences with the liberty of persons to attempt suicide and the question is whether they are justifiable.

Using my argument schema the question is whether rational individuals would consent to such limitations. I see no reason for them to consent to an absolute prohibition but I do think it is reasonable for them to agree to some kind of enforced waiting period. . . .

A third class of decisions—these are not supposed to be disjoint—involves dangers which are either not sufficiently understood or appreciated correctly by the persons involved. Let me illustrate, using the example of cigarette smoking, a number of possible cases.

1.   A man may not know the facts—e.g. smoking between 1 and 2 packs a day shortens life expectancy 6.2 years, the costs and pain of the illness caused by smoking, etc.

2. A man may know the facts, wish to stop smoking, but not have the requisite willpower.

3. A man may know the facts but not have them play the correct role in his calculation because, say, he discounts the danger psychologically because it is remote in time and/or inflates the attractiveness of other consequences of his decision which he regards as beneficial.

In case 1 what is called for is education, the posting of warnings, etc. In case 2 there is no theoretical problem. We are not imposing a good on someone who rejects it. We are simply using coercion to enable people to carry out their own goals. (Note: There obviously is a difficulty in that only a subclass of the individuals affected wish to be prevented from doing what they are doing.) In case 3 there is a sense in which we are imposing a good on someone since given his current appraisal of the facts he doesn't wish to be restricted. But in another sense we are not imposing a good since what is being claimed—and what must be shown or at least argued for—is that an accurate accounting on his part would lead him to reject his current course of action. Now we all know that such cases exist, that we are prone to disregard dangers that are only possibilities, that immediate pleasures are often magnified and distorted.

If in addition the dangers are severe and far-reaching we could agree to allowing the state a certain degree of power to intervene in such situations. The difficulty is in specifying in advance, even vaguely, the class of cases in which intervention will be legitimate.

A related difficulty is that of drawing a line so that it is not the case that all ultra-hazardous activities are ruled out, e.g. mountain-climbing, bull-fighting, sports-car racing, etc. There are some risks—even very great ones—which a person is entitled to take with his life.

A good deal depends on the nature of the deprivation—e.g. does it prevent the person from engaging in the activity completely or merely limit his participation—and how important to the nature of the activity is the absence of restriction when this is weighed against the role that the activity plays in the life of the person? In the case of automobile seat-belts, for example, the restriction is trivial in nature, interferes not at all with the use or enjoyment of the activity, and does, I am assuming, considerably reduce a high risk of serious injury. Whereas, for example, making mountain climbing illegal prevents completely a person engaging in an activity which may play an important role in his life and his conception of the person he is.

In general the easiest cases to handle are those which can be argued about in the terms which Mill thought to be so important—a concern not just for the happiness or welfare, in some broad sense, of the individual but rather a concern for the autonomy and freedom of the person. I suggest that we would be most likely to consent to paternalism in those instances in which it preserves and enhances for the individual his ability to rationally consider and carry out his own decisions.

I have suggested in this essay a number of types of situations in which it seems plausible that rational men would agree to granting the legislative powers of a society the right to impose restrictions on what Mill calls "self-regarding" conduct. However, rational men knowing something about the resources of ignorance, ill-will and stupidity available to the law-makers of a society—a good case in point is the history of drug legislation in the United States—will be concerned to limit such intervention to a minimum. I suggest in closing two principles designed to achieve this end.

In all cases of paternalistic legislation there must be a heavy and clear burden of proof placed on the authorities to demonstrate the exact nature of the harmful effects (or beneficial consequences) to be avoided (or achieved) and the probability of their occurrence. The burden of proof here is twofold—what lawyers distinguish as the burden of going forward and the burden of persuasion. That the authorities have the burden of going forward means that it is up to them to raise the question and bring forward evidence of the evils to be avoided. Unlike the case of new drugs where the manufacturer must produce some evidence that the drug has been tested and found not harmful, no citizen has to show with respect to self-regarding conduct that it is not harmful or promotes his best interests. In addition the nature and cogency of the evidence for the harmfulness of the course of action must be set at a high level. To paraphrase a formulation of the burden of proof for criminal proceedings—better 10 men ruin themselves than one man be unjustly deprived of liberty.

Finally I suggest a principle of the least restrictive alternative. If there is an alternative way of accomplishing the desired end without restricting liberty then although it may involve great expense, inconvenience, etc. the society must adopt it.

A Critique
of Paternalism
Tom L. Beauchamp

Recently ethical and legal philosophers have shown a revival of interest in whether paternalistic reasons are ever good reasons for the limitation of individual liberties in the form of coercive laws. A special target has been John Stuart Mill, whose searching criticisms of paternalism in *On Liberty* are now widely regarded as too sweeping and insufficiently guarded.

From Tom L. Beauchamp, "Paternalism and Bio-Behavioral Control," *The Monist* 60 (January 1977), pp.62–64, 66–68, 70–71, 74–78.

Against these recent trends in philosophy I argue in this paper that: (1) Mill's critique of paternalism is in all essentials sustainable; (2) Even his most sympathetic critics (especially Dworkin and Hart) have not demonstrated that paternalism is justified; (3) Paternalistic reasons for behavioral control are both common and dangerous, yet are, like all forms of paternalism, irrelevant to the justification of coercive limitation of liberty.

I shall first briefly survey a few selected examples of paternalistic justifications. ... I then pass on to general philosophical concerns about the nature and merit of paternalism, including a defense of Mill against Dworkin and other critics.

EXAMPLES OF PATERNALISTIC JUSTIFICATIONS

Dworkin has provided many useful examples of paternalistic justifications, and there is no need to repeat them. However, I do wish to point out that paternalistic justifications are not only common, as Hart rightly points out, but potentially dangerous as well. I will mention two examples to illustrate this point.

(A) Involuntary Commitment and Therapy on Grounds of Insanity

Involuntary commitment to therapeutic environments is common. The justification offered for both commitment and forced therapy is often overtly paternalistic. Sometimes language as vague as the "patient's need for treatment" is used, and at other times "dangerous to self" and in "need of custody" suffice by law as criteria of commitment. Forced bio-behavioral therapeutic techniques are legally permitted after the patient has been committed. The first and most crucial coercive act requiring justification, however, is the commitment itself. A typical problem case is that of Mrs. Catherine Lake, who suffered from arteriosclerosis causing temporary confusion and mild loss of memory, interspersed with times of mental alertness and rationality. All parties agreed that Mrs. Lake never harmed anyone or presented any threat of danger, yet she was committed to a mental institution because she often seemed in a confused and defenseless state. At her trial, while apparently fully rational, she testified that she knew the risk of living outside the hospital and preferred to take that risk rather than be in the hospital environment. The Court of Appeals denied her petition, arguing that she is "mentally ill," "is a danger to herself ... and is not competent to care for herself." The legal justification cited by the Court was a statute which "provides for involuntary hospitalization of a person who is 'mentally ill and, because of that illness, is likely to injure himself.' . . ."[1] Such reasoning is widespread today, despite forceful arguments by psychiatrists that the harmless "mentally sick" are often competent to make rational judgments.

(B) Eugenic Sterilization

Eugenic sterilization laws are still in effect in over half the states in the U.S. The retarded have been a special target, since they along with criminals, epileptics, alcoholics, and other vulnerable groups have been alleged to have genetically rooted mental and physical disabilities. Since the retarded are often childlike and unaware of their responsibilities, the rearing of children is frequently a heavy burden. For such reasons it has been considered in their own best interest that they be sterilized, even if they do not agree or fail to comprehend the decision.[2] Irvin B. Hill, writing about the sterilization of mentally deficient persons in prison, argues as follows:

> A mentally deficient person is not a suitable parent for either a normal or a subnormal child, and children would be an added burden to an already handicapped individual, who does well to support himself. It would be unfair to the state, *to the individual,* and particularly *to his potential children,* to permit his release without the *protection* of sterilization. . . .
> . . . It has been the policy of the State of Oregon to sterilize mentally deficient persons before releasing them from its institution and . . . this program has been of benefit from economic, social, *and eugenic* standpoints. . . . It *assists the individual* in his transition to a non-institutional life, and it relieves the state of the financial burden. . . .[3]

While not a pure paternalistic justification for eugenic control, it is partially paternalistic and is the kind of reasoning which, once canonized into law, can easily become purely paternalistic in coercive environments. Free and informed consent is unlikely in the context of penal institutions, especially when one is dealing with mentally deficient persons. They can be bribed with offers of freedom and intimidated by threats that their confinement will be extended. Although we now know both that most retarded persons are born from parents of normal intelligence and that the retarded often have children of normal intelligence, prison and other

[1] The relevant court documents are found in Jay Katz, Joseph Goldstein, and Alan M. Dershowitz, *Psychoanalysis, Psychiatry, and the Law* (New York: Free Press, 1967), pp. 552–554, 710–713. Informed sources have told me that Mrs. Lake was freed after repeated petitioning.

[2] The history of such justifications in American society can be found in Kenneth M. Ludmerer, *Genetics and American Society* (Baltimore: The Johns Hopkins University Press, 1972), and in Mark H. Haller, *Eugenics* (New Brunswick, N.J.: Rutgers University Press, 1963).

[3] Irvin B. Hill, "Sterilizations in Oregon," *American Journal of Mental Deficiency* **54** (1950), p. 403. Italics added.

custodial environments continue to give rise to the sort of paternalistically motivated interventions suggested by Hill.

I have intentionally chosen two examples of paternalism where the use of paternalistic justifications can have serious and even devastating effects. No doubt there are many innocuous cases of paternalistic justifications, including most of those cited by Dworkin. But, as we shall see, perhaps the major question about paternalism arises because of the harmful consequences produced by its use. My only point thus far is that *some* of those consequences cannot be classified as innocuous.

THE NATURE AND TYPES OF PATERNALISM

Paternalistically motivated laws are thought to be justified because they work to prevent persons from harming themselves. This justification for limiting individual liberty presumably supplements more widely accepted justifications such as the prevention of harm by others and the maintenance of public order. Whether paternalistic reasons are *good* reasons will occupy us momentarily, but first some agreement must be reached concerning proper use of the word "paternalism." If one operates with a definition as loose as H.L.A. Hart's—"the protection of people against themselves"[4]—misunderstandings readily follow. Legislation intended to help citizens protect themselves from inadvertent acts, such as mutilating their hands in garbage disposals, would on this definition seem paternalistic. Dworkin has provided a better definition, which I accept with only two innocuous modifications (in brackets): Paternalism is "the [coercive] interference with a person's liberty of action justified by [protective or beneficent] reasons referring exclusively to the welfare, good, happiness, needs, interests or values of the person being coerced."[5]

Joel Feinberg has quite properly distinguished two types of paternalism,[6] strong and weak. He explains the weak form as follows:

> The state has the right to prevent self-regarding harmful conduct only when it is substantially nonvoluntary or when temporary intervention is necessary to establish whether it is voluntary or not.[7]

[4]H.L.A. Hart, *Law, Liberty, and Morality* (Stanford, Calif.: Stanford University Press, 1963), p. 31.

[5]Gerald Dworkin, "Paternalism," *The Monist* **56** (January 1972), p. 65.

[6]Joel Feinberg, "Legal Paternalism," *Canadian Journal of Philosophy* **1** (1971), pp. 105–124. This paper is reworked in *Social Philosophy* (Englewood Cliffs, N.J.: Prentice-Hall, 1973). The distinction mentioned above is best made in *Social Philosophy*, p. 33, and in his "'Harmless Immoralities' and Offensive Nuisances," in N.S. Care and T.K. Trelogan (eds.), *Issues in Law and Morality* (Cleveland: Case Western Reserve Press, 1973), pp. 83f.

[7]Feinberg, "Legal Paternalism," pp. 113, 116.

The class of nonvoluntary cases includes cases where there is consent but not adequately informed consent. The strong form holds that the state has the right to coercively protect or benefit a person even when his contrary choices are informed and voluntary. The problem with this distinction, as Feinberg himself argues, is that "weak paternalism" is not paternalism in any interesting sense, because it is not a liberty limiting principle *indepen-dent* of the "harm to others" principle.[8] For this reason I restrict use of the term "paternalism" to strong paternalism. However, it is important to see that the "temporary intervention" mentioned above is both coercive and justified on what might deceptively appear to be paternalistic grounds. Mill believed that a person ignorant of a potential danger which might befall him could justifiably be restrained, so long as the coercion was temporary and only for the purpose of rendering the person informed, in which case he would be free to choose whatever course he wished. Mill regarded this—correctly, I think—as temporary but justified coercion which is not "real infringement" of liberty:

> If either a public officer or anyone else saw a person attempting to cross a bridge which had been ascertained to be unsafe, and there were no time to warn him of his danger, they might seize him and turn him back, without any real infringement of his liberty; for liberty consists in doing what one desires, and he does not desire to fall into the river.[9]

It is not a question of protecting a man *against himself* or of interfering with his *liberty of action*. He is not *acting* at all in regard to his danger. He needs protection from something which is precisely *not himself*, not his intended action, not in any remote sense of his own making. While I am here embellishing Mill, this seems to me clearly the direction of his argument. Mill goes on to say that once the man has been fully informed and understands the dangers of the bridge, then he should be free to traverse it, if he wishes. I shall be arguing in support of Mill's conclusions, and I shall call this justification of *temporary* intervention "Mill's proviso."

MILL'S ANTIPATERNALISTIC INDIVIDUALISM AND "JUSTIFIED PATERNALISM"

Dworkin, Hart, and any supporter of a limited paternalism attempt to specify with care precisely which goods, needs, interests, etc. are acceptable as reasons for intervention with one's liberty of action. Dworkin and Hart largely agree that the state is justified in coercively interfering with a person's liberty if by its interference it protects the person against his own

[8]Feinberg, "Legal Paternalism," pp. 113, 124.

[9]J.S. Mill, *On Liberty* (Indianapolis, Ind. Liberal Arts Press, 1956), p. 117. Feinberg deals with this example in "Legal Paternalism," p. 112, and in "'Harmless Immoralities,'" p. 49, but I am unsure whether he believes Mill's conclusion correct.

actions where those actions are extremely and unreasonably risky (waterfall-rafting, e.g.), or are genuinely not in the person's own best interest when his best interest is knowable by the state (as some believe in the case of suicide), or are potentially dangerous and irreversible in effect (as some drugs are). Perhaps Dworkin's fundamental condition justifying interference is that the state justifiably protects a subject against himself if the interference avoids serious evils which the person might cause to himself through decisions which are far-reaching, potentially dangerous and irreversible, and where no rational alternative is more highly valued by the person.

Dworkin and Hart proceed by citing practices most would agree are justified and sometimes spring from paternalistic motives. It is then assumed that if the conditions justifying these (paternalistically motivated) practices can be listed, they are independent of the harm principle, and paternalism has been justified. Accordingly, no Mill-supportive example can dent or falsify such an analysis, because it has already been assumed (not, I think, *argued*) that instances of *justified paternalism* have been given. Now *if* the methodology and the assumptions just mentioned are admitted, I do not believe this thesis can be gainsaid. The defender of Mill must capitulate.

AN ALTERNATIVE
TO PATERNALISM

But it is precisely these assumptions that should be challenged. The coercive measures these philosophers cite do generally seem to me justified. Their tactic goes wrong, I suggest, in assuming that the actual justifying conditions in these cases are *paternalistic* ones rather than Mill's original standard of individual harm. Mill's harm principle may need rigorous embellishment, but, properly qualified, it seems to me to specify the only valid grounds for intervention. The allegedly independent liberty limiting principle called "paternalism" is gratuitous. I now proceed to an argument for this contention.

I propose in defense of Mill and as the proper account, that one of the following two conditions, as applicable, is necessary for, and (*prima facie*) sufficient for, the justification of coercive interventions (though I shall here be concerned to defend their necessity only against paternalism and not against all possible alternative justifying principles):

(I)   There exist supportable grounds for believing that an individual or group or institution serving the public interest has been or will be *injured* (wrongfully harmed) by the actions or negligence of others. (Deliberately exploitative actions provide the strongest, though not the only grounds for injury claims. Informed consent only negatives injury, not harm; however, one might give informed consent and still be injured if treated in a way not specifically consented to.)

(II)   There exist supportable grounds for believing that an individual or group of individuals has been or will be physically or mentally harmed by some cause or condition which is to that party not known or not within its control or both (and which has not been intentionally manipulated by other persons, in which case the event would fall under I rather II).

I have intentionally used the concept of injury in (I) rather than the concept of harm. My intention is to evade certain difficulties with Mill's notion of harm. As Feinberg has pointed out, one may consent to actions and still be *harmed,* whether those actions are his own or others'. However, we might still want to say that such a person was not *injured,* i.e., not done an injustice or wrongfully harmed, because he consented.

Dworkin and Hart present troublesome cases which center on situations where persons are (a) ignorant and (b) less than fully voluntary in acting. All ignorance cases can be handled, I believe, by Mill's proviso. Once someone is adequately informed (assuming this is possible and assuming the person is able to act on the information), the decision should rest with the agent. Cases of involuntary acts or less than fully voluntary acts are more troublesome only because there are degrees of voluntariness. Fully involuntary acts are not especially difficult, however, nor did they seem so to Mill. Feinberg has this point just right:

> Neither should we expect anti-paternalistic individualism to deny protection to a person from his own nonvoluntary choices, for insofar as the choices are not voluntary they are just as alien to him as the choices of someone else.[10]

Such harmful "actions" involve harms caused by conditions either unknown to the relevant persons or beyond their control, and *for this reason* are subject to coercive intervention, as condition II specifies.

Still, what are we to say about those actions which are partially voluntary and partially involuntary—e.g., those performed under behavior control devices such as subliminal advertising and drug therapy, or in circumstances involving alcoholic stimulation, mob-inspired enthusiasm, retardation, and neurotic compulsion? I see no reason why all these cases should not be treated like ignorance cases. We may (assuming objectivity and knowledge on our part) justifiably protect a man from harm which might result directly from his drunkenness or retardation. To the extent one protects him from causes beyond his knowledge and control, to that extent (subject perhaps to further specific qualifications) one justifiably intervenes. If a potentially injurable person genuinely has "cloudy judgment" or is being deceived through ignorance, his choices are substantially nonvoluntary. And if he can be injured *because* of these conditions, we may justifiably restrain his action. But once informed of the dangers of

---

[10]Feinberg, "Legal Paternalism," p. 112 and "'Harmless Immoralities,'" p. 48.

this action, if and when a context can be provided where voluntary choice is meaningfully possible, he cannot justifiably be further restrained.

Mrs. Lake provided us earlier with an excellent anti-paternalistic example where coercion is *not* justified. Severely retarded persons provide a useful example where coercion *is* justified. Those with minimal or no language skills are not capable of voluntary choice. It is sometimes contended, however, that they must be protected against themselves by involuntary sterilization, in order that they not enter into sexual relations. This piece of paternalism has matters reversed. Such persons seldom have sexual relations unless exploited by others. Any coercion should be aimed at protecting them from exploitation and should be justified by the harm principle. There are less intrusive means to the end of protection than sterilization. Also, if such persons can be taught language skills and acquire a meaningful measure of free choice, our obligations to them are altered, and coercion would no longer be justified. The case is similar with nonrational behavior control techniques, which typically are used to alter the "choices" a man makes, without his understanding or consenting to the alterations. To the extent such actions truly are controlled, it is meaningless to say they are chosen, though no doubt the degree of control and voluntariness rest on a multilevel continuum.

It might be thought that my objections to Dworkin and Hart are pseudo-objections because these philosophers *mean* by "paternalism" something closely akin to, if not in fact identical with, what I take to be justifications on the grounds of harm and injury. There is some evidence to support this objection. Hart, for example, uses cases of paternalism where interventions are justified because the protection is against exploitation or harm.[11] However, it does seem to me unlikely that the boundaries drawn by Hart and Dworkin could be construed to coincide with my own. The reason is simple. Each of these philosophers argues that Mill's conclusions led to restrictions which are too strict. Since I have drawn my boundaries in a manner relevantly similar to Mill's, theirs must be different and their objections to Mill's analysis also objections to my analysis.

A more promising objection is that the same coercive paternalistic interferences which I presumably would disallow on harm principle grounds are allowed, through the back door, on grounds of injury by exploitation (in condition I). I think this too cannot be correct. As I am using the word "exploitation" it is simply a special means of producing injury. It is not something different from the process of injuring. Hence it cannot allow all the same coercive interferences as Hart and Dworkin allow. Their whole purpose in sanctioning paternalism is to *supplement* Mill's harm principle with an *independent* liberty limiting principle. I have been attempting to combat this extension. It is, of course, theoretically

[11]Hart, pp. 33*f.*

possible that *extensionally* all or many cases of "justified paternalism" happen to involve cases of exploitation. I doubt this, but even if it were so, either it would be only accidentally so or it would indicate that we do not need a principle to supplement the harm principle.

THE JUSTIFICATION
OF JUSTIFYING PRINCIPLES

Reasonable and informed persons differ concerning those actions which should and should not be coercively restrained; they also differ over the acceptability of those justifying principles invoked as grounds for such interventions. They can disagree vigorously over the proper interpretation of cases such as those I have advanced. Nowhere do they disagree more than in the area of cases which some take to be (1) *hard cases* in test of the sufficiency of a particular principle to justify interference (as, say, suicide and slavery are hard cases for the harm principle) or (2) *hard core cases* favoring the sufficiency of a principle (as, say, the mentally ill needing treatment are considered by some hard core cases for paternalistic principles). One person's clinching paradigm may be the butt of another's attack. In such cases we often say that two disputants cannot bring their moral intuitions into harmony. So in the present dispute over paternalism, it might be argued, I am simply unable to bring my Mill-aligned intuitions into accord with those of Dworkin and Hart; yet there are cases which have an attractive moral sway in the direction of paternalism. Cases of suicide, slavery, treatment of the retarded, and drug controls are examples. So can anything be done to adjudicate our differences?

First, a couple of methodological points are in order. I would agree that the systematic use of examples has its limits and may yield inconclusive results. I share the scepticism of those contemporary philosophers who believe that reliance upon intuition and upon quasi-legal notions such as the "outweighing" of one right or principle by another may ultimately fail to resolve important issues. Also, I am prepared to agree that ethical argument by analysis of examples is not purely descriptive of our common ethical beliefs, and hence is not simply a matter of systematically bringing general intuitions into harmony. Often such argument is *revisionary* of our ethical beliefs. Examples shock intuition and alter belief. In the end disagreements such as, say, mine with Dworkin, may largely reduce to arguments concerning why moral beliefs ought to be readjusted. To argue, then, that paternalism is never justified may well be a way of arguing that we ought to regard it as never justified. I accept the view that moral philosophy should be in the business of providing such arguments.

Why, then, ought paternalism to be judged unacceptable? The dominant reason is that paternalistic principles are too broad and hence justify too much. Robert Harris has correctly pointed out that Hart's description of paternalism would in principle "justify the imposition of a Spartan-like regimen requiring rigorous physical exercise and abstention from smoking, drinking, and hazardous pastimes."[12] The more thoughtful restrictions on paternalism proposed by Dworkin and Feinberg would disallow this sort of extreme, but still leave unacceptable latitude, especially in contexts where biobehavioral controls are most likely to be abused. Prison environments and therapeutic agencies have thrived on the use of paternalistic justifications. Paternalism potentially gives prison wardens, psychosurgeons, and state officials a good reason for coercively using most any means in order to achieve ends they believe in the subject's best interest. It is demonstrable that allowing this latitude of judgment is dangerous and acutely uncontrollable. This is as true of Feinberg, Hart, and Dworkin's hard core cases in favor of paternalism as it is elsewhere.

Paternalists, then, leave us with unresolved problems concerning the scope of the principle. Suppose, for example, that a man risks his life for the advance of medicine by submitting to an unreasonably risky experiment, an act which most would think not in his own interest. Are we to commend him or coercively restrain him? Paternalism strongly suggests that it would be permissible to coercively restrain such a person. Yet if that is so, then the state is permitted to restrain coercively its morally heroic citizens, not to mention its martyrs, if they act—as such people frequently do—in a manner "harmful" to themselves. I do not see how paternalism can be patched up by adding further conditions about the actions of heroes and martyrs. It would increasingly come to bear the marks of an ad hoc and gratuitous principle which is not genuinely independent of the harm principle.

It is universally acknowledged that the harm principle justifiably permits coercive interventions. No other justifying principle occupies such a noncontroversial status. Perhaps this will and ought to change. But before we agree to supplementary liberty limiting principles, it would seem the better part of caution to be as certain as possible that the harm principle will not suffice and that the evils the supplementary principles enable us to prevent are greater than the evils they inadvertently permit.

[12]Robert Harris, "Private Consensual Adult Behavior: The Requirement of Harm to Others in the Enforcement of Morality," *UCLA Law Review* **14** (1967), p. 585n.

SELECTED SUPPLEMENTARY READINGS

Paternalism

BAYLES, MICHAEL D., "Criminal Paternalism," in *The Limits of Law: Nomos XV*, eds., J. Roland Pennock and John W. Chapman. New York: Lieber-Atherton, 1974, pp. 174–88.

BEAUCHAMP, TOM L., AND JAMES F. CHILDRESS, *Principles of Biomedical Ethics.* New York: Oxford University Press, 1979, chaps. 3, 5.
————, "Paternalism," in *Encyclopedia of Bioethics,* ed. Warren T. Reich. New York: Free Press, 1978, vol. 3, pp. 1194–1200.
BUCHANAN, ALLEN, "Medical Paternalism," *Philosophy and Public Affairs* **7** (1978).
CARTER, ROSEMARY, "Justifying Paternalism," *Canadian Journal of Philosophy* **7** (1977).
CHILDRESS, JAMES F., *Priorities in Biomedical Ethics.* Philadelphia, Pa.: Westminster Press, 1981, chap. 1.
ENGELHARDT, H. TRISTRAM, JR., "Rights and Responsibilities of Patients and Physicians," in *Medical Treatment of the Dying: Moral Issues,* eds. Michael D. Bayles and Dallas M. High. Cambridge, Mass.: Schenkman Publishing Co., 1976.
FEINBERG, JOEL, "Legal Paternalism," *Canadian Journal of Philosophy* **1** (1971).
————, *Social Philosophy.* Englewood Cliffs, N.J.: Prentice-Hall, 1973, chaps. 2–3.
GERT, BERNARD AND CHARLES M. CULVER, "Paternalistic Behavior," *Philosophy and Public Affairs* **6** (1976).
————, "The Justification of Paternalism," in *Medical Responsibility,* eds. W. Robison and M. Pritchard. Clifton, N.J.: Humana Press, 1979.
GUTMANN, AMY, "Children, Paternalism, and Education," *Philosophy and Public Affairs* **9** (1980).
HODSON, JOHN D., "The Principle of Paternalism," *American Philosophical Quarterly* **14** (1977).
KITTRIE, NICHOLAS, *The Right to Be Different: Deviance and Enforced Therapy.* Baltimore, Md.: The Johns Hopkins University Press, 1971.
MURPHY, JEFFRIE G., "Incompetence and Paternalism," *Archives for Philosophy of Law and Social Philosophy* **40** (1974).
SZASZ, THOMAS, *Ideology and Insanity.* Garden City, N.Y.: Doubleday, 1970, chaps. 2, 9.
WIKLER, DANIEL, "Paternalism and the Mildly Retarded," *Philosophy and Public Affairs* **8** (1979).
————, "Persuasion and Coercion for Health: The Rights and Wrongs of Government's Role in Changing Lifestyles," *Milbank Memorial Fund Quarterly* **56** (1978).

General: On Liberty-Limiting Principles

ACTON, J., *Essays on Freedom and Power.* Boston: Beacon Press, 1948.
BERLIN, I., *Four Essays on Liberty.* New York: Oxford University Press, 1970.
HART, H.L.A., *Law, Liberty, and Morality.* Stanford, Calif.: Stanford University Press, 1963.
MCCLOSKEY, H.J., "Mill's Liberalism," *Philosophical Quarterly* **13** (1963). (See also the reply by A. Ryan in *Philosophical Quarterly* **14** [1964].)
POPPER, K.R., *The Open Society and Its Enemies.* Princeton, N.J.: Princeton University Press, 1966.
RADCLIFF, PETER, ed., *Limits of Liberty.* Belmont, Calif.: Wadsworth, 1966.
REES, J.C., *Mill and His Early Critics.* Leicester: University College, 1956.
RUSSELL, BERTRAND, *John Stuart Mill, Lecture on a Master Mind.* Published for the British Academy by the Oxford University Press, 1955, from the *Proceedings of the British Academy* **41.**

chapter four

Rights of the Free Press

A Theory of Freedom
of Expression

Thomas Scanlon

I will now state the principle of freedom of expression which seems to me
to be a natural extension of the thesis Mill defends in Chapter II of *On Liberty,* and which I will therefore call the Millian Principle:

> There are certain harms which, although they would not occur but for cer-
> tain acts of expression, nonetheless cannot be taken as part of a justification
> for legal restrictions on these acts. These harms are: (a) harms to certain
> individuals which consist in their coming to have false beliefs as a result of
> those acts of expression; (b) harmful consequences of acts performed as a
> result of those acts of expression, where the connection between the acts of
> expression and the subsequent harmful acts consists merely in the fact that
> the act of expression led the agents to believe (or increased their tendency to
> believe) these acts to be worth performing.

Thomas Scanlon, "A Theory of Freedom of Expression," *Philosophy and Public Affairs*,
vol. 1, no. 2 (Winter 1972). Copyright © 1972 by Princeton University Press, pp. 204–26.
Reprinted by permission of Princeton University Press. Professor Scanlon has modified his
views somewhat on the issues in this article subsequent to its original publication. Readers
are advised to consult a more recent and very detailed presentation of his views in "Freedom
of Expression and Categories of Expression."

This paper is derived from one presented to the Society for Ethical and Legal Philosophy, and I am grateful to the members of that group, as well as to a number of other audi-
ences willing and unwilling, for many helpful comments and criticisms.

I would like to believe that the general observance of the Millian Principle by governments would, in the long run, have more good consequences than bad. But my defence of the principle does not rest on this optimistic outlook. I will argue in the next section that the Millian Principle, as a general principle about how governmental restrictions on the liberty of citizens may be justified, is a consequence of the view, coming down to us from Kant and others, that a legitimate government is one whose authority citizens can recognize while still regarding themselves as equal, autonomous, rational agents. Thus, while it is not a principle about legal responsibility, the Millian Principle has its origins in a certain view of human agency from which many of our ideas about responsibility also derive.

Taken by itself, the Millian Principle obviously does not constitute an adequate theory of freedom of expression. Much more needs to be said about when the kinds of harmful consequences which the principle allows us to consider can be taken to be sufficient justification for restrictions on expression. Nonetheless, it seems to me fair to call the Millian Principle the basic principle of freedom of expression. This is so, first, because a successful defence of the principle would provide us with an answer to the charge of irrationality by explaining why certain of the most obvious consequences of acts of expression cannot be appealed to as a justification for legal restrictions against them. Second, the Millian Principle is the only plausible principle of freedom of expression I can think of which applies to expression in general and makes no appeal to special rights (e.g., political rights) or to the value to be attached to expression in some particular domain (e.g., artistic expression or the discussion of scientific ideas). It thus specifies what is special about acts of expression as opposed to other acts and constitutes in this sense the usable residue of the distinction between speech and action. . . .

As I have already mentioned, I will defend the Millian Principle by showing it to be a consequence of the view that the powers of a state are limited to those that citizens could recognize while still regarding themselves as equal, autonomous, rational agents. Since the sense of autonomy to which I will appeal is extremely weak, this seems to me to constitute a strong defence of the Millian Principle as an exceptionless restriction on governmental authority. . . .

To regard himself as autonomous in the sense I have in mind a person must see himself as sovereign in deciding what to believe and in weighing competing reasons for action. He must apply to these tasks his own canons of rationality, and must recognize the need to defend his beliefs and decisions in accordance with these canons. This does not mean, of course, that he must be perfectly rational, even by his own standard of rationality, or that his standard of rationality must be exactly ours. Obviously the content of this notion of autonomy will vary according to the range of variation we are willing to allow in canons of rational decision. If just anything counts as such a canon then the requirements I have mentioned will become mere tautologies: an autonomous man believes what he believes and decides to do what he decides to do. I am sure I could not describe a set of limits on what can count as canons of rationality which would secure general agreement, and I will not try, since I am sure that the area of agreement on this question extends far beyond anything which will be relevant to the applications of the notion of autonomy that I intend to make. For present purposes what will be important is this. An autonomous person cannot accept without independent consideration the judgment of others as to what he should believe or what he should do. He may rely on the judgment of others, but when he does so he must be prepared to advance independent reasons for thinking their judgment likely to be correct, and to weigh the evidential value of their opinion against contrary evidence.

The requirements of autonomy as I have so far described them are extremely weak. They are much weaker than the requirements Kant draws from essentially the same notion,[1] in that being autonomous in my sense (like being free in Hobbes's) is quite consistent with being subject to coercion with respect to one's actions. A coercer merely changes the considerations which militate for or against a certain course of action; weighing these conflicting considerations is still up to you.

An autonomous man may, if he believes the appropriate arguments, believe that the state has a distinctive right to command him. That is, he may believe that (within certain limits, perhaps) the fact that the law requires a certain action provides him with a very strong reason for performing that action, a reason which is quite independent of the consequences, for him or others, of his performing it or refraining. How strong this reason is—what, if anything, could override it—will depend on his view of the arguments for obedience to law. What is essential to the person's remaining autonomous is that in any given case his mere recognition that a certain action is required by law does not settle the question of whether he will do it. That question is settled only by his own decision, which may take into account his current assessment of the general case for obedience and the exceptions it admits, consideration of his other duties and obligations, and his estimate of the consequences of obedience and disobedience in this particular case.[2]

---

[1]Kant's notion of autonomy goes beyond the one I employ in that for him there are special requirements regarding the reasons which an autonomous being can act on. (See the second and third sections of *Foundations of the Metaphysics of Morals.*) While his notion of autonomy is stronger than mine, Kant does not draw from it the same limitations on the authority of states (see *Metaphysical Elements of Justice*, sections 46–49).

[2]I am not certain whether I am here agreeing or disagreeing with Robert Paul Wolff (*In Defense of Anarchism*, New York: Harper & Row, 1970). At any rate I would not call what I am maintaining anarchism. The limitation on state power I have in mind is that described by John Rawls in the closing paragraphs of "The Justification of Civil Disobedience," in Hugo Bedau, ed., *Civil Disobedience: Theory and Practice* (New York: Pegasus, 1969).

Thus, while it is not obviously inconsistent with being autonomous to recognize a special obligation to obey the commands of the state, there are limits on the *kind* of obligation which autonomous citizens could recognize. In particular, they could not regard themselves as being under an "obligation" to believe the decrees of the state to be correct, nor could they concede to the state the right to have its decrees obeyed without deliberation. The Millian Principle can be seen as a refinement of these limitations.

The apparent irrationality of the doctrine of freedom of expression derives from its apparent conflict with the principle that it is the prerogative of a state—indeed, part of its duty to its citizens—to decide when the threat of certain harms is great enough to warrant legal action, and when it is, to make laws adequate to meet this threat. (Thus Holmes's famous reference to "substantive evils that Congress has a right to prevent."[3]) Obviously this principle is not acceptable in the crude form in which I have just stated it; no one thinks that Congress can do *anything* it judges to be required to save us from "substantive evils." The Millian Principle specifies two ways in which this prerogative must be limited if the state is to be acceptable to autonomous subjects. The argument for the first part of the principle is as follows.

The harm of coming to have false beliefs is not one that an autonomous man could allow the state to protect him against through restrictions on expression. For a law to provide such protection it would have to be in effect and deterring potential misleaders while the potentially misled remained susceptible to persuasion by them. In order to be protected by such a law a person would thus have to concede to the state the right to decide that certain views were false and, once it had so decided, to prevent him from hearing them advocated even if he might wish to. The conflict between doing this and remaining autonomous would be direct if a person who authorized the state to protect him in this way necessarily also bound himself to accept the state's judgment about which views were false. The matter is not quite this simple, however, since it is conceivable that a person might authorize the state to act for him in this way while still reserving to himself the prerogative of deciding, on the basis of the arguments and evidence left available to him, where the truth was to be found. But such a person would be "deciding for himself" only in an empty sense, since in any case where the state exercised its prerogative he would be "deciding" on the basis of evidence preselected to include only that which supported one conclusion. While he would not be under an obligation to accept the state's judgment as correct, he would have conceded to the state the right to deprive him of grounds for making an independent judgment.

The argument for the second half of the Millian Principle is parallel to this one. What must be argued against is the view that the state, once it

[3]In *Schenck* v. *United States.*

has declared certain conduct to be illegal, may when necessary move to prevent that conduct by outlawing its advocacy. The conflict between this thesis and the autonomy of citizens is, just as in the previous case, slightly oblique. Conceding to the state the right to use this means to secure compliance with its laws does not immediately involve conceding to it the right to require citizens to believe that what the law says ought not to be done ought not to be done. None the less, it is a concession that autonomous citizens could not make, since it gives the state the right to deprive citizens of the grounds for arriving at an independent judgment as to whether the law should be obeyed.

These arguments both depend on the thesis that to defend a certain belief as reasonable a person must be prepared to defend the grounds of his belief as not obviously skewed or otherwise suspect. There is a clear parallel between this thesis and Mill's famous argument that if we are interested in having truth prevail we should allow all available arguments to be heard.[4] But the present argument does not depend, as Mill's may appear to, on an empirical claim that the truth is in fact more likely to win out if free discussion is allowed. Nor does it depend on the perhaps more plausible claim that, given the nature of people and governments, to concede to governments the power in question would be an outstandingly poor strategy for bringing about a situation in which true opinions prevail.

It is quite conceivable that a person who recognized in himself a fatal weakness for certain kinds of bad arguments might conclude that everyone would be better off if he were to rely entirely on the judgment of his friends in certain crucial matters. Acting on this conclusion, he might enter into an agreement, subject to periodic review by him, empowering them to shield him from any sources of information likely to divert him from their counsel on the matters in question. Such an agreement is not obviously irrational, nor, if it is entered into voluntarily, for a limited time, and on the basis of the person's own knowledge of himself and those he proposes to trust, does it appear to be inconsistent with his autonomy. The same would be true if the proposed trustees were in fact the authorities of the state. But the question we have been considering is quite different: Could an autonomous individual regard the state as having, not as part of a special voluntary agreement with him but as part of its normal powers *qua* state, the power to put such an arrangement into effect without his consent whenever *it* (i.e., the legislative authority) judged that to be advisable? The answer to this question seems to me to be quite clearly no.

Someone might object to this answer on the following grounds. I have allowed for the possibility that an autonomous man might accept a general argument to the effect that the fact that the state commands a cer-

---

[4]In Chapter II of *On Liberty*.

tain thing is in and of itself a reason why that thing should be done. Why couldn't he also accept a similar argument to the effect that the state *qua* state is in the best position to decide when certain counsel is best ignored?

I have already argued that the parallel suggested here between the state's right to command action and a right to restrict expression does not hold. But there is a further problem with this objection. What saves temporary, voluntary arrangements of the kind considered above from being obvious violations of autonomy is the fact that they can be based on a first-hand estimation of the relative reliability of the trustee's judgment and that of the "patient." Thus the person whose information is restricted by such an arrangement has what he judges to be good grounds for thinking the evidence he does receive to be a sound basis for judgment. A principle which provided a corresponding basis for relying on the state *qua* state would have to be extremely general, applying to all states of a certain kind, regardless of who occupied positions of authority in them, and to all citizens of such states. Such a principle would have to be one which admitted variation in individual cases and rested its claim on what worked out best "in the long run." Even if some generalization of this kind were true, it seems to me altogether implausible to suppose that it could be rational to rely on such a general principle when detailed knowledge of the individuals involved in a particular case suggested a contrary conclusion.

A more limited case for allowing states the power in question might rest not on particular virtues of governments but on the recognized fact that under certain circumstances individuals are quite incapable of acting rationally. Something like this may seem to apply in the case of the man who falsely shouts "fire" in a crowded theatre. Here a restriction on expression is justified by the fact that such acts would lead others (give them reason) to perform harmful actions. Part of what makes the restriction acceptable is the idea that the persons in the theatre who react to the shout are under conditions that diminish their capacity for rational deliberation. This case strikes us as a trivial one. What makes it trivial is, first, the fact that only in a very far-fetched sense is a person who is prevented from hearing the false shout under such circumstances prevented from making up his own mind about some question. Second, the diminished capacity attributed to those in the theatre is extremely brief, and applies equally to anyone under the relevant conditions. Third, the harm to be prevented by the restriction is not subject to any doubt or controversy, even by those who are temporarily "deluded." In view of all these facts, the restriction is undoubtedly one which would receive unanimous consent if that were asked.[5]

This is not true, however, of most of the other exceptions to the Millian Principle that might be justified by appeal to "diminished rationality." It is

[5]This test is developed as a criterion for justifiable paternalism by Gerald Dworkin in his essay "Paternalism," reprinted above in this text.

doubtful, for example, whether any of the three conditions I have mentioned would apply to a case in which political debate was to be suspended during a period of turmoil and impending revolution. I cannot see how nontrivial cases of this kind could be made compatible with autonomy.

The arguments I have given may sound like familiar arguments against paternalism, but the issue involved is not simply that. First, a restriction on expression justified on grounds contrary to the Millian Principle is not necessarily paternalistic, since those who are to be protected by such a restriction may be other than those (the speaker and his audience) whose liberty is restricted. When such a restriction is paternalistic, however, it represents a particularly strong form of paternalism, and the arguments I have given are arguments against paternalism only in this strong form. It is quite consistent with a person's autonomy, in the limited sense I have employed, for the law to restrict his freedom of action "for his own good," for instance by requiring him to wear a helmet while riding his motorcycle. The conflict arises only if compliance with this law is then promoted by forbidding, for example, expression of the view that wearing a helmet isn't worth it, or is only for sissies.

It is important to see that the argument for the Millian Principle rests on a limitation of the authority of states to command their subjects rather than on a right of individuals. For one thing, this explains why this particular principle of freedom of expression applies to governments rather than to individuals, who do not have such authority to begin with. There are surely cases in which individuals have the right not to have their acts of expression interfered with by other individuals, but these rights presumably flow from a general right to be free from arbitrary interference, together with considerations which make certain kinds of expression particularly important forms of activity.

If the argument for the Millian Principle were thought to rest on a right, "the right of citizens to make up their own minds," then that argument might be thought to proceed as follows. Persons who see themselves as autonomous see themselves as having a right to make up their own minds, hence also a right to whatever is necessary for them to do this; what is wrong with violations of the Millian Principle is that they infringe this right.

A right of this kind would certainly support a healthy doctrine of freedom of expression, but it is not required for one. The argument given above was much more limited. Its aim was to establish that the authority of governments to restrict the liberty of citizens in order to prevent certain harms does not include authority to prevent these harms by controlling people's sources of information to ensure that they will maintain certain beliefs. It is a long step from this conclusion to a right which is violated whenever someone is deprived of information necessary for him to make an informed decision on some matter that concerns him.

There are clearly cases in which individuals have a right to the information necessary to make informed choices and can claim this right against the government. This is true in the case of political decisions, for example, when the right flows from a certain conception of the relation between a democratic government and its citizens. Even where there is no such right, the provision of information and other conditions for the exercise of autonomy is an important task for states to pursue. But these matters take us beyond the Millian Principle.

The Millian Principle is obviously incapable of accounting for all of the cases that strike us as infringements of freedom of expression. On the basis of this principle alone we could raise no objection against a government that banned all parades or demonstrations (they interfere with traffic), outlawed posters and handbills (too messy), banned public meetings of more than ten people (likely to be unruly), and restricted newspaper publication to one page per week (to save trees). Yet such policies surely strike us as intolerable. That they so strike us is a reflection of our belief that free expression is a good which ranks above the maintenance of absolute peace and quiet, clean streets, smoothly flowing traffic, and rock-bottom taxes.

Thus there is a part of our intuitive view of freedom of expresssion which rests upon a balancing of competing goods. By contrast with the Millian Principle, which provides a single defence for all kinds of expression, here it does not seem to be a matter of the value to be placed on expression (in general) as opposed to other goods. The case seems to be different for, say, artistic expression than for the discussion of scientific matters, and different still for expression of political views.

Within certain limits, it seems clear that the value to be placed on having various kinds of expression flourish is something which should be subject to popular will in the society in question. The limits I have in mind here are, first, those imposed by considerations of distributive justice. Access to means of expression for whatever purposes one may have in mind is a good which can be fairly or unfairly distributed among the members of a society, and many cases which strike us as violations of freedom of expression are in fact instances of distributive injustice. This would be true of a case where, in an economically inegalitarian society, access to the principal means of expression was controlled by the government and auctioned off by it to the highest bidders, as is essentially the case with broadcasting licences in the United States today. The same might be said of a parade ordinance which allowed the town council to forbid parades by unpopular groups because they were too expensive to police.

But to call either of these cases instances of unjust distribution tells only part of the story. Access to means of expression is in many cases a necessary condition for participation in the political process of the country, and therefore something to which citizens have an independent right.

At the very least the recognition of such rights will require governments to ensure that means of expression are readily available through which individuals and small groups can make their views on political issues known, and to ensure that the principal means of expression in the society do not fall under the control of any particular segment of the community. But exactly what rights of access to means of expression follow in this way from political rights will depend to some extent on the political institutions in question. Political participation may take different forms under different institutions, even under equally just institutions.

The theory of freedom of expression which I am offering, then, consists of at least four distinguishable elements. It is based upon the Millian Principle, which is absolute but serves only to rule out certain justifications for legal restrictions on acts of expression. Within the limits set by this principle the whole range of governmental policies affecting opportunities for expression, whether by restriction, positive intervention, or failure to intervene, are subject to justification and criticism on a number of diverse grounds. First, on grounds of whether they reflect an appropriate balancing of the value of certain kinds of expression relative to other social goods; second, whether they ensure equitable distribution of access to means of expression throughout the society; and third, whether they are compatible with the recognition of certain special rights, particularly political rights.

This mixed theory is somewhat cumbersome, but the various parts seem to me both mutually irreducible and essential if we are to account for the full range of cases which seem intuitively to constitute violations of "free speech."

The failure of the Millian Principle to allow certain kinds of exceptions may seem to many the most implausible feature of the theory I have offered. In addition to the possibility mentioned earlier, that exceptions should be allowed in cases of diminished rationality, there may seem to be an obvious case for allowing deviations from the principle in time of war or other grave emergency.

It should be noticed that because the Millian Principle is much narrower than, say, a blanket protection of "speech," the theory I have offered can already accommodate some of the restrictions on expression which wartime conditions may be thought to justify. The Millian Principle allows one, even in normal times, to consider whether the publication of certain information might present serious hazards to public safety by giving people the capacity to inflict certain harms. It seems likely that risks of this kind which are worth taking in time of peace in order to allow full discussion of, say, certain scientific questions, might be intolerable in wartime.

But the kind of emergency powers that governments feel entitled to invoke often go beyond this and include, for example, the power to cut off political debate when such debate threatens to divide the country or otherwise to undermine its capacity to meet a present threat. The obvious justification for such powers is clearly disallowed by the Millian Principle, and the theory I have offered provides for no exceptions of this kind.

It is hard for me at the present moment to conceive of a case in which I would think the invocation of such powers by a government right. I am willing to admit that there might be such cases, but even if there are I do not think that they should be seen as "exceptions" to be incorporated within the Millian Principle.

That principle, it will be recalled, does not rest on a right of citizens but rather expresses a limitation on the authority governments can be supposed to have. The authority in question here is that provided by a particular kind of political theory, one which has its starting point in the question: How could citizens recognize a right of governments to command them while still regarding themselves as equal, autonomous, rational agents? The theory is normally thought to yield the answer that this is possible if, but only if, that right is limited in certain ways, and if certain other conditions, supposed to ensure citizen control over government, are fulfilled. I have argued that one of the necessary limitations is expressed by the Millian Principle. If I am right, then the claim of a government to rule by virtue of this particular kind of authority is undermined, I think completely, if it undertakes to control its citizens in the ways that the Millian Principle is intended to exclude.

This does not mean, however, that it could not in an extreme case be right for certain people, who normally exercised the kind of authority held to be legitimate by democratic political theory, to take measures which this authority does not justify. These actions would have to be justified on some other ground (e.g., utilitarian), and the claim of their agents to be obeyed would not be that of a legitimate government in the usual (democratic) sense. None the less most citizens might, under the circumstances, have good reason to obey.

There are a number of different justifications for the exercise of coercive authority. In a situation of extreme peril to a group, those in the group who are in a position to avert disaster by exercising a certain kind of control over the others may be justified in using force to do so, and there may be good reason for their commands to be obeyed. But this kind of authority differs both in justification and extent from that which, if democratic political theory is correct, a legitimate democratic government enjoys. What I am suggesting is that if there are situations in which a general suspension of civil liberties is justified—and, I repeat, it is not clear to me that there are such—these situations constitute a shift from one kind of authority to another. The people involved will probably continue to wear the same hats, but this does not mean that they still rule with the same title.

It should not be thought that I am here giving governments licence to kick over the traces of constitutional rule whenever this is required by the "national interest." It would take a situation of near catastrophe to justify a move of the kind I have described, and if governments know what they are doing it would take such a situation to make a move of this sort inviting. For a great deal is given up in such a move, including any notion that the commands of government have a claim to be obeyed which goes beyond the relative advantages of obedience and disobedience.

When the situation is grave and the price of disorder enormous, such utilitarian considerations may give the government's commands very real binding force. But continuing rule on this basis would be acceptable only for a society in permanent crisis or for a group of people who, because they could see each other only as obedient servants or as threatening foes, could not be ruled on any other.

Is the Press Losing the First Amendment?

Ronald Dworkin

I

Writers have had an up and down time in the courts recently. The press is worried about a series of new judicial deicisons that it believes will sharply decrease its powers and shrink the role of the First Amendment in American society. The latest of these is the amazing case of *US* v. *Snepp*, in which the Supreme Court ordered an author to turn over all his profits to the government without even holding a hearing on the issue. But the press has also won what it regards as important victories. The most recent of these is the *Richmond Newspapers* case, decided [in 1979], in which the Court reversed its decision in an earlier case and held that reporters, at least in principle, have a right to attend criminal trials even when the defendant wishes to exclude them.[1]

US v. *Snepp* is much the more important of the two cases. Frank Snepp signed a contract when he joined the CIA, promising to submit to

From Ronald Dworkin, "Is the Press Losing the First Amendment?" *New York Review of Books* (December 4, 1980). Reprinted by permission of the author.

[1]The earlier case was *Gannett* v. *DePasquale*, decided only last year, which the press especially resented. That decision permitted a judge to exclude reporters from a pre-trial hearing, and Chief Justice Burger's opinion in the *Richmond Newspapers* case states that the earlier decision was intended to apply only to such hearings and not to actual trials. But Burger's own opinion in the *Gannett* case, as well as the opinions of other justices, seemed to cover actual trials as well, so that the *Richmond Newspapers* decision was probably a change of mind, as Mr. Justice Blackmun says it was in his own separate opinion in the latter case.

it, before publication, anything he later wrote about it. The CIA argues that that agreement, which it obtains from every agent, is necessary so that it can make its own judgment, in advance, about whether any of the material an author proposes to publish is classified, and take legal action to enjoin what it does consider classified if the author does not accept its judgment. Snepp wrote a book called *Decent Interval*, after leaving the agency, in which he sharply criticized the CIA's behavior in Vietnam during the final months of the war. He feared that the agency would use its right to review his manuscript to delay and harass him by claiming that matters of no importance to security were classified, as the agency had certainly done in the case of Victor Marchetti, another former agent who had written and submitted a book.[2] After much indecision Snepp decided to publish his book without submitting it to the CIA first.

The agency sued him under the contract. Snepp argued that the First Amendment made his contractual agreement null and void because it was a form of censorship. But neither the federal district court nor the Circuit Court of Appeals, to which Snepp appealed, accepted that claim. The district court ordered Snepp, by way of remedy, to hand over to the government all his profits on the book—his only earnings for several years of work—but the Circuit Court did reverse the district court on this point. It said that the government must be content with such actual financial damages as it could prove it suffered because Snepp had broken his contract, which is the normal remedy in breach of contract cases.

Snepp appealed to the Supreme Court on the First Amendment point. The government asked the Court *not* to take the case for review, and said that it was satisfied under the circumstances with the damage remedy the Circuit Court had ordered. But it added that if the Court did take the case, it would like the opportunity to argue that the Court should reinstate the district court's much more onerous remedy. In the end the Court did accept the case, against the government's wishes, but, as it turned out, only for the purpose of reinstating the harsher penalty. The Court did that, contrary to all traditions of judicial fairness, without offering opportunity for argument to anyone. A court that is supposedly dominated by the ideal of judicial restraint twisted principles of procedural fairness to reach a result for which no party had asked.

Some journalists speculate that the Court is furious with the press over *The Brethren*, Woodward and Armstrong's "inside story" of the Court published [in 1979], and took this opportunity for revenge. But many First Amendment lawyers take the more worrying view that the case is only the latest and most dramatic example of the decline of free speech in the United States.

It is worth describing the evidence for this gloomy opinion in some

---

[2]Victor Marchetti and John D. Marks, *The CIA and the Cult of Intelligence* (Knopf, 1974).

detail. No leading constitutional lawyer (except Mr. Justice Black) has ever thought that the First Amendment bars the government from any conceivable regulation of speech. It has always been possible for people to sue one another in American courts for libel and slander, for example, and even the most famous defenders of free speech have conceded that no one has a constitutional right to cry "fire" in a crowded theater or publish information about troop movements in time of war. Nevertheless there have been tides in the Court's concern for speech as against other interests, and the present moment strikes many commentators as very low tide indeed.

The Warren Court moved very far, for example, toward protecting pornography from the censor, on the ground that it is not part of the state's concern to decide what people, in private, should or should not find tasteless or embarrassing. But the Burger Court endorsed the idea of censorship in accordance with local standards of decency, and though this test has posed no problems for the pornographers of Times Square it has made many movie theaters in small towns very cautious indeed. Defamation suits brought by public figures against newspapers provide another example. The Warren Court, in its famous decision in *Times* v. *Sullivan*, held that a public figure could not sue a paper for libel even if what that paper had published was both false and damaging, unless the public figure succeeded in showing that the paper had been not merely wrong but either malicious or reckless in what it published. The Court held that public figures must be supposed to have waived their common law right to sue for ordinary misrepresentation.

The Burger Court has not overruled the *Sullivan* decision, but it has narrowed the class of people who count as public figures for this purpose, and in the recent case of *Herbert v. Landau* it held that even when a public figure sues, reporters may be examined, under oath, about their methods of investigation and editorial judgment, in an effort to show their malice or recklessness. The Court rejected the protests of newspapers and networks that the threat of such examinations, in which reporters would be forced to defend largely subjective judgments, would inhibit reporters' freedom of inquiry and so make them less effective servants of the public.

Two of the most important recent judicial decisions involving First Amendment claims never reached the Supreme Court. The first of these was the much publicized case of the *New York Times* reporter Myron Farber, which I discussed some time ago in these pages.[3] The New Jersey courts held that Farber could be jailed for contempt because he refused to turn over his files, which might well have contained information useful to a defendant accused of murder, to defense attorneys. The *Times* (supported by other papers) argued that unless reporters are able to promise

---

[3]Ronald Dworkin, "The Rights of Myron Farber," *New York Review of Books*, October 26, 1978.

confidentiality to informers, for example, their sources will disappear and the public will lose an important source of its information. But the courts did not accept that argument.[4]

The second was the case of *The Progressive*, which ended in comedy, but was nevertheless the occasion for the first preliminary injunction ever granted in the United States against publication in advance. That magazine proposed to publish an article entitled "The H-Bomb Secret: How We Got It—Why We're Telling It," and submitted it to the Atomic Energy Commission for informal clearance. The author had in fact used only public and legally available information. But the Commission, relying on its claim that all information relating to atomic weapons is "born classified" under the Atomic Energy Act, and cannot be published unless it is affirmatively cleared for publication by the Commission, refused to pass the article and sued to enjoin it. The Commission persuaded a district court judge, who listened to government testimony in secret, that publication would be damaging to national security, because it might enable a smaller nation (Idi Amin's Uganda was the example of the day) to construct a hydrogen bomb.

The Progressive appealed the district court's injunction to the Circuit Court, but before that Court acted it became apparent that all the information the author used was in fact available at a public library maintained by the Commission, and several newspapers then published the contents of the proposed article without seeking clearance. The government withdrew in some embarrassment, and *The Progressive's* article was finally published. Nevertheless it was ominous that the First Amendment provided so little protection in this case. The Commission's "born classified" argument—that it is illegal to publish any information about atomic weapons that it has not specifically cleared—is absurdly overbroad, and would not have been sustained, I think, by higher courts. But the courts might well have sustained a procedure that allows a judge to decide particular censorship cases in secret proceedings where the judge may be unduly impressed by government technical "experts." The Atomic Age is not a healthy environment for free speech.

Not all the evidence of the present decline of free speech is drawn from judicial decisions. The Freedom of Information Act, which was strengthened by Congress after the Watergate scandal, provides that anyone can obtain any information in the hands of the federal government, with certain exceptions to protect personal privacy, trade secrets, national security, and the like. We owe much valuable information—for example, parts of William Shawcross's book on Cambodia—to that Act. But pressure has been building for substantial amendment. Doctors point out that double-blind experiments testing new drugs and procedures are ruined

---

[4]Nor did the British House of Lords in a recent case in which British Steel Corporation sued Granada television to discover the name of an informer in the Steel Corporation's management.

when reporters discover information that destroys the confidentiality that makes the experiments statistically significant. Scientists argue that the incentive to carry on research may be jeopardized when newspapers publish details of interesting grant applications. The National Disease Control Center finds that hospitals will not seek its aid in locating hospital infections when journalists can make the Center's reports to the hospitals available to potential litigants.

The CIA already benefits from a specific exception to the Freedom of Information Act allowing it to withhold information on grounds of national security. It now seeks much more confidentiality—and, in the atmosphere of concern for better intelligence that has followed the seizure of the American embassy in Iran, it may get it. The Justice Department, for example, is sponsoring an amendment (HR 7056) that would exempt from the Act whatever the CIA deems to be information obtained from nongovernment sources, or information that tends to identify intelligence sources, or information concerning intelligence-collecting systems. The proposed amendment expressly provides that the CIA's decisions to withhold information by declaring that it belongs to one of these categories will *not* be reviewable in any court. So far, however, the Senate committee concerned with the CIA has resisted such restrictions.

Congress is now moving toward passage, however, of a new bill that would make it a crime for a former CIA agent or anyone else to publish the name of a present agent. The Senate version, as amended in the Intelligence Committee, now provides that those other than present or former agents who publish names are not liable unless they do so as part of a "pattern or practice" of such disclosure. The report of that committee indicates that this qualification is to protect "mainline journalists." But the qualification is so vague as to offer little protection indeed, and the bill, if constitutional, would surely constrain journalists' investigation of the agency.

The press has not, as I said, lost all its battles. The Burger Court unanimously rejected the Nixon administration's attempt to prevent the publication of the Pentagon Papers, and has just affirmed, in the *Richmond Newspapers* case, that the press does have some constitutionally protected position under the First Amendment, strong enough so that a trial judge must show some special reason for excluding reporters from a criminal trial. But the press nevertheless believes that it is losing ground overall.

II

Nat Hentoff, in his comprehensive book on the history of the First Amendment,[5] describes the rise of the idea of free speech and a free press in America from Peter Zenger on, and notices, in apparent sadness, the

[5]Nat Hentoff, *The First Freedom: The Tumultuous History of Free Speech in America* (Delacorte, 1979).

symptoms of what he plainly takes to be its present slump. The book is remarkably readable and broad. It has the great merit of showing how the idea of free speech takes on different content as the underlying substantive issues change from educational policy to obscenity to reporting of criminal trials. The tone of the book seems dispassionate. Hentoff argues mostly by quoting others. But there is no doubt where he stands. He is a partisan of free speech, and in this book there are victories and defeats for freedom, heroes, and cowards of the press, friends, and enemies of liberty.

But there is not much attempt at analysis of the philosophical grounds of free speech or freedom of the press, or much effort to find the limits of the freedoms and powers Hentoff wants to defend. In this respect he is typical of journalists who complain about the fate of the First Amendment in the courts, though he writes better and with more enthusiasm and knowledge than most. The press takes the Amendment as a kind of private charter, and attacks more or less automatically every refusal of the courts to find some further protection in that charter. The newspapers and networks denounced the decisions in the *Farber* and *Herbert* cases as fiercely—indeed even more fiercely—than those in the cases of *The Progressive* and *Snepp*. But this strategy of automatic appeal to the First Amendment is, I think, a poor strategy, even if the press is concerned only to expand its legal powers as far as possible. For if the idea becomes popular that the Amendment is an all-purpose shield for journalists, warding off libel suits, depositions, and searches as well as censorship, then it must become a weaker shield, because it will seem obvious that so broad a power in the press must be balanced against other private and social interests in the community. What will then suffer is the historically central function of the First Amendment, which is simply to ensure that those who wish to speak on matters of political and social controversy are free to do so. Perhaps the surprising weakness of the First Amendment in protecting the defendants in *The Progressive* and *Snepp* cases, for example, is partly a consequence of the very effectiveness of the press in persuading the courts, in an earlier day, that the power of the First Amendment extends well beyond straight censorship cases.

In order to test this suspicion, we must consider an issue that Hentoff and other friends of the First Amendment neglect. What is the First Amendment for? Whom is it meant to protect? A variety of views is possible. The dominant theory among American constitutional lawyers assumes that the constitutional rights of free speech—including free press which, in the constitutional language, means published speech in general rather than journalists in particular—are directed at protecting the audience. They protect, that is, not the speaker or writer himself but the audience he wishes to address. On this view journalists and other writers are protected from censorship in order that the public at large may have access to the information it needs to vote and conduct its affairs intelligently.

In his famous essay *On Liberty*, John Stuart Mill offered a similar but more fundamental justification for the right of free speech. He said that if everyone is free to advance any theory of private or public morality, no matter how absurd or unpopular, truth is more likely to emerge from the resulting marketplace of ideas, and the community as a whole will be better off than it would be if unpopular ideas were censored. Once again, on this account, particular individuals are allowed to speak in order that the community they address may benefit in the long run.

But other theories of free speech—in the broad sense including free press—hold that the right is directed at the protection of the speaker, that is, that individuals have the right to speak, not in order that others benefit, but because they would themselves suffer some unacceptable injury or insult if censored. Anyone who holds this theory must, of course, show why censorship is a more serious injury than other forms of regulation. He must show why someone who is forbidden to speak his mind on politics suffers harm that is graver than when he is forbidden, for example, to drive at high speeds or trespass on others' property or combine to restrain trade.

Different theories might be proposed: that censorship is degrading because it suggests that the speaker or writer is not worthy of equal concern as a citizen, or that his ideas are not worthy of equal respect; that censorship is insulting because it denies the speaker an equal voice in politics and therefore denies his standing as a free and equal citizen; or that censorship is grave because it inhibits an individual's development of his own personality and integrity. Mill makes something like this last claim in *On Liberty*, in addition to his market-place-of-ideas argument, and so his theory can be said to be concerned to protect the speaker as well as the audience.

Theories concerned to protect the audience generally make what I have called an argument of policy for free speech and a free press.[6] They argue, that is, that a reporter must have certain powers, not because he or anyone else is entitled to any special protection, but in order to secure some general benefit to the community as a whole, just as farmers must sometimes have certain subsidies, not for their own sakes, but also to secure some benefit for the community. Theories concerned to protect the speaker, on the other hand, make arguments of principle for free speech. They argue that the speaker's special position, as someone wanting to express his convictions on matters of political or social importance, entitles

---

[6]See *Taking Rights Seriously* (Harvard University Press, 1977).

him, in fairness, to special consideration, even though the community as a whole may *suffer* from allowing him to speak. So the contrast is great: in the former case the community's welfare provides the ground for the protection, but in the latter the community's welfare is disregarded in order to provide it.

The distinction is relevant to the present discussion in many ways. If free speech is justified on grounds of policy, then it is plausible that journalists should be given special privileges and powers not available to ordinary citizens, because they have a special and indeed indispensable function in providing information to the public at large. But if free speech is justified on principle, then it would be outrageous to suppose that journalists should have special protection not available to others, because that would claim that they are, as individuals, more important or worthier of more concern than others.

Since the powers the press claims, like the power to attend criminal trials, must be special to it, it is natural that the press favors a view of free speech based on the policy argument concerned to protect the audience: that the press is essential to an informed public. But there is a corresponding danger in this account. If free speech is justified as a matter of policy, then whenever a decision is to be made about whether free speech requires some further exception or privilege, competing dimensions of the public's interest must be balanced against its interest in information.

Suppose the question arises, for example, whether the Freedom of Information Act should be amended so that the Disease Control Center is not required to make its reports available to reporters, or whether the Atomic Energy Commission should be allowed to enjoin a magazine from publishing an article that might make atomic information more readily available to foreign powers. The public's general interest in being well informed argues against confidentiality and for publication in both cases. But the public also has an interest in infection-free hospitals and in atomic security, and these two kinds of interests must be balanced, as in a cost-benefit analysis, in order to determine where the public's overall interest lies. Suppose that in the long term (and taking side effects into account) the public would lose more overall if the information in question were published. Then it would be self-contradictory to argue that it must be published in the public's interest, and the argument for free speech, on grounds of policy, would be defeated.

The problem is quite different, of course, if we take free speech to be a matter of principle instead. For now any conflict between free speech and the public's welfare is not a pseudo conflict between two aspects of the public's interest that may be dissolved in some judgment of its overall interest. It is a genuine conflict between the rights of a particular speaker as an individual and the competing interests of the community as a whole. Unless that competing interest is very great—unless publication threatens some emergency or other grave risk—the individual's right must outweigh the social interest, because that is what it means to suppose that he has this sort of right.

So it is important to decide, when the press claims some special privilege or protection, whether that claim is based on policy or principle. The importance of the distinction is sometimes obscured, however, by a newly fashionable idea, which is that the public has what is called a "right to know" the information that reporters might collect. If that means simply that the public has an interest in knowledge—that the community is better off, all things being equal, if it knows more rather than less about, say, criminal trials or grant applications or atomic secrets—then the phrase is simply another way of stating the familiar argument of policy in favor of a free and powerful press: a better informed public will result in a better society generally. But the suggestion that the public has a *right* to know suggests something stronger than that, which is that there is an audience-protective argument of *principle* in favor of any privilege that improves the press's ability to gather news.

But that stronger suggestion is, in fact, deeply misleading. It is wrong to suppose that individual members of the community have, in any strong sense, a right to learn what reporters might wish to discover. No citizen's equality or independence or integrity would have been denied had Farber, for example, chosen not to write any of his *New York Times* stories about Dr. Jascalevich, and no citizen could have sued Farber requiring him to do so, or seeking damages for his failure to write. It may be that the average citizen would have been worse off if the stories had not been written, but that is a matter of the general welfare, not of any individual right.

In any case the alleged right to know is supposed to be a right, not of any individual citizen, but of the public as a whole. That is almost incoherent, because "the public," in this context, is only another name for the community as a whole. And it is bizarre to say that even if the community, acting through its legislators, wishes to amend the Freedom of Information Act to exempt preliminary reports of medical research, because it believes that the integrity of such research is more important than the information it gives up, it must not do so because of its own right to have that information. Analysis of First Amendment issues would be much improved if the public's interest in information, which might well be outbalanced by its interest in secrecy, were not mislabeled a "right" to know.

It is now perhaps clearer why I believe that the press's strategy of expanding the scope of the First Amendment is a bad strategy. There is always a great risk that the courts—and the legal profession generally—will settle on one theory of a particular constitutional provision. If First Amendment protection is limited to the principle that no one who wishes to speak out on matters or in ways he deems important may be censored, then the single theory of the First Amendment will be a theory of individual rights. And this means that the commands of free speech cannot be outbalanced by some argument that the public interest is better served by censorship or regulation on some particular occasion.

But if the Amendment's protection is claimed when the claim must be based on some argument concerned to protect the audience—if it is said that reporters must not be examined about their editorial judgment in libel actions because they will then be less effective in gathering news for the public to read—the single theory that might justify so broad an Amendment must be a theory of policy. It is not surprising that the dissenting opinions in the cases about which the press complains—the opinions that argue that the press should have had what it asked—contain many arguments of policy but few arguments of principle. In the *Herbert* case, for example, Mr. Justice Brennan based his dissenting opinion on a theory of the First Amendment strikingly like Mill's theory concerned to protect the audience. Brennan cited the following well-known remark of Zechariah Chafee: "The First Amendment protects . . . a social interest in the attainment of truth, so that the country may not only adopt the wisest course of action, but carry it out in the wisest way. . . ."

But of course these appeals to the general welfare of the public invite the reply that in some cases the public's real interest would be better served, on balance, by censorship than by publication. By contrast, if the Amendment is limited to its core protection of the speaker, it can provide, in its appeal to individual rights rather than the general welfare, a principle of law strong enough to provide important protection in a true First Amendment case, like that of *The Progressive*. But if the Amendment becomes too broad it can be defended only on grounds of policy like those Brennan provided. It can be defended, that is, only on grounds that leave it most vulnerable just when it is most necessary.

III

If we attend only to the core of the First Amendment, which protects the speaker as a matter of principle, then the recent record of the Court and Congress looks better, though far from perfect. Before the *Snepp* case, that core of principle was threatened, even arguably, only by the obscenity decisions, about which most of the press cares very little, and in the case of *The Progressive*, which was only a district court decision, and which ended in victory for the press anyway. The other decisions that so angered journalists—like the *Farber* and *Herbert* cases—were all decisions that simply refused to recognize reporters' arguments of policy that the public would generally be better off if reporters had special privileges. The chilling effect the press predicted for these decisions has not materialized—

indeed Mike Wallace, one of the reporters who resisted examination in the *Herbert* case, recently said that the press might have deserved to lose that case.

In any event, if democracy works with even rough efficiency, and if the reporters' arguments of policy are sound, then they will gain the powers they seek through the political process in the long run anyway, and so they have lost nothing of lasting importance by being denied these powers in the courts. For if the public really is generally better off when the press is powerful, the public might be expected to realize where its self-interest lies sooner or later—perhaps aided by the press's own advice. Except in cases like the *Farber* case, when the rights of individuals—in that case the right to a fair trial—would be infringed by expanding the power of the press, the public can then give the press what it wants by legislation.

The question arises, however, whether the *Richmond Newspapers* decision (in which, as I said, the Supreme Court held that in the absence of strong countervailing interests reporters have a right to attend criminal trials) shows that the Court is now committed to a theory of the First Amendment that goes beyond the core of principle and extends to the protection of the general welfare of the audience. It is certainly true that the result in that case might be justified by an argument of policy like the argument Brennan made in the *Herbert* case. Burger's opinion in the *Richmond Newspapers* case points out, for example, that the public is better off if its deep interest in the criminal process, and even its inevitable desire for retribution, is served by newspaper accounts of trials. But a careful reading of the several opinions in the case shows that though the seven justices who voted for the press (Mr. Justice Rehnquist dissented and Mr. Justice Powell took no part in the case) proceeded on somewhat different theories, two arguments were dominant, neither of which was a straightforward argument of policy of the type advanced by Mill.

The first, emphasized especially by Burger and, apparently, by Blackmun, ties the protection of the First Amendment to history. It argues that if any important process of government has been open to the public by longstanding traditions of Anglo-American jurisprudence, then citizens have a right, secured by the First Amendment, to information about that process, and the press therefore has a derivative right to secure and provide that information. The citizens' right is not absolute, because it must yield before competing rights of the defendant, for example. But it stands in a case, like the *Richmond Newspapers* case, in which either no important interests of the defendant are in play, or the court can protect these interests by means other than barring reporters.

This argument from history seems to me a weak argument, for there is no reason why custom should ripen into a right unless there is some independent argument of principle why people have a right to what custom gives them. But it is in any case not an argument that requires the courts to decide whether the general welfare is, on balance, served by denying the press access to information or otherwise chilling speech on any particular occasion. It holds that the press must be admitted unless some special reason, and not simply the balance of general welfare, argues against it.

The second argument, stressed particularly in Brennan's opinion, is both more important and more complex. It urges that some special protection for the press is necessary in order not simply to advance the general good but to preserve the very structure of democracy. Madison's classic statement of this argument is often cited in the briefs the press submits in constitutional cases. He said that "a popular government, without popular information or the means of acquiring it, is but a prologue to a farce or a tragedy; or perhaps both...a people who mean to be their own governors, must arm themselves with the power knowledge gives."

This is not Mill's argument, that the more information people have the more likely they are to secure, overall, what they most want. It is rather the argument that the people need some information in order even to be able to form conceptions of what they want, and in order to participate as equals in the process of governing themselves. Mill's policy argument is open-ended: the more information the better. But the Madisonian argument from the structure of democracy cannot be open-ended, for then it will end in paradox and self-contradiction.

That is so because every extension of the First Amendment is, from the standpoint of democracy, a double-edged sword. It enhances democracy because public information increases the general power of the public. But it also contracts democracy because any constitutional right disables the popularly elected legislature from enacting some legislation it might otherwise wish to enact, and this decreases the general power of the public. Democracy implies that the majority has the power to govern effectively in what it takes to be the general interest. If so, then any extension of constitutional protection of speech and the press will both increase and decrease that power, in these two different ways. Any particular person may be more effective politically because he will know more about, for example, atomic energy installations. But he may also be less effective politically, because he will lose the power to elect congressmen who will vote for censorship of atomic information. He may well count this trade-off, on balance, a loss in political power overall, particularly if he himself would prefer to sacrifice knowledge of atomic information in order to have the increased security that comes from no one else having that information either.

Every decision about censorship confronts each citizen with that sort of cost-benefit issue, and it cannot be said that he inevitably gains in political power when the matter is taken out of politics and decided by the Supreme Court instead. Indeed it is tempting to argue, on the contrary, that genuine, full-blooded democracy would require no First Amendment at all, for then every single issue of censorship would be decided by majority will through Congress and the state legislatures. But that goes too far, because, as Madison warned, people need some general and protected structure of public information even intelligently to decide whether they want more of it. There is no democracy among slaves who could seize power if they only knew how.

The opposite mistake is just as serious, however, because it is absurd to suppose that the American electorate, which already has access to a great deal more, and more sophisticated, public information than it shows any disposition to use, would gain in democratic power if the Supreme Court decided, for example, that Congress could not amend the Freedom of Information Act so as to exempt Disease Control Center reports, no matter how many people thought that such an exemption was a good idea. So the argument from the structure of democracy requires, by its own internal logic, some threshold line to be drawn between interpretations of the First Amendment that would protect and those that would invade democracy.

There is one evident, if difficult, way to draw that threshold line. It requires the Supreme Court to describe, in at least general terms, what manner of invasion of the powers of the press would so constrict the flow of information to the public as to leave the public unable intelligently to decide whether to overturn that limitation of the press by further legislation. The Court might decide, for example, that a general and arbitrary refusal of some agency of government to provide any information or opportunity for investigation to the press at all, so as to leave the public wholly uninformed whether the practices of that agency required further investigation, fell on the wrong side of that threshold.[7] But it is extremely implausible to suppose that the public would be disabled in this dramatic way if the press were excluded from those few criminal trials in which the defendant requested such exclusion, the prosecution agreed to it, and the judge thought the interests of justice would on balance be served by it. The public of a state that adopted that practice would remain competent to decide whether it disapproved that arrangement and, if so, to outlaw it through the political process. So if Madison's argument from the structure of democracy is applied to particular cases through the idea of a threshold of public competence, the *Richmond Newspapers* case should have been decided the other way.

There is another way to apply the argument from structure however, and this is suggested in Brennan's opinion in that case. He said that

[7]The Court faced that issue in the recent case of *Houhins* v *KGBX*, in which prison administrators refused a television station all opportunities to investigate prison conditions. Perhaps because two justices were unable to participate in the case, the Court reached no effective disposition of the issues of legal principle.

though the press should have full access to information in principle, some line needed to be drawn in practice, and he proposed to draw the line, not through a threshold of the sort just discussed, but through balancing the facts of each individual case. He would assume, that is, that any constraint on the press's access to information is unconstitutional, unless there are competing interests justifying that constraint, in which case the question would be which set of interests—the public's interest in information or the competing interests—were of greater weight. In the *Richmond Newspapers* case he found no such competing interests at all, and therefore found it unnecessary to discuss how much the structure of democracy would be damaged by the exclusion in question.

All this brings Brennan's argument from structure dangerously close to an argument of policy of the kind made by Mill. Though Brennan has himself been one of the most passionate advocates of free speech, his argument invites censorship in those cases in which the general welfare, on balance, would benefit from it, or rather when the public thinks that it would. For the balance Brennan describes could fall against rather than for *The Progressive,* for example. It is not absurd to suppose that publication of atomic data increases public risk to some degree. But it is absurd to think that a constraint on such publication, considered in itself as Brennan recommends, would impair the structure of American democracy to any noticeable degree, or leave the public, which has considerable general knowledge of atomic dangers, unable to decide whether to change its mind and remove the constraint through ordinary political action. Brennan would himself distinguish between cases concerning access to information, like the *Richmond Newspapers* case, and cases of straight censorship, like *The Progressive* case. But the theory he described to cover the former cases might all too easily develop into a general structural theory of the First Amendment, and freedom would then suffer.

IV

The Supreme Court's procedures in Frank Snepp's case were extraordinary and indefensible. But the decision was also, I think, wrong on the merits, and not simply as a matter of procedure and remedy. We may, for purposes of isolating the precise constitutional issue in question, suppose the following facts, some of which I stated earlier. When Snepp joined the CIA he signed a contract calling upon him to submit for clearance any materials he might later publish about the agency. He would not have been offered the position had he refused to sign that agreement. *Decent Interval,* the book he ultimately published without submitting it, contained no classified information. If he had never worked for the CIA and had never signed such an agreement, he would have been free to publish a book containing the same information without prior clearance, and he would have been subject to no legal penalty whatever. Indeed, if Congress passed a law requiring authors of books about the CIA to submit manuscripts to that agency for advance clearance, that law would be unconstitutional because it would violate authors' First Amendment rights.[8]

So the question is this: When Snepp joined the CIA, and signed the agreement, did he waive his constitutional rights to publish unclassified information about the agency, a right that anyone else, not in his position, would plainly have? I put the question that way to show that one of the arguments the CIA pressed against Snepp is not in point. The agency argued that the requirement of prior clearance it imposed on him by contract did him no harm. If the review disclosed that he wished to publish classified information, then the agency would indeed act to prevent that. But Snepp, as the CIA rightly claimed, has no constitutional rights to publish classified information. He remained free to publish any nonclassified information once the review was completed, just as anyone else would be free to do. The contractual requirement of clearance (the CIA argues) merely gave the agency a legitimate opportunity to assess for itself whether the material proposed to be published was classified, and to take any steps to deter publication of any that was. So the contract was not a waiver of any constitutional right.

But if (as I assume) even Congress could not require those who had no connection with the CIA to submit manuscripts about it for prior review, then it is not open to the agency to argue that prior review has nothing to do with censorship. Victor Marchetti's experience with the CIA after he submitted his manuscript shows (if any demonstration were needed) how a requirement of prior review makes what an author may say a matter of compromise, negotiation, and delay, all under the shadow of the threat of litigation, rather than a matter of what the author *wants* to say, which the First Amendment insists it should be.[9]

So the question is simply whether Snepp waived whatever First Amendment rights he would otherwise have had. Once again everything depends on what view one takes of the point and force of the right of free speech. Snepp's lawyers argued, in his petition for rehearing in the

---

[8]It is of course a different question, which I cannot consider now, how far Congress may constitutionally forbid citizens in general, and former agents in particular, from publishing information that may be genuinely secret and dangerous, like the names of present agents, as the bill I described earlier proposes to do.

[9]The CIA initially listed 339 sections of Marchetti's book that it said disclosed classified information. These included a statement about Richard Helms's briefing of the National Security Council, in which Marchetti reported that "his otherwise flawless performance was marred by his mispronunciation of Malagasy, formerly Madagascar, when referring to the young republic." Marchetti and Knopf took the issue to litigation, during which the CIA itself conceded that 171 of these sections were not classified.

Supreme Court, that "the unreviewed memoirs of former government officials who held positions of trust with access to the most sensitive national security information have made invaluable contributions to public debate and understanding. The publication of scores of such works without any demonstrated harm to the nation's welfare belies the need for prior restraint of CIA officials." That argument is unpersuasive if it is meant to suggest that allowing Snepp to waive the First Amendment would be wrong because it would work against the general welfare.

It is true that if the CIA and other security agencies are allowed to impose requirements of prior clearance of publication as a condition of employment, then the public will undoubtedly, over the years, lose some information it would otherwise gain. But the CIA's arguments of policy against this point—that the efficiency of its intelligence gathering operations would be compromised if it did not have opportunity to review publications by ex-agents in advance—are not frivolous. No doubt the agency has exaggerated the importance of this review. It says, for example, that foreign agencies would stop giving intelligence to the United States if Snepp had won his case. These foreign agencies are not so stupid as to think that books by ex-agents are the principal sources of leaks from the CIA. Nevertheless, even if we discount the exaggeration, it is still plausible to suppose that the CIA will be more efficient if it has a chance to argue about this or that passage in advance, and alert its friends, including foreign intelligence agencies, about what will soon be in the bookstores.

But that means that there is a genuine cost-benefit issue of policy to decide: does the public welfare gain or lose more, in the long run, if books like Snepp's are delayed and harassed? The question whether Snepp waived his rights is a fresh question of constitutional law. It is not settled by any earlier decision of the Supreme Court, or by any embedded constitutional policy favoring speech. If we assume that it is to be settled by some cost-benefit calculation about what will make the community better off as a whole in the long run, as the argument of Snepp's lawyers may suggest, then the argument that it must be settled by the courts in favor of Snepp, rather than left to Congress and the people, is not very strong.

But the argument of his lawyers is much stronger, and seems to me right, if it means to call attention not to the general welfare but to the rights of those who want to listen to what Snepp wants to say. For these citizens believe that they will be in a better position to exercise their influence on political decisions affecting the CIA if they know more about the agency's behavior, and their constitutional right to listen should not be cut off by Snepp's private decision to waive his right to speak to them.

I must now say something about this constitutional right to listen. The constitution, as a whole, defines as well as commands the conditions under which citizens live in a just society, and it makes central to these conditions that each citizen be able to vote and participate in politics as the equal of any other. Free speech is essential to equal participation, but so is the right of each citizen that others, whose access to information may be superior to his, not be prevented from speaking to him. That is distinctly not a matter of policy: it is not a matter of protecting the majority will or of securing the general welfare over the long run. Just as the majority violates the right of the speaker when it censors him, even when the community would be better off were he censored, so it violates the right of every potential listener who believes that his own participation in politics would gain, either in effectiveness or in its meaning for him, were he to listen to that speaker.

The right to listen is generally parasitic upon the right to speak that forms the core of the First Amendment, and it is normally adequately protected by an uncompromising enforcement of that core right to speak. For the right to listen is not the right to learn what no one wants to tell.[10] But the right to listen would be seriously compromised if all government agencies were free to make it a condition of employment that officials waive their rights later to reveal nonclassified information without checking with the agency first.

The law does allow private citizens or firms to extract promises of confidentiality, of course, about revealing commercial secrets or the contents of personal diaries or the like. But Snepp's case is different. The right to listen is part of the right to participate in politics as an equal, and information about the conduct of the CIA in Vietnam is plainly more germane to political activity than information about business secrets or the personal affairs of private citizens.[11]

So the issue of whether to enforce contractual waivers of the right to speak, given the constitutionally protected right of others to listen, is one that, like so many other legal issues, requires lines to be drawn. Two different lines were available to the Supreme Court in *Snepp*. It might have said that government agencies, as distinct from private persons or firms, may never make any waiver of First Amendment rights a condition of employment. That distinction would be justified on the ground that information about government agencies is presumptively information highly relevant to participation in politics, while information about private firms, while it may be, is not presumptively so.

Or the Court might have said that a government agency may never make such a waiver a condition of employment unless that condition is

[10]As a legal matter, it is necessary to recognize an independent constitutional right in order to protect those who want to listen to someone who does not himself have a constitutional right to speak. The Supreme Court has held, for example, that the First Amendment protects Americans who want to receive political material from foreign authors who are not, of course, themselves protected by the United States Constitution.

[11]Of course in particular cases differences of this character may be differences in degree only. Commercial secrets, for example, may be matters of political importance. But if so, then the argument against enforcing waivers in such cases is correspondingly stronger.

expressly imposed by Congress rather than by the agency itself. That weaker requirement would be justified on the ground that this decision—the decision whether the gravity of the threat to national security posed by former agents publishing material without prior review is sufficiently great to justify overriding the right to listen—is a decision that should be taken by the national legislature itself, rather than by an agency whose own interests in confidentiality might affect its judgment. It may well be doubted whether this second, weaker requirement is sufficient to meet the standards of the First Amendment. But it is not necessary to speculate further on that question here, because either the weaker or the stronger requirement would have argued for a decision in favor of Snepp.

It is worth asking, however, whether a different argument, not relying on the rights of others to listen, but instead relying directly on Snepp's own First Amendment right to speak, would also have justified a decision refusing to enforce his contractual waiver. It might seem that such an argument, relying directly on Snepp's own rights, must fail, because his choice to accept a job at the price of the waiver was a free and informed choice. If Snepp (who knew, as the lawyer for the CIA succinctly put it, that he was not joining the Boy Scouts) freely bargained away his full First Amendment rights by agreeing to a prior review, why should the courts now release him from his bargain when it proves inconvenient? Why should the courts now disable others from making the same bargain in the future, as they would by finding for Snepp now?

That was the CIA's argument, and it prevailed. But it is not so strong as it looks, because it rests on a mistaken analogy between a constitutional right and a piece of property. The First Amendment does not deal out rights like trading stamps whose point is to increase the total wealth of each citizen. The Constitution as a whole states, as I said, the conditions under which citizens shall be deemed to form a community of equals. An individual citizen is no more able to redefine these conditions than the majority is. The Constitution does not permit him to sell himself into slavery or to bargain away his rights to choose his own religion. This is not because it is never in his interests to make such a bargain, but because it is intolerable that any citizen be a slave or have his conscience mortgaged.

The question that must be asked, when we consider whether any particular constitutional right may be waived, is this: will the waiver leave any person in a condition deemed a denial of equality by the Constitution? Since the First Amendment defines equal standing to include the right to report what one believes important to one's fellow citizens, as well as the right to be faithful to conscience in matters of religion, the right of free speech should no more be freely available to trade than the right to religious belief. That is why the analogy to rights in property is such a poor one. If I make a financial bargain I later regret, I have lost money. But my standing as someone who participates in politics as an equal has not been impaired, at least according to the constitutional definition of what is essential to that standing. I have not sold myself into slavery or into a condition that the Constitution deems a part of slavery.

Once again, the argument does not justify the conclusion that a person should never have the power to agree not to publish certain information or to submit it for prior review. For not every such agreement leaves that person in a position that compromises his status as a political equal. The Supreme Court must therefore find a line to distinguish permissible from impermissible waivers of the constitutional right to speak, and either of the lines we defined when we considered, just now, the audience's right to listen might be appropriate to protect the speaker's right to speak.

The court might say, that is, either that no waiver is permissible as a condition of employment in a government agency, or that no such waiver is permissible unless specifically authorized by Congress. But the Court, in its brief and unsatisfactory *per curiam* opinion, did not consider these possible distinctions, either of which would have supported Snepp's claim. The Court assumed that anyone who is employed by a government agency might waive his First Amendment rights even without specific congressional authorization. That assumption makes the mistake of supposing that a constitutional right is simply a piece of personal property.

So Snepp should have been held not to have waived his First Amendment rights. That result is necessary to protect the rights of others to listen and also necessary to protect Snepp's own independence. But this argument for Snepp depends on the conception of free speech and of the First Amendment that I defended earlier. It depends on supposing that free speech is a matter of principle, and therefore that it is a matter of great injustice, not simply an abstract threat to the community's general well-being, when someone who wishes to speak his mind is muzzled or checked or delayed. Only if free speech is seen in that light does it become clear why it is so important to protect even an ex-CIA agent who signed a contract and knew he wasn't joining the Boy Scouts. The *Farber* and *Herbert* cases show why the First Amendment so conceived will not give the press all the powers and privileges it wants. The *Richmond Newspapers* case shows why it might even take away some of what the press has gained. But *The Progressive* and *Snepp* cases show why that conception is nevertheless essential to American constitutional democracy. The First Amendment must be protected from its enemies, but it must be saved from its best friends as well.

SELECTED SUPPLEMENTARY
READINGS

ANDERSON, DAVID A., ed., "The Ethics of Investigative Reporting," in *Investigative Reporting*. Bloomington, Ind.: Indiana University Press, 1976.

BARRON, JEROME A., *Freedom of The Press For Whom? The Right of Access to Mass Media*. Bloomington, Ind.: Indiana University Press, 1973.

BERGER, FRED R., "Pornography, Sex, and Censorship," *Social Theory and Practice* **4** (1977).
————, ed., *Freedom of Expression*. Belmont, Calif.: Wadsworth, 1980.
BRACKBILL, Y., AND A.E. HELLEGERS, "Ethics and Editors," *Hastings Center Report* **10** (April 1980).
CASEBIER, ALLAN, AND JANET J. CASEBIER, eds., *Social Responsibility of the Mass Media*. Washington, D.C.: University Press of America, 1978.
CHAFEE, ZECHARIAH, JR., *Free Speech in the United States*. Cambridge, Mass.: Harvard University Press, 1941.
CHRISTIANS, CLIFFORD G., AND CATHERINE L. COVERT, *Teaching Ethics in Journalism Education*. Hastings-on-Hudson, N.Y.: The Hastings Center, 1980.
DWORKIN, RONALD, "The Rights of Myron Farber," *New York Review of Books* **25** (October 26, 1978).
EMERSON, THOMAS I., *The System of Freedom of Expression*. New York: Random House, 1970.
EPSTEIN, EDWARD JAY, "Journalism and Truth," *Commentary* (April 1974).
FEINBERG, JOEL, "Limits to the Free Expression of Opinion," in *Philosophy of Law*, (2nd ed.), eds. Joel Feinberg and Hyman Gross. Belmont, Calif.: Wadsworth, 1980.
HEINE, WILLIAM C., *Journalism Ethics: A Case Book*. London, Ont.: University of Western Ontario Library, 1975.
HULTENG, JOHN L., *The Messenger's Motives: Ethical Problems of the News Media*. Englewood Cliffs, N.J.: Prentice-Hall, 1976.
LEVY, LEONARD, *Legacy of Suppression: Freedom of Speech and Press in Early American History*. Cambridge, Mass.: Harvard University Press, 1960.
MERRILL, JOHN C., AND RALPH D. BARNEY, *Ethics and the Press: Readings in Mass Media Morality*. Hastings-on-Hudson, N.Y.: The Hastings Center, 1975.
RUBEN, BERNARD, ed., *Questioning Media Ethics*. New York: Praeger Special Studies, 1978.
SHAPIRO, MARTIN, *Freedom of Speech: The Supreme Court and Judicial Review*. Englewood Cliffs, N.J.: Prentice-Hall, 1966.
SIMONS, HOWARD, AND JOSEPH A. CALIFANO, *The Media and The Law*. New York: Praeger Special Studies, 1976.
STERN, LAURENCE, "The Daniel Schorr Affair: A Morality Play for the Fourth Estate," *Columbia Journalism Review* (May–June 1976).
SWAIN, BRUCE M., *Reporter's Ethics*. Ames, Iowa: Iowa State University Press, 1978.
YANKAUER, ALFRED, "The Ethics of Publication," *American Journal of Public Health* **70** (March 1980).

part two

Justice

Human society is a cooperative enterprise structured by various moral, legal, and cultural rules and principles. These rules and principles form what may be called the *terms of cooperation* for that society; they are the implicit and explicit terms under which individuals feel obligated to cooperate with others. Sociology, history, cultural anthropology, and social philosophy are all interested in various ways in which rules and principles defining our terms of cooperation evolve, are adapted to new situations, and acquire legitimacy for those whom they govern.

Philosophers, however, have typically been less interested in questions of history and development than in questions concerning the *justice* of the terms of cooperation: what gives one person or group of people a right to expect cooperation from another person or group of people in some societal interchange (especially an economic one) where the former benefit from it and the latter do not? Is it just for some to have more than others? Is it right for one person to gain an economic advantage over another, even if both are abiding by existing societal rules? These are typical questions to be encountered in Part Two.

THE CONCEPTS OF JUSTICE
AND DISTRIBUTIVE JUSTICE

Many moral philosophers have argued that our basic notion of justice is more akin to the notion of fairness than to almost any other moral notion. While they are right to insist on the close conceptual connections between these terms, perhaps the single word most broadly linked to the general meaning of "justice" is "desert." One has acted justly toward a person when that person has been given what he or she is due or owed, and therefore has been given what he or she deserves or can legitimately claim. It may be that a person deserves to be awarded a prize, for example, in which case justice has been done when that person receives the prize. What persons deserve or can legitimately claim is based on certain relevant properties they possess. If a person possesses the property of being a lawbreaker or of otherwise wrongly treating others, we are justified in allocating an appropriate punishment. But it is wrong, as a matter of justice, to allocate a punishment or reward if the person does *not* possess the relevant property. Similarly, it is unjust to reward a supervisor for the work of his or her subordinates when it was not the supervisor's guidance that led to the rewardable productivity.

The expression "distributive justice" refers to the proper distribution (or intentional nondistribution, as Nozick suggests) of social benefits and burdens. Paying taxes and serving on juries are distributed burdens, while welfare checks and foundation grants are distributed benefits. Most recent literature on distributive justice dealing with issues of fair *economic* distribution has focused on unjust distributions in the form of inequalities of income among different classes of persons and unfair tax burdens on certain classes. But there are other problems of economic justice, as we shall see.

Distributive justice is a notion that applies only to the distribution of scarce benefits, where there is some competition for them. If there are plenty of fish in a river so that everyone can have as many as he or she can catch, we do not establish patterns limiting fishermen or the fishing industry. It is only when we are worried that the fish supply will be exhausted or that future fishermen will be unfairly affected by present fishing that we set limits to the number of fish they may catch. There are, of course, various patterns that could serve as models for the distribution; but that fact is irrelevant to the present point. The point is that there are no problems of distributive justice and no need of principles of distributive justice until some measure of scarcity exists. Even when burdens rather than benefits are being allocated, there is competition for the least disadvantageous distribution.

David Hume pointed out that we have developed the concept of justice in order to handle situations where claims are pressed by parties with conflicting interests. As he put it, there would be no point to having rules of justice unless society were composed of persons in competition for scarce resources. The rules of justice serve to strike a balance between conflicting interests and claims that repeatedly occur in society. This shows a close link between the lawful society and the just society, since law and morality are our explicit tools for balancing conflicting claims. Nonetheless, the law may be unjust; and there may be many rules of justice that are not connected to the law or to legal enforcement.

PRINCIPLES AND THEORIES OF DISTRIBUTIVE JUSTICE

In the philosophy of distributive justice there are a few widely discussed (so-called material) principles of distributive justice. Each principle mentions a relevant property on the basis of which burdens and benefits should be distributed. That is, each principle asserts a standard of relevance for purposes of distribution. The following is a fairly standard list of the major candidates for the position of valid principles of distributive justice (though longer lists have been proposed):

1. To each person an equal share
2. To each person according to individual need
3. To each person according to individual effort
4. To each person according to societal contribution
5. To each person according to merit

There is no obvious barrier to acceptance of more than one of these principles, and some theories of justice accept all five as valid. Most societies use several of them, applying different principles of distribution in different contexts. In the United States, for example, unemployment and welfare payments are distributed on the basis of need (and to some extent on the basis of previous length of employment); jobs and promotions are in many sectors awarded (distributed) on the basis of demonstrated achievement and merit; the higher incomes of wealthy professionals are allowed (distributed) on the grounds of superior effort or merit or social contribution (or perhaps all three); and, at least theoretically, the opportunity for elementary and secondary education is distributed equally to all citizens.

Theories of distributive justice are commonly developed by emphasizing and elaborating one or more of the above principles of distributive justice, perhaps in conjunction with other moral principles. *The utilitarian theory* holds that economic justice is viewed as merely one among a number of problems about how to maximize value in society. The ideal economic distribution, utilitarians argue, is *any* arrangement that would have this maximizing effect. In his defense of an *egalitarian theory*, John Rawls argues that a social contract account of justice is more acceptable than the utilitarian view. Rawls then attempts to justify two basic principles of justice by appeal to a hypothetical situation in which fully rational agents choose the principles of distribution they wish to govern everyone in society. Rawls's central contention is that we would choose to distribute economic goods and services *equally* except in those cases where an unequal distribution would actually work to everyone's advantage, especially to the benefit of the worst off in society. Both utilitarianism and egalitarianism are rejected in Robert Nozick's *libertarian theory*. He argues that a theory of justice should work to protect our rights not to be coerced and should not propound a thesis intended to "pattern" society through distributive arrangements that redistribute economic benefits and burdens. Any economic arrangements that we freely choose are thus just. Nozick develops an entitlement theory according to which we have a right, without interference, to economic benefits we produce for ourselves, as well as a right to our voluntary economic transactions. Both Rawls and Nozick may be seen to be arguing about the connection between *autonomy* and *justice*; each has a competing conception of what the emphasis on autonomy requires for a theory of justice.

Justice in economic distribution is of course not the only crucial issue of justice. Some groups (specifically, women and nonwhite minorities) have been effectively excluded in the past by explicit and implicit discriminatory rules, and thus have been denied equal justice. Is it just, however, for a society to take extraordinary measures to compensate for this past injustice? Specifically, may women and nonwhites be given preferential treatment in the awarding of jobs or places in universities on the basis of the past injustices or present discriminatory practice, or does this simply compound the wrong by violating the rights of white males? Let us first explore these issues by considering the general question of the idea of equality and the ideal of equal treatment. Having done so, we can turn more particularly to issues of discrimination and preferential treatment.

THE IDEAL OF EQUALITY

If we say that all people should be treated equally, what ideal of equality are we espousing? We clearly are not in *all* respects equal. We must, then, determine the *relevant* respects in terms of which everyone should be treated equally. Aristotle argued that as long as persons are equal in all the respects relevant to the type of treatment under consideration, they should be treated equally; when they are unequal, they should, in proportion, be treated as unequals. For example, if someone is being hired as a teacher, that person should receive equal consideration along with everyone else on the merits of teaching ability. Only if one is demonstrably less or more capable than others as a teacher should one be treated unequally. Here race and sex, no less than a factor such as weight, are irrelevant characteristics. This Aristotelian view is an intelligent thesis about equality, one that almost everyone would agree states a necessary condition of equality. But is it also a sufficient condition? Here there is far less agreement. At least three widely held views now exist on the nature of equality (understood as an ideal). It will be helpful to examine all three before proceeding further.

   1. Equality as a Procedural Principle.   This first view of equality does not move far beyond Aristotle, if it moves beyond him at all. According to its proponents, there is no single specifiable respect or set of respects in terms of which all people should be equally considered. Rather, there is only a procedural principle of impartiality by which we ought to abide in all circumstances: "No person should be treated unequally, despite all differences with other persons, until such time as it has been shown that there is a difference between them relevant to the treatment at stake." The point of the principle is that he who seeks to treat someone unequally must prove that the person deserves unequal treatment by showing a relevant difference between that person and others. Special favoritism and prejudice are supposedly eliminated in this way. The supporters of this view argue that particular contexts normally provide *rules* to determine differences, but where there are no rules then anyone who wishes to discriminate must provide an argument against equal treatment. This view of equality is sometimes called "formal" equality because it does not specify which *particular* differences should allow us to discriminate between people. Instead it simply treats like cases alike, where "like cases" are analyzed in terms of a given set of rules. It should be noticed that the procedural principle does not rule out hiring blacks *because* they are blacks or women *because* they are women, so long as they are equal with white or male candidates in the relevant respects (for example, teaching ability). Indeed, the principle *permits* this practice, provided that one has a good reason for hiring a woman or a black.

Does this view provide a sufficient condition of equality? Many think it does not. By not distinguishing specific relevant differences, it seems not only to be an empty theory but also to allow the institutionalization of various forms of inequality, including inequalities in the very rules determining "equal treatment." Any criteria of relevance deemed acceptable, argue opponents, seem in this view to be in moral fairness acceptable. For example, if it is judged a good reason for not interviewing women for jobs that they make male interviewers nervous, then this introduces a relevant difference. This implication of the theory, if drawn correctly here, seems to render it useless as a tool for criticizing even blatant injustice. After all, the theory so construed is perfectly compatible with tyrannical rule and with caste systems; it allows through the back door the institutional favoritisms it appears to eliminate.

2. Equality as a Set of Fundamental Rights.   Moral rights have various origins. If I swear to you that I will tell the whole truth and nothing but the truth, you acquire a right to be told the truth. Still other rights are transmitted by family ties. But do all rights rest on such contingent relations? Many philosophers have maintained that we have fundamental rights, irrespective of merit, just because we are human. This view gives rise to a second view of equality, one closely tied to the classically rooted idea that humanity is a quality possessed by all people. This humanity is said to confer rights to impartial treatment in matters of justice, freedom, equality of opportunity, and so on. Members of minority groups often complain about treatment that destroys their human dignity and self-respect. One interpretation of these complaints is to say that their fundamental human rights are being violated; stronger language has it that their very *humanity* is being violated. According to this idea of equality, these human rights are so fundamental that they take precedence over all other considerations. Of if they do not always take precedence, then anyone who challenges this equality of rights begins with an extraordinarily strong presumption against his case that must be overcome by careful impartial reasoning. If inequalities themselves are validly institutionalized, it is argued, this can only be for the purpose of ensuring the greater freedom, justice, and well-being of the individuals in society. Disagreements should be resolved not, for example, by weighing conflicting *interests*, but rather by weighing conflicting *rights,* for it is only by reference to rights that institutional structures can properly be measured.

Again, however, many philosophers have not found this an attractive alternative. What are we to do when basic rights conflict? If persons who come into conflict appeal to the right of free pursuit, how are we to arbitrate their different interests? And, perhaps most important, it is not clear that this second and supposedly stronger view of equality overcomes the main problem of the procedural principle view, for it seems entirely compatible with the institutionalization of radical inequalities. Rights are notoriously *nonspecific.* After all, haven't most people long thought that women in Western societies, for example, live in a society that provides equality of freedom and opportunity? Formally, the early feminist movement achieved all its goals: Women were admitted to universities and professions, given the right to vote, and so on. Yet the proportion of women to men in professional life has been decreasing ever since. Have women been treated equally by the mere acquisition of these "rights"? And, more specifically, is it not the case that for years segregation in schools was judged consistent with, if not in fact an instance of, *equality*? Otherwise, why was the expression "separate but equal" used?

3. Equality as Balanced Distribution.   A third view of the ideal of equality tries to connect equality with the idea of a balanced distribution of benefits and hardships. Its adherents argue that because the meritocratic conception of "equal opportunity *if* equally qualified" magnifies differences between individuals by upgrading the superior, it is ineffectual in combating natural and systematic inequalities. They argue instead both that the inequalities produced by nature or by systematic underprivilege should be minimized or overcome and that we should alter those features in individuals' circumstances which prevent them from realizing their natural abilities. For example, it seems that men are presently better employed than women because of *systems* of employment. Perhaps we should have social policies that expressly attempt to compensate for such a disadvantage (for example, by giving preferential treatment in recruitment and screening processes). Similarly, it can be argued that people with great natural physical or mental talent have too much of an advantage until we balance the circumstances. The point can be stated more generally: Those who work hard in society should not be penalized because others who work only *equally* hard are different (merely) by virtue of being born with desirable natural abilities. This is not a call for total uniformity in society (and hence for mediocrity, as some maintain), but rather is an appeal to the idea that a society will remain one of unequals so long as radical disparities in benefits, burdens, opportunities, and education are allowed to exist. The ideal of equality, then, is properly a matter of equalizing the distribution of these items.

Numerous objections have also been advanced against this treatment of equality. First, it is said that the theory misses what rightly should be its own target. "Equality," as we use the term, say opponents, is not so much a matter of overcoming inequalities as it is of meeting fundamental needs. When the state compensates citizens with special education programs, preferential hiring, and health benefits, it is in order to meet fundamental needs required for human welfare. But the meeting of basic needs is perfectly compatible with even great inequalities in income and other benefits. Second, it is often objected that there is nothing unreasonable about distributing according to merit, or need, or both merit and need. In fact, it is often argued that the incentives resulting from distribution according to merit (desert) and the handicaps overcome by distribution according to need together produce a more progressive set of economic benefits than would the economic uniformities of a welfare state. Third, it has of late frequently been maintained that to equalize by removing inequalities is to create a threat to the quality of certain institutions fundamental to the welfare and advancement of society. To equalize the number of positions for blacks and women in the business and university communities is to dilute the quality by cutting down on the total pool of available talent (white males).

PREFERENTIAL TREATMENT
AND REVERSE DISCRIMINATION

Such objections have fueled a sustained controversy in recent years about government policies that are intended to ensure fairer opportunities for women and minority groups. Target goals, timetables, and quotas seem to many citizens not merely to be *preferential treatment* but actually to discriminate against more talented applicants who are excluded yet would be hired or accepted on their merits were it not for the preferential advancement of others. Such government policies are said to create a situation of "reverse discrimination." By balancing or compensating for past discrimination against persons on the basis of (morally irrelevant) characteristics such as race, sex, nationality, and religion, these policies now require discrimination in favor of such persons and therefore against the members of other previously favored classes. These policies seem unfairly discriminatory to some because they violate basic principles of justice and equal protection. Others believe this conclusion to be incorrect for a variety of reasons. In Chapter 6 we will study whether some compulsory government policies and even some policies voluntarily adopted by private industry would result in preferential treatment of persons and, if so, whether such policies are appropriate and justifiable.

It is sometimes said in popular literature that "affirmative action" is synonymous with "reverse discrimination," but this equation of meaning is probably mistaken. Affirmative action basically means the taking of positive steps to hire persons from groups previously discriminated against in educational and employment situations. Passive nondiscrimination is not sufficient to qualify as affirmative action. Federal requirements at a minimum impose on business the responsibility to advertise jobs fairly and to seek out members of those groups discriminated against in the past for employment. The projected means for the fulfillment of these responsibilities are called employment *goals*. A "goal" in this context is a targeted employment outcome (intended to eliminate discrimination) that is planned by an institution (probably after consultation with government officials). A goal is commonly distinguished from a *quota*, which is construed in this context as a hard-and-fast figure or proportion—usually expressed in percentages. Goals and quotas sound to many ears like the same thing, and it is often difficult to know which an author has in mind. However, one fact seems clear: there is a crucial *symbolic* difference between the two. Goals have come largely to symbolize federally mandated or negotiated targets and timetables, whereas quotas have come largely to symbolize policies resulting in reverse discrimination. But what is "reverse discrimination" and how does it differ from both "affirmative action" and "preferential hiring"?

Writers on the subject of reverse discrimination often use the term "reverse discrimination" in different ways. At a minimum this term means discrimination by one person or set of persons P_1 against another set of persons P_2, where P_2 formerly had discriminated against P_1. Some also assert or assume that, by definition, reverse discrimination occurs only as a result of policies involving *blanket* preferential treatment on the basis of sex or race for whole groups of persons who are members of those classes. Yet this understanding of reverse discrimination is questionable on at least two counts. First, properties other than race or sex may be used—religion or nationality, for example. Second, and more importantly, there is no reason why (by definition) a policy of compensation resulting in a reversal of discrimination must apply in blanket fashion to whole groups rather than more restrictedly to a limited number of individuals who are members of those groups. Suppose an industry-wide preferential policy were adopted that competitively advantaged the job applications of all blacks earning less than $10,000 per year (and which discriminated against competitive whites earning equivalent amounts) but did not advantage blacks who earned more than that figure. This policy would certainly qualify as reverse discrimination (based on race), but the *entire* racial group would not have been given blanket preferential treatment.

This issue is important because it is often said that affluent women and minority group members would be advantaged, and disadvantaged poor whites or males would be discriminated against, by preferential hiring policies. Some authors have seemed to favor this possible outcome: "The mere fact of a person's being black in the United States is a sufficient reason for providing compensatory techniques even though that person may in some ways appear fortunate in his personal background."[1] But this is a particular *moral* thesis about the justifiability of reverse discrimination. It does not explicate necessary features of the term's *meaning*. Hence, one can advocate even radical policies of compensation resulting in reverse discrimination and at the same time advocate nonblanket, perhaps highly restrictive policies of preferential treatment.

We can now summarize the basic outlines of the concept of reverse discrimination as follows: reverse discrimination is a discriminatory action or practice based on a (normally) morally irrelevant property; policies resulting in reverse discrimination may also apply to individual persons and/or groups and need not involve unqualified blanket preferential treatment; and, finally, any morally irrelevant property could be used—not simply race and sex.

It should also be noted that *both* minimal affirmative action programs *and* policies possibly productive of reverse discrimination involve what is referred to as "preferential hiring." This notion refers to hiring that gives preference in recruitment and ranking to women, minority groups, and others previously discriminated against. This preference can be practiced either by the use of goals or quotas, or merely by choosing blacks, women, or other groups whenever their credentials are *equal* to those of other candidates. However, "preferential hiring" carries connotations for some persons of reverse discrimination or at least of quotas. Accordingly, one should be careful to understand the term's exact use in any document or article in which it appears.

COMPENSATORY JUSTICE

We sometimes think that a severe injustice has been done to a *group* of persons. Naturally we wish to restore the balance of justice by compensating them for their loss. The *principle of compensatory justice* says that whenever an injustice has been committed, just compensation or reparation is owed the injured parties. It is now a widespread view that minority groups discriminated against in the past, including women, blacks, North American Indians, and French Canadians, should be recompensed for these injustices by compensatory policies such as affirmative action or equal opportunity programs. Whatever one may think of this proposal, it is not difficult to understand why this view is espoused. For years deliberate barriers or quotas were placed on opportunities for blacks, women, and other groups to participate in some of society's most desirable institutions

---

[1]Graham Hughes, "Reparations for Blacks?" *New York University Law Review* **43** (December 1968), p. 1073.

(universities, business, law, and others). In addition, even when barriers were formally dropped matters often did not improve. Inequalities, many came to think, are rooted in early training in public schools or in unfair testing. They further charged that our systems of screening and promotion discriminate not intentionally *against* certain groups so much as unintentionally *in favor of* other groups. All of these factors have conspired to produce a range of government programs, all of which are in effect compensatory measures.

Because of this history of discrimination and its persistence, it is widely believed that we could restore the balance of justice by making it easier for previously discriminated-against groups to obtain admission to educational institutions and job interviews. Presumably, special programs also avoid the problem of mere *token* approval of more equal distribution. This system seems clearly, however, to involve an extensive network of preferential treatments, and many have asked the following question about it: If quotas or social policies require that, for example, a woman or a black be given preference over a white man otherwise better qualified (i.e., if the circumstances had been anonymous the white man would have been selected), is this an acceptable instance of compensatory justice or is it a pure and simple case of treating the white man unjustly? In answer to question it has been argued in various ways by some that such practices of preferential treatment are (a) just, (b) unjust, or (c) not just but permitted by principles other than our concepts of justice and equality.

a. Those who claim that such compensatory measures are just, or perhaps required by justice, argue that the past lives in the present: The victims of past discrimination against blacks are still handicapped or discriminated against, while the families of past slave owners are still being unduly enriched by inheritance laws. Those who have inherited wealth which was accumulated by iniquitous practices do not have as much right to the wealth, it is argued, as do the sons of slaves, who at least have a right of compensation. In the case of women it is argued that culture equips them with a lack of self-confidence, prejudicially excludes them from much of the work force, and treats them as a low-paid auxiliary labor unit. Hence only extraordinarily independent women can be expected to compete even psychologically with males. Sometimes a slightly stronger argument is advanced: compensation is fair even if some inequalities cannot be removed by offering the best available training measures. The compensation is said to be fair simply because it is *owed* to those who in the past suffered unjust treatment. We may, for example, think veterans are owed preferential treatment because of their service and sacrifice to country, and thus we may similarly think blacks and women are owed preferential treatment because of their economic sacrifices, systematic incapacitation, and consequent personal and group losses. The issues can thus be treated in two separate ways. We can see affirmative action programs as *compensat-*

ing some groups for *past* wrongs; or we can see these programs as attempting to compensate for *present* discriminatory practices and social structure. The former way may be seen as a kind of compensation for a past harm; the latter way may be seen as an attempt to provide for present *fair* equality of opportunity.

b. Those who claim that compensatory measures are unjust argue variously that no criteria exist for measuring compensation, that the extent of discrimination is now minor (insufficiently broad to justify preferential treatment), and that none of those actually harmed in previous eras is available now to be compensated. Instead of providing compensation, they argue, we should continue to guide justice by strict equality and merit, while attacking the roots of discrimination. Also, some now successful but once underprivileged minority groups argue that their long struggle for equality is jeopardized by programs of "favoritism" to blacks and women. Their view is that they either will suffer unfairly, having already suffered enough, or else will not suffer only because they too will be compensated for past oppressions. Is it not absurd, they say, to suggest that *all* past oppressed groups—blacks and women being only two among a great many—should receive compensatory reparations? Are we not compounding initial injustices with a vastly complicated system of further injustices? Some of these arguments are carefully developed in the article below by William Blackstone.

c. The third possible view is that some strong compensatory measures are *not just*, because they violate principles of justice, and yet *are justifiable* by appeal to principles other than justice. This view is argued in Chapter 6 by Tom Beauchamp.

INTERNATIONAL ECONOMIC JUSTICE AND WORLD POWER

In most discussions of economic justice, the framework for the discussion is a national state. We ask, should taxes in the United States be made more progressive? Should Saudi Arabia put more of its oil wealth into public works projects? However, given the wide disparity in the standard of living between the developed industrial countries and the largely underdeveloped agricultural or single-resource countries, perhaps an equally appropriate question of economic justice should focus on whether or not rich countries should sacrifice some of their standard of living (wealth) for the benefit of poorer countries. Specifically, do well-off nations have any obligation to feed starving nations?

The fact of world hunger itself needs no introduction, but the proper role of moral and political philosophy in resolving this problem is less obvious. The right to food has often been appealed to in these discussions, but such appeals seem most deeply to be problems of distribution of justice. Let us, then, begin with the idea of a right to food and move progressively to more complex and theoretical considerations of justice.

The idea of a right to food has uncertain origins, but its history is characterized far more by the rhetoric of political proposal than by careful analysis of the meaning and scope of proposed rights. Unlike rights such as the right to life, the right to liberty, and the right to property, assertions of a right to food are relatively recent phenomena. Serious modern discussions of a right to food, along with many discussions of other rights on an international level, can be traced at least to the December 10, 1948, Universal Declaration of Human Rights of the United Nations General Assembly. This document attempted to set forth "a common standard of achievement for all peoples." It specifically mentions a right to food, together with a very long list of postulated rights. This declaration also illustrates the ambiguous history of proclamations of rights at the international level, for it does not appear to construe rights as entitlements. Its preamble gives the impression that the document is to be read as a blueprint for future actions and declarations of rights rather than an assertion of rights that persons in their native states *now* possess. The declaration seems to function as a guide for progressive development, both of rights and of material security, rather than as an assertion of prevailing rights or so-called natural and human rights.

The notion that rights are guiding ideals rather than existing entitlements has been given explicit recognition in many documents subsequent to the U.N. Declaration. It might even be argued that this use of the term "rights" is the prevailing political use. Thus, in the report of the 1974 Symposium on Population and Human Rights at the World Population Conference in Bucharest, also sponsored by the United Nations, it was formally recorded by some participants that "the right to an adequate standard of living, including food ... would remain a *distant ideal* for many developing countries unless their economic growth was accelerated."[2] The word "right" is here clearly functioning to set forth a commendable or perhaps obligatory target, and not to state an entitlement held by the citizens of developing countries. Indeed, it is probably safe to say that virtually all political statements about the right to food express guiding ideals rather than entitlements. In the writings of many religious organizations interested in the right to food, the use of the term "right" also fits this pattern. For example, the policy statement of Bread for the World, a self-described "Christian citizen's lobby on world hunger" proclaims that, "As Christians we affirm the right to food: the right of every man, woman, and

---

[2]"Report of the Symposium on Population and Human Rights," World Population Conference, August 19–30, 1974. New York: United Nations, 1974, pp. 16, 19. (Italics added.)

child on earth to a nutritionally adequate diet. This right is grounded in the value God places on human life . . . ."[3]

Statements of the United States Congress invite a similar interpretation; for example, the 1976 "Right-to-Food Resolution" in the House of Representatives fits this pattern. The lengthy testimony before the Subcommittee on International Resources, Food, and Energy finds its point of departure in a resolution passed by the House and Senate (and deriving from previous statements of the United Nations) to the effect that "every person in this country and throughout the world has the right to food—the right to a nutritionally adequate diet—and that this right is henceforth to be recognized as a cornerstone of United States policy."[4] As with the above statement by a religious group, these hearings take on the sober atmosphere of tackling a job that must be done to reduce world hunger. There is no indication that individuals are now entitled to make claims for food, but rather that United States policy should be directed towards "assisting the world's poorest people."

THE PROBLEM OF TRIAGE

Problems of distributive justice and food have emerged most prominently through a controversy over whether a *triage system* ought to be used by wealthy nations when making allocation decisions. (A *method of triage* is a system of allocational criteria that specify priorities; the method specifies which goods and services are to be distributed first, which second, etc. when not all demands for the goods and services can be met. The word has come into vogue because of its history in wartime systems of medical care allocations for battle and disaster victims.) Arguments to show strong obligations to give food for famine relief—paralleling those of Peter Singer discussed in this chapter—as well as assertions of rights by such bodies as the United Nations, often do not consider the possibility that food assistance *intended* to alleviate suffering and malnutrition may eventuate in the long run in greater suffering and harm than actual benefits for nations that are the recipients of the assistance. Some writers, foreseeing precisely this disastrous possibility, through empirically based predictions of long term negative effects of food assistance, argue that no nation is morally required to assist any nation unwilling to adopt population policies that would align the size of the nation's population with available

[3]Bread for the World, "The Right to Food: A Statement of Policy," *Worldview* **18** (May 1975), p. 45.

[4]*The Right-to-Food Resolution.* Hearings before the Subcommittee on International Resources, Food, and Energy of the Committee on International Relations of the House of Representatives, Ninety-fourth Congress, 2nd Session, on H. Cong. Res. 393, June 22–29, 1976. Washington, D.C.: Government Printing Office, 1976, p. 2.

food resources. The method of triage is applied to food assistance programs by a system of allocation favoring, first, nations that are truly needy but would survive without the aid, and, second, nations that have massive needs for food and population-control assistance but that can and will bring their populations into line with food resources. The third set of nations are those with food problems that *cannot* be resolved over the long run because they will not or cannot bring their populations into alignment with food resources. Assistance to these nations will ultimately increase rather than decrease their problems. According to hard-line exponents of a triage system, the latter group of nations should receive no assistance.

This triage conception of allocation has been subjected to many impressive objections. Both factual and moral problems have been discussed. There are factual problems about how to obtain evidence for the thesis that food assistance will only be an interim solution and over the long run will increase rather than decrease problems, thereby causing more suffering for the citizens of both the donor and recipient nations. Most moral objections are based on contentions such as Singer's that we are obliged to do all that we can, perhaps up to the point that nothing of comparable moral importance must be sacrificed. Whatever the merits of such objections, two brief points moderately in defense of triage exponents deserve attention. First, the triage approach is a proposed solution to problems of distributive justice that puts forward a general program, on a principled basis, for the distribution of food. Second, the program also provides a way for delineating those who do and those who do not have a right to food. According to triage theory, citizens in nations eligible for food assistance have a right to food, because others have an obligation to provide it; but citizens in nations not eligible for food assistance do not have a right to food because others do not have an obligation to provide the food.

However the problem of triage is to be handled, it appears that the right to food weakens when the use of resources to make it available would endanger, reduce, or extinguish the supply of goods and services to which individuals can claim rights by virtue of some other, presumably equally justified allocational commitments. Because the right to food must be exercised at the international level, not domestically with nation states, moral justification of a right to food seems in the end to require a theory of justice capable of transcending national concerns and boundaries. One common criticism of triage theories presumably uses a basis in justice to show that more variables than overpopulation must be mentioned to explain malnutrition and starvation in certain underdeveloped countries. In a provocative article in Chapter 7, Onora O'Neill defends a Kantian approach to famine problems and argues that the international business activities of many corporations are at least partially responsible for the dire conditions in certain underdeveloped countries. She focuses particularly on the foreign-investment activities and on the policies of commodity pricing. Since the economic chains linking U.S. multinationals and the foreign policy of the U.S. government extend to U.S. citizens, there is a relevant sense, she claims, in which almost all of us are responsible for the deaths of famine victims. Our duty, then, is to redirect the policies of the U.S. government and the multinational corporations.

THE JUSTICE OF CRIMINAL PUNISHMENT

Recent prison riots have occasioned a crisis of conscience by bringing into the open what penologists have long known: Prisons are institutions in which severe punishment and inhuman conditions breed hardened criminals rather than reformed citizens. Public discussion in the aftermath of the riots has also made it clear that we have no very systematic reasons to justify the manner in which we treat convicted criminals. This state of affairs is not simply a contemporary phenomenon produced by the modern world of impersonal, decaying, and pressure-packed cities, for the nineteenth-century philosopher Jeremy Bentham found these same problems in his native England. Bentham diligently campaigned in an effort to show that both the *practical system* of criminal punishment and the *theoretical justification* for it were in need of major reform. He found the practice of punishment brutal, overly expensive, and its court procedure vague. He regarded the prevailing theoretical justifications as deficient because they were retributive in character; that is, punishment was thought to be justified because a criminal offender's pernicious act deserved repayment. Bentham thought that punishment could be just only if it were reformatory and deterrent in character. Since his time philosophers and legal thinkers have vigorously debated these issues, with the ethical controversies chiefly settling on questions of theoretical justification. Since it is (*prima facie*) morally wrong to inflict intended suffering and since punishment consists in such infliction, ethicists are concerned to say why we are sometimes justified in doing so. In this chapter we shall explore recent central lines of argument on the question of justification.

In its most general form the problem of justifying criminal punishment centers on the following question: "Under what *conditions* is criminal punishment justified?" The major philosophical theories that have been devised to answer the demand that punishment be justified are customarily split into two opposed camps—*retributivist* and *utilitarian*. Some philosophers, however, are more accurately described as holding some combination of these positions, and thus fall into a third category.

Retributivists characteristically emphasize the moral and legal guilt of the offender, the deserved character of a penalty, and the principle that society reciprocally has a right to punish criminal offenders. They generally deny that the consequences of sentencing are relevant to the problem of justifying punishment and stress instead that the crime itself justifies punishment. Their position here is influenced by those trends in moral philosophy that emphasize the fulfillment of obligations and the avoidance of injustices. Retributivists derive their views about punishment from an evaluation of the criminal act when placed in a context of social obligations. Society, they argue, is an integrated, law-governed system of both mutual benefits and indebtednesses. To act against this system in a criminal manner is to receive undeserved benefits. The criminal then owes society a debt for what he has taken. He deserves the punishment, which is effectively a discharging of his obligation. The punishment of criminals is justified, then, in much the same way the collecting of a debt is justified.

Utilitarians, on the other hand, typically maintain that although all suffering involved in punishment is evil, it is justified if its threat or enforcement produces positive individual and social consequences, such as deterrence of crime, reformation of character, and rehabilitation of skills. This position is dictated in large measure by a wider utilitarian philosophy, with its stress on the production of good consequences and the avoidance of suffering. Utilitarians, like retributivists, look at the criminal act in a social context. They agree with retributivists that society is a system of mutual benefits but ask whether the social benefits of punishment outweigh the suffering involved. If benefits such as deterrence and reformation do outweigh the suffering, this fact is said to *justify* punishment. On the other hand, if the suffering outweighs the benefits (so that more evil than good results), then punishment is not justified, even if a person in some respects deserves to be punished. The punishment would serve no worthwhile social function. This is clearly a consequentialist argument: One should always perform the action that produces the greatest possible balance of good over evil, whether in matters of punishment or in other moral matters.

An increasingly popular thesis recently advanced is that although each of these staple theories is individually insufficient to justify punishment, some combination of elements taken from both is sufficient. Those who espouse this reconciling view might be called *utilitarian retributivists*. They emphasize the necessity of both positive social benefits and the avoidance of excessive injustice. To cite one example of this approach, it has been maintained that punishment is justified both because it is deserved and because it has a deterrent effect, but is not justified if only one of the two criteria has been satisfied. This view aims at the result of not punishing those who do not deserve it and of not punishing at all unless the penalty serves either as an individual or as a social deterrent. Presumably this alternative escapes the central criticisms of both utilitarianism (it allows punishment of the innocent) and retributivism (it allows punishment with no worthwhile result).

In order to evaluate these attempts to justify punishment, it is useful to distinguish between the justification of punishment as an *institution* and the justification of punishment in *individual cases*—especially if one is inclined toward a reconciling position. (John Rawls has referred to a more general form of this distinction as that between "justifying a practice and justifying a particular action falling under it.") To some philosophers utilitarianism has appeared far more plausible as a theory justifying a system of punishment in general—the whole institution of punishment procedures and standards—than as a theory justifying individual cases of punishment. It seems unsatisfactory in the latter cases, because utilitarianism appears to justify the punishment of innocent persons whenever such punishment produces less social harm than their nonpunishment would produce. (In Roman law, for example, punishment for regicide was inflicted not only on the malefactor but on his or her family also.) But utilitarianism per se is not subject to this objection, and is intuitively appealing, if it is understood to justify the institution of punishment in general.

Retributivism is in the reverse situation. It seems less acceptable as a general justification of the institution because it denies the significance of evaluating the advantages and disadvantages of social institutions; yet this evaluation is normally the way we justify their existence. Nonetheless, retributivism is plausible when construed (more legalistically) as justifying individual cases of punishment, for it is a well-entrenched social belief that intentional violations of the law *deserve* penalties correlative to the offense, and similarly, that punishment seems undeserved unless there has been such an offense. Looked at from these two perspectives, then, it may be possible to reconcile the utilitarian and retributivist positions. Utilitarianism is seen as taking an *external* view of the institution in order to justify it as a body of rules, while retributivism is seen as taking an *internal* view of the institution and its rules in order to justify particular instances of punishment.

THE DEATH PENALTY

In England the following kind of death penalty was being imposed as late as 1812:

> That you and each of you, be taken to the place from whence you came, and from thence be drawn on a hurdle to the place of execution, where you shall be hanged by the neck, not till you are dead; that you be severally taken

down, while yet alive, and your bowels be taken out and burnt before your faces—that your heads be then cut off, and your bodies cut into four quarters, to be at the King's disposal. And God have mercy on your souls.[5]

There can be little reasonable doubt that this particular death sentence prescribes unjustifiably cruel and unusual punishment. Since this period in English history there have been modifications in both the methods of execution and in the number of crimes thought to deserve capital punishment. Movements to abolish the death penalty completely have gained strong footholds.

The seven major considerations traditionally used to oppose the death penalty are the following: (1) Capital punishment is a primitive retributive idea based on revenge; (2) judicial mistakes lead to the death of innocent persons; (3) the sentence is often imposed unfairly against underprivileged groups; (4) the dignity and sanctity of human life are threatened by this form of punishment; (5) no evidence shows capital punishment to have a deterrent effect; (6) judges and juries opposed to the death penalty often let criminals go free without any punishment; and (7) the right to life cannot be legitimately taken away from any person. In contrast, the five major considerations traditionally used in favor of the death penalty are the following: (1) At least some forms of crime are deterred by the threat of death; (2) society has a right to punish capital offenses with similar sentences; (3) some crimes deserve the death penalty; (4) capital punishment protects society by completely preventing recidivism in capital offenses; and (5) persons sentenced to life imprisonment should at least be able to choose death. It is plausible to suppose that those who think capital punishment can or cannot be justified divide along retributivist and utilitarian lines. This hypothesis is misleading, however. Capital punishment laws have usually been framed with the *dual* intent that they be both retributive and preventive. Moreover, although there are typical retributivist *forms* of justification that do differ discernibly from utilitarian forms, members of both camps have argued in some cases *for* and in some cases *against* capital punishment.

In their arguments utilitarians emphasize that the justification of the death penalty should focus on its deterrent effect. Those who oppose the death penalty usually argue that there is no reliable statistical evidence to indicate that the death penalty deters anyone except the person executed. (They need not argue this thesis for all criminal sanctions, of course.) Since the evidence is unreliable and since imprisonment is less cruel than death, they suggest that there is a strong presumption against killing anyone, at least until better evidence is available. They also argue that one

---

[5]As quoted in Hugo A. Bedau, *The Death Penalty in America* (Garden City, N.Y.: Doubleday, 1967), p. 30.

effect of a system of execution is to diminish the value and dignity traditionally attributed to human life. Just as a lowering of ethical standards anywhere (for example, in the world of business) leads to lesser expectations by those who must conform to the standards, so, they argue, the lowering of standards pertaining to the preservation and rehabilitation of human life leads to its general devaluation. Utilitarians of this persuasion also argue that there is a paradox in making crimes such as skyjacking, rape, and kidnapping capital offenses *along with* murder. In this case the criminal has been given an incentive to kill the best witness against him rather than a reason to abstain from a capital offense.

Other utilitarians who support the death penalty argue that although statistics do not prove either deterrence or nondeterrence, specifiable conditions indicate deterrence to any person of common sense. Consider, for example, an inmate serving a life sentence in a country with no death penalty. Why should he not wantonly kill guards during escape attempts? He cannot suffer greater punishment. No punishment could be a deterrent in this case except death. Also, far from lowering ethical standards, argue these utilitarians, the death sentence raises these standards by indicating to people the seriousness with which we value life itself. What means could possibly teach respect for life, freedom, and dignity better, they reason, than the death penalty? If the threat of death has the effect of averting any murders at all, especially of innocent persons, then is not capital punishment justified for that reason alone?

Retributivists reject the utilitarian emphasis on deterrence because they think punishing individuals as a *means* to the deterrence of others is either wrong or deficient in its theoretical grasp of the justification of punishment. They emphasize in their arguments, as we would expect, the right society has to exact retribution from offenders by meting out a penalty commensurate with the offense. Those retributivists who support the death penalty argue that homicide is always malicious except where retributively justified. In the case of a criminal who intentionally and with forethought takes the life of another, the principle of reciprocity seems at least to justify, if not to demand, the taking of the criminal's life. Should not penalties be graded, they say, precisely in accordance with the severity of the crime?

Other retributivists, however, argue that the taking of any human life is never deserved as a penalty because it is morally wrong to take a human life under any conditions. Their point is that no penalty itself morally wrong (absolutely, not merely *prima facie*) can possibly be a morally right sentence. Since the right to life is an inalienable right, they maintain, it is always wrong to take a life. They also maintain that death sentences are often unjustified ways of oppressing minority groups and the poor, and that many people deserving no penalty at all, because they were innocent, have lost their lives through systems allowing the death penalty. This terminal penalty is obviously irrevocable in a way other punishment is not.

If we are to have a system that fairly hands out what is deserved, argue these retributivists, we should hesitate to sanction the death penalty, since it robs us of the possibility of rewarding the innocent when they have, only after death, been determined to be innocent.

It is reasonably clear that these arguments often hinge on larger considerations such as whether there are inalienable human rights, whether death serves as a serious deterrent, and most important, whether retributivist criteria or utilitarian criteria, or both, rightly should serve as criteria for the justification of *capital* punishment. Although some of these considerations are straightforwardly factual—for example, whether the threat of death in fact is a serious deterrent—others are distinctly ethical.

Ernest van den Haag and Hugo Bedau, in their articles, debate the merits of two major positions on the death penalty. Van den Haag argues that any case for the death penalty must be built on its deterrent effect. He even argues that principles of justice are weighty in this case only because they implicitly depend on deterrence arguments. He further maintains that the sociological uncertainty that confronts us over the actual deterrent effect produced by executions favors the death penalty so long as future victims of murder might be saved by having the institution. Van den Haag thinks the added severity of death penalties may add to the deterrent effect, but in any case the burden of proof is on those who would abolish the penalty. He argues to the conclusion that "we have no right to risk additional future victims of murder for the sake of sparing convicted murderers; on the contrary, our moral obligation is to risk the possible ineffectiveness of executions."

Bedau contends, however, that van den Haag's arguments involve serious confusions and evasions. Bedau first argues that evidence for the deterrent effect is far less conclusive than van den Haag admits and then argues against the view that the added severity of the death penalty adds to its deterrent effect. Bedau thinks the latter claim is unempirical—on the order of a hunch. By way of positive argument, Bedau points out that advocacy of the death penalty is tantamount to advocacy of state power to take human life deliberately. All conditions being equal, he argues, one would hope supporters of this view would be able to provide considerable evidence for its efficacy. He finds no such evidence in van den Haag's article—or elsewhere, for that matter.

chapter five

Social Justice

A Contractarian Theory of Justice

John Rawls

I. THE NOTION OF A WELL-ORDERED SOCIETY

The aim of a theory of justice is to clarify and to organize our considered judgments about the justice and injustice of social forms. Thus, any account of these judgments, when fully presented, expresses an underlying conception of human society, that is, a conception of the person, of the relations between persons, and of the general structure and ends of social cooperation. Now there are, I believe, rather few such conceptions; and these are sharply distinct so that the choice between them is a choice between disparate things: one cannot continuously vary their basic features so as to pass gradually from one to another. Thus, to formulate a theory of justice, we must specify its underlying conception in a particular though still abstract way. Justice as fairness does this by bringing together certain general features of any society that it seems one would, on due reflection, wish to live in and want to shape our interests and character.

From "Reply to Alexander and Musgrave," *Quarterly Journal of Economics* **88** (November 1974) and "A Kantian Conception of Equality," Section V, *Cambridge Review* (February 1975). Reprinted with the permission of John Wiley and Sons, Inc., *Cambridge Review*, and the author.

The notion of a well-ordered society is the result: it embodies these features in a definite way and indicates how to describe the original position, which is introduced in the next section. I begin by enumerating the features of such a society.[1]

First of all, a well-ordered society is defined as one that is effectively regulated by a public conception of justice. That is, it is a society in which:

1. Everyone accepts, and knows that others accept, the same principles (the same conception) of justice.
2. Basic social institutions and their arrangement into one scheme (the basic structure of society) satisfy, and are with reason believed by everyone to satisfy, these principles.
3. The public conception of justice is founded on reasonable beliefs that have been established by generally accepted methods of inquiry.

It is assumed second that the members of a well-ordered society are, and view themselves as, free and equal moral persons. More specifically, they may be described as follows:

4. They each have, and view themselves as having, a sense of justice (the content of which is defined by the principles of the public conception) that is normally effective (the desire to act on this conception determines their conduct for the most part).
5. They each have, and view themselves as having, fundamental aims and interests (a conception of their good) in the name of which it is legitimate to make claims on one another in the design of their institutions.
6. They each have, and view themselves as having, a right to equal respect and consideration in determining the principles by which the basic structure of their society is to be regulated.

In addition, a well-ordered society is said to be stable with respect to its conception of justice. This means that, viewing the society as a going concern, its members acquire as they grow up a sufficiently strong and effective sense of justice, one that usually overcomes the temptations and stresses of social life. Thus:

7. Basic social institutions generate an effective supporting sense of justice.

Since we are interested in a theory of justice, we shall restrict our attention to well-ordered societies that exist under circumstances that require some conception of justice and give point to its peculiar role. Although natural resources and the state of technology are assumed to be such so as to make social cooperation both possible and necessary, and

---

[1]The advantage of beginning the exposition with the notion of a well-ordered society was suggested to me by Ronald Dworkin's discussion in "The Original Position," *Chicago Law Review*, **40** (1973), esp. 519–23.

mutually advantageous arrangements are indeed feasible; nevertheless, the benefits they yield fall short of the demands that people make. Therefore:

8.   Conditions of moderate scarcity exist.

But also, we assume that persons and groups have conceptions of the good that incline them in contrary directions and make claims and counter-claims on one another (see (5) above). Furthermore, people have opposing basic beliefs (religious, philosophical, and moral) and different ways of assessing evidence and arguments in many essential cases, and so:

9.   There is a divergence of fundamental interests and ends, and a variety of opposing and incompatible basic beliefs.

As for the usefulness of social institutions, we assume that the arrangements of a well-ordered society are productive; they are not, so to speak, a zero-sum game in which one person's (or group's) gain is another's loss. Thus:

10.   The scheme of basic institutions is a more or less self-sufficient and productive scheme of social cooperation for mutual good.

Given these circumstances of justice ((8)–(10)), we can delineate the role and subject of justice. Since many of their fundamental aims and beliefs stand in opposition, the members of a well-ordered society are not indifferent as to how the greater benefits produced by their cooperation are distributed. Hence a set of principles is required for adjudicating between social arrangements that shape this division of advantages. We express this by:

11.   The role of the principles of justice (the public conception) is to assign rights and duties in the basic structure of society and to specify the manner in which it is appropriate for institutions to influence the overall distribution of benefits and burdens.

To which we add finally:

12.   The members of a well-ordered society take the basic structure of society (that is, basic social institutions and their arrangement into one scheme) as the primary subject of justice (as that to which the principles of justice are in the first instance to apply).

Thus the principles of social justice are macro and not necessarily micro principles.

This enumeration of conditions shows that the notion of a well-ordered society under circumstances of justice is extremely complicated. It may help to observe that the various conditions go together. Thus, (1)–(7) specify the notion of a well-ordered society: (1), (2), and (3) characterize publicity; (4), (5), and (6) fill in the idea of free and equal moral persons; and (7), stability, concludes this part of the list. Conditions (8), (9), and (10) characterize the circumstances of justice, which restrict the class of relevant cases in the way appropriate for a theory of justice; and (11) and (12) describe the role and subject of justice.

The notion of a well-ordered society articulates a formal and abstract conception of the general structure of a just society, much as the notion of general equilibrium in price theory describes the structure of markets in the economy as a whole. The analogy with the theory of general equilibrium must, however, be used with discretion; otherwise, it may mislead us as to the nature of the theory of justice. To illustrate: the relations between members of a well-ordered society are not like the relations between buyers and sellers in competitive markets. A closer analogy is to think of a pluralistic society, divided along religious, ethnic, or cultural lines, in which the various groups and associations have managed to reach a consensus on a scheme of principles to govern their political institutions and to regulate the basic structure of society. Although there is public agreement on this framework and citizens are attached to it, they have profound differences about other things. While their inclination to press their cause makes a certain vigilance against one another necessary, their public conception of justice and their affirmation of it makes their secure association together possible. It is far better to regard the notion of a well-ordered society as an extension of the idea of religious toleration than of the idea of a competitive economy.

Clearly the value of the notion of a well-ordered society, and the force of the reasoning based upon it, depends on the assumption that those who appear to hold incompatible conceptions of justice will nevertheless find conditions (1) to (7) congenial to their moral convictions, or at least would do so after consideration. Otherwise, there would be no point in appealing to these conditions in deciding between different principles of justice. But we should recognize that they are not morally neutral (whatever that would be) and certainly they are not trivial. Those who feel no affinity for the notion of a well-ordered society, and who wish to specify the underlying conception in a different form, will be unmoved by justice as fairness (even granting the validity of its argument), except of course as it may prove a better way to systematize their judgments of justice.

II. THE ROLE OF THE ORIGINAL POSITION

The idea of the original position arises in the following way. Consider the question: Which conception of justice is most appropriate for a well-ordered society, that is, which conception best accords with the above conditions? Of course, this is a vague question. One can sharpen it by asking which of a few representative conceptions, drawn from the tradition of moral philosophy, is the closest fit. Assume, then, that we have to decide between but a few conceptions (e.g., a variant of intuitionism and of utilitarianism, and certain principles of justice). Justice as fairness holds that the particular conception that is most suitable for a well-ordered society is the one that would be unanimously agreed to in a hypothetical situation that is fair between individuals conceived as free and equal moral persons, that is, as members of such a society. Alternatively, the conception that is most appropriate for a society is the one that persons characteristic of the society would adopt when fairly situated with respect to one another. This hypothetical situation is the original position. Fairness of the circumstances under which agreement is reached transfers to the fairness of the principles agreed to; and since these principles serve as principles of justice, the name "justice as fairness" seems natural.

We assume that in the original position the parties have the general information provided by natural science and social theory. This meets condition (3). But in order to define the original position as fair between individuals conceived as free and equal moral persons, we imagine that the parties are deprived of certain morally irrelevant information. For example, they do not know their place in society, their class position or social status, their fortune in the distribution of natural talents and abilities, their deeper aims and interests, or finally, their particular psychological makeup. And to insure fairness between generations, we must add that they do not know to which generation they belong and thus information about natural resources, the level of productive techniques, and the like, is also forbidden to them. Excluding this knowledge is necessary if no one is to be advantaged or disadvantaged by natural contingencies and social chance in the adoption of principles. Since all are similarly situated, and the parties do not know how to frame principles to favor their peculiar condition, each will reason in the same way. There is no need to have a binding vote, and any agreement reached is unanimous. (Thus, being in the original position is always to be contrasted with being in society.)

The description of the original position must satisfy two conditions: first, it is to be a fair situation, and second, the parties are to be conceived as members of a well-ordered society. Thus, this description contains elements drawn from the notion of fairness, for example, that the parties are symmetrically situated and subject to the veil of ignorance. It also includes features drawn from the nature and relations of persons in a well-ordered society: the parties view themselves as having final aims and interests in the name of which they think it legitimate to make claims on one another; and that they are adopting what is to serve as a public conception of justice and must, therefore, assess principles in part by their publicity effects. They must also check for stability. So long as each part of the description of the original position has a legitimate pedigree, or we are prepared to accept certain conditions in view of their implications, everything is in order.

The aim of the description of the original position is to put together in one conception the idea of fairness with the formal conditions expressed by the notion of a well-ordered society, and then to use this conception to help us select between alternative principles of justice. A striking feature of the preceding account is that we have not said anything very specific about the content of the principles of justice in a well-ordered society. We have simply combined certain rather formal and abstract conditions. One possibility is that these conditions determine unambiguously a unique conception of justice. More likely the constraints of the original position only narrow down the class of admissible conceptions; but this is still significant if it turns out that some ostensibly plausible moral conceptions are ruled out.

Finally, that the original position is hypothetical poses no difficulty. We can simulate being in that situation simply by reasoning in accordance with the stipulated constraints. If we accept the values expressed by these constraints, and therefore the formal values embodied in the notion of a well-ordered society, the idea of fairness, and the rest, we must accept the resulting limitations on conceptions of justice and reject those principles that are excluded. The attempt to unify the more formal and abstract elements of moral thought so as to bring them to bear on questions of lesser generality is characteristic of Kantian theory.

III. THE FIRST PAIR-WISE COMPARISON: TWO PRINCIPLES OF JUSTICE VS. THE PRINCIPLE OF UTILITY

What alternative conceptions are available in the original position? We must avoid the general case where the parties are to decide between all possible conceptions of justice, since one cannot specify this class in a useful way. We need to simplify greatly if we are to gain an intuitive understanding of the combined force of the conditions that characterize the original position. Thus we imagine that the parties are to choose from a short list of conceptions drawn from the tradition of moral philosophy. Actually, I shall at this point discuss only one pair-wise comparison. Doing this serves to fix ideas and enables me to note a few points that will be required as we proceed.

Now one aim of contract theory has been to give an account of justice that is both superior to utilitarianism and a more adequate basis for a democratic society. Therefore, let us imagine a choice between (α), a conception defined by the principle that average utility (interpreted in the classical sense) is to be maximized, and (β), a conception defined by two principles that express on their face, as it were, a democratic idea of justice. These principles read as follows:

1. Each person has an equal right to the most extensive scheme of equal basic liberties compatible with a similar scheme of liberties for all.
2. Social and economic inequalities are to meet two conditions: they must be (a) to the greatest expected benefit of the least advantaged (the maximin criterion); and (b) attached to offices and positions open to all under conditions of fair equality of opportunity.

The first of these principles is to take priority over the second; and the measure of benefit to the least advantaged is in terms of an index of social primary goods. These I define roughly as rights, liberties, and opportunities, income and wealth, and the social bases of self-respect; they are things that individuals are presumed to want whatever else they want, or whatever their final ends. And the parties are to reach their agreement on this supposition. (I shall come back to primary goods below.) I assume also that everyone has normal physical needs so that the problem of special health care does not arise.

Which of these two conceptions (α) or (β), would be agreed to depends, of course, on how the persons in the original position are conceived. Since they represent free moral persons, as earlier defined, they regard themselves as having fundamental aims and interests, the claims of which they must protect, if this is possible. It is partly in the name of these interests that they have a right to equal consideration and respect in the design of society. The religious interest is a familiar historical example; the interest in the integrity of the person is another (freedom from psychological oppression and physical assault belong here). In the original position the parties do not know what particular form these interests take. But they do assume that they have such interests; and also that the basic liberties necessary for their protection are guaranteed by the first principle. Here it is essential to note that basic liberties are defined by a certain list of liberties; prominent among them are freedom of thought and liberty of conscience, freedom of the person and political liberty. These liberties have a central range of application within which they can be limited and adjusted only because they clash with other basic liberties. None of these liberties, therefore, is absolute, since they may conflict with one another; but, however they are adjusted to form one's system, this system is to be the same for all. Liberties not on the list, for example, the right to own property and freedom of contract as understood in the doctrine of laissez-faire are not basic: they are not protected by the priority of the first principle.

To consider the above pair-wise comparison, we must first say how one is to understand the principle of average utility. It is to be taken in the classical sense, which permits (by definition) interpersonal comparisons of utility that can at least be assessed at the margin; and utility is to be measured from the standpoint of individuals in society (and not from the standpoint of the original position) and means the degree of satisfaction of their interests. If accepted, this is how the principle will be understood and applied in society. But then it might sometimes lead, when consistently applied over time, to a basic structure securing the basic liberties; but there is no reason why it should do so in general. And even if this criterion often insures the necessary freedoms, it would be pointless to run the risk of encountering circumstances when it does not. The two principles of justice, however, will protect these liberties; and since in the original position the parties give a special priority to their fundamental interests (which they assume to be of certain general kinds), each would far rather adopt these principles (at least when they are the only alternative).

One must also take into account other special features of a well-ordered society. For example, the principles adopted are to serve as a public conception, and this means that the effects of publicity must be assessed. Particularly important are the effects on the social bases of self-respect; for when self-respect is lacking, we feel our ends not worth pursuing, and nothing has much value. Now it would seem that people who regard themselves as free and equal moral persons are much more likely to find their self-esteem supported and confirmed by social institutions satisfying the two principles of justice than by those answering to the standard of average utility. For such institutions announce by the principles they are publicly known to satisfy the collective intent that all should have equal basic liberty and that social and economic inequalities are to be regulated by the maximin criterion. Obviously this reasoning is highly speculative; but it illustrates the kind of considerations introduced by the publicity conditions of a well-ordered society.

The reasoning that favors the two principles can be strengthened by spelling out in more detail the notion of a free person. Very roughly, the parties regard themselves as having a highest-order interest in how all their other interests, including even their fundamental ones, are shaped and regulated by social institutions. They do not think of themselves as inevitably bound to, or as identical with, the pursuit of any particular complex of fundamental interests that they may have at any given time, although they want the right to advance such interests (provided they are admissible). Rather, free persons conceive of themselves as beings who can revise and alter their final ends and who give first priority to preserving their liberty in these matters. Hence, they not only have final ends that they are in principle free to pursue or to reject, but their original allegiance and continued devotion to these ends are to be formed and affirmed under conditions that are free. Since the two principles secure a social form that maintains these conditions, they would be agreed to. Only by this agreement can the parties be sure that their highest-order interest as free persons is guaranteed.

I shall conclude this section with a few remarks about primary goods. As noted earlier these are things that, from the standpoint of the original position, it is reasonable for the parties to assume that they want, whatever their final ends. For the description of the original position to be plausible, this motivation assumption must be plausible; and the (thin) theory of the good is intended to support it. In any case, an essential part of a conception of justice is the rules governing its application by members of a well-ordered society. When the parties adopt a conception, the understanding about these rules must be made explicit. Thus while the motivation of the persons in the original position is different from the motivation of individuals in society, the interpretation of the principles agreed to must be the same.

Now an important feature of the two principles is that they assess the basic structure in terms of certain primary goods: rights, liberties, and opportunities, income and wealth, and the social bases of self-respect. The latter are features of the basic structure that may reasonably be expected to affect people's self-esteem in important ways. In the maximin criterion (part (a) of the second principle) the measure of benefits is an index of these goods. Certainly there are difficulties in defining a satisfactory index,[2] but the points to stress here are (a) that primary goods are certain objective characteristics of social institutions and people's situation with respect to them, and therefore the index is not a measure of overall satisfaction or dissatisfaction; and (b) that the same index of these goods is used to compare everyone's social circumstances. Interpersonal comparisons are based on this index. In agreeing to the two principles, the parties agree that in making judgments of justice, they are to use such an index. Of course, the precise weights can hardly be determined in the original position; these may be determined later, for example, at the legislative stage.[3] What can be settled initially is certain constraints on these weights, as illustrated by the priority of the first principle.

Implicit in the use of primary goods is the following conception. We view persons as able to control and to adjust their wants and desires in the light of circumstances and who are to be given the responsibility for doing so (assuming that the principles of justice are fulfilled). Society on its part assumes the responsibility for maintaining certain basic liberties and opportunities and for providing a fair share of primary goods within this

[2]K.J. Arrow ("Some Ordinalist-Utilitarian Notes on Rawls' Theory of Justice," *Journal of Philosophy* **70** (1973), p. 254) has noted that special health needs, which I assume here not to arise, will be a particularly difficult problem. This question requires a separate discussion.

[3]See John Rawls, *A Theory of Justice* (Cambridge: Harvard University Press, 1971), pp. 198f. At this stage we have much more information and within the constraints can adjust the index to existing social conditions.

framework, leaving it to individuals and groups to form and to revise their aims and preferences accordingly. Thus there is an understanding among members of a well-ordered society that as citizens they will press claims only for certain kinds of things and as allowed for by the principles of justice. Strong feelings and zealous aspirations for certain goals do not, as such, give people a claim upon social resources or the design of public institutions. It is not implied that those with the same index have equal well-being, all things considered; for their ends are generally different and many other factors are relevant. But for purposes of social justice this is the appropriate basis of comparison. The theory of primary goods is a generalization of the notion of needs, which are distinct from aspirations and desires. So we could say: as citizens the members of a well-ordered society collectively take responsibility for dealing justly with one another on the basis of a public measure of (generalized) needs, while as individuals and members of associations they take responsibility for their preferences and devotions. . . .

I now take up the appropriateness of the two principles in view of the equality of the members of a well-ordered society. The principles of equal liberty and fair opportunity (part (b) of the second principle) are a natural expression of this equality; and I assume, therefore, that such a society is one in which some form of democracy exists. Thus our question is: by what principle can members of a democratic society permit the tendencies of the basic structure to be deeply affected by social chance, and natural and historical contingencies?

Now since we are regarding citizens as free and equal moral persons (the priority of the first principle of equal liberty gives institutional expression to this), the obvious starting point is to suppose that all other social primary goods, and in particular income and wealth, should be equal: everyone should have an equal share. But society must take organizational requirements and economic efficiency into account. So it is unreasonable to stop at equal division. The basic structure should allow inequalities so long as these improve everyone's situation, including that of the least advantaged, provided these inequalities are consistent with equal liberty and fair opportunity. Because we start from equal shares, those who benefit least have, so to speak, a veto; and thus we arrive at the difference principle. Taking equality as the basis of comparison those who have gained more must do so on terms that are justifiable to those who have gained the least.

In explaining this principle, several matters should be kept in mind. First of all, it applies in the first instance to the main public principles and policies that regulate social and economic inequalities. It is used to adjust the system of entitlements and rewards, and the standards and precepts that this system employs. Thus the difference principle holds, for example, for income and property taxation, for fiscal and economic policy; it does not apply to particular transactions or distributions, nor, in general, to small scale and local decisions, but rather to the background against which these take place. No observable pattern is required of actual distributions, nor even any measure of the degree of equality (such as the Gini coefficient) that might be computed from these. (What is enjoined is that the inequalities make a functional contribution to those least favoured.) Finally, the aim is not to eliminate the various contingencies, for some such contingencies seem inevitable. Thus even if an equal distribution of natural assets seemed more in keeping with the equality of free persons, the question of redistributing these assets (were this conceivable) does not arise, since it is incompatible with the integrity of the person. Nor need we make any specific assumptions about how great these variations are; we only suppose that, as realized in later life, they are influenced by all three kinds of contingencies. The question, then, is by what criterion a democratic society is to organize cooperation and arrange the system of entitlements that encourages and rewards productive efforts? We have a right to our natural abilities and a right to whatever we become entitled to by taking part in a fair social process. The problem is to characterise this process.[4]

At first sight, it may appear that the difference principle is arbitrarily biased towards the least favoured. But suppose, for simplicity, that there are only two groups, one significantly more fortunate than the other. Society could maximise the expectations of either group but not both, since we can maximise with respect to only one aim at a time. It seems plain that society should not do the best it can for those initially more advantaged; so if we reject the difference principle, we must prefer maximising some weighted mean of the two expectations. But how should this weighted mean be specified? Should society proceed as if we had an equal chance of being in either group (in proportion to their size) and determine the mean that maximises this purely hypothetical expectation? Now it is true that we sometimes agree to draw lots but normally only to things that cannot be appropriately divided or else cannot be enjoyed or suffered in common.[5] And we are willing to use the lottery principle even in matters of lasting importance if there is no other way out. (Consider the example of conscription.) But to appeal to it in regulating the basic structure itself would be extraordinary. There is no necessity for society as an enduring system to invoke the lottery principle in this case; nor is there any reason for free and equal persons to allow their relations over the whole course of their life to be significantly affected by contingencies to the greater advantage of those already favoured by these accidents. No

[4]The last part of this paragraph alludes to some objections raised by Robert Nozick in his *Anarchy, State, and Utopia* (New York: Basic Books, 1974), esp. pp. 213–229 [and below in this text, pp. 162–166. eds.]

[5]At this point I adapt some remarks of Hobbes. See the *Leviathan*, Ch. 15, under the thirteenth and fourteenth laws of nature.

one had an antecedent claim to be benefited in this way; and so to maximise a weighted mean is, so to speak, to favour the more fortunate twice over. Society can, however, adopt the difference principle to arrange inequalities so that social and natural contingencies are efficiently used to the benefit of all, taking equal division as a benchmark. So while natural assets cannot be divided evenly, or directly enjoyed or suffered in common, the results of their productive efforts can be allocated in ways consistent with an initial equality. Those favoured by social and natural contingencies regard themselves as already compensated, as it were, by advantages to which no one (including themselves) had a prior claim. Thus they think the difference principle appropriate for regulating the system of entitlements and inequalities.

A Libertarian Theory of Justice

Robert Nozick

The minimal state is the most extensive state that can be justified. Any state more extensive violates people's rights. Yet many persons have put forth reasons purporting to justify a more extensive state. It is impossible within the compass of this book to examine all the reasons that have been put forth. Therefore, I shall focus upon those generally acknowledged to be most weighty and influential, to see precisely wherein they fail. In this chapter we consider the claim that a more extensive state is justified, because necessary (or the best instrument) to achieve distributive justice.

. . .

The term "distributive justice" is not a neutral one. Hearing the term "distribution," most people presume that some thing or mechanism uses some principle or criterion to give out a supply of things. Into this process of distributing shares some error may have crept. So it is an open question, at least, whether *re*distribution should take place; whether we should do again what has already been done once, though poorly. However, we are not in the position of children who have been given portions of pie by someone who now makes last minute adjustments to rectify careless cutting. There is no *central* distribution, no person or group entitled to control all the resources, jointly deciding how they are to be doled out. What each person gets, he gets from others who give to him in exchange for something, or as a gift. In a free society, diverse persons control different resources, and new holdings arise out of the voluntary exchanges and actions of persons. . . .

THE ENTITLEMENT THEORY

The subject of justice in holdings consists of three major topics. The first is the *original acquisition of holdings*, the appropriation of unheld things. This includes the issues of how unheld things may come to be held, the process, or processes, by which unheld things may come to be held, the things that may come to be held by these processes, the extent of what comes to be held by a particular process, and so on. We shall refer to the complicated truth about this topic, which we shall not formulate here, as the principle of justice in acquisition. The second topic concerns the *transfer of holdings* from one person to another. By what processes may a person transfer holdings to another? How may a person acquire a holding from another who holds it? Under this topic come general descriptions of voluntary exchange, and gift and (on the other hand) fraud, as well as reference to particular conventional details fixed upon in a given society. The complicated truth about this subject (with placeholders for conventional details) we shall call the principle of justice in transfer. (And we shall suppose it also includes principles governing how a person may divest himself of a holding, passing it into an unheld state.)

If the world were wholly just, the following inductive definition would exhaustively cover the subject of justice in holdings.

1.   A person who acquires a holding in accordance with the principle of justice in acquisition is entitled to that holding.
2.   A person who acquires a holding in accordance with the principle of justice in transfer, from someone else entitled to the holding, is entitled to the holding.
3.   No one is entitled to a holding except by (repeated) applications of 1 and 2.

The complete principle of distributive justice would say simply that a distribution is just if everyone is entitled to the holdings they possess under the distribution.

A distribution is just if it arises from another just distribution by legitimate means. The legitimate means of moving from one distribution to another are specified by the principle of justice in transfer. The legitimate first "moves" are specified by the principle of justice in acquisition. Whatever arises from a just situation by just steps is itself just. The means of change specified by the principle of justice in transfer preserve justice. As correct rules of inference are truth-preserving, and any conclusion deduced via repeated application of such rules from only true premises is itself true, so the means of transition from one situation to another specified by the principle of justice in transfer are justice-preserving, and any situation actually arising from repeated transitions in accordance with the principle from a just situation is itself just. The parallel between justice-preserving transformations and truth-preserving transformations illuminates where it fails as well as where it holds. That a conclusion could have been deduced by truth-preserving means from premises that are true suffices to show its truth. That from a just situation a situation *could* have arisen via justice-preserving means does *not* suffice to show its justice. The fact that a thief's victims voluntarily *could* have presented him with gifts does not entitle the thief to his ill-gotten gains. Justice in holdings is historical; it depends upon what actually has happened. We shall return to this point later.

Not all actual situations are generated in accordance with the two principles of justice in holdings: the principle of justice in acquisition and the principle of justice in transfer. Some people steal from others, or defraud them, or enslave them, seizing their product and preventing them from living as they choose, or forcibly exclude others from competing in exchanges. None of these are permissible modes of transition from one situation to another. And some persons acquire holdings by means not sanctioned by the principle of justice in acquisition. The existence of past injustice (previous violations of the first two principles of justice in holdings) raises the third major topic under justice in holdings: the *rectification of injustice in holdings*. If past injustice has shaped present holdings in various ways, some identifiable and some not, what now, if anything, ought to be done to rectify these injustices? What obligations do the performers of injustice have toward those whose position is worse than it would have been had the injustice not been done? Or, than it would have been had compensation been paid promptly? How, if at all, do things change if the beneficiaries and those made worse off are not the direct parties in the act of injustice, but, for example, their descendants? Is an injustice done to someone whose holding was itself based upon an unrectified injustice? How far back must one go in wiping clean the historical slate of injustices? What may victims of injustice permissibly do in order to rectify the injustices being done to them, including the many injustices done by persons acting through their government? I do not know of a thorough or theoretically sophisticated treatment of such issues. Idealizing greatly, let us suppose theoretical investigation will produce a principle of rectification. This principle uses historical information about previous situations and injustices done in them (as defined by the first two principles of justice and rights against interference), and information about the actual course of events that flowed from these injustices, until the present, and it yields a description (or descriptions) of holdings in the society. The principle of rectification presumably will make use of its best estimate of subjunctive information about what would have occurred (or a probability distribution over what might have occurred, using the expected value) if the injustice had not taken place. If the actual description of holdings turns out not to be one of the descriptions yielded by the principle, then one of the descriptions yielded must be realized.

The general outlines of the theory of justice in holdings are that the holdings of a person are just if he is entitled to them by the principles of justice in acquisition and transfer, or by the principle of rectification of injustice (as specified by the first two principles). If each person's holdings are just, then the total set (distribution) of holdings is just. To turn these general outlines into a specific theory we would have to specify the details of each of the three principles of justice in holdings: the principle of acquisition of holdings, the principle of transfer of holdings, and the principle of rectification of violations of the first two principles. I shall not attempt that task here. (Locke's principle of justice in acquisition is discussed below.)

Historical Principles
and End-Result Principles

The general outlines of the entitlement theory illuminate the nature and defects of other conceptions of distributive justice. The entitlement theory of justice in distribution is *historical*; whether a distribution is just depends upon how it came about. In contrast, *current time-slice principles* of justice hold that the justice of a distribution is determined by how things are distributed (who has what) as judged by some *structural* principle(s) of just distribution. A utilitarian who judges between any two distributions by seeing which has the greater sum of utility and, if the sums tie, applies some fixed equality criterion to choose the more equal distribution, would hold a current time-slice principle of justice. As would someone who had a fixed schedule of trade-offs between the sum of happiness and equality. According to a current time-slice principle, all that needs to be looked at, in judging the justice of a distribution, is who ends up with what; in comparing any two distributions one need look only at the matrix presenting the distributions. No further information need be fed into a principle of justice. It is a consequence of such principles of justice that any two structurally identical distributions are equally just. (Two distributions are structurally identical if they present the same profile, but perhaps have different persons occupying the particular slots. My having ten and your having five, and my having five and your having ten are structurally identical distributions.) Welfare economics is the theory of current time-slice principles of justice. The subject is conceived as operating on matrices representing only current information about distribution. This, as well as some of the usual conditions (for example, the choice of distribution is invariant under relabeling of columns), guarantees that welfare economics will be a current time-slice theory, with all of its inadequacies.

Most persons do not accept current time-slice principles as constituting the whole story about distributive shares. They think it relevant in assessing the justice of a situation to consider not only the distribution it embodies, but also how that distribution came about. If some persons are in prison for murder or war crimes, we do not say that to assess the justice of the distribution in the society we must look only at what this person has, and that person has, and that person has, ... at the current time. We think it relevant to ask whether someone did something so that he *deserved* to be punished, deserved to have a lower share. . . .

Patterning

. . . Almost every suggested principle of distributive justice is patterned: to each according to his moral merit, or needs, or marginal product, or how hard he tries, or the weighted sum of the foregoing, and so on. The principle of entitlement we have sketched is *not* patterned. There is no one natural dimension or weighted sum or combination of a small number of natural dimensions that yields the distributions generated in accordance with the principle of entitlement. The set of holdings that results when some persons receive their marginal products, others win at gambling, others receive a share of their mate's income, others receive gifts from foundations, others receive interest on loans, others receive gifts from admirers, others receive returns on investment, others make for themselves much of what they have, others find things, and so on, will not be patterned. . . .

To think that the task of a theory of distributive justice is to fill in the blank in "to each according to his _____" is to be predisposed to search for a pattern; and the separate treatment of "from each according to his _____" treats production and distribution as two separate and independent issues. On an entitlement view these are *not* two separate questions. Whoever makes something, having bought or contracted for all other held resources used in the process (transferring some of his holdings for these cooperating factors), is entitled to it. . . .

So entrenched are maxims of the usual form that perhaps we should present the entitlement conception as a competitor. Ignoring acquisition and rectification, we might say:

> From each according to what he chooses to do, to each according to what he makes for himself (perhaps with the contracted aid of others) and what others choose to do for him and choose to give him of what they've been given previously (under this maxim) and haven't yet expended or transferred.

This, the discerning reader will have noticed, has its defects as a slogan. So as a summary and great simplification (and not as a maxim with any independent meaning) we have:

From each as they choose, to each as they are chosen.

How Liberty Upsets Patterns

It is not clear how those holding alternative conceptions of distributive justice can reject the entitlement conception of justice in holdings. For suppose a distribution favored by one of these non-entitlement conceptions is realized. Let us suppose it is your favorite one and let us call this distribution D_1; perhaps everyone has an equal share, perhaps shares vary in accordance with some dimension you treasure. Now suppose that Wilt Chamberlain is greatly in demand by basketball teams, being a great gate attraction. (Also suppose contracts run only for a year, with players being free agents.) He signs the following sort of contract with a team: In each home game, twenty-five cents from the price of each ticket of admission goes to him. (We ignore the question of whether he is "gouging" the owners, letting them look out for themselves.) The season starts, and people cheerfully attend his team's games; they buy their tickets, each time dropping a separate twenty-five cents of their admission price into a special box with Chamberlain's name on it. They are excited about seeing him play; it is worth the total admission price to them. Let us suppose that in one season one million persons attend his home games, and Wilt Chamberlain winds up with $250,000, a much larger sum than the average income and larger even than anyone else has. Is he entitled to this income? Is this new distribution D_2, unjust? If so, why? There is *no* question about whether each of the people was entitled to the control over the resources they held in D_1; because that was the distribution (your favorite) that (for the purposes of argument) we assumed was acceptable. Each of these persons *chose* to give twenty-five cents of their money to Chamberlain. They could have spent it on going to the movies, or on candy bars, or on copies of *Dissent* magazine, or of *Monthly Review*. But they all, at least one million of them, converged on giving it to Wilt Chamberlain in exchange for watching him play basketball. If D_1 was a just distribution, and people voluntarily moved from it to D_2, transferring parts of their shares they were given under D_1 (what was it for if not to do something with?), isn't D_2 also just? If the people were entitled to dispose of the resources to which they were entitled (under D_1), didn't this include their being entitled to give it to, or exchange it with, Wilt Chamberlain? Can anyone else complain on grounds of justice? Each other person already has his legitimate share under D_1. Under D_1, there is nothing that anyone has that anyone else has a claim of justice against. After someone transfers something to Wilt Chamberlain, third parties *still* have their legitimate shares; *their* shares are not changed. By what process could such a transfer among two persons give rise to a legitimate claim of distributive justice on a portion of what was transferred, by a third party who had no claim of justice on any holding of the others *before* the transfer? To cut off objections irrelevant here, we might imagine the exchanges occurring in a socialist society, after hours. After playing whatever basketball he does in his daily work, or doing whatever other daily work he does, Wilt Chamberlain decides to put in *overtime* to earn additional money. (First his work quota is set; he works time over that.) Or imagine it is a skilled juggler people like to see, who puts on shows after hours. . . .

The general point illustrated by the Wilt Chamberlain example is that no end-state principle or distributional patterned principle of justice can be continuously realized without continuous interference with people's lives. Any favored pattern would be transformed into one unfavored by the principle, by people choosing to act in various ways; for example, by people exchanging goods and services with other people, or giving things to other people, things the transferrers are entitled to under the favored distributional pattern. To maintain a pattern one must either continually interfere to stop people from transferring resources as they wish to, or continually (or periodically) interfere to take from some persons resources that others for some reason chose to transfer to them. . . .

Patterned principles of distributive justice necessitate *re*distributive activities. The likelihood is small that any actual freely-arrived-at set of holdings fits a given pattern; and the likelihood is nil that it will continue to fit the pattern as people exchange and give. From the point of view of an entitlement theory, redistribution is a serious matter indeed, involving, as it does, the violation of people's rights. (An exception is those takings that fall under the principle of the rectification of injustices.) From other points of view, also, it is serious.

Taxation of earnings from labor is on a par with forced labor. Some persons find this claim obviously true: taking the earnings of *n* hours labor is like taking *n* hours from the person; it is like forcing the person to work *n* hours for another's purpose. Others find the claim absurd. But even these, *if* they object to forced labor, would oppose forcing unemployed hippies to work for the benefit of the needy. And they would also object to forcing each person to work five extra hours each week for the benefit of the needy. But a system that takes five hours wages in taxes does not seem to them like one that forces someone to work five hours, since it offers the person forced a wider range of choice in activities than does taxation in kind with the particular labor specified. . . .

Whether it is done through taxation on wages or on wages over a certain amount, or through seizure of profits, or through there being a big *social pot* so that it's not clear what's coming from where and what's going where, patterned principles of distributive justice involve appropriating the actions of other persons. Seizing the results of someone's labor is equivalent to seizing hours from him and directing him to carry on various activities. If people force you to do certain work, or unrewarded work, for a certain period of time, they decide what you are to do and what purposes your work is to serve apart from your decisions. This process whereby they take this decision from you makes them a *part-owner* of you; it gives them a property right in you. Just as having such partial control and power of decision, by right, over an animal or inanimate object would be to have a property right in it. . . .

Locke's Theory of Acquisition

Before we turn to consider other theories of justice in detail, we must introduce an additional bit of complexity into the structure of the entitlement theory. This is best approached by considering Locke's attempt to specify a principle of justice in acquisition. Locke views property rights in an unowned object as originating through someone's mixing his labor with it. This gives rise to many questions. What are the boundaries of what labor is mixed with? If a private astronaut clears a place on Mars, has he mixed his labor with (so that he comes to own) the whole planet, the whole uninhabited universe, or just a particular plot? Which plot does an act bring under ownership? . . .

Locke's proviso that there be "enough and as good left in common for others" is meant to ensure that the situation of others is not worsened. . . .

. . . I assume that any adequate theory of justice in acquisition will contain a proviso similar to [Locke's]. A process normally giving rise to a permanent bequeathable property right in a previously unowned thing will not do so if the position of others no longer at liberty to use the thing is thereby worsened. It is important to specify *this* particular mode of worsening the situation of others, for the proviso does not encompass other modes. It does not include the worsening due to more limited opportunities to appropriate . . . and it does not include how I "worsen" a seller's position if I appropriate materials to make some of what he is selling, and then enter into competition with him. Someone whose appropriation otherwise would violate the proviso still may appropriate provided he compensates the others so that their situation is not thereby worsened; unless he does compensate these others, his appropriation will violate the proviso of the principle of justice in acquisition and will be an illegitimate one. A theory of appropriation incorporating this Lockean proviso will handle correctly the cases (objections to the theory lacking the proviso) where someone appropriates the total supply of something necessary for life.

A theory which includes this proviso in its principle of justice in acquisition must also contain a more complex principle of justice in transfer. Some reflection of the proviso about appropriation constrains later actions. If my appropriating all of a certain substance violates the Lockean proviso, then so does my appropriating some and purchasing all the rest from others who obtained it without otherwise violating the Lockean proviso. If the proviso excludes someone's appropriating all the drinkable water in the world, it also excludes his purchasing it all. (More weakly, and messily, it may exclude his charging certain prices for some of his supply.) This proviso (almost?) never will come into effect; the more someone acquires of a scarce substance which others want, the higher the price of the rest will go, and the more difficult it will become for him to acquire it all. But still, we can imagine, at least, that something like this occurs: someone makes simultaneous secret bids to the separate owners of a substance, each of whom sells assuming he can easily purchase more from the other owners; or some natural catastrophe destroys all of the supply of something except that in one person's possession. The total supply could not be permissibly appropriated by one person at the beginning. His later acquisition of it all does not show that the original appropriation violated the proviso.... Rather, it is the combination of the original appropriation *plus* all the later transfers and actions that violates the Lockean proviso.

Each owner's title to his holding includes the historical shadow of the Lockean proviso on appropriation. This excludes his transferring it into an agglomeration that does violate the Lockean proviso and excludes his using it in a way, in coordination with others or independently of them, so as to violate the proviso by making the situation of others worse than their baseline situation. Once it is known that someone's ownership runs afoul of the Lockean proviso, there are stringent limits on what he may do with (what it is difficult any longer unreservedly to call) "his property." Thus a person may not appropriate the only water hole in the desert and charge what he will. Nor may he charge what he will if he possesses one, and unfortunately it happens that all the water holes in the desert dry up, except for his. This unfortunate circumstance, admittedly no fault of his, brings into operation the Lockean proviso and limits his property rights. Similarly, an owner's property right in the only island in an area does not allow him to order a castaway from a shipwreck off his island as a trespasser, for this would violate the Lockean proviso.

Notice that the theory does not say that owners do not have these rights, but that the rights are overridden to avoid some catastrophe. (Overridden rights do not disappear; they leave a trace of a sort absent in the cases under discussion.) There is no such external (and *ad hoc?*) overriding. Considerations internal to the theory of property itself, to its theory of acquisition and appropriation, provide the means for handling such cases. . . .

I believe that the free operation of a market system will not actually run afoul of the Lockean proviso. . . . If this is correct, the proviso will not . . . provide a significant opportunity for future state action.

SELECTED SUPPLEMENTARY READINGS

Concepts and Principles of Justice

BENN, STANLEY, I., "Justice in The *Encyclopedia of Philosophy*, ed. Paul Edwards. New York: Macmillan and Free Press, 1967, vol. 4, pp. 298–302.
BOWIE, NORMAN E., *Towards a New Theory of Distributive Justice*. Amherst, Mass.: University of Massachusetts Press, 1971.
FEINBERG, JOEL, "Justice and Personal Desert," in *Nomos 6: Justice*, eds. Carl J. Friedrich and John W. Chapman. New York: Atherton, pp. 68–97.
———, *Social Philosophy*. Englewood Cliffs, N. J.: Prentice-Hall, 1973, chap. 7.
———, "Noncomparative Justice," *Philosophical Review* (1974), 297–338.
FRANKENA, W. K., "Some Beliefs About Justice," in *Perspectives on Morality: Essays of William K. Frankena*, ed. K. E. Goodpaster. Notre Dame, Ind.: University of Notre Dame Press, 1976, pp. 93–106.
LUCAS, J. R., *On Justice*. Oxford, England: Clarendon Press, 1980.
PERELMAN, CHARLES, *The Idea of Justice and the Problem of Argument*, trans. John Petrie. New York: Humanities Press, 1963.
PLATO, *The Republic*, trans. Francis Cornford. New York: Oxford University Press, 1945.
RESCHER, NICHOLAS, *Distributive Justice*. Indianapolis, Ind.: Bobbs-Merrill, 1966.
STERBA, JAMES, *The Demands of Justice*. Notre Dame, Ind.: University of Notre Dame Press, 1980.
———, ed., *Justice: Alternative Political Perspectives*. Belmont, Calif.: Wadsworth, 1980.

Libertarian Theories

ARROW, K. J., "Some Ordinalist-Utilitarian Notes on Rawls' Theory of Justice," *Journal of Philosophy* **70** (1973).
GOLDMAN, ALAN H., "The Entitlement Theory of Distributive Justice," *Journal of Philosophy* **73** (1976), 823–35.
HAYEK, FRIEDRICH, *Individualism and Economic Order*. Chicago: University of Chicago Press, 1948.
HELD, VIRGINIA, "John Locke on Robert Nozick," *Social Research* **43** (Spring 1976), 169–95.
LYONS, DAVID, 'Rights Against Humanity," *Philosophical Review* **85** (1976), 208–15.
MACK, ERIC, "Liberty and Justice," in *Justice and Economic Distribution*, eds. John Arthur and William Shaw. Englewood Cliffs, N. J.: Prentice-Hall, 1978, pp. 83–93.
NARVESON, JAN, "Justice and the Business Society," in *Ethical Theory and Business*, eds. Tom L. Beauchamp and Norman Bowie. Englewood Cliffs, N. J.: Prentice-Hall, 1979.

NOZICK, ROBERT, *Anarchy, State, and Utopia.* New York: Basic Books, 1974.

RAWLS, JOHN, *A Theory of Justice.* Cambridge, Mass.: Harvard University Press, 1971.

SCANLON, THOMAS M., "Nozick on Rights, Liberty, and Property," *Philosophy and Public Affairs* **6** (1976), 3–25.

SINGER, PETER, "The Right to Be Rich or Poor," *New York Review of Books* **6** (March 1976), 19–24.

Egalitarian Theories

BARRY, BRIAN, *The Liberal Theory of Justice, a Critical Examination of the Principal Doctrines in a Theory of Justice by John Rawls.* Oxford, England: Clarendon Press, 1973.

———, "Rawls on Average and Total Utility: A Comment," *Philosophical Studies* **31** (1977), 317–25.

BEAUCHAMP, TOM L., "Distributive Justice and the Difference Principle," in *John Rawls' Theory of Social Justice: An Introduction*, eds. H. Gene Blocker and Elizabeth Smith. Athens, Ohio: Ohio University Press, 1980.

BEDAU, HUGO A., ed., *Justice and Equality.* Englewood Cliffs, N. J.: Prentice-Hall, 1971.

BERLIN, ISAIAH, "Equality," in *Proceedings of the Aristotelian Society* **56** (1955–1956), 301–26.

BLACKSTONE, WILLIAM T., ed., *The Concept of Equality.* Minneapolis, Minn.: Burgess, 1969.

BLOCKER, H. GENE AND ELIZABETH SMITH, eds., *John Rawls' Theory of Social Justice: An Introduction.* Athens, Ohio: Ohio University Press, 1980.

DANIELS, NORMAN, ed., *Reading Rawls: Critical Studies of a Theory of Justice.* New York: Basic Books, 1975.

GAUTHIER, DAVID, "Justice and Natural Endowment: Toward a Critique of Rawls' Ideological Framework," *Social Theory and Practice* **3** (1974), 3–26.

MACINTYRE, ALASDAIR, "Justice: A New Theory and Some Old Questions," *Boston University Law Review* **52** (1972), 330–34.

NAGEL, THOMAS, "Equality," in *Mortal Questions.* Cambridge, England: Cambridge University Press, 1979.

RAWLS, JOHN, "Reply to Alexander and Musgrave," *Quarterly Journal of Economics* **88** (1974), 633–55.

———, "Fairness to Goodness," *Philosophical Review* **84** (1975), 536–54.

———, "Kantian Constructivism in Moral Theory: The Dewey Lectures 1980," *Journal of Philosophy* **77** (1980), 515–72.

———, *A Theory of Justice.* Cambridge, Mass.: Harvard University Press, 1971.

VLASTOS, GREGORY, "Justice and Equality," in *Social Justice*, ed. Richard B. Brandt. Englewood Cliffs, N. J.: Prentice-Hall, 1962.

WILLIAMS, BERNARD, "The Idea of Equality," in *Philosophy, Politics, and Society*, Second Series, eds. Peter Laslett and W. G. Runciman. New York: Barnes and Noble, 1962.

Socialist and Marxist Theories

ENGELS, FRIEDRICH, "Socialism: Utopian and Scientific," reprinted in *Essential Works of Marxism*, ed. Arthur Mendel. New York: Bantam Books, 1961, pp. 45–82.

GALLIE, W. B., "Liberal Morality and Socialist Morality," in *Philosophy, Politics, and Society*, ed. Peter Laslett. Oxford, England: Blackwell Press, 1956, pp. 116–33.

MARX, KARL, *Economic and Philosophical Manuscripts*, in *Karl Marx: Early Writings*, ed. T. B. Bottomore. London: C. A. Watts, 1963.

MILLER, DAVID, *Social Justice*. Oxford, England: Clarendon Press, 1976.

MILLER, RICHARD, "Rawls and Marxism," *Philosophy and Public Affairs* **3** (1974), 167–91.

TUCKER, ROBERT C., *The Marxian Revolutionary Idea*. New York: W. W. Norton, 1969.

Utilitarian Theories

BECKER, EDWARD F., "Justice, Utility, and Interpersonal Comparison," *Theory and Decision* **6** (1975), 471–84.

BRAYBROOKE, DAVID, "Utilitarianism with a Difference: Rawls' Position in Ethics," *Canadian Journal of Philosophy* **3** (1973), 303–31.

BROCK, DAN W., "Contractualism, Utilitarianism, and Social Inequalities," *Social Theory and Practice* **1** (1971), 33–44.

———, "Recent Work in Utilitarianism," *American Philosophical Quarterly* **10** (1973), 241–76.

LYONS, DAVID, "Rawls versus Utilitarianism," *Journal of Philosophy* **69** (1972), 535–45.

MILL, JOHN STUART, "On Liberty," in *Utilitarianism; On Liberty; Representative Government*, ed. A. D. Lindsay. London: E. P. Dutton, 1976.

MILLER, RICHARD, "Rawls, Risk, and Utilitarianism," *Philosophical Studies* **28** (1975), 55–61.

TAYLOR, PAUL W., "Justice and Utility," *Canadian Journal of Philosophy* **1** (1972), 327–50.

chapter six

Racial and Sexual Discrimination

Reverse Discrimination and Compensatory Justice

William T. Blackstone

Is reverse discimination justified as a policy of compensation or of preferential treatment for women and racial minorities? That is, given the fact that women and racial minorities have been invidiously discriminated against in the past on the basis of the irrelevant characteristics of race and sex—are we now justified in discriminating in their favor on the basis of the same characteristics? This is a central ethical and legal question today, and it is one which is quite unresolved. Philosophers, jurists, legal scholars, and the man-in-the-street line up on both sides of this issue. These differences are plainly reflected (in the Supreme Court's majority opinion and Justice Douglas's dissent) in *DeFunis* v. *Odegaard*[1]....

I will argue that reverse discrimination is improper on both moral and constitutional grounds, though I focus more on moral grounds. However, I do this with considerable ambivalence, even "existential guilt." Several reasons lie behind that ambivalence. First, there are moral and constitutional arguments on both sides. The ethical waters are very muddy

[1] 94 S. Ct. 1704 (1974).

and I simply argue that the balance of the arguments are against a policy of reverse discrimination.[2] My ambivalence is further due not only to the fact that traditional racism is still a much larger problem than that of reverse discrimination but also because I am sympathetic to the *goals* of those who strongly believe that reverse discrimination as a policy is the means to overcome th' debilitating effects of past injustice. Compensation and remedy are most definitely required both by the facts and by our value commitments. But I do not think that reverse discrimination is the proper means of remedy or compensation. . . .

I

Let us now turn to the possibility of a utilitarian justification of reverse discrimination and to the possible conflict of justice-regarding reasons and those of social utility on this issue. The category of morally relevant reasons is broader, in my opinion, than reasons related to the norm of justice. It is broader than those related to the norm of utility. Also it seems to me that the norms of justice and utility are not reducible one to the other. We cannot argue these points of ethical theory here. But, if these assumptions are correct, then it is at least possible to morally justify injustice or invidious discrimination in some contexts. A case would have to be made that such injustice, though regrettable, will produce the best consequences for society and that this fact is an overriding or weightier moral reason than the temporary injustice. Some arguments for reverse discrimination have taken this line. Professor Thomas Nagel argues that such discrimination is justifiable as long as it is "clearly contributing to the eradication of great social evils."[3] . . .

Another example of what I would call a utilitarian argument for reverse discrimination was recently set forth by Congressman Andrew Young of Georgia. Speaking specifically of reverse discrimination in the context of education, he stated: "While that may give minorities a little edge in some instances, and you may run into the danger of what we now commonly call reverse discrimination, I think the educational system needs this. Society needs this as much as the people we are trying to help . . . a society working toward affirmative action and inclusiveness is going to be a stronger and more relevant society than one that accepts the lim-

---

[2] I hasten to add a qualification—more ambivalence!—resulting from discussion with Tom Beauchamp of Georgetown University. In cases of extreme recalcitrance to equal employment by certain institutions or businesses, some quota requirement (reverse discrimination) may be justified. I regard this as distinct from a general policy of reverse discrimination.

[3] Thomas Nagel, "Equal Treatment and Compensatory Discrimination," *Philosophy and Public Affairs* **2** (Summer 1974).

ited concepts of objectivity. . . . I would admit that it is perhaps an individual injustice. But it might be necessary in order to overcome an historic group injustice or series of group injustices."[4] Congressman Young's basic justifying grounds for reverse discrimination, which he recognizes as individual injustice, are the results which he thinks it will produce: a stronger and more relevant education system and society, and one which is more just overall. His argument may involve pitting some justice-regarding reasons (the right of women and racial minorities to be compensated for past injustices) against others (the right of the majority to the uniform application of the same standards of merit to all). But a major thrust of his argument also seems to be utilitarian.

Just as there are justice-regarding arguments on both sides of the issue of reverse discrimination, so also there are utilitarian arguments on both sides. In a nutshell, the utilitarian argument in favor runs like this: Our society contains large groups of persons who suffer from past institutionalized injustice. As a result, the possibilities of social discord and disorder are high indeed. If short-term reverse discrimination were to be effective in overcoming the effects of past institutionalized injustice and if this policy could alleviate the causes of disorder and bring a higher quality of life to millions of persons, then society as a whole would benefit.

There are moments in which I am nearly convinced by this argument, but the conclusion that such a policy would have negative utility on the whole wins out. For although reverse discrimination might appear to have the effect of getting more persons who have been disadvantaged by past inequities into the mainstream quicker, that is, into jobs, schools, and practices from which they have been excluded, the cost would be invidious discrimination against majority group members of society. I do not think that majority members of society would find this acceptable, i.e., the disadvantaging of themselves for past inequities which they did not control and for which they are not responsible. If such policies were put into effect by government, I would predict wholesale rejection or noncooperation, the result of which would be negative not only for those who have suffered past inequities but also for the justice-regarding institutions of society. Claims and counter-claims would obviously be raised by other ethnic or racial minorities—by Chinese, Chicanos, American Indians, Puerto Ricans—and by orphans, illegitimate children, ghetto residents, and so on. Literally thousands of types or groups could, on similar grounds as blacks or women, claim that reverse discrimination is justified on their behalf. What would happen if government attempted policies of reverse discrimination for all such groups? It would mean the arbitrary exclusion or discrimination against all others relative to a given purpose and a given group. Such a policy would itself create an injustice for which those newly

[4]*Atlanta Journal and Constitution*, September 22, 1974, 20A.

excluded persons could then, themselves, properly claim the need for reverse discrimination to offset the injustice to them. The circle is plainly a vicious one. Such policies are simply self-destructive. In place of the ideal of equality and distributive justice based on relevant criteria, we would be left with the special pleading of self-interested power groups, groups who gear criteria for the distribution of goods, services, and opportunities to their special needs and situations, primarily. Such policies would be those of special privilege, not the appeal to objective criteria which apply to all.[5] They would lead to social chaos, not social justice.

Furthermore, in cases in which reverse discrimination results in a lowering of quality, the consequences for society, indeed for minority victims of injustice for which reverse discrimination is designed to help, may be quite bad. It is no easy matter to calculate this, but the recent report sponsored by the Carnegie Commission on Higher Education points to such deleterious consequences.[6] If the quality of instruction in higher education, for example, is lowered through a policy of primary attention to race or sex as opposed to ability and training, everyone—including victims of past injustice—suffers. Even if such policies are clearly seen as temporary with quite definite deadlines for termination, I am sceptical about their utilitarian value. . . .

II

The inappropriateness of reverse discrimination, both on utilitarian and justice-regarding grounds, in no way means that compensation for past injustices is inappropriate. It does not mean that those who have suffered past injustices and who have been disadvantaged by them are not entitled to compensation or that they have no moral right to remedy. It may be difficult in different contexts to translate that moral right to remedy into practice or into legislation. When has a disadvantaged person or group been compensated enough? What sort of allocation of resources will compensate without creating additional inequities or deleterious consequences? There is no easy answer to these questions. Decisions must be made in particular contexts. Furthermore, it may be the case that the effects of past injustices are so severe (poverty, malnutrition, and the denial of educational opportunities) that genuine compensation—the balancing of the scales—is impossible. The effects of malnutrition or the lack of education are often nonreversible (and would be so even

[5]For similar arguments see Lisa Newton, "Reverse Discrimination as Unjustified," *Ethics* **83** (1973).

[6]Richard A. Lester, *Antibias Regulation of Universities*, New York, 1974, as discussed in *Newsweek* (July 15, 1974), p. 78.

under a policy of reverse discrimination). This is one of the tragedies of injustice. But if reverse discrimination is inappropriate as a means of compensation and if (as I have argued) it is unjust to make persons who are not responsible for the suffering and disadvantaging of others to suffer for those past injuries, then other means must be employed unless overriding moral considerations of another type (utilitarian) can be clearly demonstrated. That compensation must take a form which is consistent with our constitutional principles and with reasonable principles of justice. Now it seems to me that the Federal Government's Equal Opportunity and Affirmative Action Programs are consistent with these principles, that they are not only not committed to reverse discrimination but rather absolutely forbid it.[7] However, it also seems to me that some officials authorized or required to implement these compensatory efforts have resorted to reverse discrimination and hence have violated the basic principles of justice embodied in these programs. I now want to argue both of these points: first, that these federal programs reject reverse discrimination in their basic principles; secondly, that some implementers of these programs have violated their own principles.

Obviously our country has not always been committed constitutionally to equality. We need no review of our social and political heritage to document this. But with the Fourteenth Amendment, equality as a principle was given constitutional status. Subsequently, social, political, and legal practices changed radically and they will continue to do so. The Fourteenth Amendment declares that states are forbidden to deny any person life, liberty, or property without due process of law or to deny to any person the equal protection of the laws. In my opinion the principles of the Equal Opportunity and Affirmative Action Programs reflect faithfully this constitutional commitment. I am more familiar with those programs as reflected in universities. In this context they require that employers "recruit, hire, train, and promote persons in all job classifications without regard to race, color, religion, sex or national origin, except where sex is a bona fide occupational qualification."[8] They state explicitly that "goals may not be rigid and inflexible quotas which must be met, but

---

[7]See The Civil Rights Act of 1964, especially Title VII (which created the Equal Employment Opportunity Commission), amended by The Equal Employment Opportunity Act of 1972, found in *ABC's of The Equal Employment Opportunity Act*, prepared by the Editorial Staff of The Bureau of National Affairs, Inc., 1972. Affirmative Action Programs came into existence with Executive Order 11246. Requirements for affirmative action are found in the rules and regulations 41-CFR Part 60–2, Order #4 (Affirmative Action Programs), generally known as Executive Order #4 and Revised Order #4 41-CFR 60–2 B. For discussion see Brownstein, Paul, "Affirmative Action Programs," in *Equal Employment Opportunities Compliance*, New York: Practicing Law Institute, 1972, pp. 73–111.

[8]See Brownstein, "Affirmative Action Programs," and, for example, *The University of Georgia Affirmative Action Plan*, Athens, Ga., 1973–1974, pp. viii, 67, 133.

must be targets reasonably attainable by means of good faith effort."[9] They require the active recruitment of women and racial minorities where they are "underutilized," this being defined as a context in which there are "fewer minorities or women in a particular job classification than would reasonably be expected by their availability."[10] This is sometimes difficult to determine; but some relevant facts do exist and hence the meaning of a "good faith" effort is not entirely fluid. In any event the Affirmative Action Program in universities requires that "goals, timetables and affirmative action commitment, must be designed to correct any identifiable deficiencies," with separate goals and timetables for minorities and women.[11] It recognizes that there has been blatant discrimination against women and racial minorities in universities and elsewhere, and it assumes that there are "identifiable deficiencies." But it does not require that blacks be employed because they are black or women employed because they are women; that is, it does not require reverse discrimination with rigid quotas to correct the past. It requires a good faith effort in the present based on data on the availability of qualified women and racial minorities in various disciplines and other relevant facts. (Similar requirements hold, of course, for nonacademic employment at colleges and universities.) It does not mandate the hiring of the unqualified or a lowering of standards; it mandates only equality of opportunity for all which, given the history of discrimination against women and racial minorities, requires affirmative action in recruitment.

Now if this affirmative action in recruitment, which is not only consistent with but required by our commitment to equality and social justice, is translated into rigid quotas and reverse discrimination by those who implement equal opportunity and affirmative action programs in the effort to get results immediately—and there is no doubt in my mind that this has occurred—then such action violates the principles of those programs.

This violation—this inconsistency of principle and practice—occurs, it seems to me, when employers hire with *priority emphasis* on race, sex, or minority-group status. This move effectively eliminates others from the competition. It is like pretending that everyone is in the game from the beginning while all the while certain persons are systematically excluded. This is exactly what happened recently when a judge declared that a certain quota or number of women were to be employed by a given agency regardless of their qualifications for the job,[12] when some public school

---

[9]Brownstein, and *The University of Georgia Affirmative Action Plan*, p. 71.

[10]*The University of Georgia Plan*, p. 69.

[11]*The University of Georgia Plan*, p. 71.

[12]See the *Atlanta Journal and Constitution*, June 9, 1974, p. 26-D.

officials fired a white coach in order to hire a black one,[13] when a DeFunis is excluded from law school on racial grounds, and when colleges or universities announce that normal academic openings will give preference to female candidates or those from racial minorities.

If reverse discrimination is prohibited by our constitutional and ethical commitments, what means of remedy and compensation are available? Obviously, those means which are consistent with those commitments. Our commitments assure the right to remedy to those who have been treated unjustly, but our government has not done enough to bring this right to meaningful fruition in practice. Sound progress has been made in recent years, especially since the Equal Employment Opportunity Act of 1972 and the establishment of the Equal Employment Opportunities Commission. This Act and other laws have extended anti-discrimination protection to over 60% of the population.[14] The Commission is now authorized to enforce anti-discrimination orders in court and, according to one report, it has negotiated out-of-court settlements which brought 44,000 minority workers over 46 million dollars in back-pay.[15] Undoubtedly this merely scratches the surface. But now the framework exists for translating the right to remedy into practice, not just for sloughing off race and sex as irrelevant criteria of differential treatment but other irrelevant criteria as well—age, religion, the size of hips (I am thinking of airline stewardesses), the length of nose, and so on.

Adequate remedy to overcome the sins of the past, not to speak of the present, would require the expenditure of vast sums for compensatory programs for those disadvantaged by past injustice in order to assure equal access. Such programs should be racially and sexually neutral, benefiting the disadvantaged of *whatever sex or race*. Such neutral compensatory programs would have a high proportion of blacks and other minorities as recipients, for they as members of these groups suffer more from the injustices of the past. But the basis of the compensation would be that fact, not sex or race. Neutral compensatory policies have definite theoretical and practical advantages in contrast to policies of reverse discrimination: Theoretical advantages, in that they are consistent with our basic constitutional and ethical commitments whereas reverse discrimination is not; practical advantages, in that their consistency, indeed their requirement by our constitutional and ethical commitments, means that they can marshall united support in overcoming inequalities whereas reverse discrimination, in my opinion, cannot.

[13]See the *Atlanta Journal and Constitution*, June 7, 1974, p. 13-B.

[14]*Newsweek* (June 17, 1974), p. 75.

[15]*Newsweek*, p. 75.

The Justification of Reverse Discrimination in Hiring

Tom L. Beauchamp

In recent years, government policies intended to ensure fairer employment and educational opportunities for women and minority groups have engendered alarm. Although I shall in this paper argue in support of enlightened versions of these policies, I nonetheless think there is much to be said for the opposition arguments. In general I would argue that the world of business is now overregulated by the federal government, and I therefore hesitate to support an extension of the regulative arm of government into the arena of hiring and firing. Moreover, policies that would eventuate in reverse discrimination in present North American society have a heavy presumption against them, for both justice-regarding and utilitarian reasons: The introduction of such preferential treatment on a large scale could well produce a series of injustices, economic advantages to some who do not deserve them, protracted court battles, jockeying for favored position by other minorities, congressional lobbying by power groups, a lowering of admission and work standards in vital institutions, reduced social and economic efficiency, increased racial hostility, and continued suspicion that well-placed women and minority group members received their positions purely on the basis of quotas. Conjointly these reasons constitute a powerful case against the enactment of policies productive of reverse discrimination in hiring.

I find these reasons against allowing reverse discrimination to occur both thoughtful and tempting, and I want to concede from the outset that policies of reverse discrimination can create serious and perhaps even tragic injustices. One must be careful, however, not to draw an overzealous conclusion from this admission. Those who argue that reverse discrimination creates injustices often say that, because of the injustice, such policies are *unjust*. I think by this use of "unjust" they generally mean "not justified" (rather than "not sanctioned by justice"). But a policy can create and even perpetuate injustices, as violations of the principle of formal equality, and yet be justified by other reasons. It would be an injustice in this sense to fire either one of two assistant professors with exactly similar professional credentials, while retaining the other of the two; yet the financial condition of the university or compensation owed the person retained might provide compelling reasons which justify the action. The first reason supporting the dismissal is utilitarian in character, and the other derives from the principle of compensatory justice. This shows both that there can be conflicts between different justice-regarding reasons and also that violations of the principle of formal equality are not in themselves sufficient to render an action unjustifiable.

A proper conclusion, then—and one which I accept—is that all discrimination, including reverse discrimination, is *prima facie* immoral, because a basic principle of justice creates a *prima facie* duty to abstain from such treatment of persons. But no absolute duty is created come what may, for we might have conflicting duties of sufficient weight to justify such injustices. The latter is the larger thesis I wish to defend: Considerations of compensatory justice and utility are conjointly of sufficient weight in contemporary society to neutralize and overcome the quite proper presumption of immorality in the case of some policies productive of reverse discrimination.

I

It is difficult to avoid accepting two important claims: (a) that the law ought never to sanction any discriminatory practices (whether plain old unadorned discrimination or reverse discrimination), and (b) that such practices can be eradicated by bringing the full weight of the law down on those who engage in discriminatory practices. The first claim is a moral one, the second a factual one. I contend in this section that it is unrealistic to believe, as (b) suggests, that in contemporary society discriminatory practices *can* be eradicated by legal measures which do not permit reverse discrimination. And because they cannot be eradicated, I think we ought to relax our otherwise unimpeachably sound reservations (as recorded in (a) and discussed in the first section) against allowing any discriminatory practices whatever.

My argument is motivated by the belief that racial, sexual, and no doubt other forms of discrimination are not antique relics but are living patterns which continue to warp selection and ranking procedures. In my view the difference between the present and the past is that discriminatory treatment is today less widespread and considerably less blatant. But its reduction has produced apathy; its subtleness has made it less visible and considerably more difficult to detect. Largely because of the reduced visibility of racism and sexism, I suggest, reverse discrimination now strikes us as all too harsh and unfair. After all, quotas and preferential treatment have no appeal if one assumes a just, primarily nondiscriminatory society. Since the presence or absence of seriously discriminatory conditions in our society is a factual matter, empirical evidence must be adduced to show that the set of discriminatory attitudes and selection procedures I have alleged to exist do in fact exist. The data I shall mention derive primarily from historical, linguistic, sociological, and legal sources.

Statistical imbalances in employment and admission are often discounted because so many variables can be hypothesized to explain why, for nondiscriminatory reasons, an imbalance exists. We can all think of plausible nondiscriminatory reasons why 22% of Harvard's graduate students in 1969 were women but its tenured Arts and Sciences Faculty in the Graduate School consisted of 411 males and 0 females.[1] But sometimes we are able to discover evidence which supports the claim that skewed statistics are the result of discrimination. Quantities of such discriminatory findings, in turn, raise serious questions about the real reasons for suspicious statistics in those cases where we have *not* been able to determine these reasons—perhaps because they are so subtle and unnoticed. I shall discuss each factor in turn: (a) statistics which constitute *prima facie* but indecisive evidence of discrimination; (b) findings concerning discriminatory reasons for some of these statistics; and (c) cases where the discrimination is probably undetectable because of its subtleness, and yet the statistical evidence is overwhelming.

a. A massive body of statistics constituting *prima facie* evidence of discrimination has been assembled in recent years. Here is a tiny but diverse fragment of some of these statistical findings.[2] (1) Women college teachers with identical credentials in terms of publications and experience are promoted at almost exactly one-half the rate of their male counterparts. (2) In the United States women graduates of medical schools in 1975 stood at 7%, as compared with 36% in Germany. The gap in the number of women physicians was similar. (3) Of 3,000 leading law firms surveyed in 1957 only 32 reported a woman partner, and even these women were paid much less (increasingly so for every year of employment) than their male counterparts. (4) 40% of the white-collar positions in the United States are presently held by women, but only 10% of the management positions are held by women, and their pay again is significantly less (70% of clerical workers are women). (5) 8,000 workers were employed in May 1967 in the construction of BART (Bay Area Rapid Transit), but not a single electrician, ironworker, or plumber was black. (6)

[1]Catherine R. Stimpson, ed., "Statement of Dr. Bernice Sandler," *Discrimination Against Women: Congressional Hearings on Equal Rights in Education and Employment* (New York: R.R. Bowker, 1973), pp. 61, 415.

[2]All of the statistics and quotations cited are taken from the compilations of data in the following sources: (1) Kenneth M. Davidson, Ruth B. Ginsburg, and Herma H. Kay, eds., *Sex-Based Discrimination: Text, Cases, and Materials* (Minneapolis: West Publishing, 1974), esp. Chapter 3. (2) Stimpson, esp. pp. 397–441 and 449–502. (3) Alfred W. Blumrosen, *Black Employment and the Law* (New Brunswick, N.J.: Rutgers University Press, 1971), esp. pp. 107, 122f. (4) *The Federal Civil Rights Enforcement Effort—1971*, A Report of the United States Commission on Civil Rights.

In the population as a whole in the United States, 3 out of 7 employees hold white-collar positions, but only 1 of 7 blacks holds such a position, and these latter jobs are clustered in professions which have the fewest jobs to offer in top-paying positions. (7) In the well-known AT&T case, this massive conglomerate signed a settlement giving tens of millions of dollars to women and minority employees. AT&T capitulated to this settlement based on impressive statistics indicating discriminatory treatment.

   b. I concede that such statistics are far from decisive indicators of discrimination. But when further evidence concerning the reasons for the statistics is uncovered, they are put in a perspective affording them greater power—clinching power in my view. Consider (3)—the statistics on the lack of women lawyers. A survey of Harvard Law School alumnae in 1970 provided evidence about male lawyers' attitudes.[3] It showed that business and legal firms do not generally expect the women they hire to become lawyers, that they believe women cannot become good litigators, and that they believe only limited numbers of women should be hired since clients generally prefer male lawyers. Surveys of women applicants for legal positions indicate they are frequently either told that a women will not be hired, or are warned that "senior partners" will likely object, or are told that women will be hired to do only probate, trust, and estate work. (Other statistics confirm that these are the sorts of tasks dominantly given to women.) Consider also (5)—a particular but typical case of hiring in non-white-collar positions. Innumerable studies have shown that most of these positions are filled by word-of-mouth recruitment policies conducted by all-white interviewers (usually all-male as well). In a number of decisions of the Equal Employment Opportunity Commission, it has been shown that the interviewers have racially biased attitudes and that the applications of blacks and women are systematically handled in unusual ways, such as never even being filed. So serious and consistent have such violations been that the EEOC has publicly stated its belief that word-of-mouth recruitment policies without demonstrable supplementary and simultaneous recruitment in minority group communities is in itself a "*prima facie* violation of Title VII."[4] Gertrude Ezorsky has argued, convincingly I believe, that this pattern of "special ties" is no less present in professional white-collar hiring, which is neither less discriminatory nor more sensitive to hiring strictly on the basis of merit.[5]

   c. Consider, finally, (1)—statistics pertaining to the treatment of women college teachers. The Carnegie Commission and others have assembled statistical evidence to show that in even the most favorable con-

[3]Stimpson, pp. 505f.

[4]Davidson, Ginsburg, and Kay, p. 516.

[5]Gertrude Ezorsky, "The Fight over University Women," *The New York Review of Books* (May 16, 1974), pp. 32–39.

strual of relevant variables, women teachers have been discriminated against in hiring, tenuring, and ranking. But instead of summarizing this mountain of material, I wish here to take a particular case in order to illustrate the difficulty in determining, on the basis of statistics and similar empirical data, whether discrimination is occurring even where courts have been forced to find satisfactory evidence of discrimination. In December 1974 a decision was reached by the Commission against Discrimination of the Executive Department of the State of Massachusetts regarding a case at Smith College where the two complainants were women who were denied tenure and dismissed by the English Department.[6] The women claimed sex discrimination and based their case on the following: (1) Women at the full professor level in the college declined from 54% in 1958 to 21% in 1972, and in the English department from 57% in 1960 to 11% in 1972. These statistics compare unfavorably at all levels with Mt. Holyoke's, a comparable institution (since both have an all female student body and are located in Western Massachusetts). (2) Thirteen of the department's fifteen associate and full professorships at Smith belonged to men. (3) The two tenured women had obtained tenure under "distinctly peculiar experiences," including a stipulation that one be only part-time and that the other not be promoted when given tenure. (4) The department's faculty members conceded that tenure standards were applied subjectively, were vague, and lacked the kind of precision which would avoid discriminatory application. (5) The women denied tenure were at no time given advance warning that their work was deficient. Rather, they were given favorable evaluations of their teaching and were encouraged to believe they would receive tenure. (6) Some stated reasons for the dismissals were later demonstrated to be rationalizations, and one letter from a senior member to the tenure and promotion committee contradicted his own appraisal of teaching ability filed with the department. (7) The court accepted expert testimony that any deficiencies in the women candidates were also found in male candidates promoted and given tenure during this same period, and that the women's positive credentials were at least as good as the men's.

The commissioner's opinion found that "the Complainants properly used statistics to demonstrate that the Respondents' practices operate with a discriminatory effect." Citing *Parham* v. *Southwestern Bell Telephone Co.*,[7] the commissioner argued that "in such cases extreme statistics may establish discrimination as a matter of law, without additional supportive

---

[6]*Maurianne Adams and Mary Schroeder* v. *Smith College*, Massachusetts Commission Against Discrimination, Nos. 72-S-53, 72-S-54, December 30, 1974. Hereafter referred to as *The Smith College Case*.

[7]433 F.2d 421, 426 (8 Cir. 1970).

evidence." But in this case the commissioner found abundant additional evidence in the form of "the historical absence of women," "word-of-mouth recruitment policies" which operate discriminatorily, and a number of "subtle and not so subtle, societal patterns" existing at Smith.[8] On December 30, 1974 the commissioner ordered the two women reinstated with tenure and ordered the department to submit an affirmative action program within 60 days.

This case is interesting because there is little in the way of clinching proof that the members of the English Department actually held discriminatory attitudes. Yet so consistent a pattern of *apparently* discriminatory treatment must be regarded, according to this decision, as *de facto* discrimination. The commissioner's ruling and other laws are quite explicit that "intent or lack thereof is of no consequence." If a procedure constitutes discriminatory treatment, then the parties discriminated against must be recompensed. Here we have a case where irresistible statistics and other sociological evidence of "social exclusion" and "subtle societal patterns" provide convincing evidence that strong, court backed measures must be taken because nothing short of such measures is sufficiently strong to overcome the discriminatory patterns, as the Respondents' testimony in the case verifies.[9]

Some understanding of the attitudes underlying the statistical evidence thus far surveyed can be gained by consideration of some linguistic evidence now to be mentioned. It further supports the charge of widespread discrimination in the case of women and of the difficulty in changing discriminatory attitudes.

Linguistic Evidence

Robert Baker has assembled some impressive linguistic evidence which indicates that our language is male-slanted, perhaps male chauvinistic, and that language about women relates something of fundamental importance concerning the males' most fundamental conceptions of women.[10] Baker argues that as the term "boy" once expressed a paternalistic and dominating attitude toward blacks (and was replaced in our conceptual structure because of this denigrating association), so are there other English terms which serve similar functions in regard to women (but are not replaced because not considered by men as in need of replacement). Baker assembles evidence both from the language itself and from surveys of users of the language to show the following.

---

[8]*The Smith College Case*, pp. 23, 26.

[9]*The Smith College Case*, pp. 26f.

[10]Robert Baker, "'Pricks' and 'Chicks': A Plea for Persons," in Richard Wasserstrom, ed., *Today's Moral Problems* (New York: Macmillan, 1975), pp. 152–170.

The term "woman" is broadly substitutable for and frequently inter-changed in English sentences such as "Who is that _____ over there?" by terms such as those in the following divisions:

A. *Neutral Categories*	B. *Animal Categories*	C. *Plaything Categories*	D. *Gender Categories*	E. *Sexual Categories*
lady	chick	babe	skirt	snatch
gal	bird	doll	hem	cunt
girl	fox	cuddly		ass
broad	vixen	thing		twat
(sister)	filly			piece
	bitch			lay
				pussy

Baker notes that (1) while there are differences in the frequency of usage, all of these terms are standard enough to be recognizable at least by most male users of the language; (2) women do not typically identify themselves in sexual categories; and (3) typically only males use the nonneutral categories (B–E). He takes this to be evidence—and I agree—that the male conception of women differs significantly from the female conception and that the categories used by the male in classifying women are *"prima facie* denigrating."* He then argues that it is clearly and not merely *prima facie* denigrating when categories such as C and E are used, as they are either derived from playboy male images or are outright vulgarities. Baker argues that it is most likely that B and D are similarly used in denigrating ways. His arguments center on the metaphorical associations of these terms, but the evidence cannot be further pursued here.

Although Baker does not remark that women do not have a similar language for men, it seems to me important to notice this fact. Generally, any negative categories used by women to refer to men are as frequently or more frequently used by men to apply to women. This asymmetrical relation does not hold, of course, for the language used by whites and blacks for denigrating reference. This fact perhaps says something about how blacks have caught onto the impact of the language as a tool of deni-grating identification in a way women have yet to do, at least in equal numbers. It may also say something about the image of submissiveness which many women still bear about themselves—an image blacks are no longer willing to accept.

Baker concludes from his linguistic studies that "sexual discrimina-tion permeates our conceptual structure. Such discrimination is clearly inimical to any movement toward sexual egalitarianism and virtually defeats its purpose at the outset."[11] His conclusion may somewhat over-reach his premises, but when combined with the corroborating statistical evidence previously adduced, it seems apt. Linguistic dispositions lead us

[11] Baker, p. 170.

to categorize persons and events in discriminatory ways which are some-times glaringly obvious to the categorized but accepted as "objective" by the categorizer. My contention, derived from Baker's and to be supported as we proceed, is that cautious, good faith movements towards egalitarian-ism such as affirmative action guidelines *cannot* succeed short of funda-mental conceptual and ethical revisions. And since the probability of such revisions approximates zero (because discriminatory attitudes are covertly embedded in language and cultural habit), radical expedients are required to bring about the desired egalitarian results, expedients which may result in reverse discrimination.

Conclusions

Irving Thalberg has argued, correctly I believe, that the gravest con-temporary problems with racism stem from its "protectively camouflaged" status, which he calls "visceral." Thalberg skillfully points to a number of attitudes held by those whites normally classified as unprejudiced which indicate that racism still colors their conception of social facts.[12] My alli-ance with such a position ought to be obvious by now. But my overall intentions and conclusions are somewhat different. I hold that because of the peculiarly concealed nature of the protective camouflage under which sexism and racism have so long thrived, it is not a reasonable expectation that the lightweight programs now administered under the heading of affirmative action will succeed in overcoming discriminatory treatment. I turn now directly to this topic.

II

The rawest nerve of the social and political controversy concerning reverse discrimination is exposed by the following question: What govern-ment policies are permissible and required in order to bring about a society where equal treatment of persons is the rule rather than the excep-tion? Fair-minded opponents of any government policy which might pro-duce reverse discrimination—Carl Cohen and William Blackstone, for example—seem to me to oppose them largely because and perhaps only because of their *factual belief* that present government policies not causing reverse discrimination will, if seriously and sincerely pursued, prove suffi-cient to achieve the goal of equal consideration of persons.

Once again a significant factual disagreement has emerged: what means are not only fair but also sufficient? I must again support my con-tentions by adducing factual data to show that my pessimism is sustained

[12]Irving Thalberg, "Visceral Racism," *The Monist* **56** (1972), 43–63, and reprinted in Wasserstrom.

by the weight of the evidence. The evidence cited here comes from government data concerning affirmative action programs. I shall discuss the affirmative action program in order to show that on the basis of present government guidelines (which, to my knowledge, are the best either in law or proposed as law by those who oppose reverse discrimination), discriminatory business as usual will surely prevail.

Affirmative Action

I begin with a sample of the affirmative action guidelines, as understood by those who administer them. I use the example of HEW guidelines for educational institutions receiving federal financial aid. These guidelines are not radically different from those directed at hiring practices throughout the world of business. Specifically, these guidelines cover three areas: admission, treatment of students, and employment. A sample of the sorts of requirements universities are under includes: (1) They may not advertise vacant positions as open only to or preferentially to a particular race or sex, except where sex is a legitimate occupational requirement. (2) The university sets standards and criteria for employment, but if these effectively work to exclude women or minorities as a class, the university must justify the job requirements. (3) An institution may not set different standards of admission for one sex, race, etc. (4) There must be active recruitment where there is an underrepresentation of women and minorities, as gauged by the availability of qualified members of these classes. However, the relevant government officials have from time to time made it clear that: (1) Quotas are unacceptable, either for admission or employment, though target goals and timetables intended to correct deficiencies are acceptable and to be encouraged. (2) A university is never under any obligation to dilute legitimate standards, and hence there is no conflict with merit hiring. (3) Reserving positions for members of a minority group (and presumably for the female sex) is "an outrageous and illegal form of reverse bias" (as one former director of the program wrote).[13] By affirmative action requirements I mean this latter interpretation and nothing stronger (though I have given only a sample set of qualifications, of course).

The question I am currently asking is whether these guidelines, assuming they will be vigorously pursued, can reasonably be expected to bring about their goal, which is the social circumstance of nondiscriminatory treatment of persons. If they *are* strong enough, then Cohen, Blackstone, and others are right: Reverse discrimination is not under such circumstances justified. Unfortunately the statistical and linguistic evidence previously adduced indicates otherwise. *The Smith College Case* is

[13]J. Stanley Pottinger, "Race, Sex, and Jobs: The Drive Towards Equality," *Change Magazine* **4** (October 1972), 24–29.

paradigmatic of the concealed yet serious discrimination which occurs through the network of subtle distortions, old-boy procedures, and prejudices we have accumulated. Only when the statistics become egregiously out of proportion is action taken or a finding of mistreatment possible. And that is one reason why it seems unlikely that substantial progress can be made, in any realistic sense of "can," by current government measures not productive of reverse discrimination. According to Peter Holmes, once the Director of HEW's Office for Civil Rights and in charge of interpreting affirmative action guidelines: "It has been our policy that it is the institutions' responsibility to determine nondiscriminatory qualifications in the first instance, and that such qualifications, in conjunction with other affirmative action steps, should yield results."[14] This is the received HEW view, but the last sentence contains an ambiguous use of the word "should." If the "should" in this statement is a moral "should," none will disagree. But if it is an empirical, predictive "should," as I take Mr. Holmes to intend, we are back to the core of the difficulty. I now turn to a consideration of how deficient such affirmative action steps have proven to be.

Government Data

The January 1975 Report of the United States Commission on Civil Rights contains a section on "compliance reviews" of various universities. These are government assessments of university compliance with Executive Orders pertaining to affirmative action plans. The report contains a stern indictment of the Higher Education Division (HED) of HEW—the division in charge of overseeing all HEW civil rights enforcement activities in the area of higher education. It concludes that "HED has, in large part, failed to follow the procedures required of compliance agencies under the Executive Order regulations."[15] But more interesting than this mere failure to enforce the law is the report's discussion of how very difficult it is to obtain compliance even when there is a routine attempt to enforce the law. The Commission reviewed four major campuses in the United States (Harvard, University of Michigan, University of Washington, Berkeley). They concluded that there is a pattern of inadequate compliance reviews, inordinate delays, and inexcusable failures to take enforcement action where there were clear violations of the Executive Order regulations.[16]

Consider the example of the "case history of compliance contracts" at the University of California at Berkeley. According to HED's own staff a "conciliation agreement" with this university "is now being used as a model

[14]Peter E. Holmes, "HEW Guidelines and 'Affirmative Action'" *The Washington Post*, February 15, 1975.

[15]*The Federal Civil Rights Enforcement Effort—1974* **3**, 276.

[16]*The Federal Civil Rights Enforcement Effort—1974*, 281.

for compliance activities with other campuses." When the Office for Civil Rights of HEW determined to investigate Berkeley (April 1971), after several complaints, including a class action sex discrimination complaint, the university refused to permit access to its personnel files and refused to permit the interviewing of faculty members without an administrator present. Both refusals are, as the report points out, "direct violations of the Executive Order's equal opportunity clause," under which Berkeley held contracts. Despite this clear violation of the law, no enforcement action was taken. A year and one-half later, after negotiations and more complaints, the university was instructed to develop a written affirmative action plan to correct "documented deficiencies" of "pervasive discrimination." The plan was to include target goals and timetables wherever job underutilization had been identified.[17]

In January 1973 the university, in a letter from Chancellor Albert H. Bowker, submitted a draft affirmative action plan which was judged "totally unacceptable." Throughout 1973 Berkeley received "extensive technical assistance" from the government to aid it in developing a better plan. No such plan emerged, and OCR at the end of the year began to question "the university's commitment to comply with the Executive Order." The university submitted other unacceptable plans, and finally in March 1974 "a conciliation agreement was reached." However, "the document suffered from such extreme vagueness that, as of August 1974, the university and OCR were in substantial disagreement on the meaning of a number of its provisions," and "the agreement specifically violated OFCC regulations in a number of ways." These violations are extensive and serious, and the report characterizes one part as "outrageous." Four years after this "model" compliance case began, it was unresolved and no enforcement proceedings had been taken against the university. The report concludes: "In its Title VI reviews of colleges and universities, HEW routinely finds noncompliance, but it almost never imposes sanctions; instead HEW responds by making vague recommendations. Moreover, HEW does not routinely require the submission of progress reports or conduct sufficient followup to determine if its recommendations have been followed."

III

No one could be happy about the conclusions I have reached or about the depressing and disturbing facts on which they are based. But I do take it to be a *factual* and not an *evaluative* conclusion both (1) that the camouflaged attitudes I have discussed exist and affect the social position

[17]*The Federal Civil Rights Enforcement Effort—1974*, 281–286.

of minority groups and women and (2) that they will in all likelihood continue to have this influence. It is, of course, an evaluative conclusion that we are morally permitted and even required to remedy this situation by the imposition of quotas, target goals, and timetables. But anyone who accepts my *interpretation* of the facts bears a heavy burden of moral argument to show that we ought not to use such means to that end upon which I take it we all agree, viz., the equal consideration of persons irrespective of race, sex, religion, or nationality.

By way of conclusion, it is important to set my arguments in the framework of a distinction between real reverse discrimination and merely apparent reverse discrimination. My evidence demonstrates present, ongoing barriers to the removal of discriminatory practices. My contentions set the stage for showing that *because* of the existence of what Thalberg calls "visceral racism," and because of visceral sexism as well, there will be many occasions on which we can only avoid inevitable discrimination by policies productive of reverse discrimination. Sometimes, however, persons will be hired or admitted—on a quota basis, for example—who appear to be displacing better applicants, but the appearance is the result of visceral discriminatory perceptions of the person's qualifications. In this case there will certainly appear to the visceral racist or sexist to be reverse discrimination, and this impression will be reinforced by knowledge that quotas were used; yet the allegation of reverse discrimination will be a mistaken one. On other occasions there will be genuine reverse discrimination, and on many occasions it will be impossible to determine whether or not this consequence is occurring. The evidence I have adduced is, of course, intended to support the contention that real and not merely apparent reverse discrimination is justified. But it is justified only as a means to the end of ensuring genuinely nondiscriminatory treatment of all persons.

SELECTED SUPPLEMENTARY READINGS

BAYLES, MICHAEL, "Compensatory Reverse Discrimination in Hiring," *Social Theory and Practice* **2** (1971–72).

———, "Reparations to Wronged Groups," *Analysis* **33** (1973).

BEAUCHAMP, TOM L., "Blackstone and the Problem of Reverse Discrimination," *Social Theory and Practice* **5** (1979).

BEDAU, HUGO A., "Compensatory Injustice and the Black Manifesto," *The Monist* **56** (1972).

BISHOP, SHARON, AND MARJORIE WEINZWEIG, eds., *Philosophy and Women.* Belmont, Calif.: Wadsworth, 1979.

BLACKSTONE, WILLIAM T., AND ROBERT HESLEP, eds., *Social Justice and Preferential Treatment.* Athens, Ga.: University of Georgia Press, 1977.

BOWIE, NORMAN E., AND ROBERT L. SIMON, *The Individual and the Political Order.* Englewood Cliffs, N.J.: Prentice-Hall, 1977, chap. 9.

BOXILL, BERNARD, "The Morality of Preferential Hiring," *Philosophy and Public Affairs* **7** (Spring 1978).

COHEN, CARL, "Why Racial Preference is Illegal and Immoral," *Commentary* **67** (June 1979).

COHEN, MARSHALL, THOMAS NAGEL, AND THOMAS SCANLON, eds., *Equity and Preferential Treatment.* Princeton, N.J.: Princeton University Press, 1977.

COWAN, J. L., "Inverse Discrimination," *Analysis* **32** (1972).

DWORKIN, RONALD, "The Bakke Decision: Did It Decide Anything?" *New York Review of Books* **25** (August 17, 1978).

ENGLISH, JANE, ed., *Sex Equality.* Englewood Cliffs, N.J.: Prentice-Hall, 1977.

FULLINWIDER, ROBERT K., *The Reverse Discrimination Controversy.* Totowa, N.J.: Rowman and Littlefield, 1980.

GLAZER, NATHAN, *Affirmative Discrimination: Ethnic Inequality and Public Policy.* New York: Basic Books, 1975.

GOLDMAN, ALAN, "Justice and Hiring by Competence," *American Philosophical Quarterly* (January 1977).

———, *Justice and Reverse Discrimination.* Princeton, N.J.: Princeton University Press, 1979.

GREENAWALT, KENT, "The Unresolved Problems of Reverse Discrimination," *California Law Review* **67** (January 1979).

GROSS, BARRY R., *Reverse Discrimination.* Buffalo, N.Y.: Prometheus Books, 1977.

HAACK, SUSAN, "On the Moral Relevance of Sex," *Philosophy* **49** (1974).

JAGGER, ALISON, "Relaxing the Limits of Preferential Treatment," *Social Theory and Practice* **4** (Spring 1977).

———, "On Sexual Equality," *Ethics* **84** (1974).

KATZNER, LOUIS, "Is the Favoring of Women and Blacks in Employment and Educational Opportunities Justified?" in *Philosophy of Law* (2d ed.), eds. Joel Feinberg and Hyman Gross. Belmont, Calif.: Wadsworth, 1980.

LUCAS, J.R., "Because You Are a Woman," *Philosophy* **48** (1973).

LYONS, DAVID, "Rights, Utility, and Racial Discrimination," *Philosophical Law*, ed. Richard Bronaugh. Westport, Conn.: Greenwood Press, 1978.

NAGEL, THOMAS, "Equal Treatment and Compensatory Discrimination," *Philosophy and Public Affairs* **2** (Summer 1973).

NEWTON, LISA, "Reverse Discrimination as Unjustified," *Ethics* **83** (1973).

NICKEL, J.W., "Discrimination and Morally Relevant Characteristics," *Analysis* **32** (1972).

SHER, GEORGE, "Justifying Reverse Discrimination in Employment," *Philosophy and Public Affairs* **4** (Winter 1975).

SHINER, ROGER A., "Individuals, Groups, and Inverse Discrimination," *Analysis* **33** (1973).

SILVESTRI, PHILIP, "The Justification of Inverse Discrimination," *Analysis* **33** (1973).

TAYLOR, PAUL W., "Reverse Discrimination and Compensatory Justice," *Analysis* **33** (1973).

THALBERG, IRVING, "Reverse Discrimination and the Future," *Philosophical Forum* **V** (1973–74).

THOMSON, JUDITH, "Preferential Hiring," *Philosophy and Public Affairs* **2** (1973).

WASSERSTROM, RICHARD, ed., *Moral Problems* (2nd ed.). New York: Macmillan, 1979, chaps. 2–3.

VETTERLING–BRAGGIN, MARY, FREDERICK ELLISTON, AND JANE ENGLISH, eds., *Feminism and Philosophy.* Totowa, N.J.: Littlefield, Adams, 1977.

chapter seven

World Hunger and the Right to Food

Famine, Affluence, and Morality

Peter Singer

As I write this, in November 1971, people are dying in East Bengal from lack of food, shelter, and medical care. The suffering and death that are occurring there now are not inevitable, not unavoidable in any fatalistic sense of the term. Constant poverty, a cyclone, and a civil war have turned at least nine million people into destitute refugees; nevertheless, it is not beyond the capacity of the richer nations to give enough assistance to reduce any further suffering to very small proportions. The decisions and actions of human beings can prevent this kind of suffering. Unfortunately, human beings have not made the necessary decisions. At the individual level, people have, with very few exceptions, not responded to the situation in any significant way. Generally speaking, people have not given large sums to relief funds; they have not written to their parliamentary representatives demanding increased government assistance; they have not demonstrated in the streets, held symbolic fasts, or done anything else directed toward providing the refugees with the means to satisfy their essential needs. At the government level, no government has given the sort of massive aid that would enable the refugees to survive for more

Peter Singer, "Famine, Affluence, and Morality," *Philosophy & Public Affairs*, vol. 1, no. 3 (Spring 1972). Copyright © 1972 by Princeton University Press. Reprinted by permission of Princeton University Press and the author. A postscript has been added by Professor Singer.

than a few days. Britain, for instance, has given rather more than most countries. It has, to date, given £14,750,000. For comparative purposes, Britain's share of the nonrecoverable development costs of the Anglo-French Concorde project is already in excess of £275,000,000, and on present estimates will reach £440,000,000. The implication is that the British government values a supersonic transport more than thirty times as highly as it values the lives of the nine million refugees. Australia is another country which, on a per capita basis, is well up in the "aid to Bengal" table. Australia's aid, however, amounts to less than one-twelfth of the cost of Sydney's new opera house. The total amount given, from all sources, now stands at about £65,000,000. The estimated cost of keeping the refugees alive for one year is £464,000,000. Most of the refugees have now been in the camps for more than six months. The World Bank has said that India needs a minimum of £300,000,000 in assistance from other countries before the end of the year. It seems obvious that assistance on this scale will not be forthcoming. India will be forced to choose between letting the refugees starve or diverting funds from her own development program, which will mean that more of her own people will starve in the future.[1]

These are the essential facts about the present situation in Bengal. So far as it concerns us here, there is nothing unique about this situation except its magnitude. The Bengal emergency is just the latest and most acute of a series of major emergencies in various parts of the world, arising both from natural and man-made causes. There are also many parts of the world in which people die from malnutrition and lack of food independent of any special emergency. I take Bengal as my example only because it is the present concern, and because the size of the problem has ensured that it has been given adequate publicity. Neither individuals nor governments can claim to be unaware of what is happening there.

What are the moral implications of a situation like this? In what follows, I shall argue that the way people in relatively affluent countries react to a situation like that in Bengal cannot be justified; indeed, the whole way we look at moral issues—our moral conceptual scheme—needs to be altered, and with it, the way of life that has come to be taken for granted in our society.

In arguing for this conclusion I will not, of course, claim to be morally neutral. I shall, however, try to argue for the moral position that I take, so that anyone who accepts certain assumptions, to be made explicit, will, I hope, accept my conclusion.

---

[1]There was also a third possibility: that India would go to war to enable the refugees to return to their lands. Since I wrote this paper, India has taken this way out. The situation is no longer that described above, but this does not affect my argument, as the next paragraph indicates.

I begin with the assumption that suffering and death from lack of food, shelter, and medical care are bad. I think most people will agree about this, although one may reach the same view by different routes. I shall not argue for this view. People can hold all sorts of eccentric positions, and perhaps from some of them it would not follow that death by starvation is in itself bad. It is difficult, perhaps impossible, to refute such positions, and so for brevity I will henceforth take this assumption as accepted. Those who disagree need read no further.

My next point is this: if it is in our power to prevent something bad from happening, without thereby sacrificing anything of comparable moral importance, we ought, morally, to do it. By "without sacrificing anything of comparable moral importance" I mean without causing anything else comparably bad to happen, or doing something that is wrong in itself, or failing to promote some moral good, comparable in significance to the bad thing that we can prevent. This principle seems almost as uncontroversial as the last one. It requires us only to prevent what is bad, and not to promote what is good, and it requires this of us only when we can do it without sacrificing anything that is, from the moral point of view, comparably important. I could even, as far as the application of my argument to the Bengal emergency is concerned, qualify the point so as to make it: if it is in our power to prevent something very bad from happening, without thereby sacrificing anything morally significant, we ought, morally, to do it. An application of this principle would be as follows: if I am walking past a shallow pond and see a child drowning in it, I ought to wade in and pull the child out. This will mean getting my clothes muddy, but this is insignificant, while the death of the child would presumably be a very bad thing.

The uncontroversial appearance of the principle just stated is deceptive. If it were acted upon, even in its qualified form, our lives, our society, and our world would be fundamentally changed. For the principle takes, firstly, no account of proximity or distance. It makes no moral difference whether the person I can help is a neighbor's child ten yards from me or a Bengali whose name I shall never know, ten thousand miles away. Secondly, the principle makes no distinction between cases in which I am the only person who could possibly do anything and cases in which I am just one among millions in the same position.

I do not think I need to say much in defense of the refusal to take proximity and distance into account. The fact that a person is physically near to us, so that we have personal contact with him, may make it more likely that we *shall* assist him, but this does not show that we *ought* to help him rather than another who happens to be further away. If we accept any principle of impartiality, universalizability, equality, or whatever, we cannot discriminate against someone merely because he is far away from us (or we are far away from him). Admittedly, it is possible that we are in a better position to judge what needs to be done to help a person near to us than one far away, and perhaps also to provide the assistance we judge to be necessary. If this were the case, it would be a reason for helping those near to us first. This may once have been a justification for being more concerned with the poor in one's own town than with famine victims in India. Unfortunately for those who like to keep their moral responsibilities limited, instant communication and swift transportation have changed the situation. From the moral point of view, the development of the world into a "global village" has made an important, though still unrecognized, difference to our moral situation. Expert observers and supervisors, sent out by famine relief organizations or permanently stationed in famine-prone areas, can direct our aid to a refugee in Bengal almost as effectively as we could get it to someone in our own block. There would seem, therefore, to be no possible justification for discriminating on geographical grounds.

There may be a greater need to defend the second implication of my principle—that the fact that there are millions of other people in the same position, in respect to the Bengali refugees, as I am, does not make the situation significantly different from a situation in which I am the only person who can prevent something very bad from occurring. Again, of course, I admit that there is a psychological difference between the cases; one feels less guilty about doing nothing if one can point to others, similarly placed, who have also done nothing. Yet this can make no real difference to our moral obligations.[2] Should I consider that I am less obliged to pull the drowning child out of the pond if on looking around I see other people, no further away than I am, who have also noticed the child but are doing nothing? One has only to ask this question to see the absurdity of the view that numbers lessen obligation. It is a view that is an ideal excuse for inactivity; unfortunately most of the major evils—poverty, overpopulation, pollution—are problems in which everyone is almost equally involved.

The view that numbers do make a difference can be made plausible if stated in this way: if everyone in circumstances like mine gave £5 to the Bengal Relief Fund, there would be enough to provide food, shelter, and medical care for the refugees; there is no reason why I should give more than anyone else in the same circumstances as I am; therefore I have no obligation to give more than £5. Each premise in this argument is true,

[2]In view of the special sense philosophers often give to the term, I should say that I use "obligation" simply as the abstract noun derived from "ought," so that "I have an obligation to" means no more, and no less, than "I ought to." This usage is in accordance with the definition of "ought" given by the *Shorter Oxford English Dictionary*: "the general verb to express duty or obligation." I do not think any issue of substance hangs on the way the term is used; sentences in which I use "obligation" could all be rewritten, although somewhat clumsily, as sentences in which a clause containing "ought" replaces the term "obligation."

and the argument looks sound. It may convince us, unless we notice that it is based on a hypothetical premise, although the conclusion is not stated hypothetically. The argument would be sound if the conclusion were: if everyone in circumstances like mine were to give £5, I would have no obligation to give more than £5. If the conclusion were so stated, however, it would be obvious that the argument has no bearing on a situation in which it is not the case that everyone else gives £5. This, of course, is the actual situation. It is more or less certain that not everyone in circumstances like mine will give £5. So there will not be enough to provide the needed food, shelter, and medical care. Therefore by giving more than £5 I will prevent more suffering than I would if I gave just £5.

It might be thought that this argument has an absurd consequence. Since the situation appears to be that very few people are likely to give substantial amounts, it follows that I and everyone else in similar circumstances ought to give as much as possible, that is, at least up to the point at which by giving more one would begin to cause serious suffering for oneself and one's dependents—perhaps even beyond this point to the point of marginal utility, at which by giving more one would cause oneself and one's dependents as much suffering as one would prevent in Bengal. If everyone does this, however, there will be more than can be used for the benefit of the refugees, and some of the sacrifice will have been unnecessary. Thus, if everyone does what he ought to do, the result will not be as good as it would be if everyone did a little less than he ought to do, or if only some do all that they ought to do.

The paradox here arises only if we assume that the actions in question—sending money to the relief funds—are performed more or less simultaneously, and are also unexpected. For if it is to be expected that everyone is going to contribute something, then clearly each is not obliged to give as much as he would have been obliged to had others not been giving too. And if everyone is not acting more or less simultaneously, then those giving later will know how much more is needed, and will have no obligation to give more than is necessary to reach this amount. To say this is not to deny the principle that people in the same circumstances have the same obligations, but to point out that the fact that others have given, or may be expected to give, is a relevant circumstance: those giving after it has become known that many others are giving and those giving before are not in the same circumstances. So the seemingly absurd consequence of the principle I have put forward can occur only if people are in error about the actual circumstances—that is, if they think they are giving when others are not, but in fact they are giving when others are. The result of everyone doing what he really ought to do cannot be worse than the result of everyone doing less than he ought to do, although the result of everyone doing what he reasonably believes he ought to do could be.

If my argument so far has been sound, neither our distance from a preventable evil nor the number of other people who, in respect to that evil, are in the same situation as we are, lessens our obligation to mitigate or prevent that evil. I shall therefore take as established the principle I asserted earlier. As I have already said, I need to assert it only in its qualified form: if it is in our power to prevent something very bad from happening, without thereby sacrificing anything else morally significant, we ought, morally, to do it.

The outcome of this argument is that our traditional moral categories are upset. The traditional distinction between duty and charity cannot be drawn, or at least, not in the place we normally draw it. Giving money to the Bengal Relief Fund is regarded as an act of charity in our society. The bodies which collect money are known as "charities." These organizations see themselves in this way—if you send them a check, you will be thanked for your "generosity." Because giving money is regarded as an act of charity, it is not thought that there is anything wrong with not giving. The charitable man may be praised, but the man who is not charitable is not condemned. People do not feel in any way ashamed or guilty about spending money on new clothes or a new car instead of giving it to famine relief. (Indeed, the alternative does not occur to them.) This way of looking at the matter cannot be justified. When we buy new clothes not to keep ourselves warm but to look "well-dressed" we are not providing for any important need. We would not be sacrificing anything significant if we were to continue to wear our old clothes, and give the money to famine relief. By doing so, we would be preventing another person from starving. It follows from what I have said earlier that we ought to give money away, rather than spend it on clothes which we do not need to keep us warm. To do so is not charitable, or generous. Nor is it the kind of act which philosophers and theologians have called "supererogatory"—an act which it would be good to do, but not wrong not to do. On the contrary, we ought to give the money away, and it is wrong not to do so.

I am not maintaining that there are no acts which are charitable, or that there are no acts which it would be good to do but not wrong not to do. It may be possible to redraw the distinction between duty and charity in some other place. All I am arguing here is that the present way of drawing the distinction, which makes it an act of charity for a man living at the level of affluence which most people in the "developed nations" enjoy to give money to save someone else from starvation, cannot be supported. It is beyond the scope of my argument to consider whether the distinction should be redrawn or abolished altogether. There would be many other possible ways of drawing the distinction—for instance, one might decide that it is good to make other people as happy as possible, but not wrong not to do so.

Despite the limited nature of the revision in our moral conceptual scheme which I am proposing, the revision would, given the extent of both affluence and famine in the world today, have radical implications. These implications may lead to further objections, distinct from those I have already considered. I shall discuss two of these.

One objection to the position I have taken might be simply that it is too drastic a revision of our moral scheme. People do not ordinarily judge in the way I have suggested they should. Most people reserve their moral condemnation for those who violate some moral norm, such as the norm against taking another person's property. They do not condemn those who indulge in luxury instead of giving to famine relief. But given that I did not set out to present a morally neutral description of the way people make moral judgments, the way people do in fact judge has nothing to do with the validity of my conclusion. My conclusion follows from the principle which I advanced earlier, and unless that principle is rejected, or the arguments shown to be unsound, I think the conclusion must stand, however strange it appears.

It might, nevertheless, be interesting to consider why our society, and most other societies, do judge differently from the way I have suggested they should. In a well-known article, J.O. Urmson suggests that the imperatives of duty, which tell us what we must do, as distinct from what it would be good to do but not wrong not to do, function so as to prohibit behavior that is intolerable if men are to live together in society.[3] This may explain the origin and continued existence of the present division between acts of duty and acts of charity. Moral attitudes are shaped by the needs of society, and no doubt society needs people who will observe the rules that make social existence tolerable. From the point of view of a particular society, it is essential to prevent violations of norms against killing, stealing, and so on. It is quite inessential, however, to help people outside one's own society.

If this is an explanation of our common distinction between duty and supererogation, however, it is not a justification of it. The moral point of view requires us to look beyond the interests of our own society. Previously, as I have already mentioned, this may hardly have been feasible, but it is quite feasible now. From the moral point of view, the prevention of the starvation of millions of people outside our society must be considered at least as pressing as the upholding of property norms within our society.

It has been argued by some writers, among them Sidgwick and Urmson, that we need to have a basic moral code which is not too far beyond the capacities of the ordinary man, for otherwise there will be a general breakdown of compliance with the moral code. Crudely stated, this argument suggests that if we tell people that they ought to refrain from murder and give everything they do not really need to famine relief, they

---

[3]J.O. Urmson, "Saints and Heroes," in *Essays in Moral Philosophy*, ed., Abraham I. Melden (Seattle and London, 1958), p. 214. For a related but significantly different view see also Henry Sidgwick, *The Methods of Ethics*, 7th ed. (London, 1907), pp. 220–221, 492–493.

will do neither, whereas if we tell them that they ought to refrain from murder and that it is good to give to famine relief but not wrong not to do so, they will at least refrain from murder. The issue here is: Where should we draw the line between conduct that is required and conduct that is good although not required, so as to get the best possible result? This would seem to be an empirical question, although a very difficult one. One objection to the Sidgwick-Urmson line of argument is that it takes insufficient account of the effect that moral standards can have on the decisions we make. Given a society in which a wealthy man who gives five percent of his income to famine relief is regarded as most generous, it is not surprising that a proposal that we all ought to give away half our incomes will be thought to be absurdly unrealistic. In a society which held that no man should have more than enough while others have less than they need, such a proposal might seem narrow-minded. What it is possible for a man to do and what he is likely to do are both, I think, very greatly influenced by what people around him are doing and expecting him to do. In any case, the possibility that by spreading the idea that we ought to be doing very much more than we are to relieve famine we shall bring about a general breakdown of moral behavior seems remote. If the stakes are an end to widespread starvation, it is worth the risk. Finally, it should be emphasized that these considerations are relevant only to the issue of what we should require from others, and not to what we ourselves ought to do.

The second objection to my attack on the present distinction between duty and charity is one which has from time to time been made against utilitarianism. It follows from some forms of utilitarian theory that we all ought, morally, to be working full time to increase the balance of happiness over misery. The position I have taken here would not lead to this conclusion in all circumstances, for if there were no bad occurrences that we could prevent without sacrificing something of comparable moral importance, my argument would have no application. Given the present conditions in many parts of the world, however, it does follow from my argument that we ought, morally, to be working full time to relieve great suffering of the sort that occurs as a result of famine or other disasters. Of course, mitigating circumstances can be adduced—for instance, that if we wear ourselves out through overwork, we shall be less effective than we would otherwise have been. Nevertheless, when all considerations of this sort have been taken into account, the conclusion remains: we ought to be preventing as much suffering as we can without sacrificing something else of comparable moral importance. This conclusion is one which we may be reluctant to face. I cannot see, though, why it should be regarded as a criticism of the position for which I have argued, rather than a criticism of our ordinary standards of behavior. Since most people are self-interested to some degree, very few of us are likely to do everything that we ought to do. It would, however, hardly be honest to take this as evidence that it is not the case that we ought to do it.

It may still be thought that my conclusions are so wildly out of line with what everyone else thinks and has always thought that there must be something wrong with the argument somewhere. In order to show that my conclusions, while certainly contrary to contemporary Western moral standards, would not have seemed so extraordinary at other times and in other places, I would like to quote a passage from a writer not normally thought of as a way-out radical, Thomas Aquinas.

> Now, according to the natural order instituted by divine providence, material goods are provided for the satisfaction of human needs. Therefore the division and appropriation of property, which proceeds from human law, must not hinder the satisfaction of man's necessity from such goods. Equally, whatever a man has in superabundance is owed, of natural right, to the poor for their sustenance. So Ambrosius says, and it is also to be found in the *Decretum Gratiani*: "The bread which you withhold belongs to the hungry; the clothing you shut away, to the naked; and the money you bury in the earth is the redemption and freedom of the penniless."[4]

I now want to consider a number of points, more practical than philosophical, which are relevant to the application of the moral conclusion we have reached. These points challenge not the idea that we ought to be doing all we can to prevent starvation, but the idea that giving away a great deal of money is the best means to this end. It is sometimes said that overseas aid should be a government responsibility, and that therefore one ought not to give to privately run charities. Giving privately, it is said, allows the government and the noncontributing members of society to escape their responsibilities. This argument seems to assume that the more people there are who give to privately organized famine relief funds, the less likely it is that the government will take over full responsibility for such aid. This assumption is unsupported, and does not strike me as at all plausible. The opposite view—that if no one gives voluntarily, a government will assume that its citizens are uninterested in famine relief and would not wish to be forced into giving aid—seems more plausible. In any case, unless there were a definite probability that by refusing to give one would be helping to bring about massive government assistance, people who do refuse to make voluntary contributions are refusing to prevent a certain amount of suffering without being able to point to any tangible beneficial consequence of their refusal. So the onus of showing how their refusal will bring about government action is on those who refuse to give.

I do not, of course, want to dispute the contention that governments of affluent nations should be giving many times the amount of genuine, no-strings-attached aid that they are giving now. I agree, too, that giving privately is not enough, and that we ought to be campaigning actively for entirely new standards for both public and private contributions to famine

[4]*Summa Theologica*, II–III, Question 66, Article 7, in *Aquinas, Selected Political Writings*, ed., A.P. d 'Entreves, trans., J.G. Dawson (Oxford, 1948), p. 171.

relief. Indeed, I would sympathize with someone who thought that campaigning was more important than giving oneself, although I doubt whether preaching what one does not practice would be very effective. Unfortunately, for many people the idea that "it's the government's responsibility" is a reason for not giving which does not appear to entail any political action either.

Another, more serious reason for not giving to famine relief funds is that until there is effective population control, relieving famine merely postpones starvation. If we save the Bengal refugees now, others, perhaps the children of these refugees, will face starvation in a few years' time. In support of this, one may cite the now well-known facts about the population explosion and the relatively limited scope for expanded production.

This point, like the previous one, is an argument against relieving suffering that is happening now, because of a belief about what might happen in the future; it is unlike the previous point in that very good evidence can be adduced in support of this belief about the future. I will not go into the evidence here. I accept that the earth cannot support indefinitely a population rising at the present rate. This certainly poses a problem for anyone who thinks it important to prevent famine. Again, however, one could accept the argument without drawing the conclusion that it absolves one from any obligation to do anything to prevent famine. The conclusion that should be drawn is that the best means of preventing famine, in the long run, is population control. It would then follow from the position reached earlier that one ought to be doing all one can to promote population control (unless one held that all forms of population control were wrong in themselves, or would have significantly bad consequences). Since there are organizations working specifically for population control, one would then support them rather than more orthodox methods of preventing famine.

A third point raised by the conclusion reached earlier relates to the question of just how much we all ought to be giving away. One possibility, which has already been mentioned, is that we ought to give until we reach the level of marginal utility—that is, the level at which, by giving more, I would cause as much suffering to myself or my dependents as I would relieve by my gift. This would mean, of course, that one would reduce oneself to very near the material circumstances of a Bengali refugee. It will be recalled that earlier I put forward both a strong and a moderate version of the principle of preventing bad occurrences. The strong version, which required us to prevent bad things from happening unless in doing so we would be sacrificing something of comparable moral significance, does seem to require reducing ourselves to the level of marginal utility. I should also say that the strong version seems to me to be the correct one. I proposed the more moderate version—that we should prevent bad occurrences unless, to do so, we had to sacrifice something morally significant—only in order to show that even on this surely undeniable principle a great change in our way of life is required. On the more moderate principle, it may not follow that we ought to reduce ourselves to the level of marginal utility, for one might hold that to reduce oneself and one's family to this level is to cause something significantly bad to happen. Whether this is so I shall not discuss, since, as I have said, I can see no good reason for holding the moderate version of the principle rather than the strong version. Even if we accepted the principle only in its moderate form, however, it should be clear that we would have to give away enough to ensure that the consumer society, dependent as it is on people spending on trivia rather than giving to famine relief, would slow down and perhaps disappear entirely. There are several reasons why this would be desirable in itself. The value and necessity of economic growth are now being questioned not only by conservationists, but by economists as well.[5] There is no doubt, too, that the consumer society has had a distorting effect on the goals and purposes of its members. Yet looking at the matter purely from the point of view of overseas aid, there must be a limit to the extent to which we should deliberately slow down our economy; for it might be the case that if we gave away, say, forty percent of our Gross National Product, we would slow down the economy so much that in absolute terms we would be giving less than if we gave twenty-five percent of the much larger GNP that we would have if we limited our contribution to this small percentage.

I mention this only as an indication of the sort of factor that one would have to take into account in working out an ideal. Since Western societies generally consider one percent of the GNP an acceptable level for overseas aid, the matter is entirely academic. Nor does it affect the question of how much an individual should give in a society in which very few are giving substantial amounts.

It is sometimes said, though less often now than it used to be, that philosophers have no special role to play in public affairs, since most public issues depend primarily on an assessment of facts. On questions of fact, it is said, philosophers as such have no special expertise, and so it has been possible to engage in philosophy without committing oneself to any position on major public issues. No doubt there are some issues of social policy and foreign policy about which it can truly be said that a really expert assessment of the facts is required before taking sides or acting, but the issue of famine is surely not one of these. The facts about the existence of suffering are beyond dispute. Nor, I think, is it disputed that we can do something about it, either through orthodox methods of famine relief or

[5]See, for instance, John Kenneth Galbraith, *The New Industrial State* (Boston, 1967); and E.J. Mishan, *The Costs of Economic Growth* (London, 1967).

through population control or both. This is therefore an issue on which philosophers are competent to take a position. The issue is one which faces everyone who has more money than he needs to support himself and his dependents, or who is in a position to take some sort of political action. These categories must include practically every teacher and student of philosophy in the universities of the Western world. If philosophy is to deal with matters that are relevant to both teachers and students, this is an issue that philosophers should discuss.

Discussion, though, is not enough. What is the point of relating philosophy to public (and personal) affairs if we do not take our conclusions seriously? In this instance, taking our conclusion seriously means acting upon it. The philosopher will not find it any easier than anyone else to alter his attitudes and way of life to the extent that, if I am right, is involved in doing everything that we ought to be doing. At the very least, though, one can make a start. The philosopher who does so will have to sacrifice some of the benefits of the consumer society, but he can find compensation in the satisfaction of a way of life in which theory and practice, if not yet in harmony, are at least coming together.

POSTSCRIPT

The crisis in Bangladesh that spurred me to write the above article is now of historical interest only, but the world food crisis, is, if anything, still more serious. The huge grain reserves that were then held by the United States have vanished. Increased oil prices have made both fertilizer and energy more expensive in developing countries, and have made it difficult for them to produce more food. At the same time, their population has continued to grow. Fortunately, as I write now, there is no major famine anywhere in the world; but poor people are still starving in several countries, and malnutrition remains very widespread. The need for assistance is, therefore, just as great as when I first wrote, and we can be sure that without it there will, again, be major famines.

The contrast between poverty and affluence that I wrote about is also as great as it was then. True, the affluent nations have experienced a recession, and are perhaps not as prosperous as they were in 1971. But the poorer nations have suffered as least as much from the recession, in reduced government aid (because if governments decide to reduce expenditure, they regard foreign aid as one of the expendable items, ahead of, for instance, defense or public construction projects) and in increased prices for goods and materials they need to buy. In any case, compared to the difference between the affluent nations and the poor nations, the whole recession was trifling; the poorest in the affluent nations remained incomparably better off than the poorest in the poor nations.

So the case for aid, on both a personal and a governmental level, remains as great now as it was in 1971, and I would not wish to change the basic argument that I put forward then.

There are, however, some matters of emphasis that I might put differently if I were to rewrite the article, and the most important of these concerns the population problem. I still think that, as I wrote then, the view that famine relief merely postpones starvation unless something is done to check population growth is not an argument against aid, it is only an argument against the *type* of aid that should be given. Those who hold this view have the same obligation to give to prevent starvation as those who do not; the difference is that they regard assisting population control schemes as a more effective way of preventing starvation in the long run. I would now, however, have given greater space to the discussion of the population problem; for I now think that there is a serious case for saying that if a country refuses to take any steps to slow the rate of its population growth, we should not give it aid. This is, of course, a very drastic step to take, and the choice it represents is a horrible choice to have to make; but if, after a dispassionate analysis of all the available information, we come to the conclusion that without population control we will not, in the long run, be able to prevent famine or other catastrophes, then it may be more humane in the long run to aid those countries that are prepared to take strong measures to reduce population growth, and to use our aid policy as a means of pressuring other countries to take similar steps.

It may be objected that such a policy involves an attempt to coerce a sovereign nation. But since we are not under an obligation to give aid unless that aid is likely to be effective in reducing starvation or malnutrition, we are not under an obligation to give aid to countries that make no effort to reduce a rate of population growth that will lead to catastrophe. Since we do not force any nation to accept our aid, simply making it clear that we will not give aid where it is not going to be effective cannot properly be regarded as a form of coercion.

I should also make it clear that the kind of aid that will slow population growth is not just assistance with the setting up of facilities for dispensing contraceptives and performing sterilizations. It is also necessary to create the conditions under which people do not wish to have so many children. This will involve, among other things, providing greater economic security for people, particularly in their old age, so that they do not need the security of a large family to provide for them. Thus, the requirements of aid designed to reduce population growth and aid designed to eliminate starvation are by no means separate; they overlap, and the latter will often be a means to the former. The obligation of the affluent is, I believe, to do both. Fortunately, there are now so many people in the foreign aid field, including those in the private agencies, who are aware of this.

One other matter that I should now put forward slightly differently is that my argument does, of course, apply to assistance with development, particularly agricultural development, as well as to direct famine relief. Indeed, I think the former is usually the better long-term investment. Although this was my view when I wrote the article, the fact that I started from a famine situation, where the need was for immediate food, has led some readers to suppose that the argument is only about giving food and not about other types of aid. This is quite mistaken, and my view is that the aid should be of whatever type is most effective.

On a more philosophical level, there has been some discussion of the original article which has been helpful in clarifying the issues and pointing to the areas in which more work on the argument is needed. In particular, as John Arthur has shown in "Rights and the Duty to Bring Aid," something more needs to be said about the notion of "moral significance." The problem is that to give an account of this notion involves nothing less than a full-fledged ethical theory; and while I am myself inclined toward a utilitarian view, it was my aim in writing "Famine, Affluence, and Morality" to produce an argument which would appeal not only to utilitarians, but also to anyone who accepted the initial premises of the argument, which seemed to me likely to have a very wide acceptance. So I tried to get around the need to produce a complete ethical theory by allowing my readers to fill in their own version—within limits—of what is morally significant, and then see what the moral consequences are. This tactic works reasonably well with those who are prepared to agree that such matters as being fashionably dressed are not really of moral significance; but Arthur is right to say that people could take the opposite view without being obviously irrational. Hence, I do not accept Arthur's claim that the weak principle implies little or no duty of benevolence, for it will imply a significant duty of benevolence for those who admit, as I think most nonphilosophers and even off-guard philosophers will admit, that they spend considerable sums on items that by their own standards are of no moral significance. But I do agree that the weak principle is nonetheless too weak, because it makes it too easy for the duty of benevolence to be avoided.

On the other hand, I think the strong principle will stand, whether the notion of moral significance is developed along utilitarian lines, or once again left to the individual reader's own sincere judgment. In either case, I would argue against Arthur's view that we are morally entitled to give greater weight to our own interests and purposes simply because they are our own. This view seems to me contrary to the idea, now widely shared by moral philosophers, that some element of impartiality or universalizability is inherent in the very notion of a moral judgment.[6]

[6]For a discussion of the different formulations of this idea, and an indication of the extent to which they are in agreement, see R.M. Hare, "Rules of War and Moral Reasoning," *Philosophy and Public Affairs* 1, no. 2 (1972).

Granted, in normal circumstances, it may be better for everyone if we recognize that each of us will be primarily responsible for running our own lives and only secondarily responsible for others. This, however, is not a moral ultimate, but a secondary principle that derives from consideration of how a society may best order its affairs, given the limits of altruism in human beings. Such secondary principles are, I think, swept aside by the extreme evil of people starving to death.

Kantian Approaches to Some Famine Problems
Onora O'Neill

A SIMPLIFIED ACCOUNT OF KANT'S ETHICS

Kant's moral theory has acquired the reputation of being forbiddingly difficult to understand and, once understood, excessively demanding in its requirements. I don't believe that this reputation has been wholly earned, and I am going to try to undermine it . . . I shall try to reduce some of the difficulties, and [then] I shall try to show the implications of a Kantian moral theory for action toward those who do or may suffer famine. Finally, I shall compare Kantian and utilitarian approaches and assess their strengths and weaknesses.

The main method by which I propose to avoid some of the difficulties of Kant's moral theory is by explaining only one part of the theory. This does not seem to me to be an irresponsible approach in this case. One of the things that makes Kant's moral theory hard to understand is that he gives a number of different versions of the principle that he calls the Supreme Principle of Morality, and these different versions don't look at all like one another. They also don't look at all like the utilitarians' Greatest Happiness Principle. But the Kantian principle is supposed to play a similar role in arguments about what to do.

Kant calls his Supreme Principle the *Categorical Imperative*; its various versions also have sonorous names. One is called the Formula of Universal

Law; another is the Formula of the Kingdom of Ends. The one on which I shall concentrate is known as the *Formula of the End in Itself*. To understand why Kant thinks that these picturesquely named principles are equivalent to one another takes quite a lot of close and detailed analysis of Kant's philosophy. I shall avoid this and concentrate on showing the implications of this version of the Categorical Imperative.

THE FORMULA OF THE END IN ITSELF

Kant states the Formula of the End in Itself as follows:

> Act in such a way that you always treat humanity, whether in your own person or in the person of any other, never simply as a means but always at the same time as an end.[1]

To understand this we need to know what it is to treat a person as a means or as an end. According to Kant, each of our acts reflects one or more *maxims*. The maxim of the act is the principle on which one sees oneself as acting. A maxim expresses a person's policy, or if he or she has no settled policy, the principle underlying the particular intention or decision on which he or she acts. Thus, a person who decides "This year I'll give 10 percent of my income to famine relief" has as a maxim the principle of tithing his or her income for famine relief. In practice, the difference between intentions and maxims is of little importance, for given any intention, we can formulate the corresponding maxim by deleting references to particular times, places, and persons. In what follows I shall take the terms "maxim" and "intention" as equivalent.

　　Whenever we act intentionally, we have at least one maxim and can, if we reflect, state what it is. (There is of course room for self-deception here—"I'm only keeping the wolf from the door" we may claim as we wolf down enough to keep ourselves overweight, or, more to the point, enough to feed someone else who hasn't enough food.)

　　When we want to work out whether an act we propose to do is right or wrong, according to Kant, we should look at our maxims and not at how much misery or happiness the act is likely to produce, and whether it does better at increasing happiness than other available acts. We just have to check that the act we have in mind will not use anyone as a mere means, and, if possible, that it will treat other persons as ends in themselves.

---

[1]Immanuel Kant, *Groundwork of the Metaphysics of Morals*, trans. H.J. Paton (New York: Harper & Row, 1964), p. 96.

USING PERSONS
AS MERE MEANS

To use someone as a *mere means* is to involve them in a scheme of action *to which they could not in principle consent.* Kant does not say that there is anything wrong about using someone as a means. Evidently we have to do so in any cooperative scheme of action. If I cash a check I use the teller as a means, without whom I could not lay my hands on the cash; the teller in turn uses me as a means to earn his or her living. But in this case, each party consents to her or his part in the transaction. Kant would say that though they use one another as means, they do not use one another as *mere* means. Each person assumes that the other has maxims of his or her own and is not just a thing or a prop to be manipulated.

But there are other situations where one person uses another in a way to which the other could not in principle consent. For example, one person may make a promise to another with every intention of breaking it. If the promise is accepted, then the person to whom it was given must be ignorant of what the promisor's intention (maxim) really is. If one knew that the promisor did not intend to do what he or she was promising, one would, after all, not accept or rely on the promise. It would be as though there had been no promise made. Successful false promising depends on deceiving the person to whom the promise is made about what one's real maxim is. And since the person who is deceived doesn't know that real maxim, he or she can't in principle consent to his or her part in the proposed scheme of action. The person who is deceived is, as it were, a prop or a tool—a mere means—in the false promisor's scheme. A person who promises falsely treats the acceptor of the promise as a prop or a thing and not as a person. In Kant's view, it is this that makes false promising wrong.

One standard way of using others as mere means is by deceiving them. By getting someone involved in a business scheme or a criminal activity on false pretenses, or by giving a misleading account of what one is about, or by making a false promise or a fraudulent contract, one involves another in something to which he or she in principle cannot consent, since the scheme requires that he or she doesn't know what is going on. Another standard way of using others as mere means is by coercing them. If a rich or powerful person threatens a debtor with bankruptcy unless he or she joins in some scheme, then the creditor's intention is to coerce; and the debtor, if coerced, cannot consent to his or her part in the creditor's scheme. To make the example more specific: If a moneylender in an Indian village threatens not to renew a vital loan unless he is given the debtor's land, then he uses the debtor as a mere means. He coerces the debtor, who cannot truly consent to this "offer he can't refuse." (Of course the outward form of such transactions may look like ordinary commercial dealings, but we know very well that some offers and demands couched in that form are coercive.)

In Kant's view, acts that are done on maxims that require deception or coercion of others, and so cannot have the consent of those others (for consent precludes both deception and coercion), are wrong. When we act on such maxims, we treat others as mere means, as things rather than as ends in themselves. If we act on such maxims, our acts are not only wrong but unjust: such acts wrong the particular others who are deceived or coerced.

TREATING PERSONS
AS ENDS IN THEMSELVES

Duties of justice are, in Kant's view (as in many others'), the most important of our duties. When we fail in these duties, we have used some other or others as mere means. But there are also cases where, though we do not use others as mere means, still we fail to use them as ends in themselves in the fullest possible way. To treat someone as an end in him or herself requires in the first place that one not use him or her as mere means, that one respect each as a rational person with his or her own maxims. But beyond that, one may also seek to foster others' plans and maxims by sharing some of their ends. To act beneficently is to seek others' happiness, therefore to intend to achieve some of the things that those others aim at with their maxims. If I want to make others happy, I will adopt maxims that not merely do not manipulate them but that foster some of their plans and activities. Beneficent acts try to achieve what others want. However, we cannot seek everything that others want; their wants are too numerous and diverse, and, of course, sometimes incompatible. It follows that beneficence has to be selective.

There is then quite a sharp distinction between the requirements of justice and of beneficence in Kantian ethics. Justice requires that we act on *no* maxims that use others as mere means. Beneficence requires that we act on *some* maxims that foster others' ends, though it is a matter for judgment and discretion which of their ends we foster. Some maxims no doubt ought not to be fostered because it would be unjust to do so. Kantians are not committed to working interminably through a list of happiness-producing and misery-reducing acts; but there are some acts whose obligatoriness utilitarians may need to debate as they try to compare total outcomes of different choices, to which Kantians are stringently bound. Kantians will claim that they have done nothing wrong if none of their acts is unjust, and that their duty is complete if in addition their life plans have in the circumstances been reasonably beneficent.

In making sure that they meet all the demands of justice, Kantians do not try to compare all available acts and see which has the best effects. They consider only the proposals for action that occur to them and check that these proposals use no other as mere means. If they do not, the act is permissible; if omitting the act would use another as mere means, the act is obligatory. Kant's theory has less scope that utilitarianism. Kantians do not claim to discover whether acts whose maxims they don't know fully are just. They may be reluctant to judge others' acts or policies that cannot be regarded as the maxim of any person or institution. They cannot rank acts in order of merit. Yet, the theory offers more precision than utilitarianism when data are scarce. One can usually tell whether one's act would use others as mere means, even when its impact on human happiness is thoroughly obscure.

KANTIAN DELIBERATIONS ON FAMINE PROBLEMS

The theory I have just sketched may seem to have little to say about famine problems. For it is a theory that forbids us to use others as mere means but does not require us to direct our benevolence first to those who suffer most. A conscientious Kantian, it seems, has only to avoid being unjust to those who suffer famine and can then be beneficent to those nearer home. He or she would not be obliged to help the starving, even if no others were equally distressed.

Kant's moral theory does make less massive demands on moral agents than utilitarian moral theory. On the other hand, it is somewhat clearer just what the more stringent demands are, and they are not negligible. We have here a contrast between a theory that makes massive but often indeterminate demands and a theory that makes fewer but less unambiguous demands and leaves other questions, in particular the allocation of beneficence, unresolved. We have also a contrast between a theory whose scope is comprehensive and one that is applicable only to persons acting intentionally and to those institutions that adopt policies, and so maxims. Kantian ethics is silent about the moral status of unintentional action; utilitarians seek to assess all consequences regardless of the intentions that led to them.

KANTIAN DUTIES OF JUSTICE IN TIMES OF FAMINE

In famine situations, Kantian moral theory requires unambiguously that we do no injustice. We should not act on any maxim that uses another as mere means, so we should neither deceive nor coerce others. Such a requirement can become quite exacting when the means of life are scarce, when persons can more easily be coerced, and when the advantage of gaining more than what is justly due to one is great. I shall give a list of acts that on Kantian principles it would be unjust to do, but that one might be strongly tempted to do in famine conditions.

I will begin with a list of acts that one might be tempted to do as a member of a famine-stricken population. First, where there is a rationing scheme, one ought not to cheat and seek to get more than one's share— any scheme of cheating will use someone as mere means. Nor may one take advantage of others' desperation to profiteer or divert goods onto the black market or to accumulate a fortune out of others' misfortunes. Trans-actions that are outwardly sales and purchases can be coercive when one party is desperate. All the forms of corruption that deceive or put pres-sure on others are also wrong: hoarding unallocated food, diverting relief supplies for private use, corruptly using one's influence to others' disad-vantage. Such requirements are far from trivial and frequently violated in hard times. In severe famines, refraining from coercing and deceiving may risk one's own life and require the greatest courage.

Second, justice requires that in famine situations one still try to fulfill one's duties to particular others. For example, even in times of famine, a person has duties to try to provide for dependents. These duties may, tragically, be unfulfillable. If they are, Kantian ethical theory would not judge wrong the acts of a person who had done her or his best. There have no doubt been times in human history where there was nothing to be done except abandon the weak and old or to leave children to fend for themselves as best they might. But providing the supporter of dependents acts on maxims of attempting to meet their claims, he or she uses no others as mere means to his or her own survival and is not unjust. A conscientious attempt to meet the particular obligations one has undertaken may also require of one many further maxims of self-restraint and of endeavor— for example, it may require a conscientious attempt to avoid having (further) children; it may require contributing one's time and effort to programs of economic development. Where there is no other means to fulfill particular obligations, Kantian principles may require a generation of sacrifice. They will not, however, require one to seek to maximize the happiness of later generations but only to establish the modest security and prosperity needed for meeting present obligations.

The obligations of those who live with or near famine are undoubt-edly stringent and exacting; for those who live further off it is rather harder to see what a Kantian moral theory demands. Might it not, for example, be permissible to do nothing at all about those suffering famine? Might one not ensure that one does nothing unjust to the victims of fam-ine by adopting no maxims whatsoever that mention them? To do so would, at the least, require one to refrain from certain deceptive and coer-cive practices frequently employed during the European exploration and economic penetration of the now under-developed world and still not unknown. For example, it would be unjust to "purchase" valuable lands and resources from persons who don't understand commercial transactions or exclusive property rights or mineral rights, so do not understand that their acceptance of trinkets destroys their traditional economic pattern and way of life. The old adage "trade follows the flag" reminds us to how great an extent the economic penetration of the less-developed countries involved elements of coercion and deception, so was on Kantian principles unjust (regardless of whether or not the net effect has benefited the citizens of those countries).

Few persons in the developed world today find themselves faced with the possibility of adopting on a grand scale maxims of deceiving or coercing persons living in poverty. But at least some people find that their jobs require them to make decisions about investment and aid policies that enormously affect the lives of those nearest to famine. What does a commitment to Kantian moral theory demand of such persons?

It has become common in writings in ethics and social policy to distinguish between one's *personal responsibilities* and one's *role responsibilities*. So a person may say, "As an individual I sympathize, but in my official capacity I can do nothing"; or we may excuse persons' acts of coercion because they are acting in some particular capacity—e.g., as a soldier or a jailer. On the other hand, this distinction isn't made or accepted by everyone. At the Nuremberg trials of war criminals, the defense "I was only doing my job" was disallowed, at least for those whose command position meant that they had some discretion in what they did. Kantians generally would play down any distinction between a person's own responsibilities and his or her role responsibilities. They would not deny that in any capacity one is accountable for certain things for which as a private person one is not accountable. For example, the treasurer of an organization is accountable to the board and has to present periodic reports and to keep specified records. But if she fails to do one of these things for which she is held accountable she will be held responsible for that failure—it will be imputable to her as an individual. When we take on positions, we *add* to our responsibilities those that the job requires; but we do not lose those that are already required of us. Our social role or job gives us, on Kant's view, no license to use others as mere means; even business executives and aid officials and social revolutionaries will act unjustly, so wrongly, if they deceive or coerce—however benevolent their motives.

If persons are responsible for all their acts, it follows that it would be unjust for aid officials to coerce persons into accepting sterilization, wrong for them to use coercive power to achieve political advantages (such as military bases) or commercial advantages (such as trade agreements that will harm the other country). It would be wrong for the executives of large corporations to extort too high a price for continued operation employment and normal trading. Where a less-developed country is pushed to exempt a multinational corporation from tax laws, or to construct out of its meager tax revenues the infrastructure of roads, harbors, or airports (not to mention executive mansions) that the corporation—but perhaps not the country—needs, then one suspects that some coercion has been involved.

The problem with such judgments—and it is an immense problem—is that it is hard to identify coercion and deception in complicated institutional settings. It is not hard to understand what is coercive about one person threatening another with serious injury if he won't comply with the first person's suggestion. But it is not at all easy to tell where the outward forms of political and commercial negotiation—which often involve an element of threat—have become coercive. I can't here explore this fascinating question. But I think it is at least fairly clear that the preservation of the outward forms of negotiation, bargaining, and voluntary consent do *not* demonstrate that there is no coercion, especially when one party is vastly more powerful or the other in dire need. Just as our judiciary has a long tradition of voiding contracts and agreements on grounds of duress or incompetence of one of the parties, so one can imagine a tribunal of an analogous sort rejecting at least some treaties and agreements as coercive, despite the fact that they were negotiated between "sovereign" powers or their representatives. In particular, where such agreements were negotiated with some of the cruder deceptions and coercion of the early days of European economic expansion or the subtler coercions and deceptions of contemporary superpowers, it seems doubtful that the justice of the agreement could be sustained.

Justice, of course, is not everything, even for Kantians. But its demands are ones that they can reasonably strive to fulfill. They may have some uncertain moments—for example, does advocating cheap raw materials mean advocating an international trade system in which the less developed will continue to suffer the pressures of the developed world—or is it a benevolent policy that will maximize world trade and benefit all parties, while doing no one an injustice? But for Kantians, the important moral choices are above all those in which one acts directly, not those in which one decides which patterns of actions to encourage in others or in those institutions that one can influence. And such moral decisions include decisions about the benevolent acts that one will or will not do.

KANTIAN DUTIES
OF BENEFICENCE IN TIMES
OF FAMINE

The grounds of duties of beneficence are that such acts not merely don't use others as mere means but are acts that develop or promote others' ends and that, in particular, foster others' capacities to pursue ends, to be autonomous beings.

Clearly there are many opportunities for beneficence. But one area in which the *primary* task of developing others' capacity to pursue their own ends is particularly needed is in the parts of the world where extreme poverty and hunger leave people unable to pursue *any* of their other ends. Beneficence directed at putting people in a position to pursue whatever ends they may have has, for Kant, a stronger claim on us than beneficence directed at sharing ends with those who are already in a position to pursue varieties of ends. It would be nice if I bought a tennis racquet to play with my friend who is tennis mad and never has enough partners; but it is more important to make people able to plan their own lives to a minimal extent. It is nice to walk a second mile with someone who requests one's company; better to share a cloak with someone who may otherwise be too cold to make any journey. Though these suggestions are not a detailed set of instructions for the allocation of beneficence by Kantians, they show that relief of famine must stand very high among duties of beneficence.

THE LIMITS OF KANTIAN ETHICS: INTENTIONS AND RESULTS

Kantian ethics differs from utilitarian ethics both in its scope and in the precision with which it guides action. Every action, whether of a person or of an agency, can be assessed by utilitarian methods, provided only that information is available about all the consequences of the act. The theory has unlimited scope, but, owing to lack of data, often lacks precision. Kantian ethics has a more restricted scope. Since it assesses actions by looking at the maxims of agents, it can only assess intentional acts. This means that it is most at home in assessing individuals' acts; but it can be extended to assess acts of agencies that (like corporations and governments and student unions) have decision-making procedures. It can do nothing to assess patterns of action that reflect no intention or policy, hence it cannot assess the acts of groups lacking decision-making procedures, such as the student movement, the women's movement, or the consumer movement.

It may seem a great limitation of Kantian ethics that it concentrates on intentions to the neglect of results. It might seem that all conscientious Kantians have to do is to make sure that they never intend to use others as mere means, and that they sometimes intend to foster others' ends. And, as we all know, good intentions sometimes lead to bad results, and correspondingly, bad intentions sometimes do no harm, or even produce good.[2] If [Hardin] is right, the good intentions of those who feed the starving lead to dreadful results in the long run. If some traditional arguments

[2]G. Hardin, "Lifeboat Ethics: The Case Against Helping The Poor," *Psychology Today* (September 1974).

in favor of capitalism are right, the greed and selfishness of the profit motive have produced unparalleled prosperity for many.

But such discrepancies between intentions and results are the exception and not the rule. For we cannot just *claim* that our intentions are good and do what we will. Our intentions reflect what we expect the immediate results of our action to be. Nobody credits the "intentions" of a couple who practice neither celibacy nor contraception but still insist "we never meant to have (more) children." Conception is likely (and known to be likely) in such cases. Where people's expressed intentions ignore the normal and predictable results of what they do, we infer that (if they are not amazingly ignorant) their words do not express their true intentions. The Formula of the End in Itself applies to the intentions on which one acts—not to some prettified version that one may avow. Provided this intention—the agent's real intention—uses no other as mere means, he or she does nothing unjust. If some of his or her intentions foster others' ends, then he or she is sometimes beneficent. It is therefore possible for people to test their proposals by Kantian arguments even when they lack the comprehensive causal knowledge that utilitarianism requires. Conscientious Kantians can work out whether they will be doing wrong by some act even though they know that their foresight is limited and that they may cause some harm or fail to cause some benefit. But they will not cause harms that they can foresee without this being reflected in their intentions. . . .

LIFEBOAT EARTH

If in the fairly near future millions of people die of starvation, will those who survive be in any way to blame for those deaths? Is there anything which people ought to do now, and from now on, if they are to be able to avoid responsibility for unjustifiable deaths in famine years? I shall argue from the assumption that persons have a right not to be killed unjustifiably to the claim that we have a duty to try to prevent and postpone famine deaths. A corollary of this claim is that if we do nothing we shall bear some blame for some deaths.

I shall assume that persons have a right not to be killed and a corresponding duty not to kill. . . .

Let us imagine six survivors on a lifeboat. There are two possible levels of provisions:

1. Provisions are on all reasonable calculations sufficient to last until rescue. Either the boat is near land, or it is amply provisioned or it has gear for distilling water, catching fish, etc.
2. Provisions are on all reasonable calculations unlikely to be sufficient for all six to survive until rescue.

We can call situation (1) *the well-equipped lifeboat situation;* situation (2) *the under-equipped lifeboat situation.* . . . On an under-equipped lifeboat it is not possible for all to survive until rescue. . . . Lifeboat situations do not occur very frequently. We are not often confronted starkly with the choice between killing or being killed by the application of a decision to distribute scarce rations in a certain way. Yet this is becoming the situation of the human species on this globe. The current metaphor "spaceship Earth" suggests more drama and less danger; if we are feeling sober about the situation, "lifeboat Earth" may be more suggestive.

Some may object to the metaphor "lifeboat Earth." A lifeboat is small; all aboard have equal claims to be there and to share equally in the provisions. Whereas the earth is vast and while all may have equal rights to be there, some also have property rights which give them special rights to consume, while others do not. The starving millions are far away and have no right to what is owned by affluent individuals or nations, even if it could prevent their deaths. If they die, it will be said, this is a violation at most of their right not to be allowed to die. And this I have not established or assumed.

I think that this could reasonably have been said in times past. The poverty and consequent deaths of far-off persons was something which the affluent might perhaps have done something to prevent, but which they had (often) done nothing to bring about. Hence they had not violated the right not to be killed of those living far off. But the economic and technological interdependence of today alters this situation. Sometimes deaths are produced by some persons or groups of persons in distant, usually affluent, nations. Sometimes such persons and groups of persons violate not only some persons' alleged right not to be allowed to die but also their more fundamental right not to be killed. . . .

If we imagine a lifeboat in which special quarters are provided for the (recently) first-class passengers, and on which the food and water for all passengers are stowed in those quarters, then we have a fair, if crude, model of the present human situation on lifeboat Earth. For even on the assumption that there is at present sufficient for all to survive, some have control over the means of survival and so, indirectly, over others' survival. Sometimes the exercise of control can lead, even on a well-equipped lifeboat, to the starvation and death of some of those who lack control. On an ill-equipped lifeboat some must die in any case. . . . Corresponding situations can, do, and will arise on lifeboat Earth, and it is to these that we should turn our attention, covering both the presumed present situation of global sufficiency of the means of survival and the expected future situations of global insufficiency.

Aboard a well-equipped lifeboat any distribution of food and water which leads to a death is a killing and not just a case of permitting a death. For the acts of those who distribute the food and water are the causes of a death which would not have occurred had those agents either had no causal influence or done other acts. . . .

It is not far-fetched to think that at present the economic activity of some groups of persons leads to others' deaths. I shall choose a couple of examples of the sort of activity which can do so, but I do not think that these examples do more than begin a list of cases of killing by economic activities. Neither of these examples depends on questioning the existence of unequal property rights; they assume only that such rights do not override a right not to be killed. Neither example is one for which it is plausible to think that the killing could be justified as undertaken in self-defense.

Case one might be called the *foreign investment* situation. A group of investors may form a company which invests abroad—perhaps in a plantation or in a mine—and so manage their affairs that a high level of profits is repatriated, while the wages for the laborers are so minimal that their survival rate is lowered, that is, their expectation of life is lower than it might have been had the company not invested there. In such a case the investors and company management do not act alone, do cause immediate deaths, and do not know in advance who will die; it is also likely that they intend no deaths. But by their involvement in the economy of an underdeveloped area they cannot claim, as can another company which has no investments there that they are "doing nothing." On the contrary, they are setting the policies which determine the living standards which determine the survival rate. When persons die because of the lowered standard of living established by a firm or a number of firms which dominate a local economy and either limit persons to employment on their terms or lower the other prospects for employment by damaging traditional economic structures, and these firms could either pay higher wages or stay out of the area altogether, then those who establish these policies are violating some persons' rights not to be killed. Foreign investment which *raises* living standards, even to a still abysmal level, could not be held to kill, for it causes no additional deaths, unless there are special circumstances, as in the following example.

Even when a company investing in an underdeveloped country establishes high wages and benefits and raises the expectation of life for its workers, it often manages to combine these payments with high profitability only by having achieved a tax-exempt status. In such cases the company is being subsidized by the general tax revenue of the underdeveloped economy. It makes no contribution to the infrastructure—e.g., roads and harbors and airports—from which it benefits. In this way many underdeveloped economies have come to include developed enclaves whose development is achieved in part at the expense of the poorer majority. In such cases, government and company policy combine to produce a high wage sector at the expense of a low wage sector; in consequence, some of the persons in the low wage sector, who would not otherwise have died, may die; these persons, whoever they may be, are killed and not merely allowed to die. Such killings may sometimes be justifiable—perhaps, if they are outnumbered by lives saved through having a developed sector—but they are killings nonetheless, since the victims might have survived if not burdened by transfer payments to the developed sector.

But, one may say, the management of such a corporation and its investors should be distinguished more sharply. Even if the management may choose a level of wages, and consequently of survival, the investors usually know nothing of this. But the investors, even if ignorant, are responsible for company policy. They may often fail to exercise control, but by law they have control. They choose to invest in a company with certain foreign investments; they profit from it; they can, and others cannot, affect company policy in fundamental ways. To be sure the investors are not murderers—they do not intend to bring about the deaths of any persons; nor do the company managers usually intend any of the deaths company policies cause. Even so, investors and management acting together with the sorts of results just described do violate some persons' rights not to be killed and usually cannot justify such killings either as required for self-defense or as unavoidable.

Case two, where even under sufficiency conditions some persons' economic activities result in the deaths of other persons, might be called the *commodity pricing* case. Underdeveloped countries often depend heavily on the price level of a few commodities. So a sharp drop in the world price of coffee or sugar or cocoa may spell ruin and lowered survival rates for whole regions. Yet such drops in price levels are not in all cases due to factors beyond human control. Where they are the result of action by investors, brokers, or government agencies, these persons and bodies are choosing policies which will kill some people. Once again, to be sure, the killing is not single-handed, it is not instantaneous, the killers cannot foresee exactly who will die, and they may not intend anybody to die.

Because of the economic interdependence of different countries, deaths can also be caused by rises in the prices of various commodities. For example, . . . famine in the Sahelian region of Africa and in the Indian subcontinent is attributed by agronomists partly to climatic shifts and partly to the increased prices of oil and hence of fertilizer, wheat, and other grains.

> The recent doubling in international prices of essential foodstuffs will, of necessity, be reflected in higher death rates among the world's lowest income groups, who lack the income to increase their food expenditures proportionately, but live on diets near the subsistence level to begin with.[3]

[3]Lester R. Brown and Erik P. Eckholm, "The Empty Breadbasket," *Ceres* (F.A.O. Review on Development), March-April 1974, p. 59. See also N. Borlaug and R. Ewell, "The Shrinking Margin," in the same issue.

Of course, not all of those who die will be killed. Those who die of drought will merely be allowed to die, and some of those who die because less has been grown with less fertilizer will also die because of forces beyond the control of any human agency. But to the extent that the raising of oil prices is an achievement of Arab diplomacy and oil company management rather than a windfall, the consequent deaths are killings. Some of them may perhaps be justifiable killings (perhaps if outnumbered by lives saved within the Arab world by industrialization), but killings nonetheless. Even on a sufficiently equipped earth some persons are killed by others' distribution decisions. The causal chains leading to death-producing distributions are often extremely complex. Where they can be perceived with reasonable clarity we ought, if we take seriously the right not to be killed and seek not merely to avoid killing others but to prevent third parties from doing so, to support policies which reduce deaths. For example—and these are only examples—we should support certain sorts of aid policies rather than others; we should oppose certain sorts of foreign investments; we should oppose certain sorts of commodity speculation, and perhaps support certain sorts of price support agreements for some commodities (e.g., those which try to maintain high prices for products on whose sale poverty stricken economies depend).

If we take the view that we have no duty to enforce the rights of others, then we cannot draw so general a conclusion about our duty to support various economic policies which might avoid some unjustifiable killings. But we might still find that we should take action of certain sorts either because our own lives are threatened by certain economic activities of others or because our own economic activities threaten others' lives. Only if we knew that we were not part of any system of activities causing unjustifiable deaths could we have no duties to support policies which seek to avoid such deaths. Modern economic causal chains are so complex that it is likely that only those who are economically isolated and self-sufficient could know that they are part of no such systems of activities. Persons who believe that they are involved in some death-producing activities will have some of the same duties as those who think they have a duty to enforce others' rights not to be killed.

SELECTED SUPPLEMENTARY READINGS

AIKEN, WILLIAM, AND HUGH LA FOLLETTE, eds., *World Hunger and Moral Obligation.* Englewood Cliffs, N.J.: Prentice-Hall, 1977.

ARTHUR, JOHN, AND WILLIAM H. SHAW, eds., *Justice and Economic Distribution.* Englewood Cliffs, N.J.: Prentice-Hall, 1978.

BAYLES, MICHAEL D., ed., *Ethics and Population.* Cambridge, Mass.: Schenkman Press, 1976.

BEAUCHAMP, TOM L.,"The Right To Food," in *Values in Conflict*, ed. Burton Leiser. New York: Macmillan, 1981.

BRANDT, RICHARD B., "The Concept of Welfare," in *Talking About Welfare: Readings in Philosophy and Public Policy*, eds. Noel Timms and David Watson. London: Routledge and Kegan Paul, 1976.

BROWN, PETER G., AND DOUGLAS MACLEAN, eds., *Human Rights and U.S. Foreign Policy*. Lexington, Mass.: Lexington Books, 1979.

BROWN, PETER G., AND HENRY SHUE, eds., *Food Policy: The Responsibility of the United States in the Life and Death Choices*. New York: Free Press, 1977.

BUCK, PEARL S., *The Good Earth*. New York: J. Day, 1934.

CALLAHAN, DANIEL, "Doing Well by Doing Good: Garrett Hardin's 'Lifeboat Ethic'," *The Hastings Center Report* **4** (December 1974).

EBERSTADT, NICK, "Myths About Starvation," *The New York Review of Books* **23** (February 19, 1976).

GREEN, WADE, "Triage," *New York Times Magazine* (January 5, 1975).

HARDIN, GARRETT, "Living on a Lifeboat," *Bioscience* **24** (October 1974).

————, "The Tragedy of the Commons," *Science* **162** (December 13, 1968).

HENRIOT, P. J., AND M. DANIEL, "Population and Ecology: An Overview," in *Occasional Population Paper*, New York: The Hastings Center, 1976.

LAPPE, FRANCES, "The World Food Problem," *Commonweal* **99** (February 8, 1974).

LUCAS, GEORGE R., AND THOMAS W. OGLETREE, eds., *Lifeboat Ethics*. New York: Harper and Row, 1976. Reprinted from a special issue of *Soundings*, cited below.

PADDOCK, PAUL, AND WILLIAM PADDOCK, *Famine—1975!* Boston: Little, Brown, 1968).

SIMON, LAURENCE, "The Ethics of Triage," *Christian Century* **95** (January 8, 1975).

SOUNDINGS LIX (Spring 1976). A special issue on "World Famine and Lifeboat Ethics: Moral Dilemmas in the Formation of Public Policy." (See LUCAS above).

WARWICK, DONALD P., "Contraceptives in the Third World," *The Hastings Center Report* **5** (August 1975).

chapter eight

Punishment and the Death Penalty

On Deterrence and the Death Penalty

Ernest van den Haag

I

If rehabilitation and the protection of society from unrehabilitated offenders were the only purposes of legal punishment the death penalty could be abolished: it cannot attain the first end, and is not needed for the second. No case for the death penalty can be made unless "doing justice," or "deterring others," are among our penal aims.[1] Each of these purposes can justify capital punishment by itself; opponents, therefore, must show that neither actually does, while proponents can rest their case on either.

Although the argument from justice is intellectually more interesting, and, in my view, decisive enough, utilitarian arguments have more appeal: the claim that capital punishment is useless because it does not deter others, is most persuasive. I shall, therefore, focus on this claim. Lest

[1]Social solidarity of "community feeling" (here to be ignored) might be dealt with as a form of deterrence.

the argument be thought to be unduly narrow, I shall show, nonetheless, that some claims of injustice rest on premises which the claimants reject when arguments for capital punishment are derived therefrom; while other claims of injustice have no independent standing: their weight depends on the weight given to deterrence.

II

Capital punishment is regarded as unjust because it may lead to the execution of innocents, or because the guilty poor (or disadvantaged) are more likely to be executed than the guilty rich.

Regardless of merit, these claims are relevant only if "doing justice" is one purpose of punishment. Unless one regards it as good, or, at least, better, that the guilty be punished rather than the innocent, and that the equally guilty be punished equally,[2] unless, that is, one wants penalties to be just, one cannot object to them because they are not. However, if one does include justice among the purposes of punishment, it becomes possible to justify any one punishment—even death—on grounds of justice. Yet, those who object to the death penalty because of its alleged injustice, usually deny not only the merits, or the sufficiency, of specific arguments based on justice, but the propriety of justice as an argument: they exclude "doing justice" as a purpose of legal punishment. If justice is not a purpose of penalties, injustice cannot be an objection to the death penalty, or to any other; if it is, justice cannot be ruled out as an argument for any penalty.

Consider the claim of injustice on its merits now. A convicted man may be found to have been innocent; if he was executed, the penalty cannot be reversed. Except for fines, penalties never can be reversed. Time spent in prison cannot be returned. However, a prison sentence may be remitted once the prisoner serving it is found innocent; and he can be compensated for the time served (although compensation ordinarily cannot repair the harm). Thus, though (nearly) all penalties are irreversible, the death penalty, unlike others, is irrevocable as well.

Despite all precautions, errors will occur in judicial proceedings: the innocent may be found guilty;[3] or the guilty rich may more easily escape conviction, or receive lesser penalties than the guilty poor. However, these injustices do not reside in the penalties inflicted but in their maldistribution. It is not the penalty—whether death or prison—which is unjust when

---

[2] Certainly a major meaning of *suum cuique tribue.*

[3] I am not concerned here with the converse injustice, *which I regard as no less grave.*

inflicted on the innocent, but its imposition on the innocent. Inequity between poor and rich also involves distribution, not the penalty distributed.[4] Thus injustice is not an objection to the death penalty but to the distributive process—the trial. Trials are more likely to be fair when life is at stake—the death penalty is probably less often unjustly inflicted than others. It requires special consideration not because it is more, or more often, unjust than other penalties, but because it is always irrevocable.

Can any amount of deterrence justify the possibility of irrevocable injustice? Surely injustice is unjustifiable in each actual individual case; it must be objected to whenever it occurs. But we are concerned here with the process that may produce injustice, and with the penalty that would make it irrevocable—not with the actual individual cases produced, but with the general rules which may produce them. To consider objections to a general rule (the provision of any penalties by law) we must compare the likely net result of alternative rules and select the rule (or penalty) likely to produce the least injustice. For however one defines justice, to support it cannot mean less than to favor the least injustice. If the death of innocents because of judicial error is unjust, so is the death of innocents by murder. If some murders could be avoided by a penalty conceivably more deterrent that others—such as the death penalty—then the question becomes: which penalty will minimize the number of innocents killed (by crime and by punishment)? It follows that the irrevocable injustice sometimes inflicted by the death penalty would not significantly militate against it, if capital punishment deters enough murders to reduce the total number of innocents killed so that fewer are lost than would be lost without it.

In general, the possibility of injustice argues against penalization of any kind only if the expected usefulness of penalization is less important than the probable harm (particularly to innocents) and the probable inequities. The possibility of injustice argues against the death penalty only inasmuch as the added usefulness (deterrence) expected from irrevocability is thought less important than the added harm. (Were my argument specifically concerned with justice, I could compare the injustice inflicted by the courts with the injustice—outside the courts—avoided by the judicial process. *I.e.,* "important" here may be used to include everything to which importance is attached.)

We must briefly examine now the general use and effectiveness of deterrence to decide whether the death penalty could add enough deterrence to be warranted.

---

[4]Such inequity, though likely, has not been demonstrated. Note that, since there are more poor than rich, there are likely to be more guilty poor; and, if poverty contributes to crime, the proportion of the poor who are criminals also should be higher than that of the rich.

III

Does any punishment "deter others" at all? Doubts have been thrown on this effect because it is thought to depend on the incorrect rationalistic psychology of some of its 18th and 19th century proponents. Actually deterrence does not depend on rational calculation, on rationality or even on capacity for it; nor do arguments for it depend on rationalistic psychology. Deterrence depends on the likelihood and on the regularity—not on the rationality—of human responses to danger; and further on the possibility of reinforcing internal controls by vicarious external experiences.

Responsiveness to danger is generally found in human behavior; the danger can, but need not, come from the law or from society; nor need it be explicitly verbalized. Unless intent on suicide, people do not jump from high mountain cliffs, however tempted to fly through the air; and they take precautions against falling. The mere risk of injury often restrains us from doing what is otherwise attractive; we refrain even when we have no direct experience, and usually without explicit computation of probabilities, let alone conscious weighing of expected pleasure against possible pain. One abstains from dangerous acts because of vague, inchoate, habitual and, above all, preconscious fears. Risks and rewards are more often felt than calculated; one abstains without accounting to oneself, because "it isn't done," or because one literally does not conceive of the action one refrains from. Animals as well refrain from painful or injurious experiences presumably without calculation; and the threat of punishment can be used to regulate their conduct.

Unlike natural dangers, legal threats are constructed deliberately by legislators to restrain actions which may impair the social order. Thus legislation transforms social into individual dangers. Most people further transform external into internal danger: they acquire a sense of moral obligation, a conscience, which threatens them, should they do what is wrong. Arising originally from the external authority of rulers and rules, conscience is internalized and becomes independent of external forces. However, conscience is constantly reinforced in those whom it controls by the coercive imposition of external authority on recalcitrants and on those who have not acquired it. Most people refrain from offenses because they feel an obligation to behave lawfully. But this obligation would scarcely be felt if those who do not feel or follow it were not to suffer punishment.

Although the legislators may calculate their threats and the responses to be produced, the effectiveness of the threats neither requires nor depends on calculations by those responding. The predictor (or producer) of effects must calculate; those whose responses are predicted (or produced) need not. Hence, although legislation (and legislators) should be rational, subjects, to be deterred as intended, need not be: they need only be responsive.

Punishments deter those who have not violated the law for the same reasons—and in the same degrees (apart from internalization: moral obligation) as do natural dangers. Often natural dangers—all dangers not deliberately created by legislation (e.g., injury of the criminal inflicted by the crime victim) are insufficient. Thus, the fear of injury (natural danger) does not suffice to control city traffic; it must be reinforced by the legal punishment meted out to those who violate the rules. These punishments keep most people observing the regulations. However, where (in the absence of natural danger) the threatened punishment is so light that the advantage of violating rules tends to exceed the disadvantage of being punished (divided by the risk), the rule is violated (i.e., parking fines are too light). In this case the feeling of obligation tends to vanish as well. Elsewhere punishment deters.

To be sure, not everybody responds to threatened punishment. Non-responsible persons may be (a) self-destructive or (b) incapable of responding to threats, or even of grasping them. Increases in the size, or certainty, of penalties would not affect these two groups. A third group (c) might respond to more certain or more severe penalties.[5] If the punishment threatened for burglary, robbery, or rape were a $5 fine in North Carolina, and 5 years in prison in South Carolina, I have no doubt that the North Carolina treasury would become quite opulent until vigilante justice would provide the deterrence not provided by law. Whether to increase penalties (or improve enforcement) depends on the importance of the rule to society, the size and likely reaction of the group that did not respond before, and the acceptance of the added punishment and enforcement required to deter it. Observation would have to locate the points—likely to differ in different times and places—at which diminishing, zero, and negative returns set in. There is no reason to believe that all present and future offenders belong to the *a priori* nonresponsive groups, or that all penalties have reached the point of diminishing, let alone zero returns.

IV

Even though its effectiveness seems obvious, punishment as a deterrent has fallen into disrepute. Some ideas which help explain this progressive heedlessness were uttered by Lester Pearson, then Prime Minister of

---

[5]I neglect those motivated by civil disobedience or, generally, moral or political passion. Deterring them depends less on penalties than on the moral support they receive, though penalties play a role. I also neglect those who may belong to all three groups listed, some successively, some even simultaneously, such as drug addicts. Finally, I must altogether omit the far from negligible role problems of apprehension and conviction play in deterrence—beyond saying that by reducing the government's ability to apprehend and convict, courts are able to reduce the risks of offenders.

Canada, when, in opposing the death penalty, he proposed that instead "the state seek to eradicate the causes of crime—slums, ghettos and personality disorders."[6]

"Slum, ghettos and personality disorders" have not been shown, singly or collectively, to be "the causes" of crime.

1. The crime rate in the slums is indeed higher than elsewhere; but so is the death rate in hospitals. Slums are no more "causes" of crime, than hospitals are of death; they are locations of crime, as hospitals are of death. Slums and hospitals attract people selectively; neither is the "cause" of the condition (disease in hospitals, poverty in slums) that leads to the selective attraction.

As for poverty which draws people into slums, and, sometimes, into crime, any relative disadvantage may lead to ambition, frustration, resentment and, if insufficiently restrained, to crime. Not all relative disadvantages can be eliminated; indeed very few can be, and their elimination increases the resentment generated by the remaining ones; not even relative poverty can be removed altogether. (Absolute poverty—whatever that may be—hardly affects crime.) However, though contributory, relative disadvantages are not a necessary or sufficient cause of crime: most poor people do not commit crimes, and some rich people do. Hence, "eradication of poverty" would, at most, remove one (doubtful) cause of crime.

In the United States, the decline of poverty has not been associated with a reduction of crime. Poverty measured in dollars of constant purchasing power, according to present government standards and statistics, was the condition of ½ of all our families in 1920; of ⅕ in 1962; and of less than ⅙ in 1966. In 1967, 5.3 million families out of 49.8 million were poor—⅑ of all families in the United States. If crime has been reduced in a similar manner, it is a well kept secret.

Those who regard poverty as a cause of crime often draw a wrong inference from a true proposition: the rich will not commit certain crimes—Rockefeller never riots; nor does he steal. (He mugs, but only on TV.) Yet while wealth may be the cause of not committing (certain) crimes, it does not follow that poverty (absence of wealth) is the cause of committing them. Water extinguishes or prevents fire; but its absence is not the cause of fire. Thus, if poverty could be abolished, if everybody had all "necessities" (I don't pretend to know what this would mean), crime would remain, for, in the words of Aristotle "the greatest crimes are committed not for the sake of basic necessities but for the sake of superfluities." Superfluities cannot be provided by the government; they would be what the government does not provide.

2. Negro ghettos have a high, Chinese ghettos have a low crime rate.

---

[6]*New York Times*, November 24, 1967, p. 22. The actual psychological and other factors which bear on the disrepute—as distinguished from the rationalizations—cannot be examined here.

Ethnic separation, voluntary or forced, obviously has little to do with crime; I can think of no reason why it should.[7]

3. I cannot see how the state could "eradicate" personality disorders even if all causes and cures were known and available. (They are not.) Further, the known incidence of personality disorders within the prison population does not exceed the known incidence outside—though our knowledge of both is tenuous. Nor are personality disorders necessary, or sufficient causes for criminal offenses, unless these be identified by means of (moral, not clinical) definition with personality disorders. In this case, Mr. Pearson would have proposed to "eradicate" crime by eradicating crime—certainly a sound, but not a helpful idea.

Mr. Pearson's views are part as well of the mental furniture of the former U.S. Attorney General, Ramsey Clark, who told a congressional committee that ". . . only the elimination of the causes of crime can make a significant and lasting difference in the incidence of crime." Uncharitably interpreted, Mr. Clark revealed that only the elimination of causes eliminates effects—a sleazy cliche and wrong to boot. Given the benefit of the doubt, Mr. Clark probably meant that the causes of crime are social; and that therefore crime can be reduced "only" by nonpenal (social) measures.

This view suggests a fireman who declines fire-fighting apparatus by pointing out that "in the long run only the elimination of the causes" of fire "can make a significant and lasting difference in the incidence" of fire, and that fire-fighting equipment does not eliminate "the causes"—except that such a fireman would probably not rise to fire chief. Actually, whether fires are checked depends on equipment and on the efforts of the firemen using it no less than on the presence of "the causes": inflammable materials. So with crimes. Laws, courts and police actions are no less important in restraining them, than "the causes" are in impelling them. If firemen (or attorneys general) pass the buck and refuse to use the means available, we may all be burned while waiting for "the long run" and "the elimination of the causes."

Whether any activity—be it lawful or unlawful—takes place depends on whether the desire for it, or for whatever is to be secured by it, is stronger than the desire to avoid the costs involved. Accordingly people work, attend college, commit crimes, go to the movies—or refrain from any of these activities. Attendance at a theatre may be high because the show is entertaining and because the price of admission is low. Obviously the attendance depends on both—on the combination of expected gratification and cost. The wish, motive or impulse for doing anything—the experienced, or expected, gratification—is the cause of doing it; the wish

---

[7]Mixed areas, incidentally, have higher crime rates than segregated ones. See, e.g., Ross and van den Haag, *The Fabric of Society*, 192–4 (1957). Because slums are bad (morally) and crime is, many people seem to reason that "slums spawn crime"—which confuses some sort of moral with a causal relation.

to avoid the cost is the cause of not doing it. One is no more and no less "cause" than the other. (Common speech supports this use of "cause" no less than logic: "Why did you go to Jamaica?" *"Because* it is such a beautiful place." "Why didn't you go to Jamaica?" *"Because* it is too expensive."— "Why do you buy this?" *"Because* it is so cheap." "Why don't you buy that?" *"Because* it is too expensive.") Penalties (costs) are causes of lawfulness, or (if too low or uncertain) of unlawfulness, of crime. People do commit crimes because, given their conditions, the desire for the satisfaction sought prevails. They refrain if the desire to avoid the cost prevails. Given the desire, low cost (penalty) causes the action, and high cost restraint. Given the cost, desire becomes the causal variable. Neither is intrinsically more causal than the other. The crime rate increases if the cost is reduced or the desire raised. It can be decreased by raising the cost or by reducing the desire.

The cost of crime is more easily and swiftly changed than the conditions producing the inclination to it. Further, the costs are very largely within the power of the government to change, whereas the conditions producing propensity to crime are often only indirectly affected by government action, and some are altogether beyond the control of the government. Our unilateral emphasis on these conditions and our undue neglect of costs may contribute to an unnecessarily high crime rate.

V

The foregoing suggests the question posed by the death penalty: is the deterrence added (return) sufficiently above zero to warrant irrevocability (or other, less clear, disadvantages)? The question is not only whether the penalty deters, but whether it deters more than alternatives and whether the difference exceeds the cost of irrevocability. (I shall assume that the alternative is actual life imprisonment so as to exclude the complication produced by the release of the unrehabilitated.)

In some fairly infrequent but important circumstances the death penalty is the only possible deterrent. Thus, in case of acute *coups d'etat*, or of acute substantial attempts to overthrow the government, prospective rebels would altogether discount the threat of any prison sentence. They would not be deterred because they believe the swift victory of the revolution will invalidate a prison sentence and turn it into an advantage. Execution would be the only deterrent because, unlike prison sentences, it cannot be revoked by victorious rebels. The same reasoning applies to deterring spies or traitors in wartime. Finally, men who, by virtue of past acts, are already serving, or are threatened, by a life sentence, could be deterred from further offenses only by the threat of the death penalty.[8]

What about criminals who do not fall into any of these (often ignored) classes? Prof. Thorsten Sellin has made a careful study of the available statistics: he concluded that they do not yield evidence for the deterring effect of the death penalty.[9] Somewhat surprisingly, Prof. Sellin seems to think that this lack of evidence for deterrence is evidence for the lack of deterrence. It is not. It means that deterrence has not been demonstrated statistically—not that nondeterrence has been.

It is entirely possible, indeed likely (as Prof. Sellin appears willing to concede), that the statistics used, though the best available, are nonetheless too slender a reed to rest conclusions on. They indicate that the homicide rate does not vary greatly between similar areas with or without the death penalty, and in the same area before and after abolition. However, the similar areas are not similar enough; the periods are not long enough; many social differences and changes, other than the abolition of the death penalty, may account for the variation (or lack of it) in homicide rates with and without, before and after abolition: some of these social differences and changes are likely to have affected homicide rates. I am unaware of any statistical analysis which adjusts for such changes and differences. And logically, it is quite consistent with the postulated deterrent effect of capital punishment that there be less homicide after abolition: with retention there might have been still less.

Homicide rates do not depend exclusively on penalties any more than do other crime rates. A number of conditions which influence the propensity to crime, demographic, economic or generally social, changes or differences—even such matters as changes of the divorce laws or of the cotton price—may influence the homicide rate. Therefore variation or constancy cannot be attributed to variations or constancy of the penalties, unless we know that no other factor influencing the homicide rate has changed. Usually we don't. To believe the death penalty deterrent does not require one to believe that the death penalty, or any other, is the only, or the decisive causal variable; this would be as absurd as the converse mistake that "social causes" are the only, or always the decisive factor. To favor capital punishment, the efficacy of neither variable need be denied. It is enough to affirm that the severity of the penalty may influence some potential criminals, and that the added severity of the death penalty adds to deterrence, or may do so. It is quite possible that such a deterrent effect may be offset (or intensified) by nonpenal factors which affect propensity; its presence or absence therefore may be hard, and perhaps impossible to demonstrate.

[8]Cautious revolutionaries, uncertain of final victory, might be impressed by prison sentences—but not in the acute stage, when faith in victory is high. And one can increase even the severity of a life sentence in prison. Finally, harsh punishment of rebels can intensify rebellious impulses. These points, though they qualify it, hardly impair the force of the argument.

[9]Prof. Sellin considered mainly homicide statistics. His work may be found in his *Capital Punishment* (1967), or, most conveniently, in Bedau, *The Death Penalty in America* (1964), which also offers other material, mainly against the death penalty.

Contrary to what Prof. Sellin *et al.* seem to presume, I doubt that offenders are aware of the absence or presence of the death penalty state by state or period by period. Such unawareness argues against the assumption of a calculating murderer. However, unawareness does not argue against the death penalty if by deterrence we mean a preconscious, general response to a severe, but not necessarily specifically and explicitly apprehended, or calculated threat. A constant homicide rate, despite abolition, may occur because of unawareness and not because of lack of deterrence: people remain deterred for a lengthy interval by the severity of the penalty in the past, or by the severity of penalties used in similar circumstances nearby.

I do not argue for a version of deterrence which would require me to believe that an individual shuns murder while in North Dakota, because of the death penalty, and merrily goes to it in South Dakota since it has been abolished there; or that he will start the murderous career from which he had hitherto refrained, after abolition. I hold that the generalized threat of the death penalty may be a deterrent, and the more so, the more generally applied. Deterrence will not cease in the particular areas of abolition or at the particular times of abolition. Rather, general deterrence will be somewhat weakened, through local (partial) abolition. Even such weakening will be hard to detect owing to changes in many offsetting, or reinforcing, factors.

For all of these reasons, I doubt that the presence or absence of a deterrent effect of the death penalty is likely to be demonstrable by statistical means. The statistics presented by Prof. Sellin *et al.*, show only that there is no statistical proof for the deterrent effect of the death penalty. But they do not show that there is no deterrent effect. Not to demonstrate presence of the effect is not the same as to demonstrate its absence; certainly not when there are plausible explanations for the non-demonstrability of the effect.

It is on our uncertainty that the case for deterrence must rest.[10]

VI

If we do not know whether the death penalty will deter others, we are confronted with two uncertainties. If we impose the death penalty, and achieve no deterrent effect thereby, the life of a convicted murderer has

---

[10]In view of the strong emotions aroused (itself an indication of effectiveness to me: might murderers not be as upset over the death penalty as those who wish to spare them?) and because I believe penalties must reflect community feeling to be effective, I oppose mandatory death sentences and favor optional recommendations by juries after their finding of guilt. The opposite course risks the nonconviction of guilty defendants by juries who do not want to see them executed.

been expended in vain (from a deterrent viewpoint). There is a net loss. If we impose the death sentence and thereby deter some future murderers, we spared the lives of some future victims (the prospective murderers gain too; they are spared punishment because they were deterred). In this case, the death penalty has led to a net gain, unless the life of a convicted murderer is valued more highly than that of the unknown victim, or victims (and the nonimprisonment of the deterred nonmurderer).

The calculation can be turned around, of course. The absence of the death penalty may harm no one and therefore produce a gain—the life of the convicted murderer. Or it may kill future victims of murderers who could have been deterred, and thus produce a loss—their life.

To be sure, we must risk something certain—the death (or life) of the convicted man, for something uncertain—the death (or life) of the victims of murderers who may be deterred. This is in the nature of uncertainty—when we invest, or gamble, we risk the money we have for an uncertain gain. Many human actions, most commitments—including marriage and crime—share this characteristic with the deterrent purpose of any penalization, and with its rehabilitative purpose (and even with the protective).

More proof is demanded for the deterrent effect of the death penalty than is demanded for the deterrent effect of other penalties. This is not justified by the absence of other utilitarian purposes such as protection and rehabilitation; they involve no less uncertainty than deterrence.[11]

Irrevocability may support a demand for some reason to expect more deterrence than revocable penalties might produce, but not a demand for more proof of deterrence, as has been pointed out above. The reason for expecting more deterrence lies in the greater severity, the terrifying effect inherent in finality. Since it seems more important to spare victims than to spare murderers, the burden of proving that the greater severity inherent in irrevocability adds nothing to deterrence lies on those who oppose capital punishment. Proponents of the death penalty need show only that there is no more uncertainty about it than about greater severity in general.

The demand that the death penalty be proved more deterrent than alternatives can not be satisfied any more than the demand that six years in prison be proved to be more deterrent than three. But the uncertainty which confronts us favors the death penalty as long as by imposing it we might save future victims of murder. This effect is as plausible as the gen-

---

[11]Rehabilitation or protection are of minor importance in our actual penal system (though not in our theory). We confine many people who do not need rehabilitation and against whom we do not need protection (e.g., the exasperated husband who killed his wife); we release many unrehabilitated offenders against whom protection is needed. Certainly rehabilitation and protection are not, and deterrence is, the main actual function of legal punishment, if we disregard nonutilitarian purposes.

eral idea that penalties have deterrent effects which increase with their severity. Though we have no proof of the positive deterrence of the penalty, we also have no proof of zero, or negative effectiveness. I believe we have no right to risk additional future victims of murder for the sake of sparing convicted murderers; on the contrary, our moral obligation is to risk the possible ineffectiveness of executions. However rationalized, the opposite view appears to be motivated by the simple fact that executions are more subjected to social control than murder. However, this applies to all penalties and does not argue for the abolition of any.

Deterrence and the Death Penalty: A Reconsideration

Hugo Adam Bedau

Professor Van den Haag's recent article "On Deterrence and the Death Penalty,"[1] raises a number of points of that mixed (i.e., empirical-and-conceptual-and-normative) character which typifies most actual reasoning in social and political controversy but which (except when its purely formal aspects are in question) tends to be ignored by philosophers. This discussion will pass by any number of tempting points in his critique in order to focus in detail only on those which affect his asserted major topic—the issue of deterrence as it bears on the retention of abolition of the death penalty.

Van den Haag's main contentions appear to be the following:

1. Abolitionists of a utilitarian persuasion "claim that capital punishment is useless because it does not deter others. . . ."[2]
2. There are some classes of criminals and some circumstances for which "the death penalty is the only possible deterrent."[3]

[1] Ernest Van den Haag, "On Deterrence and the Death Penalty," *Journal of Criminal Law, Criminology, and Police Science* **61** (no. 4) (1971). This is a "revised version" under the same title of an article which first appeared in *Ethics* **78** (1968), p. 280. The author is grateful to Professor Van den Haag for the provision of a reprint of each version of the article.

[2] *Journal of Criminal Law, Criminology, and Police Science* **60** (1969), 141.

[3] *J.C.L.C.P.S.*, p. 145.

3. As things currently stand, "deterrence [of criminal homicide by the death penalty] has not been demonstrated statistically"; but it is erroneous to assume that "non-deterrence" has been demonstrated statistically.[4]
4. The death penalty is to be favored over imprisonment because "the added severity of the death penalty adds to deterrence, or may do so."[5]
5. "Since it seems more important to spare victims than to spare murderers, the burden of proving that the greater severity inherent in irrevocability adds nothing to deterrence lies on those who oppose capital punishment."[6]

The refutation of the foregoing assertions will constitute the task of this article. The rebuttal arguments may be succinctly summarized as follows: regarding (1), utilitarian abolitionists do not argue as Van den Haag claims, and they would be in error if they did; his assertion in (2), that situations exist in which the death penalty is the only possible deterrent, is misleading and, in the interesting cases, is empirically insignificant; concerning (3), the heart of the dispute, Van den Haag is correct in affirming that deterrence has not been determined statistically, but he is incorrect in denying that that non-deterrence has been demonstrated statistically; his suggestion, (4), that the added severity of the death penalty contributes to its deterrent function, is unempirical and one-sided as well; finally, his contention regarding the burden of proof, (5), which he would impose entirely upon abolitionists, is a dodge and is based on a muddled analysis.

The reason for pursuing in some detail what at first might appear to be mere polemical controversy is not that Professor Van den Haag's essay is so persuasive nor that it is likely to be of unusual influence. The reason is that the issues he raises, even though they are familiar, have not been adequately discussed, despite a dozen state, congressional, and foreign government investigations into capital punishment in recent years. In Massachusetts, for example, several persons under sentence of death have been granted stays of execution pending the final report of a special legislative commission to investigate the death penalty. The exclusive mandate of this commission is to study the question of deterrence.[7] Its provisional conclusions, published late in 1968, though not in line with Professor Van den Haag's views, are open to the kind of criticism he makes. This suggests that his reasoning may be representative of many who have tried to understand the arguments and research studies brought forward by those who would abolish the death penalty, and therefore that his errors are worth exposure and correction.

[4]*J.C.L.C.P.S.*, p. 145.
[5]*J.C.L.C.P.S.*, p. 146.
[6]*J.C.L.C.P.S.*, p. 147.

[7]See ch. 150, Mass. Acts & Resolves 929 (1969); *Mass. Legislative Report, Interim Report of the Special Commission Established to Make an Investigation and Study Relative to the Effectiveness of Capital Punishment as a Deterrent to Crime* (1968) (unpublished).

The claim Van den Haag professes to find "most persuasive"—capital punishment is useless because it does not deter others"—is strange, and it is strange that he finds it so persuasive. Anyone who would make this claim must assume that only deterrent efficacy is relevant to assessing the utility of a punishment. In a footnote, Van den Haag implicitly concedes that deterrence may not be the only utilitarian consideration, when he asserts that whatever our penal "theory" may tell us, "deterrence is . . . the *main actual* function of legal punishment if we disregard nonutilitarian ones."[8] But he does not pursue this qualification. It may be conceded that if "the main actual function" means the main intended or professed function of a punishment for those responsible for instituting it, deterrence is probably the main function of punishment. His definition of deterrence, however, remains vulnerable. According to Van den Haag, it is "a preconscious, general response to a severe but not necessarily specifically and explicitly apprehended or calculated threat."[9]

This definition of deterrence has two merits and at least one fatal defect. First, it preserves the idea that "a law can have no deterrent effect upon a potential criminal if he is unaware of its existence."[10] Surely, this is a truism necessary to the establishment of a definition of "deterrence." Second, by emphasizing threats, it avoids the errors in defining deterrence as "the preventive effect which actual or theoretical punishment of offenders has upon potential offenders."[11] On such a definition, one could not distinguish between the *deterrent* effect of the death penalty and its more inclusive *preventive* effects. Obviously, an executed criminal is prevented from further crimes, but not by having been deterred from them.[12]

Only rarely will the preventive and the deterrent effects of a given punishment be equivalent. Van den Haag's definition, however, falls before a similar objection upon consideration of the general, though by no means universal, desire of persons to avoid capture and punishment for the crimes they commit. Some criminologists have thought this desire to be the primary outcome of severe punishments. If so, then the outcome can

[8]Van den Haag, p. 147 n. 11 (emphasis added).

[9]Van den Haag, p. 146.

[10]Ball, "The Deterrence Concept in Criminology and Law," *Journal of Criminal Law, Criminology and Police Science* **46** (1955), pp. 347, 351.

[11]Ball, p. 347.

[12]Ball writes that "Capital punishment can be totally effective as a deterrent. . . . The executed murderer is no longer a threat to society. He has been permanently deterred." (Ball, p. 353.) This is an erroneous conclusion to reach, and when Ball goes on to use it to argue in favor of the deterrent efficacy of the death penalty, it reveals the menace which lies hidden in a faulty definition.

result whether or not the deterrent function succeeds. Yet such a desire to avoid punishment is embraced by Van den Haag's rubric of "general response" and therefore could count as evidence for the deterrent efficacy of a punishment! Since Van den Haag's conception of deterrence does not discriminate between such fundamentally different types of "general response" to the threat of punishment, it is too ill-formulated as a definition to be of any serious use.

Among the ideas to be incorporated into any definition of deterrence are a pair of truisms: if someone has been deterred then he doesn't commit the crime, and conversely if someone does commit a crime then he hasn't been deterred. Likewise, the key notion in deterrence is prevention by threat of punishment. Therefore, assume (Definition 1) that a given punishment (P) is a *deterrent* for a given person (A) with respect to a given crime (C) at a given time (t) if and only if A does not commit C at t because he believes he runs some risk of P if he commits C, and A prefers, *ceteris paribus*, not to suffer P for committing C. This definition does not presuppose that P really is the punishment for C (a person could be deterred through a mistaken belief); it does not presuppose that A runs a high risk of incurring P (the degree of risk could be zero); or that A consciously thinks of P prior to t (the theory needed to account for the operation of A's beliefs and preferences on his conduct is left open). Nor does it presuppose that anyone ever suffers P (P could be a "perfect" deterrent), nor that only P could have deterred A from C (some sanction less severe than P might have worked as well). Finally, it does not presuppose that because P deters A at t from C, therefore P would deter A at any other time or anyone else at t. The definition insures that we cannot argue erroneously from the fact that A does not commit C to the conclusion that P has succeeded as a deterrent: the definition contains conditions which prevent this. Further, the definition prevents the commission of the more subtle converse error of arguing from the fact that A has not been deterred by P to the conclusion that A will (or must have) commit(ted) C. Both these errors arise from supposing that "the educative, moralizing and habituative effects of punishment,"[13] which serve to prevent the bulk of the public from committing crime, are euphemisms for "deterrence" or operate by the same mechanisms that deterrence does.

Definition 1 suggests a general functional analogue appropriate to express scientific measurements of *differential deterrent efficacy* of a given punishment for a given crime with respect to a given population (Definition 2). Let us say that a given punishment P deters a given population H from a crime C to the degree D that the members of H do not commit C

---

[13]Zimring and Hawkins, "Deterrence and Marginal Groups," *Journal of Research in Crime and Delinquency,* **5** (1968), p. 100.

because they believe that they run some risk of P if they commit C and, *ceteris paribus*, they prefer not to suffer P for committing C. If D = 0, then P has completely failed as a deterrent, whereas if D = 1, P has proved to be a perfect deterrent. Given this definition and the appropriate empirical results for various values of P, C, and H, it should be possible to establish on inductive grounds the relative effectiveness of a given punishment (the value of D) as a deterrent.

Definition 2 in turn suggests the following corollary for assertions of relative superior deterrent efficacy of one punishment over another: a given punishment P_1 is a superior deterrent to another punishment P_2 with respect to some crime C and some population H if and only if: the members of H believe that they are liable to P_1 upon committing C, then they commit C to the degree d_1; whereas if the members of H believe that they are liable to P_2 upon committing C, then they commit C to the degree d_2; and, $d_1 < d_2$. This formulation plainly allows that P_1 may be a more effective deterrent than P_2 for C_1 and yet less effective as a deterrent than P_2 for a different crime C_2 (with H constant), and so forth for other possibilities. When speaking about deterrence in the sections which follow, these definitions and this corollary are presupposed.

Even if Van den Haag's notion of deterrence did not need to be reformulated to incorporate the above improvements, there would still be a decisive objection to his claim. Neither classic nor contemporary utilitarians have argued for or against the death penalty *solely* on the ground of deterrence, nor would their ethical theory entitle them to do so. One measure of the nondeterrent utility of the death penalty derives from its elimination (through death of a known criminal) of future possible crimes from that source; another arises from the elimination of the criminal's probable adverse influence upon others to emulate his ways; another lies in the generally lower budgetary outlays of tax monies needed to finance a system of capital punishment as opposed to long-term imprisonment. There are still further consequences apart from deterrence which the scrupulous utilitarian must weigh, along with the three previously mentioned. Therefore, it is incorrect to assume that a demonstrated failure of the deterrent effect of the death penalty would generate an inference, on utilitarian assumptions, that "the death penalty is useless" and therefore ought to be abolished. The problem for the utilitarian is to make commensurable such diverse social utilities as those measured by deterrent efficacy, administrative costs, etc., and then to determine which penal policy in fact maximizes utility. Finally, inspection of sample arguments actually used by abolitionists[14] will show that Van den Haag has attacked a straw

[14]See the several essays reprinted in Hugo Bedau, *The Death Penalty in America* (Rev. ed. 1967), pp. 166–170.

man: there are few if any contemporary abolitionists (and Van den Haag names none) who argue solely from professedly utilitarian assumptions, and there is none among the nonutilitarians who would abolish the death penalty solely on grounds of its deterrent inefficacy.

II

Governments faced by incipient rebellion or threatened by a *coup d'état* may well conclude, as Van den Haag insists they should, that rebels (as well as traitors and spies) can be deterred, if at all, by the threat of death, since "swift victory" of the revolution "will invalidate [the deterrent efficacy] of a prison sentence."[15] But this does not reveal the importance of providing such deterrence, any more than the fact that a threat of expulsion is the severest deterrent available to university authorities reveals whether they should insist on expelling campus rebels. Also, since severe penalties might have the effect of creating martyrs for the cause, they could provoke attempts to overthrow the government to secure a kind of political sainthood. This possibility Van den Haag recognizes but claims in a footnote that it "hardly impairs the force of the argument."[16] From a logical point of view, it impairs the argument considerably; from an empirical point of view, since one is wholly without any reliable facts or hypotheses on politics in such extreme situations, the entire controversy remains quite speculative.

The one important class of criminals deterrable, if at all, by the death penalty consists, according to Van den Haag, of those already under "life" sentence or guilty of a crime punishable by "life." In a trivial sense, he is correct; a person already suffering a given punishment, P, for a given crime, C_1, could not be expected to be deterred by anticipating the reinfliction of P were he to commit C_2. For if the dread of P did not deter him from committing C_1, how could the dread of P deter him from committing C_2 given that he is already experiencing P? This generalization seems to apply whenever P = "life" imprisonment. Actually, the truth is a bit more complex, because in practice (as Van den Haag concedes, again in a footnote) so-called "life" imprisonment always has its aggravations (e.g., solitary confinement) and its mitigations (parole eligibility). These make it logically possible to deter a person already convicted of criminal homicide and serving "life" imprisonment from committing another such crime. The aggravations available are not, in practice, likely to provide much added deterrent effect; but exactly how likely or unlikely this effect is remains a matter for empirical investigation, not idle guesswork. Van den

[15]Van den Haag, p. 145. The same argument has been advanced earlier in Hook, *The New York Law Forum* 7 (1961), pp. 278–283. For the revised version of this argument, see Bedau, pp. 150–151.
[16]Van den Haag, p. 145, no. 8.

Haag's seeming truism, therefore, relies for its plausibility on the false assumption that "life" imprisonment is a uniform punishment not open to further deterrence-relevant aggravations and mitigations.

Empirically, the objection to his point is that persons already serving a "life" sentence do not in general constitute a source of genuine alarm to custodial personnel. Being already incarcerated and integrated into the reward structure of prison life, they do not seem to need the deterrent controls allegedly necessary for other prisoners and the general public.[17] There are convicts who are exceptions to this generalization, but there is no known way of identifying them in advance, and their number has proved to be small. It would be irrational, therefore, to design a penal policy which invokes the death penalty for the apparent purpose of deterring such convicted offenders from further criminal homicide.[18] Van den Haag cites no evidence that such policies accomplish their alleged purpose, and a review of authorities reveals none. The real question which Van den Haag's argument raises is: Is there any class of actual or potential criminals for which the death penalty exerts a marginally superior deterrent effect over every less severe alternative? With reference to this question there is no evidence at all, one way or the other. Until a determination is made as to whether there is a "marginal group" for whom the death penalty serves as a superior deterrent, there is no reason to indulge Van den Haag in his speculations.[19]

III

It is not clear why Van den Haag is so anxious to discuss whether there is evidence that the death penalty is a deterrent, or whether, as he thinks, there is no evidence that it is not a deterrent. For the issue over abolishing the death penalty, as all serious students of the subject have known for decades, is not whether (1) *the death penalty is a deterrent*, but whether (2) *the death penalty is a superior deterrent to "life" imprisonment*, and consequently the evidential dispute is also not over (1) but only over (2). As this author has argued elsewhere,[20] abolitionists have reason to contest (1) only if they are against *all* punitive alternatives to the death penalty. Since few abolitionists (and none cited by Van den Haag) take this extreme view, and since most

[17]See, e.g., Sellin, "Prison Homicides," in *Capital Punishment*, ed. T. Sellin (1967), pp. 154–60.

[18]Rhode Island (1852), North Dakota (1915), New York (1965), Vermont (1965), and New Mexico (1969), have all qualified their abolition of the death penalty by enacting such a policy. See Bedau, p. 12.

[19]Zimring and Hawkins, pp. 104–105, explain that by a marginal group they mean "the entire class of persons who are objectively on the margin of a particular form of criminal behavior, or, in other words, the class of persons 'next most likely' to engage in criminal behavior in question."

[20]Bedau, pp. 260–261.

are, in fact, reconciled to a punitive alternative of "life" imprisonment, we may concentrate on (2) here. It should be noticed in passing, however, that if (1) could be demonstrated to be false, there would be no need for abolitionists to marshall evidence against (2). Since the truth of (1) is a presupposition of (2), the falsity of (1) would obviate (2) entirely. While it is true that some abolitionists may be faulted for writing as if the falsity of (1) followed from the falsity of (2), this is not a complaint Van den Haag makes nor is it an error of inference upon which the argument against the death penalty depends. Similar considerations inveigh against certain pro-death penalty arguments. Proponents must do more than establish (1), they must also provide evidence in favor of (2); and they cannot infer from evidence which establishes (1) that (2) is true or even probable (unless, of course, that evidence would establish (2) independently). These considerations show us how important it is to distinguish (1) and (2) and the questions of evidence which each raises. Van den Haag never directly discusses (2); he only observes in passing that "the question is not only whether the death penalty deters but whether it deters more than alternatives...."[21] Since he explicitly argues over the evidential status of (1), it is unclear whether he chose to ignore (2) or whether he thinks that his arguments regarding the evidence for (1) also have consequences for (2). Perhaps Van den Haag thinks that if there is no evidence disconfirming (1), then there can be no evidence disconfirming (2); or perhaps he thinks that none of the evidence disconfirming (2) also disconfirms (1). (If he thinks either, he is wrong.) Or perhaps he is careless, conceding on the one hand that (2) is important to the issue of abolition of the death penalty, only to slide back into a discussion exclusively about (1).

Van den Haag writes as if his chief contentions were these two: first, we must not confuse (a) the assertion that there is no evidence that (1), with (b) the assertion that there is evidence that not-(1), i.e., evidence that (1) is false; and second, abolitionists have asserted (b) whereas all they are entitled to assert is (a).[22] I grant, as anyone must, that the distinction between (a) and (b) is legitimate and important. But since, as I have argued, (1) need not be at issue in the death penalty controversy, neither

[21]Van den Haag, p. 145.

[22]Van den Haag accuses Professor Thorsten Sellin, a criminologist "who has made a careful study of the available statistics," of appearing to "think that this lack of evidence for deterrence is evidence for the lack of deterrence." (Van den Haag, p. 145). That is, Van den Haag claims Sellin thinks that (a) is (b)! Sellin's writings, see, e.g., Sellin, "Prison Homicides," do not support the contention that he "thinks" the one "is" the other. A review of his writings, which span the years from 1953–1967, will reveal a certain vacillation between the two manners of stating his conclusion. His most recent statement is unqualified in the (b) form. (See Sellin, p. 138.) Since Van den Haag also cited this author's *The Death Penalty in America*, though not in this connection, it should be added that the distinction between (a) and (b) was there made; but it was not insisted, as it is here, that the argument entitles abolitionists to

are (a) and (b). What is at issue, even though Van den Haag's discussion obscures the point, is whether abolitionists must content themselves with asserting that there is no evidence against (2), or whether they may go further and assert that there is evidence that not-(2), (evidence that (2) is false). Whereas Van den Haag would presumably confine abolitionists to the former, weaker assertion, it shall be argued that they may make the stronger, latter, assertion.

In order to see the issue fairly it is necessary to see how (2) has so far been submitted to empirical test. First of all, the issue has been confined to the death penalty for criminal homicide; consequently, it is not (2) but a subsidiary proposition which critics of the death penalty have tested—(2a) *the death penalty is a superior deterrent to "life" imprisonment for the crime of criminal homicide.* The falsification of (2a) does not entail the falsity of (2); the death penalty could still be a superior deterrent to "life" imprisonment for the crime of burglary, etc. However, the disconfirmation of (2a) would be obviously a significant partial disconfirmation of (2). Secondly, (2a) has not been tested directly but only indirectly. No one has devised a way to count or estimate directly the number of persons in a given population who have been deterred from criminal homicide by the fear of the penalty. The difficulties in doing so are plain enough. For instance, it would be possible to infer from the countable numbers who have not been deterred (because they did commit a given crime) that everyone else in the population was deterred, but only on the assumption that the only reason why a person did not commit a given crime is because he was deterred. Unfortunately for this argument (though happily enough otherwise) this assumption is almost certainly false, as we have noted above in section I. Other methods which might be devised to test (2a) directly have proved equally unfeasible. Yet it would be absurd to insist that there can be no *evidence* for or against (2a) unless it is *direct* evidence for or against it. Because Van den Haag nowhere indicated what he thinks would count as evidence, direct or indirect, for or against (1), much less (2), his insistence upon the distinction between (a) and (b) and his rebuke to abolitionists is in danger of implicitly relying upon just this absurdity.

assert (b). (See Bedau, pp. 264–65.) For the views of writers, all criminologists, who have recently stated the same or a stronger conclusion, see, e.g., Chambliss, "Types of Deviance and the Effectiveness of Legal Sanctions," *Wisconsin Law Review* (1967), pp. 703, 706 ("Capital punishment does not act as an effective deterrent to murder"); Morris and Zimring, "Deterrence and Correction," *The Annals* **381** (1969), pp. 137, 143 ("The capital punishment controversy has produced the most reliable information on the general deterrent effect of a criminal sanction. It now seems established and accepted that . . . the death penalty makes no difference to the homicide rate . . . ."); Reckless, "The Use of the Death Penalty," *Crime and Delinquency* **15** (1969), pp. 43, 52 ("[T]he evidence indicates that [the death penalty for murder] has no discernible effects in the United States . . . ."); Doleschal, "The Deterrent Effect of Legal Punishment," *Information Review on Crime and Delinquency* **1** (1969), 1, 7 ("Capital punishment is ineffective in deterring murder").

How, then, has the indirect argument for (2a) proceeded? During the past generation, at least six different hypotheses have been formulated, as corollaries of (2a), as follows:[23]

i.   Death penalty jurisdictions should have a lower annual rate of criminal homicide than abolition jurisdictions;

ii.   Jurisdictions which abolished the death penalty should show an increased annual rate of criminal homicide after abolition;

iii. Jurisdictions which reintroduced the death penalty should show a decreased annual rate of criminal homicide after reintroduction;

iv.   Given two contiguous jurisdictions differing chiefly in that one has the death penalty and the other does not, the latter should show a higher annual rate of criminal homicide;

v.   Police officers on duty should suffer a higher annual rate of criminal assault and homicide in abolition jurisdictions than in death penalty jurisdictions;

vi.   Prisoners and prison personnel should suffer a higher annual rate of criminal assault and homicide from life-term prisoners in abolition jurisdictions than in death penalty jurisdictions.

It could be objected to these six hypotheses that they are, as a set, insufficient to settle the question posed by (2a) no matter what the evidence for them may be—that the falsity of (i)–(vi) does not entail the falsity of (2a). Or it could be objected that each of (i)–(vi) has been too inadequately tested or insufficiently disconfirmed to establish any disconfirmation of (2a), even though it is conceded that if (i)–(vi) were highly disconfirmed they would disconfirm (2a). Van den Haag's line of attack is not entirely clear as between these two alternatives. It appears that he should take the former line of criticism in its most extreme version. How else could he argue his chief point, that the research used by abolitionists has so far failed to produce *any* evidence against (1)—we may take him to mean (2) or (2a)? Only if (i)–(vi) were *irrelevant* to (2a) could it be fairly concluded from the evidential disconfirmation of (i)–(vi) that there is still no disconfirmation of (2a). And this is Van den Haag's central contention.

---

[23]The relevant research, regarding each of the six hypotheses in the text, is as follows:

(i) Schuessler, "The Deterrent Influence of the Death Penalty," *The Annals* **284** (1952), 54, 57; Reckless, "The Use of the Death Penalty—A Factual Statement," *Crime and Delinquency* **15** (1969), pp. 43, 52 (Table No. 9).

(ii) Thorsten Sellin, *The Death Penalty*, reprinted in Bedau, pp. 135–38.

(iii) Sellin, pp. 34–38; reprinted in Bedau, pp. 339–43.

(iv) See works cited in (iii).

(v) *Canada, Minutes and Proceedings of Evidence, Joint Committee of the Senate and House of Commons of Capital Punishment and Corporeal Punishment and Lotteries* and *The State Police and the Death Penalty*, app. F pt. I, pp. 718–35 (1955); "The Death Penalty and Police Safety," in Bedau, pp. 284–301; and in *Capital Punishment*, ed. Sellin, pp. 138–54.

(vi) *Massachusetts, Report and Recommendations of the Special Commission on the Death Penalty*, 1958, in Bedau, p. 400; Sellin, "Prison Homicides," in *Capital Punishment*, ed. Sellin, pp. 154–60.

The other ways to construe Van den Haag's reasoning are too implausible to be considered: he cannot think that the evidence is indifferent to or *confirms* (i)–(vi); nor can he think that there has been no *attempt* at all to disconfirm (2a); nor can he think that the evidence which disconfirms (i)–(vi) is not therewith also evidence which confirms the negations of (i)–(vi). If any of these three were true it would be a good reason for saying that there is "no evidence" against (2a); but each is patently false. If one inspects (i)–(vi) and (2a), it is difficult to see how one could argue that disconfirmation of the former does not constitute disconfirmation of the latter, even if it might be argued that verification of the former does not constitute verification of the latter. Therefore, there is nothing to be gained by further pursuit of this first line of attack.

Elsewhere, Van den Haag seems to adopt the alternative criticism, albeit rather crudely, as when he argues (against (iv), seemingly, since he nowhere formulated (i)–(vi)) that "the similar areas are not similar enough."[24] He fails to explain why the rates of criminal homicide in Michigan and in Illinois from 1920 to 1960 are not relevant, but simply alleges that the states aren't "similar enough." His criticism does, however, tacitly concede that if the jurisdictions *were* "similar enough," then it would be logically possible to argue from the evidence against (iv) to the disconfirmation of (2a). And this seems to be in keeping with the nature of the case. Thus it is this second line of attack which needs closer examination.

Van den Haag's own position and objections apart, what is likely to strike the neutral observer who studies the ways in which (i)–(vi) have been tested and declared disconfirmed is that their disconfirmation, and *a fortiori*, the disconfirmation of (2a), is imperfect for two related reasons. First, all the tests rely upon *unproved empirical assumptions*; second, it is not known whether there is any *statistical significance* to the results of the tests. It is important to make these concessions, and abolitionists and other disbelievers in the deterrent efficacy of the death penalty have not always done so.

It is not possible here to review all the evidence and reach a judgment on the empirical status of (i)–(vi). But it is possible and desirable to illustrate how the two qualifications cited above must be understood, and then to assess their effect on the empirical status of (2a). The absence of statistical significance may be illustrated by reference to hypothesis (v). According to the published studies, the annual rate of assaults upon on-duty policemen in abolition jurisdictions is lower than in death penalty jurisdictions.[25] But the studies do not answer whether the difference is statistically significant because the data were not submitted to tests of statistical significance. Nor is there any known method by which the data could be

---

[24] Van den Haag, p. 146.

[25] A rate of 1.2 attacks per 100,000 population in abolition jurisdictions as opposed to 1.3 per 100,000 population in death penalty jurisdictions.

subjected to any such tests. This is, of couse, no reason to suppose that the evidence is really not evidence after all, or that though it is evidence against (i) it is not evidence against (2a). Statistical significance is, after all, only a measure of the strength of evidence, not a *sine qua non* of evidential status.

The qualification concerning unproved assumptions is more important, and is worth examining somewhat more fully (though, again, only illustratively). Consider hypothesis (i). Is one entitled to infer that (i) is disconfirmed because in fact a study of the annual homicide rates (as measured by vital statistics showing cause of death) unquestionably indicates that the rate in all abolition states is consistently lower than in all death penalty states? To make this inference one must assume that (A_1) homicides as measured by vital statistics are in a generally constant ratio to criminal homicides, (A_2) the years for which the evidence has been gathered are representative and not atypical, (A_3) however much fluctuations in the homicide rate owe to other factors, there is a non-negligible proportion which is a function of the severity of the penalty, and (A_4) the deterrent effect of a penalty is not significantly weakened by its infrequent imposition. There are, of course, other assumptions, but these are central and sufficiently representative here. Assumption A_1 is effectively unmeasurable because the concept of a criminal homicide is the concept of a homicide which *deserves* to be criminally prosecuted. Nevertheless, A_1 has been accepted by criminologists for over a generation.[26] A_2 is confirmable, on the other hand, and bit by bit, a year at a time, seems to be being confirmed. Assumption A_3 is rather more interesting. To the degree to which it is admitted or insisted that other factors than the severity of the penalty affect the rate of homicide, to that degree A_3 becomes increasingly dubious; but at the same time testing (2a) by (i) becomes increasingly unimportant. The urgency of testing (2a) rests upon the assumption that it is the deterrent efficacy of penalties which is the chief factor in the rate of crimes, and it is absurd to hold that assumption and at the same time doubt A_3. On the other hand, A_4 is almost certainly false (and has been believed so by Bentham and other social theorists for nearly two hundred years). The falsity of A_4, however, is not of fatal harm to the disconfirmation of (i) because it is not known how infrequently a severe penalty such as death or life imprisonment may be imposed without decreasing its deterrent efficacy. The available information on this point leads one to doubt that for the general population the frequency with which the death sentence is imposed makes any significant difference to the volume of criminal homicide.[27]

[26]For a discussion surrounding this point, see Bedau, pp. 56–74.

[27]See R. Dann, *The Deterrent Effect of Capital Punishment* (1935); Savitz, "A Study in Capital Punishment, *Journal of Criminal Law, Criminology, and Police Science* **49** (1958), pp. 338–341 (reprinted in Bedau, pp. 315–332), Graves, "A Doctor Looks at Capital Punishment," *Medical Arts and Sciences* **10** (1956), pp. 137–141 (reprinted in Bedau, pp. 322–332).

These four assumptions and the way in which they bear upon interpretation and evaluation of the evidence against (i), and therefore the disconfirmation of (2a), are typical of what one finds as one examines the work of criminologists as it relates to the rest of these corollaries of (2a). Is it reasonable, in the light of these considerations, to infer that there is no evidence against (i)–(vi), or that although there may be evidence against (i)–(vi), there is none against (2a)? Probably not. Short of unidentified and probably unobtainable "crucial experiments," it is impossible to marshall evidence for (2a) or for (i)–(vi) except by means of certain additional assumptions such as A_1–A_4. To reason otherwise is to rely on nothing more than the fact that it is logically possible to grant the evidence against (i)–(vi) and yet deny that (2a) is false; or it is to insist that the assumptions which the inference relies upon are not plausible assumptions at all (or though plausible are themselves not confirmed) and that no other assumptions can be brought forward which will both be immune to objections and still preserve the linkage between the evidence, (i)–(vi), and (2a). The danger now is that one will repudiate assumptions such as A_1–A_4, so as to guarantee the failure of efforts to disconfirm (2a) via disconfirmation of (i)–(vi): or else that one will place the standards of evidence too high before one accepts the disconfirmation. In either case one has begun to engage in the familiar but discreditable practice of "protecting the hypothesis" by making it in effect immune to any kind of disconfirmation.

In sum, then, the abolitionist's argument regarding deterrence has the following structure: an empirical proposition not directly testable, (2), has a significant corollary, (2a), which in turn suggests a number of corollaries, (i)–(vi), each of which is testable with varying degrees of indirectness. Each of (i)–(vi) has been tested. To accept the results as evidence disconfirming (i)–(vi) and as therefore disconfirming (2a), it is necessary to make certain assumptions, of which A_1–A_4, are typical. These assumptions in turn are not all testable much less directly confirmed; some of them, in their most plausible formulation, may even be false (but not in that formulation necessary to the inference, however). Since this structure of indirect testing, corollary hypotheses, unproved assumptions, is typical of the circumstances which face us when we wish to consider the evidence for or against any complex empirical hypothesis such as (2), I conclude that while (2) has by no means been disproved (whatever that might mean), it is equally clear that (2) has been disconfirmed, rather than confirmed or left untouched, by the inductive arguments surveyed.

An attempt has been made to review and appraise the chief "statistical" arguments, as Van den Haag calls them, marshalled during the past fifteen years or so in this country by those critical of the death penalty. But in order to assess these arguments more adequately, it is helpful to keep in mind two other considerations. First, most of the criminologists sceptical of (1) are led to this attitude not by the route we have examined—the argument against (2)—but by a general theory of the causation of crimes of personal violence. Given their confidence in that theory, and the evidence for it, they tend not to credit seriously the idea that the death penalty deters (very much), much less the idea that it is a superior deterrent to a severe alternative such as "life" imprisonment (which may not deter very much, either).[28] The interested reader should consult in particular Professor Marvin Wolfgang's monograph on this subject.[29] Second, very little of the empirical research purporting to establish the presence or absence of deterrent efficacy of a given punishment is entirely reliable, because almost no effort has been made to isolate the relevant variables. Surely, it is platitudinously true that *some* persons in *some* situations considering *some* crimes can be deterred from commiting them by *some* penalties. To go beyond this, however, and supplant these variables with a series of well-confirmed functional hypotheses about the deterrent effect of current legal sanctions is not possible today.[30]

Even if one cannot argue, as Van den Haag does, that there is no evidence against the claim that the death penalty is a better deterrent than life imprisonment, this does not yet settle the reliability of the evidence. Van den Haag could, after all, give up his extreme initial position and retreat to the concession that although there is evidence against the superior deterrent efficacy of the death penalty, still, the evidence is not very good, indeed, not good enough to make reasonable the policy of abolishing the death penalty. The reply, so far as there is one, short of further empirical studies (which undoubtedly are desirable), is twofold: the evidence against (i)–(vi) is uniformly confirmatory; and this evidence is in turn made intelligible by the chief current sociological theory of the causation of crimes of personal violence. Finally, there do not seem to be any good empirical reasons in favor of keeping the death penalty, as a deterrent or for any other reason, a point to be amplified in the next section.

IV

Van den Haag rests considerable weight on the claims that "the added severity of the death penalty adds to deterrence, or may do so"; and that "the generalized threat of the death penalty may be a deterrent, and the more so, the more generally applied." These claims are open to criticism on at least three grounds.

---

[28]See, for an excellent critique of a recent study in deterrence, Zimring and Hawkins, pp. 111–114.

[29]M. Wolfgang, *Patterns of Criminal Homicide* (1958).

[30]For a general review, see Doleschal, "The Deterrent Effect of Legal Punishment: A Review of the Literature," *Information Review on Crime and Delinquency* 1 (1969), 1–17, and the many research studies cited therein, especially the survey by Morris and Zimring, pp. 137–46.

First, as the modal auxiliaries signal, Van den Haag has not really committed himself to any affirmative empirical claim, but only to a truism. It is always logically possible, no matter what the evidence, that a given penalty which is *ex hypothesi* more severe than an alternative, may be a better deterrent under some conditions not often realized and be proven so by evidence not ever detectable. For this reason, there is no possible way to prove that Van den Haag's claims are false, no possible preponderance of evidence against his conclusions which must, logically, force him to give them up. One would have hoped those who believe in the deterrent superiority of the death penalty could, at this late date, offer their critics something more persuasive than logical possibilities. As it is, Van den Haag's appeal to possible evidence comes perilously close to an argument from ignorance: the possible evidence one might gather is used to offset the actual evidence that has been gathered.

Second, Van den Haag rightly regards his conclusion above as merely an instance of the general principle that, *ceteris paribus*, The Greater the Severity the Greater the Deterrence, a "plausible" idea, as he says. Yet the advantage on behalf of the death penalty produced by this principle is a function entirely of the evidence for the principle itself. But no evidence at all is offered to make this plausible principle into a confirmed hypothesis of contemporary criminological theory of special relevance to crimes of personal violence. Until evidence concerning specific crimes, specific penalties, and specific criminal populations is brought forward to show that in general The Greater the Severity the Greater the Deterrence, the risk of being stupefied by the merely plausible is run. Besides, without any evidence for this principle there will be a complete standoff with the abolitionist (who, of course, can play the same game), because he has his own equally plausible first principle: The Greater the Severity of Punishment the Greater the Brutality Provoked Throughout Society. When at last, exhausted and frustrated by mere plausibilities, one once again turns to study the evidence, he will find that the current literature on deterrence in criminology does not encourage a belief in Van den Haag's principle.[31]

Third, Van den Haag has not given any reason why, in the quest for deterrent efficacy, one should fasten, as he does, on the severity of the punishments in question, rather than, as Bentham long ago counselled, on all the relevant factors, notably the ease, speed, and reliability with which the punishment can be inflicted. Van den Haag cannot hope to convince anyone who has studied the matter that the death penalty and "life" imprisonment differ only in their severity and that in all other respects affecting deterrent efficacy they are equivalent; and if he believes this himself it would be interesting to have seen his evidence for it. The only

[31]See authorities cited notes 22 and 30 above.

thing to be said in favor of fastening exclusively upon the question of severity in the appraisal of punishments for their relative deterrent efficacy is this: to augment the severity of a punishment usually imposes little if any added direct cost to operate the penal system; it even may be cheaper. This is bound to please the harried taxpayer, and at the same time gratify the demand on government to "do something" about crime. Beyond that, emphasizing the severity of punishments as the main, or indeed the sole, variable relevant to deterrent efficacy is unbelievably superficial.

V

Van den Haag's final point concerning where the burden of proof lies is based, he admits, on playing off a certainty (the death of the persons executed) against a risk (that innocent persons, otherwise the would-be victims of those deterrable only by the death penalty, would be killed).[32] This is not analogous, as he seems to think it is, with the general nature of gambling, investment, and other risk-taking enterprises. In none of them is death deliberately inflicted, as it is, for instance, when carrot seedlings are weeded out to enable those remaining to grow larger (a eugenic analogy, by the way, which might be more useful to Van den Haag's purpose). In none, is it necessary to *sacrifice* a present loss in the hope of securing a future net gain; there is only the risk of a loss in that hope. Moreover, in gambling ventures one recoups what he risked if he wins, whereas in executions society must lose something (the lives of persons executed) no matter if it loses or wins (the lives of innocents protected). Van den Haag's attempt to locate the burden of proof by appeal to principles of gambling is a failure.

Far more significantly, Van den Haag frames the issue in such a way that the abolitionist has no chance of discharging the burden of proof once he accepts it. For what evidence could be marshalled to prove what Van den Haag wants proved, that "the greater severity inherent in irrevocability [of the death penalty]...adds nothing to deterrence"? The evidence alluded to at the end of section IV does tend to show that this generalization (the negation of Van den Haag's own principle) is indeed true, but it does not prove its unqualified validity. It must be concluded therefore, that either Van den Haag is wrong in his argument which shows the locus of burden of proof to lie on the abolitionist, or one must accept less than proof in order to discharge this burden (in which case, the very argument Van den Haag advances shows that the burden of proof now lies on those who would retain the death penalty).

[32]The same objection has been previously raised in Feinberg, "Review of the Death Penalty in America," *Ethics* **76** (1965), p. 63.

"Burden of proof" in areas outside judicial precincts, where evidentiary questions are at stake, tends to be a rhetorical phrase and nothing more. Anyone interested in the truth of a matter will not defer gathering evidence pending a determination of where the burden of proof lies. For those who do think there is a question of burden of proof, as Van den Haag does, they should consider this: Advocacy of the death penalty is advocacy of a rule of penal law which empowers the state to deliberately take human life and in general to threaten the public with the taking of life. *Ceteris paribus*, one would think anyone favoring such a rule would be ready to offer considerable evidence for its necessity and efficacy. Surely, some showing of neccessity, some evidentiary proof, is to be expected to satisfy the sceptical. Exactly when and in what circumstances have the apologists for capital punishment offered evidence to support their contentions? Where is that evidence recorded for us to inspect, comparable to the evidence cited in section III against the superior deterrent efficacy of the death penalty? Van den Haag conspicuously cited no such evidence, and so it is with all other proponents of the death penalty. The insistence that the burden of proof lies on abolitionists, therefore, is nothing but the rhetorical demand of every defender of the status quo who insists upon evidence from those who would effect change, while reserving throughout the right to dictate criteria and standards of proof and refusing to offer evidence for his own view.

The death penalty is a sufficiently momentous matter and of sufficient controversy that the admittedly imperfect evidence assembled over the past generation by those friendly to abolition should by now be countered by evidence tending to support the opposite, retentionist, position. It remains a somewhat sad curiosity that nothing of the sort has happened; no one has ever published research tending to show, however inconclusively, that the death penalty after all is a deterrent and a superior deterrent to "life" imprisonment. Among scholars at least, if not among legislators and other politicians, the perennial appeal to burden of proof really ought to give way to offering of proof by those interested enough to argue the issue.

SELECTED SUPPLEMENTARY READINGS

BEDAU, HUGO ADAM, "Capital Punishment," in *Matters of Life and Death*, ed. Tom Regan. New York: Random House, 1980.
——, "The Courts, the Constitution, and Capital Punishment," *Utah Law Review* (1968).
——, ed.,*The Death Penalty in America* (rev. ed.). Garden City, N.Y.: Doubleday, 1967.

————, "The Death Penalty as a Deterrent," and "A Concluding Note on Deterrence and the Death Penalty," *Ethics* **80, 81** (1970).

————, *The Right to Life and Other Essays on the Death Penalty*. New York: Pegasus, 1969.

————, "A Social Philosopher Looks at the Death Penalty," *American Journal of Psychiatry* **123** (1967).

BEDAU, HUGO ADAM AND CHARLES M. PIERCE, eds., *Capital Punishment in the United States*. New York: AMS Press, 1976.

BENN, S.I., "Punishment," in *The Encyclopedia of Philosophy*, ed. P. Edwards. New York: Macmillan, 1967.

BERNS, WALTER, *For Capital Punishment*. New York: Basic Books, 1979.

BLACK, CHARLES L., JR., *Capital Punishment: The Inevitability of Caprice and Mistake*. New York: W.W. Norton, 1974.

CAMUS, ALBERT, *Reflections on the Guillotine: An Essay on Capital Punishment*, trans. Richard Howard. Michigan City, Ind.: Fridtjof-Karla Press, 1959.

DARROW, CLARENCE, "Why Capital Punishment?" *The Story of My Life*. New York: Scribner's, 1932, chap. 10.

EZORSKY, GERTRUDE, ed., *Philosophical Perspectives on Punishment*. Albany, N.Y.: State University of New York Press, 1972.

FEINBERG, JOEL, "Crime, Clutchability, and Individual Treatment," in *Doing and Deserving*. Princeton, N.J.: Princeton University Press, 1970.

GOLDBERG, STEVEN, "On Capital Punishment," *Ethics* **85** (1974).

HART, H.L.A., *Punishment and Responsibility*. Oxford, England: Clarendon Press, 1968.

HOCHKAMMER, WILLIAM O., "The Capital Punishment Controversy," *The Journal of Criminal Law, Criminology, and Police Science* **60** (1969).

HOOK, SIDNEY, "The Death Sentence," in *The Death Penalty in America* (rev. ed.). Garden City, N.Y.: Doubleday, 1967.

KALVEN, HARRY JR. AND HANS ZEISEL, "The American Jury and the Death Penalty," *University of Chicago Law Review* **33** (1966).

LEISER, BURTON M., *Liberty, Justice, and Morals* (2nd ed.). New York: Macmillan, 1979.

LONG, THOMAS A., "Capital Punishment—Cruel and Unusual?" *Ethics* **83** (1973).

McCAFFERTY, JAMES A., ed., *Capital Punishment*. New York: Lieber-Atherton, 1972.

MAPPES, THOMAS A. AND JANE S. ZEMBATY, eds., *Social Ethics: Morality and Social Policy* (2nd ed.). New York: McGraw-Hill, 1981.

RACHELS, JAMES, ed., *Moral Problems* (3rd ed.). New York: Harper & Row, 1979.

RADIN, MARGARET JANE, "The Jurisprudence of Death: Evolving Standards for the Cruel and Unusual Punishments Clause," *University of Pennsylvania Law Review* (May 1978).

VAN DEN HAAG, E., "On Deterrence and the Death Penalty," and "Deterrence and the Death Penalty: A Rejoinder," *Ethics* **78, 81** (1968, 1970).

WASSERSTROM, RICHARD, ed., *Today's Moral Problems* (2nd ed.). New York: Macmillan, 1979.

ZEISEL, HANS, "The Deterrent Effect of the Death Penalty: Facts v. Faith," in *The Supreme Court Review 1976*, ed. P.B. Kurland. Chicago: University of Chicago Press, 1977.

part three

Respect for Life

Modern medicine and biology have prompted reflection on a number of ethical issues about death, dying, and experimentation with live subjects. Each of the chapters in this section treats such a problem. In particular, the problems of abortion, euthanasia, experimentation involving humans, and experimentation involving animals are discussed. These problems suggest a need to reflect on the exact nature of permissible and impermissible treatments of fetuses, animals, and human persons from infancy through the final stages of adulthood. These reflections all center on an attempt to analyze what is meant by often invoked expressions such as "respect for life."

ABORTION

The central moral problem of abortion is "Under what conditions, if any, is abortion ethically permissible?" Some contend that abortion is never acceptable, or at most is permissible only if abortion is required to save the pregnant woman's life. This view is commonly called the *conservative theory of abortion*, and Baruch Brody defends one version of it in Chapter 9. Others hold that abortion is always permissible if a pregnant woman freely chooses it. This view is commonly termed the *liberal theory of abortion* and has frequently been advocated by those who emphasize the right of a woman to make decisions which affect her own body. H. Tristram Engelhardt, Jr. defends some aspects of such a liberal theory below. Finally, many defend *intermediate* or *moderate theories*, according to which abortion is ethically permissible up to a certain stage of fetal development or for some limited set of moral reasons which is sufficient to warrant the taking of fetal life in certain circumstances. Judith Thomson defends an intermediate theory which has generally been interpreted as leaning toward liberalism.

The Ontological Status of the Fetus. Recent controversies about abortion focus on what rights, if any, are possessed by fetuses. But a more basic issue is that of the *kind of entity* a human fetus is. Following current usage, including that used by Engelhardt, we shall refer to this as the problem of *ontological status*. Questions such as the following are discussed under this heading: (1) Is the fetus an *individual organism?* (2) Is the fetus *biologically a human being?* (3) Is the fetus *psychologically a human being?* and (4) Is the fetus a *person?* Some who write on problems of ontological status attempt to develop a theory which specifies the conditions under which the fetus can be said to be independent, individual, and alive, while others focus on the conditions, if any, under which the fetus is human, and still others are concerned to explain the conditions, if any, under which the fetus is a person. It would be generally agreed that one attributes a more significant status to the fetus by saying that it is a human being than by simply saying that it is an individual organism, and that one enhances its status still further by describing it as a person.

The Concept of Humanity. The concept of human life plays a central role in discussions of abortion, yet it is an especially perplexing concept, for it can have at least two starkly different meanings. On the one hand, it can mean (a) *biological human life*, that set of biological characteristics—for example, genetic ones—that set the human species apart from nonhuman species. On the other hand, the term "human life" can also be used to mean (b) *distinctively human life*—that is, a life characterized by those properties that define the essence of humanity as an advanced species. These are largely psychological, as contrasted with biological properties. It is often said, for example, that the ability to use symbols, to imagine, to love, and to perform various higher intellectual skills are the most distinctive human properties—those that define humans as human. To have these properties, we sometimes say, is truly to be a "human being."

A simple example will illustrate the differences between these two senses. Some infants with various diseases are born and die after a short period of time—as both Engelhardt and Brandt discuss in their Part Three essays. These infants are classifiable in all relevant biological respects as human. However, they never exhibit "distinctively" human traits, and do not have the potential for doing so. For these individuals it is not possible for human life in the "biological" sense to become human in the "distinctively human" or "psychological" sense. We do not differentiate these two levels of life in discourse about any other animal species. We do not, for example, speak of making feline life feline. But we do meaningfully speak of making human life human, and this usage makes sense precisely because there exists in the language the dual meaning just mentioned. In discussions of abortion, it is imperative that one be specific about which meaning is being employed when using an expression such as the "taking of human life." A great many proponents of abortion, and opponents as well, would agree that while biological human life is taken by abortions, human life in the second or psychological sense is not.

The Concept of Personhood. The concept of personhood may or may not be different from either the biological sense or the psychological sense of "human life" discussed above. One might claim that what it means to be a person is simply to have some properties making an organism human in one or both of these senses. But other writers, including Engelhardt, suggest a list of more demanding criteria for being a person. A list of conditions for being a person similar to the following has been supported by several recent writers:

1. consciousness
2. self-consciousness
3. capacity to communicate with other persons
4. capacity to make moral judgments
5. rationality

Sometimes it is said by those who propose such a list that in order to be a person an entity need only satisfy some one criterion on the list—for example, it must be conscious (1) but need not also satisfy the other conditions (2)–(5). Others suggest that all of these conditions must be satisfied in order to be a person. It makes a major difference which of these two views one accepts, but the dominant and prior question is whether one needs to accept anything like this list at all.

The Problem of Line-Drawing.   The problem of ontological status is complicated by a further factor related to the biological development of the fetus. It is important to state at what point of development an entity is to be distinguished as individual, as human, or as a person. This involves specifying at what point each of these stages in ontological status is gained. One position is that the fetus never fits into any of the categories mentioned, and therefore has no human ontological status. The opposite position is that the fetus falls into all of the categories discussed above. Those who hold this view usually claim that the line distinguishing human ontological status must be drawn at conception.

Obviously there can be many intermediate positions as well. These are generally defended by drawing the line somewhere between the two extremes of conception and birth. For example, the line may be drawn at quickening or viability—or perhaps when brain waves are first present. Whichever point is chosen, it is essential that any theory be clear on two matters: (1) It should be specified whether the ontological status of persons, human beings, or some other category is under discussion; and (2) Whatever the point at which the line is drawn (conception, viability, birth, and so on), it should be argued that the line can be justifiably drawn at that point so that the theory is a nonarbitrary one.

As we have seen, the *ontological* status of the fetus remains controversial. We shall now see that the fetus' *moral* status is equally controversial.

The Moral Status of the Fetus.   The notion of *moral status* might be explicated in several ways, but probably is most easily understood in terms of rights. (See the discussion of rights in Part One.) Accordingly, to say that a fetus possesses moral status is to say that it possesses rights. But which rights, if any? Conservatives hold that unborn fetuses possess the same rights as those who are born and therefore have *full moral status*. At least some moderates contend that fetuses have only some rights and therefore have only a *partial moral status*. Liberals, on the other hand, maintain that fetuses possess no rights and therefore have *no moral status*. If this liberal account is accepted, then the unborn have no more right to life than a bodily cell or a tumor, and an abortion would seem to be no more morally objectionable than surgery to remove the tumor. On the other hand, if the conservative account is accepted, then the unborn possess all the rights possessed by other human beings; and an abortion would appear to be as objectionable as any other act of killing an innocent person.

Theories of moral status tend to complement theories of ontological status. The conservative holds that since the line between the human and the nonhuman must be drawn at conception, the fetus has both full human ontological status and full moral status from the moment of conception. Liberals generally tie their theory of moral status to an ontological account by contending that since the line between the human and the nonhuman must be drawn at birth, the fetus has no significant ontological status and therefore no moral status as well. However, a rather different approach has recently become popular. Liberals have argued that even though the fetus is biologically human, it nonetheless is not human in a morally significant sense and hence has no significant moral status. Moderates, on the other hand, use a wide mixture of arguments, which sometimes do and sometimes do not combine an ontological account with a moral one. Typical of moderate views is the claim that the line between the human and the nonhuman or the line between persons and nonpersons should be drawn at some point between conception and birth, and therefore that the fetus has no significant moral status during some stages of growth but acquires significant moral status at some later stage.

The Problem of Conflicting Rights.   If either the liberal or the conservative view of the moral status of the fetus is adopted, the problem of morally justifying abortion may appear to admit of rather easy solution. If one endorses the liberal theory—that a fetus does not enjoy an ethically significant claim to treatment as a human being—the problem may seem to disappear quickly, for it is then arguable that abortions are not morally reprehensible and are prudentially justified much as other surgical procedures are. On the other hand, if one endorses the conservative theory—that a fetus at any stage of development is a human life with full moral status, and possibly a person—the equation "abortion is murder" might be accepted. By this reasoning abortion is never justified under any conditions, or at least could be permitted only if it were an instance of justified homicide.

It has of course been argued that there are cases of justified homicide involving the unborn. For example, it has been argued that a pregnant woman may legitimately "kill" the fetus in "self-defense" if only one of the two may survive or if both will die unless the life of the fetus is terminated. In order to claim that abortion is always wrong, conservatives must justify the position that the fetus' "right to life" always overrides—or at least is equal to—the pregnant woman's rights, including her rights to life and liberty. Judith Thomson explores these issues in her essay in Chapter 9, and Brody offers a response to her views.

Even if the conservative theory is construed so that it entails that human fetuses have equal rights because of their moral status, nothing in the theory requires that these moral rights always override all other moral rights. Here a defender of the conservative theory confronts the problem of the morality of abortion on the level of conflicting rights: the unborn possess some rights (including a right to life) and pregnant women also possess rights (including rights to life and liberty). Those who possess the rights have a (*prima facie*) moral claim to be treated in accordance with their rights. But what is to be done when these rights conflict? This same problem confronts those who hold a moderate theory of the moral status of the fetus. These theories provide moral grounds against arbitrary termination of fetal life (the fetus has some claim to protection against the actions of others), yet do not grant to the unborn (at least in some conditions or at some points in development) the same right to life possessed by those already born. Accordingly, advocates of these theories are faced with the problem of specifying which rights or claims are sufficiently weighty to override the rights or claims of others.

These are only a few of the dilemmas and considerations that emerge in the three essays on abortion in Chapter 9.

EUTHANASIA

By comparison to the topic of abortion, issues about euthanasia are concerned with problems of death and dying from infancy to old age. Nonetheless, some of the problems are the same. For example, the conditions under which killing is permitted and the role of the concept of personhood are as relevant in this section as in the last.

The Nature and Types of Euthanasia.   Many moral and legal disputes concerning euthanasia may be the result of different conceptions or definitions of euthanasia. Certainly it is an elusive and difficult concept, marked by recent changes of meaning. In its original meaning the term "euthanasia" derived from the Greek for "good death," a notion so broad as to be useless. Until rather recently the term was used for the act of painlessly and mercifully putting to death incurably ill persons. But with recent advances in biomedical equipment, which make it possible to sustain life much beyond what formerly was the natural point of death, the meaning has shifted. It now refers both to the active and intentional putting to death of the incurably ill and to the withdrawing or withholding of artificial means used merely to prolong life. Accordingly, "euthanasia" is now generally understood as the action of intentionally bringing about a seriously suffering person's death by at least one other person, where the motive for ending the life is merciful and the means chosen is as painless as possible.

Perhaps because of the recently extended scope of the concept of euthanasia, a distinction is commonly drawn between *active* and *passive* euthanasia. Active or positive euthanasia results when death is directly and intentionally caused by another person (as, for example, when a lethal injection of a drug is administered), while passive or negative euthanasia occurs when death results because others intentionally refrain from actions that might prolong life (usually though not necessarily by withholding or withdrawing artificial life supports). Often in literature on euthanasia this distinction is associated with the distinction between killing and letting die. Another widely used distinction is that between *voluntary* and *involuntary* euthanasia. "Voluntary" here refers to voluntary consent by the patient, and hence the distinction is between euthanasia with patient consent and euthanasia without patient consent—for example, where someone is irreversibly comatose but not dead. These two distinctions, if accepted, generate four different types of euthanasia, which may be diagrammed as follows:

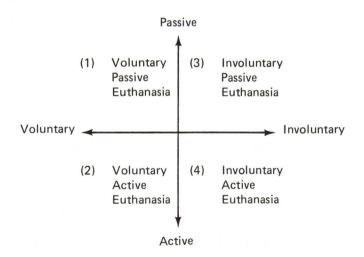

Active or positive euthanasia is illegal in all states in the United States, but physicians may lawfully remove life-prolonging therapy (one form of passive euthanasia) in a variety of cases. The American Medical Association generally supports the latter position, as do many religious groups. However, it is a debated question whether cessation of therapy under all such conditions is or is not truly a form of euthanasia, and also whether its being passive justifies one's failure to act. Similarly there is much debate concerning what does and does not constitute an active causing of death—for example, whether the actual shutting down of a respirator is active.

Ordinarily we distinguish between "causing death" and "permitting death to occur." But is this distinction morally relevant? Is it morally permissible to allow a patient to die, but never morally permissible to kill a patient actively? There would certainly seem to be an important psychological difference between standing aside and letting someone die and actively pushing that person toward death. When a person is allowed to die it is his or her disease or condition that causes death; but if a physician administers a toxic drug, then the physician actively causes the patient's death. In the one case death seems to be natural while in the other it is artificially induced.

James Rachels argues in Chapter 10 that discontinuing treatment with the intent that the patient die is an act, not merely an omission. He goes on to challenge the moral relevance of the killing/letting die distinction. According to Rachels, if it is permissible to intend that a patient die, then acting directly to terminate a patient's life is justified if it is more humane than simply allowing the patient to die. Tom Beauchamp, by contrast, argues that the active/passive distinction may be a relevant moral consideration under some social conditions because of social consequences that might occur if such a distinction were viewed as morally irrelevant.

Arguments for and Against Euthanasia

Quite apart from arguments about the active/passive distinction, the literature on euthanasia reveals three pervasive arguments in favor of voluntary euthanasia:

1. An Argument from Individual Liberty.   Many argue that a primary moral principle, which ought to be incorporated into law whenever possible, is the right of free choice. They argue that state coercion is never permissible unless an individual's actions produce harm to others. Since the sufferer's choice to accelerate death does not harm others, it is a permissible exercise of individual liberty and ought not to be subject to the compulsion of law. (This right of free choice seems to be what is often meant by "the right to die.")

2. An Argument from Loss of Human Dignity. As we have seen, medical technology has increased, and will continue to increase, our capacity to prolong lives. Sometimes dying persons see themselves gradually stripped of their former character and of all the activities they formerly enjoyed. Such patients are not only subjected to intense and abiding pain, they are often aware of their own deterioration, as well as of the burden they have become to others. To some it seems uncivilized and incompassionate, under these conditions, not to allow them to choose their own death.

3. An Argument from the Reduction of Suffering. Some kinds of suffering are so intense and others so protracted as to be unendurable. This suffering can be borne by patient and family alike. As in argument 2, it seems to some immoral under such circumstances not to allow a patient (and in some cases family members) to elect his or her death. Euthanasia is here said to be justified on grounds of prevention of cruelty.

Those in favor of *involuntary* euthanasia must of course provide criteria for its justified application. Some criteria that have been proposed strikingly resemble criteria in support of abortion: for example, the individual must have no potentiality for partaking in human relationships; the suffering the person is likely to endure must outweigh the quality of life the patient can be anticipated to enjoy; and the harm to the family or society must outweigh the benefits of continued existence to the patient. In Chapter 10, R. B. Brandt advocates involuntary euthanasia involving handicapped infants and incompetent patients. Conversely, of course, many oppose any form of involuntary euthanasia, including being allowed to die. They argue that no one should be authorized to make life and death decisions on behalf of another. (Those subscribing to this position need not, however, be opposed to voluntary euthanasia.)

General arguments against the moral legitimacy (and/or the legalization) of voluntary as well as involuntary euthanasia include the following:

1. An Argument from the Sanctity of Human Life. Those opposed to euthanasia often claim that human life is inviolable, and for this reason ought not to be taken under any circumstances. The reasons for this appeal to the value of human life vary. Some reasons are religiously based; others are rooted in the conviction that an obligation to respect life or a sanctity of life principle forms the pillar of social order. Still other reasons derive from reflection on various ancient and modern periods in human history when human lives were disposed of at the whim of the state or family.

2. The Wedge Argument. Some who fear euthanasia appeal to the danger of deteriorating standards. If we once permit the taking of human life by the consent of patients to be a permissible practice, this will erode other strictures against the taking of life. Such euthanasia proposals are said to be the "thin end of a wedge" leading to euthanasia without consent, infanticide, and so on. Euthanasia proposals must be resisted in the beginning, it is argued, or we will ultimately be unable to draw the line ending practices that take human life; for it is not so distant a move from the incurably ill to the socially deviant.

3. Arguments from Probable Abuse.   This argument appeals to the likelihood of abuse by doctors, members of the family, and other interested parties. The claim is that provision of wide discretion to medical practitioners concerning the methods of terminating life introduces a risk of abuse so serious that it outweighs any possible benefits of euthanasia. There are also problems concerning whether the conditions under which a patient gives his or her consent are appropriate, especially when one considers possible family and financial pressures.

4. Arguments from Wrong Diagnoses and New Treatments.   Another argument is encapsulated in the saying, "Where there's life there's hope." It is well known that doctors often misdiagnose maladies. This is not so serious when the diagnoses are correctable, but in cases of euthanasia if the information given is wrong, or if a new treatment appears shortly after death, the case is not correctable. And there are many cases on record of "hopelessly incurable" patients who recovered.

The several arguments listed above are not the only arguments for and against euthanasia, but they do seem the most influential and widely discussed. In the articles in this volume the issue of active and passive euthanasia is most thoroughly explored. These articles must, however, be placed in the context of the broader set of arguments we have just canvassed.

RESEARCH INVOLVING HUMAN SUBJECTS

Much medical, biological, and social scientific knowledge is the result of research conducted on both animals and humans, and in the next two sections we will take up issues pertaining to these forms of research. But, first, let us explore the meaning of the expression "research involving human or animal subjects." *Research* is generally contrasted with *therapy*, where "therapy" refers to a medical or behavioral benefit provided to an individual patient. Such benefits can derive from preventive services, diagnostic procedures, the actual treatment of a disease, or treatment for an injury. "Research," by contrast, refers to an organized scientific procedure intended to produce generalizable knowledge. While research is performed more extensively on animals and other nonhuman biological systems, the study of humans for purposes of generalizable knowledge is a pervasive feature of modern medicine.

Direct benefits to human subjects involved in research can sometimes be provided to them through the research process. On the other hand, some research only produces benefits for individuals who are *not* participants in the research. In still other cases, it is highly uncertain until the research has been completed whether individuals involved in the research will or will not benefit. The main ethical issues about research involving human subjects center on research involving some level of risk and research that does not hold out the prospect of direct benefit to subjects.

Various ethical problems of research involving human subjects were called to the public's attention by documented abuses of human subjects that occurred during World War II. At the Nuremberg Trials, a set of principles known as the Nuremberg Code was devised in order to judge the actions of physicians and legal authorities who had been responsible for experimentation on concentration camp victims. This code became the first in a series of codes issued by various bodies around the world in an attempt to provide ethical standards for research involving human subjects. Extremely important documents in this history were issued, for example, at Helsinki in 1964 and by the United States government in 1971. Subsequently, many professional organizations have issued their own codes to guide the research of their members, perhaps the best known being the American Psychological Association's Code.

During the late nineteenth and early twentieth centuries, research predominantly involved ward patients of no financial means; at the same time, the positive benefits resulting from such research largely accrued to the wealthy, who in some cases could alone afford the medical treatments. Also, a famous case that occurred over a 30-year period from the 1940s into the early 1970s became a celebrated case in the United States. Commonly known as the Tuskegee Syphilis Experiments, this case involved the use of poor, rural, black men in Alabama, some of whom were intentionally not treated for syphilis. The intentional nontreatment was part of a research design to discover facts about the effective treatment of syphilis. This research was heavily criticized in later ethical literature on research involving human subjects and became a paradigm of what is morally proscribed.

Ethical issues involving research on human subjects usually center on one of two areas. The first area is that of adequate standards for the informed consent of subjects or of legal guardians who represent subjects. If a person gives an informed consent to be a subject of research, it is widely believed that this consent justifies the involvement of the person. But what constitutes a truly informed consent, and do subjects ever in fact know enough to give a consent? Questions have been raised about whether research investigators can transmit the proper information to patients and parents or guardians, and other questions have been raised about whether most subjects can actually comprehend the information that has been provided to them. How, for example, are we to interpret the "consent" of children, and if they cannot consent, how can we justify their involvement in research? This question is a focal consideration of the Engelhardt and Wellman articles in Chapter 11.

The voluntariness of such a consent has also been questioned. For example, research with prisoners was one of the most celebrated issues in the last decade about research involving human subjects. Previously, almost all research on new drugs had been carried out on prisoners, and many observers and participants came to doubt that adequate information about the drugs was being conveyed to prisoners. They also doubted whether most prisoners could understand the information provided by drug companies. Perhaps the most severe criticism came from those who regarded it as patently immoral to use persons nonvoluntarily confined for research purposes. Eventually, the arguments against research involving prisoners were accepted at the federal level in the United States, and the research was ended. However, the controversy did not thereby end, for many remain convinced that prisoners can be given sufficient information and can voluntarily consent.

The second area of issues about research involving human subjects is that of how to assess risks and benefits to the human subjects involved. It is often difficult to determine risks of new research, and these risks have sometimes turned out to be much greater than formerly had been expected—for example, there may be unanticipated side effects that result for some subjects of research. The benefits too are very often uncertain. Where there is a high level of uncertainty regarding risks and benefits, some have argued that the research cannot be justified. Others have maintained, however, that the most we can ask is a careful scrutiny of risks and benefits, in order to ascertain whether the foreseen benefits outweigh the unforeseen risks. These problems raise the general issue of the conditions under which research is justified—an issue addressed by both Wellman and Donagan.

Let us now turn to major arguments that have in the past been used to delineate these conditions. Because research involving human subjects involves sensitive and serious issues, it is appropriate to ask for a general justification of such research. In the literature on the subject, three different justifications have been offered. The first is a utilitarian argument to the conclusion that there are broad social advantages gained through research and that the benefits outweigh any attached risks. According to the proponents of this argument, substantial benefits would never have been realized were it not for research, and many risks run in common medical practice would also never have been discovered. For example, in medicine it is common to use so-called "innovative therapies." These are newly emerging therapies whose safety and efficacy are still not well determined. If controlled research on such therapies could not be conducted, the medical community might continue for many years using such "therapies," while in ignorance of the serious risks they present to patients. Research serves the function of reducing such ignorance about risks, improving treatments, and eliminating nonefficacious practices. Without research many discoveries might never have been made at all, or at least would have been appreciably delayed. For example, if research had not been conducted on infants, far less information would be available regarding the diagnosis, monitoring, prevention, and treatment of diseases that affect infants. According to this utilitarian argument, these benefits enormously outweigh the rather low-level risks that might have been presented to the infants involved in past research.

A second argument favorable to research is based on a reciprocity account of social obligations. The argument is that each of us is the beneficiary of a substantial amount of medical research—everyone who has been successfully vaccinated against a disease being an example. Thus, we owe a reciprocal obligation to society to become involved as subjects of research. Otherwise, we would fail to repay the benefits that have been conferred upon us by past research.

A third justification is based on the consent of subjects and the freedom of investigators to do as they choose. If a subject involved in research proffers a free and informed consent to be a subject of research, then, according to this argument, no one can rightfully restrict either that individual or scientific researchers by preventing them from carrying out the research. Here the contention is that one is justified in doing whatever one freely undertakes, so long as it does not present a risk to others who have *not consented* to become involved in the research.

Those who object to research involving human subjects are unimpressed with arguments that defend the freedom of research investigators, though they too emphasize the freedom of individuals. They maintain that society has no right except possibly in emergencies to demand that an individual become a subject of research. As they see it, the pursuit of knowledge through research is not a mandatory goal, but rather one that is optional; there is neither a utilitarian nor a reciprocity basis for asserting an obligation to assume the burden of being a subject of research. Those who accept such arguments effectively see justifiable research involving human subjects as analogous to public health emergencies: whereas in normal times we strictly abstain from imposing quarantines, when a public health emergency occurs such quarantines are quickly accepted as justified. However, so this argument continues, under normal conditions there is nothing parallel to a public health emergency or even to a medical emergency that requires research with human subjects, and so we can do without the knowledge for the moment, while continuing to work on animal or other nonhuman systems.

Many who voice these objections are not morally opposed to research involving human subjects under *all* conditions. They simply view it as properly reserved for limited contexts: Emergency contexts can justify mandatory involvement, while voluntary involvement justifies other research. Moreover, many of the most important breakthroughs in the history of clinical medicine have come as the result of a small group of medical investigators who undertook research either on themselves or on a small group of associated medical colleagues. Those who object to research note that such subjects were involved in the research not because they had a social *obligation* but rather because they volunteered, based on what they believed to be important, and for no other reason. Obviously, the opponents of research regard this distinction between a justification based on obligation and a justification based on voluntary choice as critical.

These emphases on individual freedom and nonobligation are often conjoined with the famous Kantian maxim that we must never treat other persons merely as means to our own ends—a thesis given considerable attention in the articles by Donagan and Wellman. On this basis some have found research involving humans inherently degrading. As those who object to research point out, nontherapeutic research is not undertaken with the research subjects' own welfare primarily in mind. They serve as means to the end of scientific knowledge. Some would even say more strongly that such research subjects are not being respected as persons, for they are effectively conscripted into research. Research involving children and infants again provides a useful example. In cases of nontherapeutic research, infants are by definition not involved in research for their own welfare; they are involved for the goals of society and scientific research investigators. Thus, those who believe in a strong Kantian maxim see nontherapeutic research involving human subjects as without justification even if it produces valuable information. At the threat of overgeneralization, we might say that this problem is at the center of controversy in the essays in Chapter 11.

ANIMAL RIGHTS
AND ANIMAL RESEARCH

A recent debate on animal rights and research held at the University of Virginia Medical School framed issues about research involving animal subjects as follows:

> The original claim of 19th century antivivisectionists that animal experiments should be discontinued because of their failure to yield practical medical results has been refuted by the phenomenal medical advances made in

the 20th century, many of which were directly dependent on animal experimentation. A new antivivisectionism based on the ethics of animal use has now been developed and is exerting increasing pressure on the scientific community from within and without.

Federal regulatory agencies, national and international organizations of scientists, accreditation associations and local peer review systems have all moved in recent years to require ever more stringent controls over the amount and type of distress to animals permissible in any given experiment. These moves have, for the most part, failed to satisfy the advocates of animal rights. It is their belief that the experimental use of fellow-species is both morally repugnant and ethically reprehensible. This places them in direct confrontation with the medical research community.[1]

As the quotation indicates, it is widely believed among biomedical scientists that new scientific investigations and advances would come to a halt unless animal subjects were extensively used. Animals, as well as creatures lower on the phylogenetic scale, are obviously more convenient to use as research subjects than are humans—and such research has gone largely, though not completely, unchallenged in the past. On the other hand, many have come to challenge this use of animals, for reasons to be explored in this section.

These issues are dramatically introduced in the following exchange (which occurred after the showing of a film on animal research) between David Baltimore, a molecular biologist who argues that moral considerations are irrelevant to animal research, and Robert Nozick, a philosopher who maintains that certain moral considerations are relevant to research involving animals.

GRAHAM CHEDD: Dr. Baltimore, you're a cancer researcher at MIT and you work with, not primates, I believe, but rodents and rabbits. Do you find the film shocking in any way?

DAVID BALTIMORE: No. I didn't. I'm a little at a loss to understand the nature of the controversy which has been generated.

. . .

ROBERT NOZICK: I found it disturbing because of the assumption that it was perfectly all right to do this. There was no indication [from the scientists] in the film and I think, perhaps in the scientific community generally, that there's a great cost that's being paid; namely, animals are suffering. Their lives are being taken. And I think it was a virtue of the film that it forcefully presented the question of why is this being done and did the reasons justify it? If we got into the explanation of why it was being done at the same time as seeing what was being done, then we might have been lulled into thinking, well, it's perfectly

---

[1]*The Medical Center Hour*, The University of Virginia School of Medicine, November 19, 1980.

CHEDD:

RICHARD
LEWONTIN:

ADRIAN PERACHIO:

LEWONTIN:

NOZICK:

CHEDD:

BALTIMORE:

NOZICK:
PERACHIO:

all right. But when you see it starkly without knowing why it's being done, you're forced to ask yourself the question—and I hope we all will do so—the reasons which will justify doing that to those animals.

Do you think we would have reacted differently to the film had they been rats? Dr. Lewontin, you grind up flies for a living, apart from other things.

I grind them up. I crush them. I gas them. I do all sorts of things and they seem not to be animals to me. But I would have a difficult time doing that to a thing that looked so human.

Where is that line drawn then? At what point does morality enter into the picture? Is a rat beneath your concern or above it? And how does one arrive at such fine distinctions?

I think that misconceives the question. The question is not morality toward the animals; the question is, what does our activity in this sphere predispose us to? How does it alter our perception of human beings? It's the whole question of the predisposition for behavior toward people.

But I don't think the only issue is the spillover from animals to human beings. The animals count for something themselves. Primates are just an especially hard case, because the usual dividing line that's drawn is something about intelligence or linguistic behavior. And out of Yerkes laboratory and other places, we now have indications of serious evidence that nonhumans are capable of linguistic behavior.... The question among the scientists seems to be: How much is it costing and will it be useful enough to justify its financial cost? But this wasn't just a film about money being spent. People are stunned or shocked by seeing what's being done to the animals. Now that's a cost also, and I would like the scientists to speak to the question of how they estimate how heavy a cost that is, and how they think that should be taken into account in deciding the justification of new research.

Is it true that scientists do feel there's a moral cost? Do you feel there's a moral cost?

Well, I think I'd answer no. Gratuitous killing of animals has been going on for centuries; hunting, that kind of thing.

But we would condemn that, wouldn't we? . . .

Then if you're going to find a cure for cancer, should experimentation, because of its moral cost, be limited to humans? Because it's a given that some form of experimentation has to take place.

> If that cost is much too high, then some alternative has to be found, not necessarily at the abandonment of any moral standard system, but with the realization that there is a need that supersedes some of those moral values.

NOZICK: But there's no sense that any cost is being taken into account at all. . . .

Have we ever heard, in the scientific community—

Have we ever heard people saying, there are these experiments that can be done on animals, but, in fact . . . though we'll learn something, it won't be important enough to justify killing . . . five hundred animals. Has that ever occurred in the scientific community? . . .

BALTIMORE: I don't think it really is a moral question. It's a question of, here we all sit, we want to survive; we get some pleasure out of it and we therefore have drawn some sort of line about human experimentation, in which we've defined humans—in a loose but reasonable fashion—and we live with that definition. To go over that line, we ask a whole series of different questions, and if we lose that [line between animal and human experimentation] then I think you will take apart the research establishment. There certainly is a large movement in the country to try to take apart the scientific research establishment on the basis of an antivivisectionist approach and I consider it both wrong and basically wrong-headed in the way that the question is approached.[2]

The general term "respect for life" is sufficiently broad that it could as easily cover "animal life" as "human life." While many philosophers have maintained that only human life deserves the special protection afforded by moral principles, others have urged that we not restrict the special protection of life to human life. Recently a number of philosophers have argued that there is no morally relevant difference between human life and animal life sufficient to justify the claim that only human life deserves extensive protections. What is it, these philosophers ask, that distinguishes the life of a human infant from the life of an adult chimpanzee so that infants are protected in ways that chimpanzees are not? This question has been taken to be equivalent in many of these discussions to the question, "Do animals have rights?" Let us now explore these questions.

There are many issues raised in the above discussion between Nozick and others, but the crucial one seems to be: Do we have any moral obligation to take the interests of animals into account when conducting research? To many, such as some of the scientists quoted, the question

[2]*Hastings Center Report* **5** (February 1975).

seems so wrongheaded as to be silly; if we do not perform research on animals, we would have to do it on humans, and the latter is morally unacceptable.

However, to many others this approach begs the question. The same reasons that forbid such research on humans, they argue, are strong enough to forbid research on animals. The idea is that there is no consistent way to draw a line between human and animal life that will exclude one and include the other. It cannot be merely the capacity to feel pleasure and pain that makes the difference, for many animals share that capacity almost equally with humans. Nor can it be, for example, that humans have "reason," the "use of language," or "the capacity to interact with the human community" in ways animals do not. If one takes those considerations as relevant to drawing a line between humans and animals, then one will also have to hold that, for example, retarded or irreversibly comatose infants fall into the same categories as animals. No matter where one draws the line between animals and humans, one is going to let in too much or exclude too little.

The challenge, then, is to find some morally relevant property of human beings that will justify restricting the "sanctity of life" to *human* life. If this restriction cannot be appropriately and fairly delineated, then humans may perhaps justifiably be charged with a kind of moral blindness. The *only* reason we would have for excluding animals would be *merely* that they are not human, and that would amount to mere "speciesism," a blind prejudice in favor of one's own species—and one dangerously akin to racism and sexism. This view provides the force behind Nozick's complaint that "there's no sense that any cost is being taken into account at all"; that is, the moral issues are not even being considered. Perhaps research on animals is indeed morally justified, but even if it is, so these philosophers argue, it will be so after the animals' interests have been weighed fairly in a moral balancing of burdens and benefits, and where humans are a part of the balancing process.

An argument from principles of justice supports this case against the exclusion of animals' interests from moral consideration. The formal principle of justice requires us to treat relevantly similar cases equally. If some animals share an equal capacity with humans to experience pleasure and pain, then whatever other differences there may be between animals and humans, that feature will require us to treat animals as we would humans if we are to remain consistent with our moral principles.

A more radical version of this argument holds that the rights of animals, and not merely their interests must be taken into account. Philosophers such as Peter Singer (see Chapter 12) have advanced the claim that the basis of ascription of rights to any entity lies in the entity's capacity to be harmed or benefited—especially in the capacity to suffer pleasure or pain. Since clearly some animals have virtually the same capacities for such experiences as do humans, it would follow that animals are indeed capable of having rights. They need not, of course, be ceded *all* the rights that humans have. They need not, for example, be given a right to vote, nor need one worry about their freedom of religion. But they should share rights with humans if there are relevant capacities that they share equally with humans. Thus, they would have rights to freedom from cruel treatment, which derive from a more general right to freedom from having pain inflicted on them. It would also follow that where research is concerned, animals share with humans the right that the risk of harm be minimized by the research design.

This more radical line of argument has been subjected to attack on the grounds that we only have certain limited obligations to animals, whereas they have no rights. We have, for example, a society for the prevention of cruelty to animals, but support of this society does not entail our having moral obligations to animals or their having rights of any sort. This argument is based on the idea that animals are not the kind of beings which have rights or to which we have more than very limited obligations. Here we must explain on what basis certain entities should be classified as the kinds of things about which it is proper to have moral concerns.

It is, of course, another matter whether animals are capable of *having* moral concerns. We can, for example, think that it is proper to have moral concerns about inflicting unnecessary cruelty on dogs without holding that dogs are themselves capable of entertaining such concerns—just as we can have obligations to irreversibly comatose patients without their having the capacity to know it. Many philosophers would argue, however, that to be an entity capable of *having* moral concerns is a necessary condition of being the kind of entity that can have rights. To be capable of having rights is to be capable of entering into the moral community—that is, the community of entities capable of having moral concerns about each other. Animals fall outside of this community, and thus have no rights. Some philosophers have extended this argument to hold that since animals have no rights, we do not even have stringent obligations to them. At best, we can have self-imposed duties toward them—for example, to treat them well. It is thus right if we so treat animals, but not wrong if we do not, according to these philosophers.

chapter nine

Abortion

A Defense of Abortion

Judith Jarvis Thomson

Most opposition to abortion relies on the premise that the fetus is a human being, a person, from the moment of conception. The premise is argued for, but, as I think, not well. Take, for example, the most common argument. We are asked to notice that the development of a human being from conception through birth into childhood is continuous; then it is said that to draw a line, to choose a point in this development and say "before this point the thing is not a person, after this point it is a person" is to make an arbitrary choice, a choice for which in the nature of things no good reason can be given. It is concluded that the fetus is, or anyway that we had better say it is, a person from the moment of conception. But this conclusion does not follow. Similar things might be said about the development of an acorn into an oak tree, and it does not follow that acorns are oak trees, or that we had better say they are. Arguments of this form are sometimes called "slippery slope arguments"—the phrase is perhaps self-

Judith Jarvis Thomson, "A Defense of Abortion," *Philosophy & Public Affairs*, vol. 1, no. 1 (Fall 1971). Copyright © 1971 by Princeton University Press. Reprinted by permission of Princeton University Press.

I am very much indebted to James Thomson for discussion, criticism, and many helpful suggestions.

explanatory—and it is dismaying that opponents of abortion rely on them so heavily and uncritically.

I am inclined to agree, however, that the prospects for "drawing a line" in the development of the fetus look dim. I am inclined to think also that we shall probably have to agree that the fetus has already become a human person well before birth. Indeed, it comes as a surprise when one first learns how early in its life it begins to acquire human characteristics. By the tenth week, for example, it already has a face, arms and legs, fingers and toes; it has internal organs, and brain activity is detectable.[1] On the other hand, I think that the premise is false, that the fetus is not a person from the moment of conception. A newly fertilized ovum, a newly implanted clump of cells, is no more a person than an acorn is an oak tree. But I shall not discuss any of this. For it seems to me to be of great interest to ask what happens if, for the sake of argument, we allow the premise. How, precisely, are we supposed to get from there to the conclusion that abortion is morally impermissible? Opponents of abortion commonly spend most of their time establishing that the fetus is a person, and hardly any time explaining the step from there to the impermissibility of abortion. Perhaps they think the step too simple and obvious to require much comment. Or perhaps instead they are simply being economical in argument. Many of those who defend abortion rely on the premise that the fetus is not a person, but only a bit of tissue that will become a person at birth; and why pay out more arguments than you have to? Whatever the explanation, I suggest that the step they take is neither easy nor obvious, that it calls for closer examination than it is commonly given, and that when we do give it this closer examination we shall feel inclined to reject it.

I propose, then, that we grant the fetus is a person from the moment of conception. How does the argument go from here? Something like this, I take it. Every person has a right to life. So the fetus has a right to life. No doubt the mother has a right to decide what shall happen in and to her body; everyone would grant that. But surely a person's right to life is stronger and more stringent than the mother's right to decide what happens in and to her body, and so outweighs it. So the fetus may not be killed; an abortion may not be performed.

It sounds plausible. But now let me ask you to imagine this. You wake up in the morning and find yourself back to back in bed with an unconscious violinist. A famous unconscious violinist. He has been found to have a fatal kidney ailment, and the Society of Music Lovers has canvassed all the available medical records and found that you alone have the right

---

[1]Daniel Callahan, *Abortion: Law, Choice and Morality* (New York, 1970), p. 373. This book gives a fascinating survey of the available information on abortion. The Jewish tradition is surveyed in David M. Feldman, *Birth Control in Jewish Law* (New York, 1968), Part 5, the Catholic tradition in John T. Noonan, Jr., "An Almost Absolute Value in History," in *The Morality of Abortion* (Cambridge, Mass., 1970).

blood type to help. They have therefore kidnapped you, and last night the violinist's circulatory system was plugged into yours, so that your kidneys can be used to extract poisons from his blood as well as your own. The director of the hospital now tells you, "Look, we're sorry the Society of Music Lovers did this to you—we would never have permitted it if we had known. But still, they did it, and the violinist now is plugged into you. To unplug you would be to kill him. But never mind, it's only for nine months. By then he will have recovered from his ailment, and can safely be unplugged from you." Is it morally incumbent on you to accede to this situation? No doubt it would be very nice of you if you did, a great kindness. But do you *have* to accede to it? What if it were not nine months, but nine years? Or longer still? What if the director of the hospital says, "Tough luck, I agree, but you've now got to stay in bed, with the violinist plugged into you, for the rest of your life. Because remember this. All persons have a right to life, and violinists are persons. Granted you have a right to decide what happens in and to your body, but a person's right to life outweighs your right to decide what happens in and to your body. So you cannot ever be unplugged from him." I imagine you would regard this as outrageous, which suggests that something really is wrong with that plausible-sounding argument I mentioned a moment ago.

In this case, of course, you were kidnapped; you didn't volunteer for the operation that plugged the violinist into your kidneys. Can those who oppose abortion on the ground I mentioned make an exception for a pregnancy due to rape? Certainly. They can say that persons have a right to life only if they didn't come into existence because of rape; or they can say that all persons have a right to life, but that some have less of a right to life than others, in particular, that those who came into existence because of rape have less. But these statements have a rather unpleasant sound. Surely the question of whether you have a right to life at all, or how much of it you have, shouldn't turn on the question of whether or not you are the product of a rape. And in fact the people who oppose abortion on the ground I mentioned do not make this distinction, and hence do not make an exception in case of rape.

Nor do they make an exception for a case in which the mother has to spend the nine months of her pregnancy in bed. They would agree that would be a great pity, and hard on the mother; but all the same, all persons have a right to life, the fetus is a person, and so on. I suspect, in fact, that they would not make an exception for a case in which, miraculously enough, the pregnancy went on for nine years, or even the rest of the mother's life.

Some won't even make an exception for a case in which continuation of the pregnancy is likely to shorten the mother's life; they regard abortion as impermissible even to save the mother's life. Such cases are nowadays very rare, and many opponents of abortion do not accept this extreme view. All the same, it is a good place to begin: a number of points of interest come out in respect to it.

1. Let us call the view that abortion is impermissible even to save the mother's life "the extreme view." I want to suggest first that it does not issue from the argument I mentioned earlier without the addition of some fairly powerful premises. Suppose a woman has become pregnant, and now learns that she has a cardiac condition such that she will die if she carries the baby to term. What may be done for her? The fetus, being a person, has a right to life, but as the mother is a person too, so has she a right to life. Presumably they have an equal right to life. How is it supposed to come out that an abortion may not be performed? If mother and child have an equal right to life, shouldn't we perhaps flip a coin? Or should we add to the mother's right to life her right to decide what happens in and to her body, which everybody seems to be ready to grant—the sum of her rights now outweighing the fetus' right to life?

The most familiar argument here is the following. We are told that performing the abortion would be directly killing[2] the child, whereas doing nothing would not be killing the mother, but only letting her die. Moreover, in killing the child, one would be killing an innocent person, for the child has committed no crime and is not aiming at his mother's death. And then there are a variety of ways in which this might be continued. (1) But as directly killing an innocent person is always and absolutely impermissible, an abortion may not be performed. Or, (2) as directly killing an innocent person is murder, and murder is always and absolutely impermissible, an abortion may not be performed.[3] Or, (3) as one's duty to refrain from directly killing an innocent person is more stringent than one's duty to keep a person from dying, an abortion may not be performed. Or, (4) if one's only options are directly killing an innocent person or letting a person die, one must prefer letting the person die, and thus an abortion may not be performed.[4]

---

[2]The term "direct" in the arguments I refer to is a technical one. Roughly, what is meant by "direct killing" is either killing as an end in itself, or killing as a means to some end, for example, the end of saving someone else's life. See footnote 5 for an example of its use.

[3]Cf. *Encyclical Letter of Pope Pius XI on Christian Marriage*, Boston: St. Paul Editions, n.d., p. 32: "however much we may pity the mother whose health and even life is gravely imperiled in the performance of the duty allotted to her by nature, nevertheless what could ever be a sufficient reason for excusing in any way the direct murder of the innocent? This is precisely what we are dealing with here." Noonan (*The Morality of Abortion*, p. 43) reads this as follows: "What cause can ever avail to excuse in any way the direct killing of the innocent? For it is a question of that."

[4]The thesis in (4) is in an interesting way weaker than those in (1), (2), and (3): they rule out abortion even in cases in which both mother *and* child will die if the abortion is not performed. By contrast, one who held the view expressed in (4) could consistently say that one needn't prefer letting two persons die to killing one.

Some people seem to have thought that these are not further premises which must be added if the conclusion is to be reached, but that they
follow from the very fact that an innocent person has a right to life.[5] But
this seems to me to be a mistake, and perhaps the simplest way to show this
is to bring out that while we must certainly grant that innocent persons
have a right to life, the theses in (1) through (4) are all false. Take (2), for
example. If directly killing an innocent person is murder, and thus is
impermissible, then the mother's directly killing the innocent person
inside her is murder, and thus is impermissible. But it cannot seriously be
thought to be murder if the mother performs an abortion on herself to
save her life. It cannot seriously be said that she *must* refrain, that she *must*
sit passively by and wait for her death. Let us look again at the case of you
and the violinist. There you are, in bed with the violinist, and the director
of the hospital says to you, "It's all most distressing, and I deeply sympathize, but you see this is putting an additional strain on your kidneys, and
you'll be dead within the month. But you *have* to stay where you are all the
same. Because unplugging you would be directly killing an innocent violinist, and that's murder, and that's impermissible." If anything in the
world is true, it is that you do not commit murder, you do not do what is
impermissible, if you reach around to your back and unplug yourself from
that violinist to save your life.

The main focus of attention in writings on abortion has been on what
a third party may or may not do in answer to a request from a woman for
an abortion. This is in a way understandable. Things being as they are,
there isn't much a woman can safely do to abort herself. So the question
asked is what a third party may do, and what the mother may do, if it is
mentioned at all, is deduced, almost as an afterthought, from what it is
concluded that third parties may do. But it seems to me that to treat the
matter in this way is to refuse to grant to the mother that very status of
person which is so firmly insisted on for the fetus. For we cannot simply
read off what a person may do from what a third party may do. Suppose
you find yourself trapped in a tiny house with a growing child. I mean a
very tiny house, and a rapidly growing child—you are already up against
the wall of the house and in a few minutes you'll be crushed to death. The
child on the other hand won't be crushed to death; if nothing is done to
stop him from growing he'll be hurt, but in the end he'll simply burst
open the house and walk out a free man. Now I could well understand it if

[5]Cf. the following passage from Pius XII, *Address to the Italian Catholic Society of
Midwives*: "The baby in the maternal breast has the right to life immediately from God.—
Hence there is no man, no human authority, no science, no medical, eugenic, social, economic
or moral 'indication' which can establish or grant a valid juridical ground for a direct deliberate disposition of an innocent human life, that is a disposition which looks to its destruction
either as an end or as a means to another end perhaps in itself not illicit.—The baby, still not
born, is a man in the same degree and for the same reason as the mother" (quoted in
Noonan, *The Morality of Abortion*, p. 45).

a bystander were to say, "There's nothing we can do for you. We cannot choose between your life and his, we cannot be the ones to decide who is to live, we cannot intervene." But it cannot be concluded that you too can do nothing, that you cannot attack it to save your life. However innocent the child may be, you do not have to wait passively while it crushes you to death. Perhaps a pregnant woman is vaguely felt to have the status of house, to which we don't allow the right of self-defense. But if the woman houses the child, it should be remembered that she is a person who houses it.

I should perhaps stop to say explicitly that I am not claiming that people have a right to do anything whatever to save their lives. I think, rather, that there are drastic limits to the right of self-defense. If someone threatens you with death unless you torture someone else to death, I think you have not the right, even to save your life, to do so. But the case under consideration here is very different. In our case there are only two people involved, one whose life is threatened, and one who threatens it. Both are innocent: the one who is threatened is not threatened because of any fault, the one who threatens does not threaten because of any fault. For this reason we may feel that we bystanders cannot intervene. But the person threatened can.

In sum, a woman surely can defend her life against the threat to it posed by the unborn child, even if doing so involves its death. And this shows not merely that the theses in (1) through (4) are false; it shows also that the extreme view of abortion is false, and so we need not canvass any other possible ways of arriving at it from the argument I mentioned at the outset.

2. The extreme view could of course be weakened to say that while abortion is permissible to save the mother's life, it may not be performed by a third party, but only by the mother herself. But this cannot be right either. For what we have to keep in mind is that the mother and the unborn child are not like two tenants in a small house which has, by an unfortunate mistake, been rented to both: the mother *owns* the house. The fact that she does adds to the offensiveness of deducing that the mother can do nothing from the supposition that third parties can do nothing. But it does more than this: it casts a bright light on the supposition that third parties can do nothing. Certainly it lets us see that a third party who says "I cannot choose between you" is fooling himself if he thinks this is impartiality. If Jones has found and fastened on a certain coat, which he needs to keep him from freezing, but which Smith also needs to keep him from freezing, then it is not impartiality that says "I cannot choose between you" when Smith owns the coat. Women have said again and again "This body is *my* body!" and they have reason to feel angry, reason to feel that it has been like shouting into the wind. Smith, after all, is hardly likely to bless us if we say to him, "Of course it's your coat, anybody would

grant that it is. But no one may choose between you and Jones who is to have it."

We should really ask what it is that says "no one may choose" in the face of the fact that the body that houses the child is the mother's body. It may be simply a failure to appreciate this fact. But it may be something more interesting, namely the sense that one has a right to refuse to lay hands on people, even where it would be just and fair to do so. This justice might call for somebody to get Smith's coat back from Jones, and yet you have a right to refuse to be the one to lay hands on Jones, a right to refuse to do physical violence to him. This, I think, must be granted. But then what should be said is not "no one may choose," but only "*I* cannot choose," and indeed not even this, but "*I* will not *act*," leaving it open that somebody else can or should, and in particular that anyone in a position of authority, with the job of securing people's rights, both can and should. So this is no difficulty. I have not been arguing that any given third party must accede to the mother's request that he perform an abortion to save her life, but only that he may.

I suppose that in some views of human life the mother's body is only on loan to her, the loan not being one which gives her any prior claim to it. One who held this view might well think it impartiality to say "I cannot choose." But I shall simply ignore this possibility. My own view is that if a human being has any just, prior claim to anything at all, he has a just, prior claim to his own body. And perhaps this needn't be argued for here anyway, since, as I mentioned, the arguments against abortion we are looking at do grant that the woman has a right to decide what happens in and to her body.

But although they do grant it, I have tried to show that they do not take seriously what is done in granting it. I suggest the same thing will reappear even more clearly when we turn away from cases in which the mother's life is at stake, and attend, as I propose we now do, to the vastly more common cases in which a woman wants an abortion for some less weighty reason than preserving her own life.

3. Where the mother's life is not at stake, the argument I mentioned at the outset seems to have a much stronger pull. "Everyone has a right to life, so the unborn person has a right to life." And isn't the child's right to life weightier than anything other than the mother's own right to life, which she might put forward as ground for an abortion?

This argument treats the right to life as if it were unproblematic. It is not, and this seems to me to be precisely the source of the mistake.

For we should now, at long last, ask what it comes to, to have a right to life. In some views having a right to life includes having a right to be given at least the bare minimum one needs for continued life. But suppose that what in fact *is* the bare minimum a man needs for continued life is something he has no right at all to be given? If I am sick unto death, and the only thing that will save my life is the touch of Henry Fonda's cool hand on my fevered brow, then all the same, I have no right to be given the touch of Henry Fonda's cool hand on my fevered brow. It would be frightfully nice of him to fly in from the West Coast to provide it. It would be less nice, though no doubt well meant, if my friends flew out to the West Coast and carried Henry Fonda back with them. But I have no right at all against anybody that he should do this for me. Or again, to return to the story I told earlier, the fact that for continued life that violinist needs the continued use of your kidneys does not establish that he has a right to be given the continued use of your kidneys. He certainly has no right against you that *you* should give him continued use of your kidneys. For nobody has any right to use of your kidneys unless you give him such a right; and nobody has the right against you that you shall give him this right—if you do allow him to go on using your kidneys, this is a kindness on your part, and not something he can claim from you as his due. Nor has he any right against anybody else that *they* should give him continued use of your kidneys. Certainly he had no right against the Society of Music Lovers that they should plug him into you in the first place. And if you now start to unplug yourself, having learned that you will otherwise have to spend nine years in bed with him, there is nobody in the world who must try to prevent you, in order to see to it that he is given something he has a right to be given.

Some people are rather stricter about the right to life. In their view, it does not include the right to be given anything, but amounts to, and only to, the right not to be killed by anybody. But here a related difficulty arises. If everybody is to refrain from killing that violinist, then everybody must refrain from doing a great many different sorts of things. Everybody must refrain from slitting his throat, everybody must refrain from shooting him—and everybody must refrain from unplugging you from him. But does he have a right against everybody that they shall refrain from unplugging you from him? To refrain from doing this is to allow him to continue to use your kidneys. It could be argued that he has a right against us that *we* should allow him to continue to use your kidneys. That is, while he had no right against us that we should give him the use of your kidneys, it might be argued that he anyway has a right against us that we shall not now intervene and deprive him of the use of your kidneys. I shall come back to third-party interventions later. But certainly the violinist has no right against you that *you* shall allow him to continue to use your kidneys. As I said, if you do allow him to use them, it is a kindness on your part, and not something you owe him.

The difficulty I point to here is not peculiar to the right to life. It reappears in connection with all the other natural rights; and it is something which an adequate account of rights must deal with. For present purposes it is enough just to draw attention to it. But I would stress that I am not arguing that people do not have a right to life—quite to the contrary, it seems to me that the primary control we must place on the acceptability of an account of rights is that it should turn out in that account to be a truth that all persons have a right to life. I am arguing only that having a right to life does not guarantee having either a right to be given the use of or a right to be allowed continued use of another person's body—even if one needs it for life itself. So the right to life will not serve the opponents of abortion in the very simple and clear way in which they seem to have thought it would.

4. There is another way to bring out the difficulty. In the most ordinary sort of case, to deprive someone of what he has a right to is to treat him unjustly. Suppose a boy and his small brother are jointly given a box of chocolates for Christmas. If the older boy takes the box and refuses to give his brother any of the chocolates, he is unjust to him, for the brother has been given a right to half of them. But suppose that, having learned that otherwise it means nine years in bed with that violinist, you unplug yourself from him. You surely are not being unjust to him, for you gave him no right to use your kidneys, and no one else can have given him any such right. But we have to notice that in unplugging yourself, you are killing him; and violinists, like everybody else, have a right to life, and thus in the view we were considering just now, the right not to be killed. So here you do what he supposedly has a right you shall not do, but you do not act unjustly to him in doing it.

The emendation which may be made at this point is this: the right to life consists not in the right not to be killed, but rather in the right not to be killed unjustly. This runs a risk of circularity, but never mind: it would enable us to square the fact that the violinist has a right to life with the fact that you do not act unjustly toward him in unplugging yourself, thereby killing him. For if you do not kill him unjustly, you do not violate his right to life, and so it is no wonder you do him no injustice.

But if this emendation is accepted, the gap in the argument against abortion stares us plainly in the face: it is by no means enough to show that the fetus is a person, and to remind us that all persons have a right to life—we need to be shown also that killing the fetus violates its right to life, i.e., that abortion is unjust killing. And is it?

I suppose we may take it as a datum that in a case of pregnancy due to rape the mother has not given the unborn person a right to the use of her body for food and shelter. Indeed, in what pregnancy could it be supposed that the mother has given the unborn person such a right? It is not as if there were unborn persons drifting about the world, to whom a woman who wants a child says "I invite you in."

But it might be argued that there are other ways one can have acquired a right to the use of another person's body than by having been invited to use it by that person. Suppose a woman voluntarily indulges in intercourse, knowing of the chance it will issue in pregnancy, and then she does become pregnant; is she not in part responsible for the presence, in fact the very existence, of the unborn person inside her? No doubt she did not invite it in. But doesn't her partial responsibility for its being there itself give it a right to the use of her body?[6] If so, then her aborting it would be more like the boy's taking away the chocolates, and less like your unplugging yourself from the violinist—doing so would be depriving it of what it does have a right to, and thus would be doing it an injustice.

And then, too, it might be asked whether or not she can kill it even to save her own life: If she voluntarily called it into existence, how can she now kill it, even in self-defense?

The first thing to be said about this is that it is something new. Opponents of abortion have been so concerned to make out the independence of the fetus, in order to establish that it has a right to life, just as its mother does, that they have tended to overlook the possible support they might gain from making out that the fetus is *dependent* on the mother, in order to establish that she has a special kind of responsibility for it, a responsibility that gives it rights against her which are not possessed by any independent person—such as an ailing violinist who is a stranger to her.

On the other hand, this argument would give the unborn person a right to its mother's body only if her pregnancy resulted from a voluntary act, undertaken in full knowledge of the chance a pregnancy might result from it. It would leave out entirely the unborn person whose existence is due to rape. Pending the availability of some further argument, then, we would be left with the conclusion that unborn persons whose existence is due to rape have no right to the use of their mothers' bodies, and thus that aborting them is not depriving them of anything they have a right to and hence is not unjust killing.

And we should also notice that it is not at all plain that this argument really does go even as far as it purports to. For there are cases and cases, and the details make a difference. If the room is stuffy, and I therefore open a window to air it, and a burglar climbs in, it would be absurd to say, "Ah, now he can stay, she's given him a right to the use of her house—for she is partially responsible for his presence there, having voluntarily done what enabled him to get in, in full knowledge that there are such things as burglars, and that burglars burgle." It would be still more absurd to say this if I had had bars installed outside my windows, precisely to prevent burglars from getting in, and a burglar got in only because of a defect in the bars. It remains equally absurd if we imagine it is not a burglar who climbs in, but an innocent person who blunders or falls in. Again, suppose it were like this: people-seeds drift about in the air like pollen, and if you

---

[6]The need for a discussion of this argument was brought home to me by members of the Society for Ethical and Legal Philosophy, to whom this paper was originally presented.

open your windows, one may drift in and take root in your carpets or upholstery. You don't want children, so you fix up your windows with fine mesh screens, the very best you can buy. As can happen, however, and on very, very rare occasions does happen, one of the screens is defective; and a seed drifts in and takes root. Does the person-plant who now develops have a right to the use of your house? Surely not—despite the fact that you voluntarily opened your windows, you knowingly kept carpets and upholstered furniture, and you knew that screens were sometimes defective. Someone may argue that you are responsible for its rooting, that it does have a right to your house, because after all you *could* have lived out your life with bare floors and furniture, or with sealed windows and doors. But this won't do—for by the same token anyone can avoid a pregnancy due to rape by having a hysterectomy, or anyway by never leaving home without a (reliable!) army.

It seems to me that the argument we are looking at can establish at most that there are *some* cases in which the unborn person has a right to the use of its mother's body, and therefore *some* cases in which abortion is unjust killing. There is room for much discussion and argument as to precisely which, if any. But I think we should sidestep this issue and leave it open, for at any rate the argument certainly does not establish that all abortion is unjust killing.

5. There is room for yet another argument here, however. We surely must all grant that there may be cases in which it would be morally indecent to detach a person from your body at the cost of his life. Suppose you learn that what the violinist needs is not nine years of your life, but only one hour; all you need do to save his life is to spend one hour in that bed with him. Suppose also that letting him use your kidneys for that one hour would not affect your health in the slightest. Admittedly you were kidnapped. Admittedly you did not give anyone permission to plug him into you. Nevertheless it seems to me plain you *ought* to allow him to use your kidneys for that hour—it would be indecent to refuse.

Again, suppose pregnancy lasted only an hour, and constituted no threat to life or health. And suppose that a woman becomes pregnant as a result of rape. Admittedly she did not voluntarily do anything to bring about the existence of a child. Admittedly she did nothing at all which would give the unborn person a right to the use of her body. All the same it might well be said, as in the newly emended violinist story, that she *ought* to allow it to remain for that hour—that it would be indecent in her to refuse.

Now some people are inclined to use the term "right" in such a way that it follows from the fact that you ought to allow a person to use your body for the hour he needs, that he has a right to use your body for the hour he needs, even though he has not been given that right by any person or act. They may say that it follows also that if you refuse, you act unjustly toward him. This use of the term is perhaps so common that it cannot be called wrong; nevertheless it seems to me to be an unfortunate loosening of what we would do better to keep a tight rein on. Suppose that box of chocolates I mentioned earlier had not been given to both boys jointly, but was given only to the older boy. There he sits, stolidly eating his way through the box, his small brother watching enviously. Here we are likely to say "You ought not to be so mean. You ought to give your brother some of those chocolates." My own view is that it just does not follow from the truth of this that the brother has any right to any of the chocolates. If the boy refuses to give his brother any, he is greedy, stingy, callous—but not unjust. I suppose that the people I have in mind will say it does follow that the brother has a right to some of the chocolates, and thus that the boy does act unjustly if he refuses to give his brother any. But the effect of saying this is to obscure what we should keep distinct, namely the difference between the boy's refusal in this case and the boy's refusal in the earlier case, in which the box was given to both boys jointly, and in which the small brother thus had what was from any point of view clear title to half.

A further objection to so using the term "right" that from the fact that A ought to do a thing for B, it follows that B has a right against A that A do it for him, is that it is going to make the question of whether or not a man has a right to a thing turn on how easy it is to provide him with it; and this seems not merely unfortunate, but morally unacceptable. Take the case of Henry Fonda again. I said earlier that I had no right to the touch of his cool hand on my fevered brow, even though I needed it to save my life. I said it would be frightfully nice of him to fly in from the West Coast to provide me with it, but that I had no right against him that he should do so. But suppose he isn't on the West Coast. Suppose he has only to walk across the room, place a hand briefly on my brow—and lo, my life is saved. Then surely he ought to do it, it would be indecent to refuse. Is it to be said "Ah, well, it follows that in this case she has a right to the touch of his hand on her brow, and so it would be an injustice in him to refuse"? So that I have a right to it when it is easy for him to provide it, though no right when it's hard? It's rather a shocking idea that anyone's rights should fade away and disappear as it gets harder and harder to accord them to him.

So my own view is that even though you ought to let the violinist use your kidneys for the one hour he needs, we should not conclude that he has a right to do so—we should say that if you refuse, you are, like the boy who owns all the chocolates and will give none away, self-centered and callous, indecent in fact, but not unjust. And similarly, that even supposing a case in which a woman pregnant due to rape ought to allow the unborn person to use her body for the hour he needs, we should not conclude that he has a right to do so; we should conclude that she is self-centered, callous, indecent, but not unjust, if she refuses. The complaints are no less grave; they are just different. However, there is no need to insist on this point. If anyone does wish to deduce "he has a right" from "you ought," then all the same he must surely grant that there are cases in which it is not morally required of you that you allow that violinist to use your kidneys, and in which he does not have a right to use them, and in which you do not do him an injustice if you refuse. And so also for mother and unborn child. Except in such cases as the unborn person has a right to demand it—and we were leaving open the possibility that there may be such cases—nobody is morally *required* to make large sacrifices, of health, of all other interests and concerns, of all other duties and commitments, for nine years, or even for nine months, in order to keep another person alive.

6. We have in fact to distinguish between two kinds of Samaritan: the Good Samaritan and what we might call the Minimally Decent Samaritan. The story of the Good Samaritan, you will remember, goes like this:

> A certain man went down from Jerusalem to Jericho, and fell among thieves, which stripped him of his raiment, and wounded him, and departed, leaving him half dead.
>
> And by chance there came down a certain priest that way; and when he saw him, he passed by on the other side.
>
> And likewise a Levite, when he was at the place, came and looked on him, and passed by on the other side.
>
> But a certain Samaritan, as he journeyed, came where he was; and when he saw him he had compassion on him.
>
> And went to him, and bound up his wounds, pouring in oil and wine, and set him on his own beast, and brought him to an inn, and took care of him.
>
> And on the morrow, when he departed, he took out two pence, and gave them to the host, and said unto him, "Take care of him; and whatsoever thou spendest more, when I come again, I will repay thee." (Luke 10:30–35)

The Good Samaritan went out of his way, at some cost to himself, to help one in need of it. We are not told what the options were, that is, whether or not the priest and the Levite could have helped by doing less than the Good Samaritan did, but assuming they could have, then the fact they did nothing at all shows they were not even Minimally Decent Samaritans, not because they were not Samaritans, but because they were not even minimally decent.

These things are a matter of degree, of course, but there is a difference, and it comes out perhaps most clearly in the story of Kitty Genovese, who, as you will remember, was murdered while thirty-eight people watched or listened, and did nothing at all to help her. A Good Samaritan would have rushed out to give direct assistance against the murderer. Or perhaps we had better allow that it would have been a Splendid Samaritan who did this, on the ground that it would have involved a risk of death for himself. But the thirty-eight not only did not do this, they did not even trouble to pick up a phone to call the police. Minimally Decent Samaritanism would call for doing at least that, and their not having done it was monstrous.

After telling the story of the Good Samaritan, Jesus said "Go, and do thou likewise." Perhaps he meant that we are morally required to act as the Good Samaritan did. Perhaps he was urging people to do more than is morally required of them. At all events it seems plain that it was not morally required of any of the thirty-eight that he rush out to give direct assistance at the risk of his own life, and that it is not morally required of anyone that he give long stretches of his life—nine years or nine months—to sustaining the life of a person who has no special right (we were leaving open the possibility of this) to demand it.

Indeed, with one rather striking class of exceptions, no one in any country in the world is *legally* required to do anywhere near as much as this for anyone else. The class of exceptions is obvious. My main concern here is not the state of the law in respect to abortion, but it is worth drawing attention to the fact that in no state in this country is any man compelled by law to be even a Minimally Decent Samaritan to any person; there is no law under which charges could be brought against the thirty-eight who stood by while Kitty Genovese died. By contrast, in most states in this country women are compelled by law to be not merely Minimally Decent Samaritans, but Good Samaritans to unborn persons inside them. This doesn't by itself settle anything one way or the other, because it may well be argued that there should be laws in this country—as there are in many European countries—compelling at least Minimally Decent Samaritanism.[7] But it does show that there is a gross injustice in the existing state of the law. And it shows also that the groups currently working against liberalization of abortion laws, in fact working toward having it declared unconstitutional for a state to permit abortion, had better start working for the adoption of Good Samaritan laws generally, or earn the charge that they are acting in bad faith.

I should think, myself, that Minimally Decent Samaritan laws would be one thing, Good Samaritan laws quite another, and in fact highly improper. But we are not here concerned with the law. What we should ask is not whether anybody should be compelled by law to be a Good Samaritan, but whether we must accede to a situation in which somebody is being compelled—by nature, perhaps—to be a Good Samaritan. We have, in other words, to look now at third-party interventions. I have been arguing that no person is morally required to make large sacrifices to sustain the life of another who has no right to demand them, and this even where the sacrifices do not include life itself; we are not morally required

[7]For a discussion of the difficulties involved, and a survey of the European experience with such laws, see *The Good Samaritan and the Law*, ed. James M. Ratcliffe (New York, 1966).

to be Good Samaritans or anyway Very Good Samaritans to one another. But what if a man cannot extricate himself from such a situation? What if he appeals to us to extricate him? It seems to me plain that there are cases in which we can, cases in which a Good Samaritan would extricate him. There you are, you were kidnapped, and nine years in bed with that violinist lie ahead of you. You have your own life to lead. You are sorry, but you simply cannot see giving up so much of your life to the sustaining of his. You cannot extricate yourself, and ask us to do so. I should have thought that—in light of his having no right to the use of your body—it was obvious that we do not have to accede to your being forced to give up so much. We can do what you ask. There is no injustice to the violinist in our doing so.

7. Following the lead of the opponents of abortion, I have throughout been speaking of the fetus merely as a person, and what I have been asking is whether or not the argument we began with, which proceeds only from the fetus' being a person, really does establish its conclusion. I have argued that it does not.

But of course there are arguments and arguments, and it may be said that I have simply fastened on the wrong one. It may be said that what is important is not merely the fact that the fetus is a person, but that it is a person for whom the woman has a special kind of responsibility issuing from the fact that she is its mother. And it might be argued that all my analogies are therefore irrelevant—for you do not have that special kind of responsibility for that violinist, Henry Fonda does not have that special kind of repsonsibility for me. And our attention might be drawn to the fact that men and women both *are* compelled by law to provide support for their children.

I have in effect dealt (briefly) with this argument in section 4 above; but a (still briefer) recapitulation now may be in order. Surely we do not have any such "special responsibility" for a person unless we have assumed it, explicitly or implicitly. If a set of parents do not try to prevent pregnancy, do not obtain an abortion, and then at the time of birth of the child do not put it out for adoption, but rather take it home with them, then they have assumed responsibility for it, they have given it rights, and they cannot *now* withdraw support from it at the cost of its life because they now find it difficult to go on providing for it. But if they have taken all reasonable precautions against having a child, they do not simply by virtue of their biological relationship to the child who comes into existence have a special responsibility for it. They may wish to assume responsibility for it, or they may not wish to. And I am suggesting that if assuming responsibility for it would require large sacrifices, then they may refuse. A Good Samaritan would not refuse—or anyway, a Splendid Samaritan, if the sacrifices that had to be made were enormous. But then so would a Good Samaritan assume responsibility for that violinist; so would Henry Fonda, if he is a Good Samaritan, fly in from the West Coast and assume responsibility for me.

8. My argument will be found unsatisfactory on two counts by many of those who want to regard abortion as morally permissible. First, while I do argue that abortion is not impermissible, I do not argue that it is always permissible. There may well be cases in which carrying the child to term requires only Minimally Decent Samaritanism of the mother, and this is a standard we must not fall below. I am inclined to think it a merit of my account precisely that it does *not* give a general yes or a general no. It allows for and supports our sense that, for example, a sick and desperately frightened fourteen-year-old schoolgirl, pregnant due to rape, may *of course* choose abortion, and that any law which rules this out is an insane law. And it also allows for and supports our sense that in other cases resort to abortion is even positively indecent. It would be indecent in the woman to request an abortion and indecent in a doctor to perform it, if she is in her seventh month, and wants the abortion just to avoid the nuisance of postponing a trip abroad. The very fact that the arguments I have been drawing attention to treat all cases of abortion, or even all cases of abortion in which the mother's life is not at stake, as morally on a par ought to have made them suspect at the outset.

Second, while I am arguing for the permissibility of abortion in some cases, I am not arguing for the right to secure the death of the unborn child. It is easy to confuse these two things in that up to a certain point in the life of the fetus it is not able to survive outside the mother's body; hence removing it from her body guarantees its death. But they are importantly different. I have argued that you are not morally required to spend nine months in bed, sustaining the life of that violinist; but to say this is by no means to say that if, when you unplug yourself, there is a miracle and he survives, you then have a right to turn round and slit his throat. You may detach yourself even if this costs him his life; you have no right to be guaranteed his death, by some other means, if unplugging yourself does not kill him. There are some people who will feel dissatisfied by this feature of my argument. A woman may be utterly devastated by the thought of a child, a bit of herself, put out for adoption and never seen or heard of again. She may therefore want not merely that the child be detached from her, but more, that it die. Some opponents of abortion are inclined to regard this as beneath contempt—thereby showing insensitivity to what is surely a powerful source of despair. All the same, I agree that the desire for the child's death is not one which anybody may gratify, should it turn out to be possible to detach the child alive.

At this place, however, it should be remembered that we have only been pretending throughout that the fetus is a human being from the moment of conception. A very early abortion is surely not the killing of a person, and so is not dealt with by anything I have said here.

The Morality of Abortion

Baruch Brody

Perhaps our must fundamental moral intuition is that it is wrong to take the life of another human being. Nearly as fundamental, however, is the intuition that under certain circumstances it is permissible to do so. Such exceptions have historically been very difficult of definition—that observation is apparent from the most casual inspection of the exceptions condoned in the past. There are obvious conflicts among them, and one suspects that at least some of these exceptions have been allowed out of political or other special interests.

The clearest exception is self-defense. If the life of one human being is threatened by the actions of another, then the first human being may, all else failing, defend himself, even to the point of taking the life of the second. I should like to explore, in this chapter, the following issue: let us suppose that there is some point (and now it is not necessary to try to establish that point) in the development of the fetus when that fetus is properly regarded as a human being; and let us imagine, further, a case in which the woman carrying the fetus discovers, at some time after that point, that she herself will die unless she aborts the fetus. Is it permissible for her to abort the fetus in order to save her own life? Is this one of the extreme circumstances in which it is permissible to take the life of another human being? Is this, in short, legitimate self-defense?

ABORTION AND SELF-DEFENSE

Why would not it be permissible for the mother to have an abortion in order to save her life even after that point at which the fetus becomes a human being? After all, the fetus's continued existence poses a threat to the life of the mother, and why can't she void that threat by taking the life of the fetus, as an ultimate act of defense?

To be sure, it may be the physician, or other agent, who will cause the abortion, and not the mother herself, but that difference seems to be irrelevant. Our intuition is that the person whose life is threatened (call

From Baruch Brody, *Abortion and the Sanctity of Human Life: A Philosophical View.* Cambridge, Mass.: MIT Press, 1975, pp. 6–11, 26–30, 37–39 and from "Fetal Humanity and the Theory of Essentialism" in *Philosophy and Sex*, ed. Robert Baker and Frederick Elliston. Buffalo, N.Y.: Prometheus Books, 1975, pp. 207, 210–213. Reprinted by permission of the MIT Press, Cambridge, Massachusetts, Prometheus Books, and the author.

that person *A*) may either take the life of the person (*B*) who threatens his life or call upon someone else (*C*) to do so. And more important, it seems permissible (and perhaps even obligatory in some cases) for *C* to take *B*'s life in order to save *A*'s life. Put in traditional terms, we are really speaking of the mother's right as the pursued, or anyone else's right as an onlooker, to take the life of the fetus who is the pursuer.

Pope Pius XI observed,[1] in objecting to this argument from self-defense, that in the paradigm case of killing the pursuer, *B* is unjustly attempting to take *A*'s life and is responsible for that attempt. It is the resulting guilt, based in part on *B*'s intention (found in the attempt to kill *A*), together with the fact that *A* will die unless *B* is stopped, which permits the taking of *B*'s life. The reader will notice that the abortion situation is quite different. Leaving aside for now—we shall return to it later on—the question as to whether the fetus can properly be described as attempting to take the mother's life, we can certainly agree that the fetus is not responsible for such an attempt (if it is occurring), that the fetus is therefore innocent, not guilty, and that the taking of fetal life cannot be compared to the paradigm case of killing the pursuer.

There is another way of putting Pope Pius's point. Consider the following case: there is, let us imagine, a medicine that *A* needs to stay alive, *C* owns some, and *C* will give it to *A* only if *A* kills *B*. Moreover, *A* has no other way of getting the medicine. In this case, the continued existence of *B* certainly poses a threat to the life of *A*; *A* can survive only if *B* does not survive. Still, it is not permissible for *A* to kill *B* in order to save *A*'s life. Why not? How does this case differ from the paradigm case of killing the pursuer? The simplest answer is that in this case, while *B*'s continued existence poses a threat to the life of *A*, *B* is not guilty of attempting to take *A*'s life because there is no attempt to be guilty about in the first place. Now if we consider the case of a fetus whose continued existence poses a threat to the life of the mother, we see that it is like the medicine case and not like the paradigm case of killing the pursuer. The fetus does pose (in our imagined situation) a threat to the life of its mother, but it is not guilty of attempting to take its mother's life. Consequently, in an analogue to the medicine case, the mother (or her agent) could not justify destroying the fetus on the ground that it would be a permissible act of killing the pursuer.

The persuasiveness of both of the preceding arguments indicates that we have to analyze the whole issue of pursuit far more carefully before we can definitely decide whether an abortion to save the life of the mother could be viewed as a permissible act of killing the pursuer. If we

---

[1]This is, essentially, his argument in Section 64 of *Casti Connubii*, reprinted in William J. Gibbons, ed., *Seven Great Encyclicals* (Glen Rock, N.J.: Paulist Press, 1939), p. 95.

look again at a paradigm case of pursuit, we see that there are three factors involved:

1. The continued existence of *B* poses a threat to the life of *A*, a threat that can be met only by the taking of *B*'s life (we shall refer to this as the condition of danger).
2. *B* is unjustly attempting to take *A*'s life (we shall refer to this as the condition of attempt).
3. *B* is responsible for his attempt to take *A*'s life (we shall refer to this as the condition of guilt).

In the medicine case, only the danger condition was satisfied. Our intuitions that it would be wrong for *A* to take *B*'s life in that case reflects our belief that the mere fact that *B* is a danger to *A* is not sufficient to establish that killing *B* will be a justifiable act of killing a pursuer. But it would be rash to conclude, as Pope Pius did, that all three conditions must be satisfied before the killing of *B* will be a justifiable act of killing a pursuer. What would happen, for example, if the first two conditions, but not the guilt condition, were satisfied?

There are good reasons for supposing that the satisfaction of the first two conditions is sufficient justification for taking *B*'s life as an act of killing the pursuer. Consider, for example, a variation of the pursuit paradigm—one in which *B* is about to shoot *A*, and the only way by which *A* can stop him is by killing him first—but one in which *B* is a minor who is not responsible for his attempt to take *A*'s life.[2] In this case, the only condition not satisfied is the condition of guilt. Still, despite that fact, it seems that *A* may justifiably take *B*'s life as a permissible act of killing a pursuer. The guilt of the pursuer, then, is not a requirement for legitimacy in killing the pursuer.

Are there any cases in which the satisfaction of the danger condition and something weaker than the attempt condition is sufficient to justify *A*'s killing *B* as an act of killing a pursuer? It seems that there may be. Consider, for example, the following case: *B* is about to press a button that turns on a light, and there is no reason for him to suspect what is the case, that is, that his doing so will also explode a bomb that will destroy *A*. Moreover, the only way in which we can stop *B* and save *A*'s life is by taking *B*'s life, for there is no opportunity to warn *B* of the actual consequences of his act. In such a case, *B* is not attempting to take *A*'s life and, a fortiori, he is neither responsible for nor guilty of any such attempt. Nevertheless, this may still be a case in which there is justification for taking *B*'s life in order to save *A*'s life; that is, this may still be a legitimate case of killing a pursuer.

---

[2]This point, and its significance, was first pointed out by R. Huna when he said (*Talmud, Sanhedrin*, 72b) that a pursuer who is a minor can be stopped even by killing him.

It is important to keep in mind that although we may kill B to save A, it does not follow—and indeed it is not true—that A should be punished if he does blow up B. As we shall see later, there is an important difference in this respect between punishment and preventive killing.

How does this case differ from the medicine case? Or, to put our question another way, what condition, in addition to the danger condition, is satisfied in this case but not in the medicine case, so that its satisfaction (together with the satisfaction of the danger condition) is sufficient to justify our killing B as an act of killing a pursuer? As we think about the two cases, the following idea suggests itself: there is, in this most recent example, some action that B is doing (pressing the button) that will result in A's death, an action that if taken in full knowledge and voluntarily would result in B's being responsible for the loss of A's life. Even if performed without full knowledge and intent, this action itself justifies the taking of B's life. In the medicine case, on the other hand, no such action is performed. C may well be to blame for the loss of A's life if he does not give A the medicine when A refuses to kill B. But this has nothing to do with B. It would seem then that A is justified in taking B's life as an act of killing a pursuer if, in addition to B's being a danger to A, the following condition is satisfied:

B is doing some action that will lead to A's death, and that action is such that if B were a responsible person who did it voluntarily knowing that this result would come about, B would be responsible for the loss of A's life (we shall refer to this as the condition of action).

To summarize, then, our general discussion of killing the pursuer, we can say the following: the mere satisfaction of the danger condition is not sufficient to justify the killing of the pursuer. If, in addition, either the attempt condition or the condition of action is satisfied, then one would be justified in killing the pursuer to save the life of the pursued. In any case, the condition of guilt, arising from full knowledge and intent, need not be satisfied.

These results wreak havoc with a very plausible analysis of why it is permissible to take the life of the pursuer to save the life of the pursued. It seemed at one point that it was the guilt of the pursuer that justified the taking of his life to save that of the pursued. This presupposes that the pursuer performs his attempt knowledgeably and intentionally. We have just seen that this is not so; the mere action is sufficient justification. So the analysis in question must be rejected.

Let us return now to the problem of abortion and apply these results to the case of the fetus whose continued existence poses a threat to the life of his mother. Is it permissible, as an act of killing a pursuer, to abort the fetus in order to save the mother? The first thing that we should note is that Pope Pius's objection to aborting the fetus as a permissible act of killing a pursuer is mistaken. His objection is that the fetus shows no

288 Respect for Life

knowledge or intention in his attempt to take the life of the mother, that the fetus is, in a word, innocent. But that only means that the condition of guilt is not satisfied, and we have seen that its satisfaction is not necessary.

Is, then, the aborting of the fetus, when necessary to save the life of the mother, a permissible act of killing a pursuer? It is true that in such cases the fetus is a danger to the mother. But it is also clear that the condition of attempt is not satisfied. The fetus has neither the beliefs nor the intentions to which we have referred. Furthermore, there is on the part of the fetus no action that threatens the life of the mother. So not even the condition of action is satisfied. It seems to follow, therefore, that aborting the fetus could not be a permissible act of killing a pursuer. . . .

THE WOMAN'S RIGHT
TO HER BODY

It is a common claim that a woman ought to be in control of what happens to her body to the greatest extent possible, that she ought to be able to use her body in ways that she wants to and refrain from using it in ways that she does not want to. This right is particularly pressed where certain uses of her body have deep and lasting effects upon the character of her life, personal, social, and economic. Therefore, it is argued, a woman should be free either to carry her fetus to term, thereby using her body to support it, or to abort the fetus, thereby not using her body for that purpose.

In some contexts in which this argument is advanced, it is clear that it is not addressed to the issue of the morality of abortion at all. Rather, it is made in opposition to laws against abortion on the ground that the choice to abort or not is a moral decision that should belong only to the mother. But that specific direction of the argument is irrelevant to our present purposes; I will consider it in Chapter 3, when I deal with the issues raised by laws prohibiting abortions. For the moment, I am concerned solely with the use of this principle as a putative ground tending to show the permissibility of abortion, with the claim that because it is the woman's body that carries the fetus and upon which the fetus depends, she has certain rights to abort the fetus that no one else may have.

We may begin by remarking that it is obviously correct that, as carrier of the fetus, the mother has it within her power to choose whether or not to abort the fetus. And, as an autonomous and responsible agent, she must make this choice. But let us notice that this in no way entails either that whatever choice she makes is morally right or that no one else has the right to evaluate the decision that she makes. It is, of course, just this type of evaluation of moral decisions that we have been making in Chapter 1.

In short, our sole and appropriate concern is with the following issue: Should we modify the conclusions we reached [previously] so as to allow some (or all) abortions as morally permissible, on the ground that a woman ought to be free to do what is necessary to retain control over her body?

At first glance, it would seem that this argument cannot be used by anyone who supposes, as we do for the moment, that there is a point in fetal development from which time on the fetus is a human being. After all, people do not have the right to do anything whatsoever that may be necessary for them to retain control over the uses of their bodies. In particular, it would seem wrong for them to kill another human being in order to do so.

In a recent article,[3] Professor Judith Thomson has, in effect, argued that this simple view is mistaken. How does Professor Thomson defend her claim that the mother has a right to abort the fetus, even if it is a human being, whether or not her life is threatened and whether or not she has consented to the act of intercourse in which the fetus is conceived? At one point,[4] discussing just the case in which the mother's life is threatened, she makes the following suggestion:

> In [abortion], there are only two people involved, one whose life is threatened and one who threatens it. Both are innocent: the one who is threatened is not threatened because of any fault, the one who threatens does not threaten because of any fault. For this reason, we may feel that we bystanders cannot intervene. But the person threatened can.

But surely this description is equally applicable to the following case: *A* and *B* are adrift on a lifeboat. *B* has a disease that he can survive, but *A*, if he contracts it, will die, and the only way that *A* can avoid that is by killing *B* and pushing him overboard. Surely, *A* has no right to do this. So there must be some special reason why the mother has, if she does, the right to abort the fetus.

There is, to be sure, an important difference between our lifeboat case and abortion, one that leads us to the heart of Professor Thomson's argument. In the case that we envisaged, both *A* and *B* have equal rights to be in the lifeboat, but the mother's body is hers and not the fetus's, and she has first rights to its use. The primacy of these rights allows an abortion whether or not her life is threatened. Professor Thomson summarizes this argument in the following way:[5]

> I am arguing only that having a right to life does not guarantee having either a right to be given the use of, or a right to be allowed continued use of, another person's body—even if one needs it for life itself.

---

[3]Judith Thomson, "A Defense of Abortion," *Philosophy and Public Affairs*, **1** (1971), pp. 47–66, and reprinted above, pp. 268–283.

[4]Thomson, p. 53, and reprinted above, p. 273.

[5]Thomson, p. 56, and reprinted above, p. 276.

One part of this claim is clearly correct. I have no duty to X to save X's life by giving him the use of my body (or my life savings, or the only home I have, and so on), and X has no right, even to save his life, to any of those things. Thus, the fetus conceived in the laboratory that will perish unless it is implanted into a woman's body has in fact no right to any woman's body. But this portion of the claim is irrelevant to the abortion issue, for in abortion of the fetus that is a human being the mother must kill X to get back the sole use of her body, and that is an entirely different matter.

This point can also be put as follows: we must distinguish the taking of X's life from the saving of X's life, even if we assume that one has a duty not to do the former and to do the latter. Now that latter duty, if it exists at all, is much weaker than the first duty; many circumstances may relieve us from the latter duty that will not relieve us from the former one. Thus, I am certainly relieved from my duty to save X's life by the fact that fulfilling it means the loss of my life savings. It may be noble for me to save X's life at the cost of everything I have, but I certainly have no duty to do that. And the same observation may be made about cases in which I can save X's life by giving him the use of my body for an extended period of time. However, I am not relieved of my duty not to take X's life by the fact that fulfilling it means the loss of everything I have and not even by the fact that fulfilling it means the loss of my life. Something more is required before rights like self-defense become applicable. A fortiori, it would seem that I am not relieved of the duty not to take life by the fact that its fulfill-ment means that some other person, who is innocently occupying my body, continues to do so.

At one point in her paper, Professor Thomson does consider this objection. She has previously imagined the following case: a famous violin-ist, who is dying from a kidney ailment, has been, without your consent, plugged into you for a period of time so that his body can use your kid-neys:

> Some people are rather stricter about the right to life. In their view, it does not include the right to be given anything, but amounts to, and only to, the right not to be killed by anybody. But here a related difficulty arises. If everybody is to refrain from killing that violinist, then everybody must refrain from doing a great many different sorts of things ... everybody must refrain from unplugging you from him. But does he have a right against everybody that they shall refrain from unplugging you from him? To refrain from doing this is to allow him to continue to use your kidneys ... certainly the violinist has no right against you that you shall allow him to con-tinue to use your kidneys.

Applying this argument to the case of abortion, we can see that Professor Thomson's argument would run as follows:

a. Assume that the fetus's right to life includes the right not to be killed by the woman carrying him.

b. But to refrain from killing the fetus is to allow him the continued use of the woman's body.

c. So our first assumption entails that the fetus's right to life includes the right to the continued use of the woman's body.

d. But we all grant that the fetus does not have the right to the continued use of the woman's body.

e. Therefore, the fetus's right to life cannot include the right not to be killed by the woman in question.

And it is also now clear what is wrong with this argument. When we granted that the fetus has no right to the continued use of the woman's body, all that we meant was that he does not have this right merely because the continued use saves his life. But, of course, there may be other reasons why he has this right. One would be that the only way to take the use of the woman's body away from the fetus is by killing him, and that is something that neither she nor we have the right to do. So, I submit, the way in which Assumption d is true is irrelevant, and cannot be used by Professor Thomson, for Assumption d is true only in cases where the saving of the life of the fetus is at stake and not in cases where the taking of his life is at stake.

I conclude therefore that Professor Thomson has not established the truth of her claims about abortion, primarily because she has not sufficiently attended to the distinction between our duty to save *X*'s life and our duty not to take it. Once one attends to that distinction, it would seem that the mother, in order to regain control over her body, has no right to abort the fetus from the point at which it becomes a human being.

It may also be useful to say a few words about the larger and less rigorous context of the argument that the woman has a right to her own body. It is surely true that one way in which women have been oppressed is by their being denied authority over their own bodies. But it seems to me that, as the struggle is carried on for meaningful amelioration of such oppression, it ought not to be carried so far that it violates the steady responsibilities all people have to one another. Parents may not desert their children, one class may not oppress another, one race or nation may not exploit another. For parents, powerful groups in society, races or nations in ascendancy, there are penalties for refraining from these wrong actions, but those penalties can in no way be taken as the justification for such wrong actions. Similarly, if the fetus is a human being, the penalty of carrying it cannot, I believe, be used as the justification for destroying it. . . .

THE MODEL
PENAL CODE CASES

All of the arguments that we have looked at so far are attempts to show that there is something special about abortion that justifies its being treated differently from other cases of the taking of human life. We shall now consider claims that are confined to certain special cases of abortion: the case in which the mother has been raped, the case in which bearing the child would be harmful to her health, and the case in which having the child may cause a problem for the rest of her family (the latter case is a particular case of the societal argument). In addressing these issues, we shall see whether there is any point to the permissibility of abortions in some of the cases covered by the Model Penal Code[6] proposals.

When the expectant mother has conceived after being raped, there are two different sorts of considerations that might support the claim that she has the right to take the life of the fetus. They are the following: (A) the woman in question has already suffered immensely from the act of rape and the physical and/or psychological aftereffects of that act. It would be particularly unjust, the argument runs, for her to have to live through an unwanted pregnancy owing to that act of rape. Therefore, even if we are at a stage at which the fetus is a human being, the mother has the right to abort it; (B) the fetus in question has no right to be in that woman. It was put there as a result of an act of aggression upon her by the rapist, and its continued presence is an act of aggression against the mother. She has a right to repel that aggression by aborting the fetus.

The first argument is very compelling. We can all agree that a terrible injustice has been committed on the woman who is raped. The question that we have to consider, however, is whether it follows that it is morally permissible for her to abort the fetus. We must make that consideration reflecting that, however unjust the act of rape, it was not the fetus who committed or commissioned it. The injustice of the act, then, should in no way impinge upon the rights of the fetus, for it is innocent. What remains is the initial misfortune of the mother (and the injustice of her having to pass through the pregnancy, and, further, to assume responsibility of at least giving the child over for adoption or assuming the burden of its care). However unfortunate that circumstance, however unjust, the misfortune and the injustice are not sufficient cause to justify the taking of the life of an innocent human being as a means of mitigation.

It is at this point that Argument B comes in, for its whole point is that the fetus, by its mere presence in the mother, is committing an act of aggression against her, one over and above the one committed by the rapist, and one that the mother has a right to repel by abortion. But we

---

[6]On the Model Penal Code provisions, see American Law Institute, *Model Penal Code: Tentative Draft No. 9* (1959).

saw [previously] that (1) the fetus is certainly innocent (in the sense of not responsible) for any act of aggression against the mother and that (2) the mere presence of the fetus in the mother, no matter how unfortunate for her, does not constitute an act of aggression by the fetus against the mother. Argument B fails then at just that point at which Argument A needs its support, and we can therefore conclude that the fact that pregnancy is the result of rape does not give the mother the right to abort the fetus.

We turn next to the case in which the continued existence of the fetus would threaten the mental and/or physical health but not necessarily the life of the mother. Again, we saw [earlier] that the fact that the fetus's continued existence poses a threat to the life of the mother does not justify her aborting it. It would seem to be true, *a fortiori*, that the fact that the fetus's continued existence poses a threat to the mental and/or physical health of the mother does not justify her aborting it either.

We come finally to those cases in which the continuation of the pregnancy would cause serious problems for the rest of the family. There are a variety of cases that we have to consider here together. Perhaps the health of the mother will be affected in such a way that she cannot function effectively as a wife and mother during, or even after, the pregnancy. Or perhaps the expenses incurred as a result of the pregnancy would be utterly beyond the financial resources of the family. The important point is that the continuation of the pregnancy raises a serious problem for other innocent people involved besides the mother and the fetus, and it may be argued that the mother has the right to abort the fetus to avoid that problem.

By now, the difficulties with this argument should be apparent. We have seen earlier that the mere fact that the continued existence of the fetus threatens to harm the mother does not, by itself, justify the aborting of the fetus. Why should anything be changed by the fact that the threatened harm will accrue to the other members of the family and not to the mother? Of course, it would be different if the fetus were committing an act of aggression against the other members of the family. But, once more, this is certainly not the case.

We conclude, therefore, that none of these special circumstances justifies an abortion from that point at which the fetus is a human being. . . .

FETAL HUMANITY
AND BRAIN FUNCTION

The question which we must now consider is the question of fetal humanity. Some have argued that the fetus is a human being with a right to life (or, for convenience, just a human being) from the moment of conception. Others have argued that the fetus only becomes a human being at the moment of birth. Many positions in between these two extremes have also been suggested. How are we to decide which is correct?

The analysis which we will propose here rests upon certain metaphysical assumptions which I have defended elsewhere. These assumptions are: (a) the question is when has the fetus acquired all the properties essential (necessary) for being a human being, for when it has, it is a human being; (b) these properties are such that the loss of any one of them means that the human being in question has gone out of existence and not merely stopped being a human being; (c) human beings go out of existence when they die. It follows from these assumptions that the fetus becomes a human being when it acquires all those characteristics which are such that the loss of any one of them would result in the fetus's being dead. We must, therefore, turn to the analysis of death. . . .

We will first consider the question of what properties are essential to being human if we suppose that death and the passing out of existence occur only if there has been an irreparable cessation of brain function (keeping in mind that that condition itself, as we have noted, is a matter of medical judgment). We shall then consider the same question on the supposition that Ramsey's more complicated theory of death (the modified traditional view) is correct.

According to what is called the brain-death theory, as long as there has not been an irreparable cessation of brain function the person in question continues to exist, no matter what else has happened to him. If so, it seems to follow that there is only one property—leaving aside those entailed by this one property—that is essential to humanity, namely, the possession of a brain that has not suffered an irreparable cessation of function.

Several consequences follow immediately from this conclusion. We can see that a variety of often advanced claims about the essence of humanity are false. For example, the claim that movement, or perhaps just the ability to move, is essential for being human is false. A human being who has stopped moving, and even one who has lost the ability to move, has not therefore stopped existing. Being able to move, and *a fortiori* moving, are not essential properties of human beings and therefore are not essential to being human. Similarly, the claim that being perceivable by other human beings is essential for being human is also false. A human being who has stopped being perceivable by other humans (for example, someone isolated on the other side of the moon, out of reach even of radio communication) has not stopped existing. Being perceivable by other human beings is not an essential property of human beings and is not essential to being human. And the same point can be made about the claims that viability is essential for being human, that independent existence is essential for being human, and that actual interaction with other human beings is essential for being human. The loss of any of these properties would not mean that the human being in question had gone out of existence, so none of them can be essential to that human being and none of them can be essential for being human.

Let us now look at the following argument: (1) A functioning brain (or at least, a brain that, if not functioning, is susceptible of function) is a property that every human being must have because it is essential for being human. (2) By the time an entity acquires that property, it has all the other properties that are essential for being human. Therefore, when the fetus acquires that property it becomes a human being. It is clear that the property in question is, according to the brain-death theory, one that is had essentially by all human beings. The question that we have to consider is whether the second premise is true. It might appear that its truth does follow from the brain-death theory. After all, we did see that that theory entails that only one property (together with those entailed by it) is essential for being human. Nevertheless, rather than relying solely on my earlier argument, I shall adopt an alternative approach to strengthen the conviction that this second premise is true: I shall note the important ways in which the fetus resembles and differs from an ordinary human being by the time it definitely has a functioning brain (about the end of the sixth week of development). It shall then be evident, in light of our theory of essentialism, that none of these differences involves the lack of some property in the fetus that is essential for its being human.

Structurally, there are few features of the human being that are not fully present by the end of the sixth week. Not only are the familiar external features and all the internal organs present, but the contours of the body are nicely rounded. More important, the body is functioning. Not only is the brain functioning, but the heart is beating sturdily (the fetus by this time has its own completely developed vascular system), the stomach is producing digestive juices, the liver is manufacturing blood cells, the kidney is extracting uric acid from the blood, and the nerves and muscles are operating in concert, so that reflex reactions can begin.

What are the properties that a fetus acquires after the sixth week of its development? Certain structures do appear later. These include the fingernails (which appear in the third month), the completed vocal chords (which also appear then), taste buds and salivary glands (again, in the third month), and hair and eyelashes (in the fifth month). In addition, certain functions begin later than the sixth week. The fetus begins to urinate (in the third month), to move spontaneously (in the third month), to respond to external stimuli (at least in the fifth month), and to breathe (in the sixth month). Moreover, there is a constant growth in size. And finally, at the time of birth the fetus ceases to receive its oxygen and food through the placenta and starts receiving them through the mouth and nose.

I will not examine each of these properties (structures and functions) to show that they are not essential for being human. The procedure would be essentially the one used previously to show that various essentialist claims are in error. We might, therefore, conclude, on the supposition that the brain-death theory is correct, that the fetus becomes a human being about the end of the sixth week after its development.

There is, however, one complication that should be noted here. There are, after all, progressive stages in the physical development and in the functioning of the brain. For example, the fetal brain (and nervous system) does not develop sufficiently to support spontaneous motion until some time in the third month after conception. There is, of course, no doubt that that stage of development is sufficient for the fetus to be human. No one would be likely to maintain that a spontaneously moving human being has died; and similarly, a spontaneously moving fetus would seem to have become human. One might, however, want to claim that the fetus does not become a human being until the point of spontaneous movement. So then, on the supposition that the brain-death theory of death is correct, one ought to conclude that the fetus becomes a human being at some time between the sixth and twelfth week after its conception.

But what if we reject the brain-death theory, and replace it with its equally plausible contender, Ramsey's theory of death? According to that theory—which we can call the brain, heart, and lung theory of death—the human being does not die, does not go out of existence, until such time as the brain, heart, and lungs have irreparably ceased functioning naturally. What are the essential features of being human according to this theory?

Actually, the adoption of Ramsey's theory requires no major modifications. According to that theory, what is essential to being human, what each human being must retain if he is to continue to exist, is the possession of a functioning (actually or potentially) heart, lung or brain. It is only when a human being possesses none of these that he dies and goes out of existence; and the fetus comes into humanity, so to speak, when he acquires one of these.

On Ramsey's theory, the argument would now run as follows: (1) The property of having a functioning brain, heart, or lungs (or at least organs of the kind that, if not functioning, are susceptible of function) is one that every human being must have because it is essential for being human. (2) By the time that an entity acquires that property it has all the other properties that are essential for being human. Therefore, when the fetus acquires that property it becomes a human being. There remains, once more, the problem of the second premise. Since the fetal heart starts operating rather early, it is not clear that the second premise is correct. Many systems are not yet operating, and many structures are not yet present. Still, following our theory of essentialism, we should conclude that the fetus becomes a human being when it acquires a functioning heart (the first of the organs to function in the fetus).

There is, however, a further complication here, and it is analogous to the one encountered if we adopt the brain-death theory: When may we properly say that the fetal heart begins to function? At two weeks, when occasional contractions of the primitive fetal heart are present? In the fourth to fifth week, when the heart, although incomplete, is beating regularly and pumping blood cells through a closed vascular system, and when the tracings obtained by an ECG exhibit the classical elements of an adult tracing? Or after the end of the seventh week, when the fetal heart is functionally complete and "normal"?

We have not reached a precise conclusion in our study of the question of when the fetus becomes a human being. We do know that it does so sometime between the end of the second week and the end of the third month. But it surely is not a human being at the moment of conception and it surely is one by the end of the third month. Though we have not come to a final answer to our question, we have narrowed the range of acceptable answers considerably.

CONCLUSION

We have argued that the fetus becomes a human being with a right to life sometime between the second and twelfth week after conception. We have also argued that abortions are morally impermissible after that point except in rather unusual circumstances. What is crucial to note is that neither of these arguments appeal to any theological considerations. We conclude, therefore, that there is a human-rights basis for moral opposition to abortions.

Viability and the Use of the Fetus

H. Tristram Engelhardt, Jr.

In its landmark case, *Roe* v. *Wade*, the Supreme Court of the United States appealed to viability (that is, the potential ability of a fetus to survive on its own outside of the womb) in signaling when it would be appropriate for

From H. Tristram Engelhardt, Jr., "Viability and the Use of the Fetus," in *Abortion and the Status of the Fetus*, ed. W. B. Bondeson, H. Tristram Engelhardt, Jr., S. F. Spicker, and Daniel Winship. Dordrecht, Holland: Reidel Publishing Company, 1982. Reprinted with permission of the publisher. The article is reprinted here only in part.

the state to proscribe abortions for other than the preservation of the life or the health of the mother. The Court stated,

> For the stage subsequent to viability the state, in promoting its interest in the potentiality of human life, may, if it chooses, regulate, and even proscribe, abortion, except where it is necessary, in appropriate medical judgment, for the preservation of the life or the health of the mother.[1]

The National Commission for the Protection of Human Subjects of Biomedical and Behavioral Research appealed as well to a distinction between viable and nonviable living fetuses in drafting its canons for regulations.

What I shall do in this essay is to explore the sense and meaning of such appeals to viability. I will attempt to indicate the extent to which the stage of viability could have moral implications for decisions about abortion or fetal research. That is, I shall attempt to delineate its moral and conceptual value. Having done that, I shall then suggest some public policy implications of such a conceptual analysis. For example, in considering policies concerning abortion and fetal research, one needs to know whether the stage of viability, as it bears upon moral discussions, is *fixed* or whether it will change as technology allows us to sustain the lives of ever more immature fetuses.

Although appeal is often made to the *criterion of viability*, there is very little helpful analysis to suggest the origin of its moral pertinence. Justice Blackmun, in delivering the opinion of the Supreme Court in *Roe* v. *Wade*, noted that physicians and their scientific colleagues placed weight upon the point at which the fetus becomes "viable." He then defined viability as the stage at which the fetus would be "potentially able to live outside the mother's womb, albeit with artificial aid. Viability is usually placed at about seven months (twenty-eight weeks) but may occur earlier, even at twenty-four weeks."[2] I argue that this statement is dangerously misleading in that it might suggest that the point of viability could be pushed ever earlier simply by the force of scientific advances in fetal medicine. Contrary to such a suggestion, I hold that the sense of viability pertinent to *moral decisions* with regard to the use of the fetus should not be so open to change in this fashion, but rather should be set, or fixed, at that point at which a near-full-term infant could survive without one providing what would be tantamount to a surrogate womb. Indeed, such a conceptualization of viability allows us to make a clear delineation between viability and nonviability, in both a biological and moral sense. Viability as a *biological* criterion I define as a point in gestation *before which* no infant has been known to survive. And, viability as a *moral* criterion is a point in gestation *after which*

---

[1] *Roe* v. *Wade*, 93 S. Ct. 705 (1973), pp. 164–165.

[2] *Roe* v. *Wade*, p. 160.

abortion may be procured only with special justification, such as considerations of the health or life of the mother, or because the fetus is probably defective. This delineation represents a balancing of various consequentialist concerns as well as the recognition of the requirement of respecting the freedom of the pregnant woman.

I will argue this point on the basis of two central considerations. The first is that fetuses, even viable fetuses, are not *persons*, and therefore need not be extended the special protection we give to persons. Second, in establishing restrictions with regard to easy access to abortion one must always be concerned not to circumscribe unduly the freedom of women who are actually and fully persons. In developing this argument, one must bear in mind that I am attempting to advance general secular considerations. Although I do not make appeal to religious or other special considerations, neither do I deny their validity for those who embrace them. Rather, I argue that a peaceable pluralist community may not make appeal to such considerations in the development of its public policies bearing on the use of the fetus. For example, this suggests that it would be immoral for a pluralist society to forbid by law abortion on request, in that consequentialist arguments (see the introduction to Part 1 of this text) against abortion could not outweigh the moral considerations regarding respect of the person of the woman, which would count in favor of avoiding such a prohibition.

I. BEING A PERSON

Why should one be interested in deciding which of the objects of this world are persons? That will, naturally, depend upon what one means by person. Our language often bewitches us in our attempts to be clear about what it is to be a person. The fact that we have but one word "person" may suggest that we have but one concept of person. Yet we use the term to describe various kinds of beings. For example, although we speak of both adults and infants as persons, it is, I argue, *not* the case that they are persons in the same sense.

In a strict context, I use the term "person" to identify those entities that are self-conscious, rational, and self-determining. But beyond such a strict conceptualization, the term "person" can be arranged on a sort of continuum of personhood:

1. *Possible persons*: persons that could under certain circumstances come into existence. As merely possible persons they have no actual rights.
2. *Potential persons*: a shorthand expression indicating entities that are not yet persons and therefore do not have any of the rights of persons, and which have a probability of "becoming" a person. The "entity" (e.g., fetus) has "continuity" with the "entity" (e.g., embodied person) who will follow it in the sense of there being a physical continuity over time. An analogous con-

tinuity exists also, for example, between the body of a person before and after total brain death. One entity is followed by another entity, although there is much physical continuity. There are, however, also special and important changes in physical structure. Thus one can distinguish between what became of a body and what became of a person.

3. *Persons in the social sense*: humans who are not persons in the strict sense, but to whom some of the special rights of persons have been *imputed* because of utilitarian and other consequentialist considerations; for example, infants.

4. *Persons in the strict sense*: persons in the sense of moral agents who are self-conscious, rational, and capable of free choice and of having interests. This includes not only normal adult humans, but possible extraterrestrials with similar powers.

This central place of persons in moral reflections flows from the very notion of a *moral community*. If one views ethics as a means of resolving moral disputes in a fashion not based upon force, but rather upon peaceable negotiation, in a context where the participants are held accountable for their actions, the only original members of that community, of the moral world, will be *persons in the strict sense*: entities who are self-conscious, rational, and self-determining, and therefore are accountable for their choices, and who have interests. Insofar as there is a sense of rights and duties irreducible to interests in particular goods and values, it will be founded on the necessary condition for such a community, namely, mutual respect of the free choice of its members. Such a view of rights is the least presumptuous and therefore the least difficult to establish. It presumes only that the ethical life is based upon peaceable negotiation and the eschewal of force against the innocent. It does not presuppose that one can discover a univocal and morally obligatory view of the good life, nor grounds for imposing such a view upon the unconsenting innocent.

A community of moral agents is invoked as soon as one begins the endeavor of determining with others what the nature of the moral life ought to be. The only possible participants in such a discussion are moral agents, or persons in the strict sense. It is for this reason that persons possess such a singular place in ethical reflections, in the moral life, and in the constitution of the moral universe. It is in terms of an appeal to such a community that general moral absolutes can be produced, such as: One should not take the lives of unconsenting innocent persons. This is not to deny that taking the life of an "unconsenting" human for sport, if that entity is not a person in the strict sense, may also be morally offensive; it will not, however, offend against the basic notion of a moral community. That is, rules concerning the termination of *human biological life* (which does not refer to a person in a strict sense, but rather denotes human zygotes and fetuses) will need to be justified in terms of whether they are in line with particular goods and values, including moral character. One may also wish to take into account here any pain involved in such taking of *life*, a consideration that is by no means restricted to *human personal life* alone (where "personal" refers to persons in the strict sense). Human biological life may therefore be a moral object. Such is the case with nonhuman life as well. In any event, whatever pain and suffering is endured by a human fetus or infant, it is surely not as severe as the pain and suffering that normal adult nonhuman mammals can experience, and is not of the same moral significance as imposing pain on an unconsenting person.

Thus, if one attempts to identify entities who are persons—members of the moral community—one is attempting to determine which objects are also self-conscious, rational, and self-determining. Not all humans will be persons in this sense. Nor will appeals to potentiality secure for potential persons the standing of actual persons. If X is a potential Y, it follows that X is not Y. Moreover, if X is only a potential Y, it follows that X does not as a consequence of that relationship have all the properties of a Y. In fact, the contrary is true. Thus, if X is a potential president, it does not follow that X has presidential rights.[3] Rather, it is the case that X *potentially* has such rights, which is far from *having* those rights.

In order to avoid the confusion often associated with the use of the term "potential," it might be wise to substitute the term "probable." Thus, one might speak of a zygote being a "0.4 probable person," indicating that it has a 40 percent chance of *becoming* a person. The extent to which an entity is a probable person would then play an important role in the value one attributed to it. In any event, even though human sperm, ova, zygotes, embryos, fetuses, and infants are potential—or probable—persons, this does not confer upon them *eo ipso* the standing of actual persons. Since the focus here is upon fetuses, this means that there is not a general secular argument that would secure for them a greater intrinsic value than the value held by adult organisms of similar sapience and responsiveness to their environment. That is to say, considered *only* in that regard, they would have a position comparable to that of lower vertebrates. However, they play a role in endeavors that do have important moral standing, and therefore secular arguments may be available to provide greater moral worth to the fetus in terms of these extrinsic conditions.[4] How human

[3] The example of presidential rights was explored by S. I. Benn in "Abortion, Infanticide, and Respect for Persons" in *The Problem of Abortion*, ed. Joel Feinberg (Belmont, Calif.: Wadsworth, 1973), p. 102.

[4] The reader should note that I stress here *secular* argument. It is important that the reader understand that here, and in fact throughout these arguments, I am indicating what can be delivered by a secular argument without special religious appeals. This distinction is important not only because it acknowledges the integrity of religious argument for religious communities, but also because it sets limits on the extent to which a secular society may impose religious values upon its members. Thus, it would be a violation of the notion of the moral community for a secular society to impose by law a religious or metaphysical view upon its unconsenting members.

fetuses will be valued will depend upon such issues as a society's interest in having more persons, or more persons of a particular sort.

Potential persons, all else being equal, have no actual rights. However, the actual persons they might become would, should they come into existence, indeed have strong moral rights and claims upon us, although they may still be regarded as disvalued and prevented from existence as long as they are merely potential persons. Generally, actions that will injure present actual persons are immoral, as are actions that injure future actual persons. However, when the injury to the future actual person is due to a causal chain that is a part of the gestational history of the body of that person, it is not clear that one is obliged to avoid causing that injury at the cost of avoiding that person's existence.

It should be clear as well, that the intention to abort alters the value of the fetus. A fetus that is to be aborted may no longer have positive significance for the mother and may indeed be of negative value for her. Thus on this point, at least, a fetus-to-be-aborted should receive different consideration than a fetus-going-to-term. This should be the case as well with regard to the use of the fetus in research, although current federal regulations fail to acknowledge this difference.[5] The value of potential persons will be determined by the benefits and costs associated with their lives, or the termination of their lives under specific circumstances, where costs are understood in the broadest sense—including psychological, financial, and such social costs as impeding the realization of moral goods. The assumption of such costs will be justifiable when they are outbalanced by other psychological, financial, moral and social goods, and insofar as the freedom of persons in the strict sense is not violated.

Thus, one could, for example, understand the moral probity of investing considerable funds per organism to ensure that all whooping crane embryos are brought to term, while not investing such energies to prevent the loss of embryos in the case of humans, reasoning that the world has far too few whooping cranes, and in general far too many human persons. Once such persons, however, come into existence, although one might wish there had been fewer of them, one will be strictly bound by duties of forbearance not to kill them, unless they act as unjust aggressors.

Such reflections require distinctions to be drawn between "human" and "person." In these reflections I use "human" to identify a particular genus. There will be a certain ambiguity as to whether under some circumstances one would mean to restrict the term "human" to only some of the species within the genus homo. In any event, "human" need not denote personal characteristics. As already indicated, there are many

---

[5]U.S. Department of Health, Education and Welfare, "Protection of Human Subjects of Biomedical and Behavioral Research," *Federal Register* **44** (August 14, 1979), p. 47733.

instances of human biological life that are not instances of human personal life. One might think here of human zygotes, fetuses, infants, and brain-dead but otherwise alive human individuals. All of these are surely instances of life and in fact of human life. They are not porcine, feline, canine, or simian. Moreover, just as not all humans are persons, not all persons need be humans, as the characters in the popular science fiction movies *Star Wars* and *The Empire Strikes Back* and in fact the general genre of science fiction and indeed religious reflection attest. Self-conscious, rational, self-determining extraterrestrials, angels, and gods are persons, although they are not humans. Thus we arrive at the distinction between *human biological life*, which is defined in terms of certain biological characteristics, and *human personal life*, which identifies those instances of human biological life that are also persons.

This would appear to do violence to many of the settled ways in which we in our culture deal with human life. We currently accord humans the status of persons at birth and remove that status at brain death. However, what are we to make of the status of infants, the severely mentally retarded, the severely senile, and the severely brain-damaged? It would appear, all else being equal, that killing them would involve the seriousness of killing an animal of a similar level of sentience. Although this would be a serious act, it would in itself not be assigned the same level of the seriousness as killing, for example, an adult higher primate. However, all else is not equal in the case of infants, the severely mentally retarded, and so on, for they play important moral roles within particular communities of persons. A plausible reconstruction of this state of affairs is that our settled practices presuppose more than one concept of person. The first would be the strict sense of a moral agent, an entity that could be a member of a moral community. It is through appeals to such a notion that we would understand certain entities to have strong, though abstract, natural rights to forbearance, so that it would be an equally heinous moral act to slay for sport and without consent an innocent human person or an innocent extraterrestrial person. Our treatment of instances of human life that are not also persons must be explained in terms of general practices established to secure important goods and interests, including the development of kindly parental attitudes to children, concern and sympathy for the weak, and protection in ambiguous circumstances for persons in the strict sense.

This practice of imputing personhood thus depends upon the moral concepts of a particular moral community. For example, one may wish to treat infants as persons in order to secure attitudes of love and attention to children. In addition one will wish to ensure that the person the infant will become will be secure against injuries that would antedate his or her personhood. Also, because one might fear false positive determinations of the fact that one was no longer a person strictly, one might, for example, treat individuals such as Karen Quinlan as if they were persons strictly, although all the available evidence suggests to the contrary—that is, their status is the consequence of a false negative test for death. That is, one would establish operational criteria for deciding in a conservative fashion what was a person strictly.

Where does this leave us, then, with regard to the concept of person? At the deepest level, one must distinguish between human *personal* and human *biological* life. Next, one must recognize that our moral concerns involve more than one sense of "person." We have drawn the line for imputation of personhood along one border at birth, conferring upon human life above that border the rights of persons as civil rights, similar to the rights possessed by persons (in the strict sense) as natural rights. The fact that birth as a moral criterion represents a line that is created, not discovered, suggests how one must proceed in examining the significance of viability. That is, one confers upon birth a moral significance because of certain practices that sustain the achievement of certain values, goods, and interests. We must now explore the possible functions of the criterion of viability in this light in terms of the goals such a moral criterion would serve.

II. THE MORAL SIGNIFICANCE OF VIABILITY

An initial reflection on the possible moral grounds for holding that the state of viability is of ethical significance in the development of practices regarding the fetus is likely to offer at least four possible accounts.

1. The point of viability is that point at which the fetus becomes a person in the strict sense of a moral agent.
2. At the point of viability the fetus has become a sufficiently well-integrated organism as to experience significant pain in the process of being aborted.
3. The point of viability identifies a stage at which the interests of the State in such goods as procuring more citizens outweigh interests in maximizing the liberty of women to decide late in their pregnancies not to carry a fetus to term. As a consequence, late-gestation fetuses may be treated as if they were persons.
4. At the point of viability, one has usually given sufficient time for a woman to decide whether she wishes to carry a pregnancy to term (if health concerns should give late grounds for abortion, one would presume, as is currently the case, that a woman would, with her physician, have total liberty in procuring an abortion) so that one can give predominance to such utilitarian and teleological considerations as the effect of late abortions on attitudes towards parenting, upon the emotional well-being of physicians and nurses, and upon the establishment of a general high regard for the value of human life.

The arguments that are advanced to this point suggest that the first position is untenable. There is no evidence that viable fetuses are self-conscious, rational, self-determining entities. They are not persons in this strict sense. Nor does there appear to be any evidence to support in a convincing fashion the second proposition. There do not appear to be any well-established arguments that society should be greatly concerned about pain in an organism at the level of sensitivity of a fetus, especially considering the serious issue of a woman being able to decide freely whether she would wish to be a mother. Indeed, newborn infants are considered to have such a limited capacity to appreciate pain that they are held not to suffer in significant fashion (it would appear that there is not full connection of the frontal lobes until some time after birth), so that, for example, circumcisions are performed without anesthetic. In any event—and what is central to the arguments here—there is not the suffering that is present in the case of a person in the strict sense, where pain can also be intellectually appreciated as suffering.

The third view can, I believe, be subsumed under the fourth. One is, after all, interested in balancing the concern to respect the decisions of the mother who is a person in the strict sense, with interests that others might have in establishing fetuses as persons because of possible benefits from such treatment. This is to say that given the argument already forwarded that the boundaries for the social concept of person are created, not discovered, one might very well imagine a utilitarian argument to the effect that human biological life should be accorded personal status from the moment of conception. However, the arguments against such a practice will be both deontological and utilitarian. The deontological argument will be based on regard for the freedom of the woman who is the only person in a strict sense immediately involved, and who possesses strong claims in the matter—that is, presuming that the woman did not promise to bring the fetus to term as a part of an agreement with her husband, her lover, or parties for whom she promised to act as a surrogate mother. Therefore, one will not be able, for utilitarian or other consequentialist considerations, to circumscribe the woman's liberty of decision so that she would not have sufficient time to consider an abortion and to determine, should she wish, whether the fetus is defective. In fact, the second consideration would likely be strong enough to preclude the proscription of abortion at a time that would interfere with the ability to acquire adequate information from prenatal diagnostic maneuvers or would cause her to risk her life or health. Due to these considerations, fetuses may not be treated as persons.

These last considerations would also form a part of a utilitarian argument. One would not wish to set the upper allowable limit in gestation for abortions at a point that would preclude women from aborting defective fetuses on the basis of prenatal diagnosis, if such fetuses would as infants not be treated anyway, or would constitute a serious burden for society. Or at least, one would wish to have an exception or a loophole in the proscription of abortion after a particular point of "viability" in gestation, should those abortions be sought on the basis that a prenatal diagnosis indicated that the fetus would be severely deformed, or to protect the life or health of the mother.

In practice these deontological and utilitarian considerations will make it possible for many women to have late abortions by disingenuously claiming (with the aid of some physicians) that carrying the fetus to term will damage their mental health. Still, requiring such a claim is itself of moral value. It is a way of requiring that women seeking abortions past the point of viability advance a reasonable justification in order to reaffirm the moral seriousness of late abortions—for example, the importance of avoiding distress to others by such procedures, and of protecting complex biological life even when it is not human personal life. This requirement allows one to acknowledge the moral consequences of late abortions, while recognizing the utilitarian considerations in favor of easy access to early abortions. These will include the role of abortion in population control and in preventing the birth of unwanted children or the birth of children under circumstances when the births themselves would be a burden to the mothers. Thus, in the creation of a secular proscription of the abortion of fetuses late in pregnancy, one would seek a line that allowed women self-determination, the effective use of prenatal diagnosis, the preservation of their lives and health, and the achievement of other societal goals such as the prevention of the births of unwanted children, while avoiding undue insult to practices of parenting.

Current notions of viability offer an appealing point for drawing such a line, in that it is also reasonable to wish to avoid the delivery of fetuses, who could then readily survive as infants. Not only may such a circumstance thwart a woman's desire not to be a mother, but it is also quite reasonable to presume that such events are likely to be traumatic for those who view them or who come to know about them. The point of viability, therefore, can function as a reasonable point after which abortion should not be performed without good reasons. Of course, although an abortion past that period would offend a moral practice and the goods it sustains, it would not involve active infanticide. Or to put the matter another way, there does not appear to be sufficient untoward consequences from later abortions so as to extend to late-gestation fetuses the status of persons. The point of birth has functioned successfully as a point at which to confer personhood in a social sense. Further, the fetus is not necessarily embedded in a social matrix. Fetuses can, unlike infants, be ignored and they will tend to go to term. It is infants that must necessarily be embedded in a social context and given a social role in terms of which they receive care. It is for this reason difficult to envisage imposing personhood upon instances of human life prior to birth; they are not necessarily placed within an active social matrix in which they themselves play an active role. Finally, the fact that one would need to allow late abortions for the life or health of the mother, or for grounds of fetal defect, would appear to be a strong bar against conferring personhood on the fetus.

The current criterion of viability appears thus to be reasonably construed as a social creation insofar as it bears moral weight. It represents a line drawn in gestation, which allows the balancing of interests in favor of abortion with those in favor of fetal life.

III. WHEN IS A FETUS VIABLE?

The advantage of the criterion of birth for conferring personhood is that it is a fairly discrete event. One can determine whether a fetus has made it outside of the mother and drawn a breath. Then and only then are the rights of person conferred, from inheriting estates to possessing a tax deduction. Viability is not as clear a criterion, even if one wishes to set it at a point at which at least one fetus has been known to survive. Moreover, if such an analysis of viability is embraced, one might then envisage developments in the neonatal care of premature infants pushing the point of viability ever earlier. Indeed, one can imagine *in vitro* fertilization and gestation advancing to the point at which a zygote could be brought to term *in vitro*. At that point, all conceptuses would be viable in the sense of being at a stage at which there were known survivors. Would such, or ought such, possible developments in science so alter the stage of viability as to forbid absolutely all abortions (except in circumstances involving the life or health of the mother, as is currently the case)?

Such a possibility would appear to be indefensible. After all, viability functions as a useful criterion as long as it is late enough in pregnancy to allow the use of prenatal diagnosis and to allow women time to reflect upon whether they would wish to be mothers. Even under the best of future possible worlds, there are likely to be contraceptive failures, failures to use adequate contraception, and revisions of judgment regarding motherhood once pregnancy has begun. Since fetuses born much earlier than 28 to 24 weeks gestation are unlikely to survive long without agressive treatment, the moral insult of allowing a fetus of, say 20 weeks gestation to die without employing aggressive treatment is unlikely to create great moral costs. Should that, however, prove to be the case (which is more unlikely the earlier in gestation the fetus is aborted), it would then be justifiable to use abortifacient techniques that guaranteed the death of the fetus. One is concerned primarily to respect the freedom of the mother. As a consequence, one would wish as well to forbid attempts, against the will of the mother, to sustain the life of an abortus prior to the established general upper limit for abortions. Or to put it another way, given the absence of a generally defensible secular argument that fetuses are persons, it will follow that a secular society will not have the right to encumber a woman's interests in not being a mother, as would be the case if biomedical science were able to push the point of viability ever earlier as a moral criterion.

As a consequence, one will be forced to distinguish between viability as a moral criterion and viability as a medical generalization. The latter is likely to move ever earlier as our ability to treat premature infants advances. However, the former should remain fixed at that point at which survival would not be possible without special intervention often tantamount to a surrogate womb. Indeed, the criterion probably should remain fixed at the level at which it was understood to be set in 1973. Again, one would need to be extremely cautious in pushing the moral criterion any earlier, in that such might hinder the woman's ability adequately to use prenatal diagnosis in her decision whether to bring a fetus to term. Such constraints would limit her freedom to control the quality of the fetuses to which she would give birth. It would in addition have some consequences of marked disutility— that is, the birth of handicapped children in need of expensive support.

One might ask whether such a policy would not lead to unequal treatment for entities that are in other circumstances equal. One would be ready to employ aggressive means to sustain the life of a wanted premature baby, but not that of an unwanted fetus at a comparable stage in development. There is not, however, parity between the premature infant and the possibly viable fetus. The first is already born and therefore already plays a role under the social rubric of *child*. Personhood has been conferred upon it through the passage of birth. Beyond that, the wanted premature infant accrues value due to the interest of its parents.

In any event, it appears unreasonable to hold that a biological criterion of viability can in some simple fashion be given moral force. As a result, if advances in biomedicine move the criterion of viability earlier as a medical generalization, it does not follow that viability as a moral guidepost should be pushed earlier. Quite to the contrary. The criterion of viability, in that it reflects a balancing of various considerations, is likely to be influenced only marginally by ever-earlier extensions of viability through new medical interventions. Viability as a moral criterion is thus, perhaps, best placed at a point at which fetuses, should they be aborted, would die, given the level of support thought to be obligatory in the case of full-term or near full-term births. That is, it indicates a line at which a fetus brought *ex utero* could reasonably be placed in the social role of child. In this way one could offer a useful interpretation of the Supreme Court's identification of viability as a point at which a fetus would be capable of meaningful life *ex utero*.[6] Again, the fact that parents interested in saving their premature children might wish to invest resources in extending the role of child to very premature infants (even though placing such a child in what would be tantamount to a surrogate womb would restrict the full realization of that role) would not defeat the legitimacy of maintaining a rather constant criterion of viability for moral decisions at somewhere between 24 and 28 weeks.

Given the considerations to be balanced in creating such a line, it would be appropriate for legislatures, should a community of interest be strong enough, to give legal force to the criterion, as long as the woman's interest in preserving her life and health, and in avoiding the birth of a defective fetus, was not compromised. Given such constraints, it would then be appropriate for a legislature to establish a criterion of viability for such purposes somewhere between 24 and 28 weeks gestation, with exception beyond that point being made for abortions sought on the basis of fetal defect or because of a risk to the health or life of the mother.

It is important to note that these considerations lead us to two distinct genres of viability. The first is a set of biological generalizations of this sort: no infant of x gestational age and/or y weight has ever survived; or infants of x gestational age and/or y weight have only survived in z (some presumably small number) percent of the recorded cases; or infants of x gestational age and/or y weight have survived, but only with special intervention of p sort. The second genre of statements about viability are not biological generalizations, but moral judgments made in part by taking into consideration empirical data, especially those concerning viability in the first genre. They are of this sort: abortions for q reasons are not allowed after r weeks of pregnancy because of reasons s through z. One might, for the sake of avoiding confusion, substitute a new phrase for the term *viability*, when viability is used as a moral criterion. In this way, one might avoid confusing viability as a biological generalization and viability as a moral criterion. One might use a phrase such as "upper limit for aborting the fetus without special justification." That phrase would identify a criterion based on a complex set of grounds, including moral judgments of the consequences of aborting fetuses after (biological) viability.

CONCLUSIONS

I have attempted through these reflections to analyze the conceptual presuppositions underlying the criterion of viability in its role as setting an upper limit for abortions, save in the case of abortions where the life and

---

[6]*Roe* v. *Wade*, pp. 164–165.

health of the mother is at stake, as is presently the case, or to avoid a defective fetus going to term, as ought to be the case. The argument I have forwarded is offered as a general secular one, appealing to considerations open to all without special appeal to religious, ideological, or metaphysical presuppositions. Again, I do not wish to suggest that such special appeals are improper. Rather, I have restricted myself to those considerations that can feasibly provide the moral cement of a pluralistic society.

To summarize, the criterion of viability can be used as a line expressing the upper limits for abortion in circumstances that do not involve the life or health of the mother, or the abortion of a defective fetus. In such circumstances no upper limit may be set. Moreover, the use of viability as a moral criterion does not indicate that personhood should be conferred on fetuses. Rather, viability expresses the point at which, in many circumstances, there has been an adequate balancing of the women's rights of self-determination with consequentialist considerations in favor of abortion or in favor of the preservation of fetal life. Therefore, one must distinguish clearly between the criterion of viability as a moral criterion and viability as expressing a medical generalization about the likely chances of a fetus surviving. It is therefore reasonable to hold that the criterion of viability should continue to function as it does now, precluding abortions after 24 to 28 weeks of gestation, save in cases involving the life or the health of the mother, and as I have argued, abortions performed to avoid bringing a defective fetus to term. In this fashion, one will be able to respect adequately the freedom of the women involved as well as to achieve important moral goals, including a moral regard for the fetus.

SELECTED SUPPLEMENTARY READINGS

BEAUCHAMP, TOM L., AND LEROY WALTERS, eds., *Contemporary Issues in Bioethics* (2nd ed.). Belmont, Calif.: Wadsworth, 1982, chaps. 2, 6.

BENNETT, JONATHAN, "Whatever the Consequences," *Analysis* **26** (January 1966).

BRANDT, R. B., "The Morality of Abortion," *The Monist* **36** (1972).

BRODY, BARUCH A., "Abortion and the Law," *Journal of Philosophy* **68** (1971).

———, "Thomson on Abortion," *Philosophy and Public Affairs* **1** (Spring 1972).

———, "Abortion and the Sanctity of Human Life," *American Philosophical Quarterly* **10** (April 1973).

CALLAHAN, DANIEL, *Abortion: Law, Choice and Morality.* New York: Macmillan, 1970.

CARRIER, L. S., "Abortion and the Right to Life," *Social Theory and Practice* **3** (Fall, 1975).

DANIELS, CHARLES B., "Abortion and Potential," *Dialogue* **18** (June 1979).

DEVINE, PHILIP E., *The Ethics of Homicide.* Ithaca, N.Y.: Cornell University Press, 1978.

DRINAN, ROBERT F., "The Inviolability of the Right to be Born," in *Abortion and the Law*, ed., David T. Smith. Cleveland, Ohio: Case Western Reserve Press, 1967.

ELY, JOHN HART, "The Wages of Crying Wolf: A Comment on *Roe v. Wade*," *Yale Law Journal* **82** (April 1973).

ENGELHARDT, H. TRISTRAM, JR., "The Ontology of Abortion," *Ethics* **84** (April 1974).

ENGLISH, JANE, "Abortion and the Concept of a Person," *Canadian Journal of Philosophy* **5** (October 1975).

FEINBERG, JOEL, ed., *The Problem of Abortion*. Belmont, Calif.: Wadsworth, 1973.

———, "Abortion," in *Matters of Life and Death*, ed. Tom Regan. New York: Random House, 1980.

FINNIS, JOHN, "The Rights and Wrongs of Abortion: A Reply to Judith Thomson," *Philosophy and Public Affairs* **2** (Winter 1973).

FOOT, PHILIPPA, "The Problem of Abortion and the Doctrine of Double Effect," *The Oxford Review* **5** (1967).

FRANKENA, WILLIAM K., "The Ethics of Respect for Life," in *Respect for Life*, ed. Stephen Barker. Baltimore: The Johns Hopkins University Press, 1976.

GLOVER, JONATHAN, *Causing Death and Saving Lives*. Harmondsworth, England: Penguin Books, 1977.

HARE, R. M., "Abortion and the Golden Rule," *Philosophy and Public Affairs* **4** (Spring 1975).

MARGOLIS, JOSEPH, "Abortion," *Ethics* **84** (1973).

MCCORMICK, RICHARD A., "Past Church Teaching on Abortion," *Proceedings of the Catholic Theological Society of America* **23** (1968).

NOONAN, JOHN T., JR., ed., *The Morality of Abortion: Legal and Historical Perspectives*. Cambridge, Mass.: Harvard University Press, 1970.

———, *How to Argue About Abortion*. Reprinted from a pamphlet published by the Ad Hoc Committee in Defense of Life, Inc., 1974.

PERKINS, ROBERT, ed., *Abortion*. Cambridge, Mass.: Schenkman, 1974.

POTTS, MALCOLM, et al., *Abortion*. Cambridge, England: Cambridge University Press, 1977.

RAMSEY, PAUL, "Abortion: A Review Article," *The Thomist* **37** (1973).

———, "The Morality of Abortion," in *Life or Death: Ethics and Options*, ed. Daniel H. Labby. Seattle, Wash.: University of Washington Press, 1968.

RUDINOW, JOEL, "On 'the slippery slope,'" *Analysis* **34** (1974).

SINGER, PETER, *Practical Ethics*. New York: Cambridge University Press, 1979, chap. 6.

STERBA, JAMES P., "Abortion, Distant Peoples and Future Generations," *Journal of Philosophy* **77** (July 1980).

SUMNER, L. W., *Abortion and Moral Theory*. Princeton, N.J.: Princeton University Press, 1981.

THOMSON, JUDITH JARVIS, "Rights and Deaths," *Philosophy and Public Affairs* **2** (Winter 1973).

TOOLEY, MICHAEL, "Abortion and Infanticide," *Philosophy and Public Affairs* **2** (Winter 1973).

TRIBE, LAURENCE H., "Toward a Model of Roles in the Due Process of Life and Law," *Harvard Law Review* **87** (1973).

WARREN, MARY ANNE, "On the Moral and Legal Status of Abortion," *The Monist* **56** (January 1973).

WERTHEIMER, ROGER, "Understanding the Abortion Argument," *Philosophy and Public Affairs* **1** (1971).

chapter ten

Euthanasia

Active and Passive Euthanasia

James Rachels

The distinction between active and passive euthanasia is thought to be crucial for medical ethics. The idea is that it is permissible, at least in some cases, to withhold treatment and allow a patient to die, but it is never permissible to take any direct action designed to kill the patient. This doctrine seems to be accepted by most doctors, and it is endorsed in a statement adopted by the House of Delegates of the American Medical Association on December 4, 1973:

> The intentional termination of the life of one human being by another—mercy killing—is contrary to that for which the medical profession stands and is contrary to the policy of the American Medical Association.
> The cessation of the employment of extraordinary means to prolong the life of the body when there is irrefutable evidence that biological death is imminent is the decision of the patient and/or his immediate family. The advice and judgment of the physician should be freely available to the patient and/or his immediate family.

However, a strong case can be made against this doctrine. In what follows I will set out some of the relevant arguments, and urge doctors to reconsider their views on this matter.

Printed by permission from the *New England Journal of Medicine*, vol. 292, pp. 78–80 (January 1975).

To begin with a familiar type of situation, a patient who is dying of incurable cancer of the throat is in terrible pain, which can no longer be satisfactorily alleviated. He is certain to die within a few days, even if present treatment is continued, but he does not want to go on living for those days since the pain is unbearable. So he asks the doctor for an end to it, and his family joins in the request.

Suppose the doctor agrees to withhold treatment, as the conventional doctrine says he may. The justification for his doing so is that the patient is in terrible agony, and since he is going to die anyway, it would be wrong to prolong his suffering needlessly. But now notice this. If one simply withholds treatment, it may take the patient longer to die, and so he may suffer more than he would if more direct action were taken and a lethal injection given. This fact provides strong reason for thinking that, once the initial decision not to prolong his agony has been made, active euthanasia is actually preferable to passive euthanasia, rather than the reverse. To say otherwise is to endorse the option that leads to more suffering rather than less, and is contrary to the humanitarian impulse that prompts the decision not to prolong his life in the first place.

Part of my point is that the process of being "allowed to die" can be relatively slow and painful, whereas being given a lethal injection is relatively quick and painless. Let me give a different sort of example. In the United States about one in 600 babies is born with Down's syndrome. Most of these babies are otherwise healthy—that is, with only the usual pediatric care, they will proceed to an otherwise normal infancy. Some, however, are born with congenital defects such as intestinal obstructions that require operations if they are to live. Sometimes, the parents and the doctor will decide not to operate, and let the infant die. Anthony Shaw describes what happens then:

> . . . When surgery is denied [the doctor] must try to keep the infant from suffering while natural forces sap the baby's life away. As a surgeon whose natural inclination is to use the scalpel to fight off death, standing by and watching a salvageable baby die is the most emotionally exhausting experience I know. It is easy at a conference, in a theoretical discussion, to decide that such infants should be allowed to die. It is altogether different to stand by in the nursery and watch as dehydration and infection wither a tiny being over hours and days. This is a terrible ordeal for me and the hospital staff— much more so than for the parents who never set foot in the nursery.[1]

I can understand why some people are opposed to all euthanasia, and insist that such infants must be allowed to live. I think I can also understand why other people favor destroying these babies quickly and painlessly. But why should anyone favor letting "dehydration and infection

---

[1] Anthony Shaw, "Doctor, Do We Have a Choice?" *New York Times Magazine* (January 30, 1972), p. 54.

wither a tiny being over hours and days?" The doctrine that says that a baby may be allowed to dehydrate and wither, but may not be given an injection that would end its life without suffering, seems so patently cruel as to require no further refutation. The strong language is not intended to offend, but only to put the point in the clearest possible way.

My second argument is that the conventional doctrine leads to decisions concerning life and death made on irrelevant grounds.

Consider again the case of the infants with Down's syndrome who need operations for congenital defects unrelated to the syndrome to live. Sometimes, there is no operation, and the baby dies, but when there is no such defect, the baby lives on. Now, an operation such as that to remove an intestinal obstruction is not prohibitively difficult. The reason why such operations are not performed in these cases is, clearly, that the child has Down's syndrome and the parents and doctor judge that because of that fact it is better for the child to die.

But notice that this situation is absurd, no matter what view one takes of the lives and potentials of such babies. If the life of such an infant is worth preserving, what does it matter if it needs a simple operation? Or, if one thinks it better that such a baby should not live on, what difference does it make that it happens to have an unobstructed intestinal tract? In either case, the matter of life and death is being decided on irrelevant grounds. It is the Down's syndrome, and not the intestine, that is the issue. The matter should be decided, if at all, on that basis, and not be allowed to depend on the essentially irrelevant question of whether the intestinal tract is blocked.

What makes this situation possible, of course, is the idea that when there is an intestinal blockage, one can "let the baby die," but when there is no such defect there is nothing that can be done, for one must not "kill" it. The fact that this idea leads to such results as deciding life or death on irrelevant grounds is another good reason why the doctrine should be rejected.

One reason why so many people think that there is an important moral difference between active and passive euthanasia is that they think killing someone is morally worse than letting someone die. But is it? Is killing, in itself, worse than letting die? To investigate this issue, two cases may be considered that are exactly alike except that one involves killing whereas the other involves letting someone die. Then, it can be asked whether this difference makes any difference to the moral assessments. It is important that the cases be exactly alike, except for this one difference, since otherwise one cannot be confident that it is this difference and not some other that accounts for any variation in the assessments of the two cases. So, let us consider this pair of cases:

In the first, Smith stands to gain a large inheritance if anything should happen to his six-year-old cousin. One evening while the child is taking his bath, Smith sneaks into the bathroom and drowns the child, and then arranges things so that it will look like an accident.

In the second, Jones also stands to gain if anything should happen to his six-year-old cousin. Like Smith, Jones sneaks in planning to drown the child in his bath. However, just as he enters the bathroom Jones sees the child slip and hit his head, and fall face down in the water. Jones is delighted; he stands by, ready to push the child's head back under if it is necessary, but it is not necessary. With only a little thrashing about, the child drowns all by himself, "accidentally," as Jones watches and does nothing.

Now Smith killed the child, whereas Jones "merely" let the child die. That is the only difference between them. Did either man behave better, from a moral point of view? If the difference between killing and letting die were in itself a morally important matter, one should say that Jones's behavior was less reprehensible than Smith's. But does one really want to say that? I think not. In the first place, both men acted from the same motive, personal gain, and both had exactly the same end in view when they acted. It may be inferred from Smith's conduct that he is a bad man, although that judgment may be withdrawn or modified if certain further facts are learned about him—for example, that he is mentally deranged. But would not the very same thing be inferred about Jones from his conduct? And would not the same further considerations also be relevant to any modification of this judgment? Moreover, suppose Jones pleaded, in his own defense, "After all, I didn't do anything except just stand there and watch the child drown. I didn't kill him; I only let him die." Again, if letting die were in itself less bad than killing, this defense should have at least some weight. But it does not. Such a "defense" can only be regarded as a grotesque perversion of moral reasoning. Morally speaking, it is no defense at all.

Now, it may be pointed out, quite properly, that the cases of euthanasia with which doctors are concerned are not like this at all. They do not involve personal gain or the destruction of normal healthy children. Doctors are concerned only with cases in which the patient's life is of no further use to him, or in which the patient's life has become or will soon become a terrible burden. However, the point is the same in these cases: the bare difference between killing and letting die does not, in itself, make a moral difference. If a doctor lets a patient die, for humane reasons, he is in the same moral position as if he had given the patient a lethal injection for humane reasons. If his decision was wrong—if, for example, the patient's illness was in fact curable—the decision would be equally regrettable no matter which method was used to carry it out. And if the doctor's decision was the right one, the method used is not in itself important.

The AMA policy statement isolates the crucial issue very well; the crucial issue is "the intentional termination of the life of one human being by another." But after identifying this issue, and forbidding "mercy killing," the statement goes on to deny that the cessation of treatment is the intentional termination of a life. This is where the mistake comes in, for what is the cessation of treatment, in these circumstances, if it is not "the intentional termination of the life of one human being by another?" Of course it is exactly that, and if it were not, there would be no point to it.

Many people will find this judgment hard to accept. One reason, I think, is that it is very easy to conflate the question of whether killing is, in itself, worse that letting die, with the very different question of whether most actual cases of killing are more reprehensible than most actual cases of letting die. Most actual cases of killing are clearly terrible (think, for example, of all the murders reported in the newspapers), and one hears of such cases every day. On the other hand, one hardly ever hears of a case of letting die, except for the actions of doctors who are motivated by humanitarian reasons. So one learns to think of killing in a much worse light than of letting die. But this does not mean that there is something about killing that makes it in itself worse than letting die, for it is not the bare difference between killing and letting die that makes the difference in these cases. Rather, the other factors—the murderer's motive of personal gain, for example, contrasted with the doctor's humanitarian motivation—account for different reactions to the different cases.

I have argued that killing is not in itself any worse than letting die; if my contention is right, it follows that active euthanasia is not any worse than passive euthanasia. What arguments can be given on the other side? The most common, I believe, is the following:

argument

> The important difference between active and passive euthanasia is that, in passive euthanasia, the doctor does not do anything to bring about the patient's death. The doctor does nothing, and the patient dies of whatever ills already afflict him. In active euthanasia, however, the doctor does something to bring about the patient's death: he kills him. The doctor who gives the patient with cancer a lethal injection has himself caused his patient's death: whereas if he merely ceases treatment, the cancer is the cause of the death.

A number of points need to be made here. The first is that it is not exactly correct to say that in passive euthanasia the doctor does nothing, for he does do one thing that is very important: he lets the patient die. "Letting someone die" is certainly different, in some respects, from other types of action—mainly in that it is a kind of action that one may perform by way of not performing certain other actions. For example, one may let a patient die by way of not giving medication, just as one may insult someone by way of not shaking his hand. But for any purpose of moral assessment, it is a type of action nonetheless. The decision to let a patient die is subject to moral appraisal in the same way that a decision to kill him would be subject to moral appraisal: it may be assessed as wise or unwise, compassionate or sadistic, right or wrong. If a doctor deliberately let a patient die who was suffering from a routinely curable illness, the doctor would certainly be to blame for what he had done, just as he would be to blame if he had needlessly killed the patient. Charges against him would then be appropriate. If so, it would be no defense at all for him to insist that he didn't "do anything." He would have done something very serious indeed, for he let his patient die.

Fixing the cause of death may be very important from a legal point of view, for it may determine whether criminal charges are brought against the doctor. But I do not think that this notion can be used to show a moral difference between active and passive euthanasia. The reason why it is considered bad to be the cause of someone's death is that death is regarded as a great evil—and so it is. However, if it has been decided that euthanasia—even passive euthanasia—is desirable in a given case, it has also been decided that in this instance death is no greater an evil than the patient's continued existence. And if this is true, the usual reason for not wanting to be the cause of someone's death simply does not apply.

Finally, doctors may think that all of this is only of academic interest—the sort of thing that philosophers may worry about but that has no practical bearing on their own work. After all, doctors must be concerned about the legal consequences of what they do, and active euthanasia is clearly forbidden by the law. But even so, doctors should also be concerned with the fact that the law is forcing upon them a moral doctrine that may well be indefensible, and has a considerable effect on their practices. Of course, most doctors are not now in the position of being coerced in this matter, for they do not regard themselves as merely going along with what the law requires. Rather, in statements such as the AMA policy statement that I have quoted, they are endorsing this doctrine as a central point of medical ethics. In that statement, active euthanasia is condemned not merely as illegal but as "contrary to that for which the medical profession stands," whereas passive euthanasia is approved. However, the preceding considerations suggest that there is really no moral difference between the two, considered in themselves (there may be important moral differences in some cases in their *consequences*, but, as I pointed out, these differences may make active euthanasia, and not passive euthanasia, the morally preferable option). So, whereas doctors may have to discriminate between active and passive euthanasia to satisfy the law, they should not do any more than that. In particular, they should not give the distinction any added authority and weight by writing it into official statements of medical ethics.

A Reply to Rachels on Active and Passive Euthanasia

Tom L. Beauchamp

James Rachels has recently argued that the distinction between active and passive euthanasia is neither appropriately used by the American Medical Association nor generally useful for the resolution of moral problems of euthanasia.[1] Indeed he believes this distinction—which he equates with the killing/letting die distinction—does not in itself have any moral importance. The chief object of his attack is the following statement adopted by the House of Delegates of the American Medical Association in 1973:

> The intentional termination of the life of one human being by another—mercy killing—is contrary to that for which the medical profession stands and is contrary to the policy of the American Medical Association.
>
> The cessation of the employment of extraordinary means to prolong the life of the body when there is irrefutable evidence that biological death is imminent is the decision of the patient and/or his immediate family. The advice and judgment of the physician should be freely available to the patient and/or his immediate family.[2]

Rachels constructs a powerful and interesting set of arguments against this statement. In this paper I attempt the following: (1) to challenge his views on the grounds that he does not appreciate the moral reasons which give weight to the active/passive distinction; and (2) to provide a constructive account of the moral relevance of the active/passive distinction; and (3) to offer reasons showing that Rachels may nonetheless be correct in urging that we *ought* to abandon the active/passive distinction for purposes of moral reasoning.

I

I would concede that the active/passive distinction is *sometimes* morally irrelevant. Of this Rachels convinces me. But it does not follow that it is *always* morally irrelevant. What we need, then, is a case where the distinc-

This paper is a heavily revised version of an article by the same title first published in T. Mappes and J. Zembaty, eds. *Social Ethics* (N.Y.: McGraw-Hill, 1976). Copyright © 1975, 1977 by Tom L. Beauchamp.

[1]James Rachels, "Active and Passive Euthanasia," *New England Journal of Medicine* **292** (January 9, 1975), pp. 78–80, and reprinted above, pp. 312–317.

[2]Rachels, p. 241, and reprinted above, p. 312.

tion is a morally relevant one and an explanation why it is so. Rachels himself uses the method of examining two cases which are exactly alike except that "one involves killing whereas the other involves letting die."[3] We may profitably begin by comparing the kinds of cases governed by the AMA's doctrine with the kinds of cases adduced by Rachels in order to assess the adequacy and fairness of his cases.

The second paragraph of the AMA statement is confined to a narrowly restricted range of passive euthanasia cases, viz., those (a) where the patients are on extraordinary means, (b) where irrefutable evidence of imminent death is available, and (c) where patient or family consent is available. Rachels' two cases involve conditions notably different from these:

> In the first, Smith stands to gain a large inheritance if anything should happen to his six-year-old cousin. One evening while the child is taking his bath, Smith sneaks into the bathroom and drowns the child, and then arranges things so that it will look like an accident.
>
> In the second, Jones also stands to gain if anything should happen to his six-year-old cousin. Like Smith, Jones sneaks in planning to drown the child in his bath. However, just as he enters the bathroom Jones sees the child slip and hit his head, and fall face down in the water. Jones is delighted; he stands by, ready to push the child's head back under if it is necessary, but it is not necessary. With only a little thrashing about, the child drowns all by himself, "accidentally," as Jones watches and does nothing.
>
> Now Smith killed the child, whereas Jones "merely" let the child die. That is the only difference between them.[4]

Rachels says there is no moral difference between the cases in terms of our moral assessments of Smith and Jones' behavior. This assessment seems fair enough, but what can Rachels' cases be said to prove, as they are so markedly disanalogous to the sorts of cases envisioned by the AMA proposal? Rachels concedes important disanalogies, but thinks them irrelevant:

> The point is the same in these cases: the bare difference between killing and letting die does not, in itself, make a moral difference. If a doctor lets a patient die, for humane reasons, he is in the same moral position as if he had given the patient a lethal injection for humane reasons.[5]

Three observations are immediately in order. First, Rachels seems to infer that from such cases we can conclude that the distinction between killing and letting die is *always* morally irrelevant. This conclusion is fallaciously derived. What the argument in fact shows, being an analogical argument, is only that in all *relevantly similar* cases the distinction does not

[3]Rachels, p. 243, and reprinted above, p. 314.

[4]Rachels, p. 243, and reprinted above, p. 314–315.

[5]Rachels, p. 244, and reprinted above, p. 315.

in itself make a moral difference. Since Rachels concedes that other cases are disanalogous, he seems thereby to concede that his argument is as weak as the analogy itself. Second, Rachels' cases involve two *unjustified* actions, one of killing and the other of letting die. The AMA statement distinguishes one set of cases of unjustified killing and another of *justified* cases of allowing to die. Nowhere is it claimed by the AMA that what makes the difference in these cases is the active/passive distinction itself. It is only implied that one set of cases, the justified set, *involves* (passive) letting die while the unjustified set *involves* (active) killing. While it is said that justified euthanasia cases are passive ones and unjustified ones active, it is not said either that what makes some acts justified is the fact of their being passive or that what makes others unjustified is the fact of their being active. This fact will prove to be of vital importance.

The third point is that in both of Rachels' cases the respective moral agents—Smith and Jones—are morally responsible for the death of the child and are morally blameworthy—even though Jones is presumably not causally responsible. In the first case death is caused by the agent, while in the second it is not; yet the second agent is no less morally responsible. While the law might find only the first homicidal, morality condemns the motives in each case as equally wrong, and it holds that the duty to save life in such cases is as compelling as the duty not to take life. I suggest that it is largely because of this equal degree of moral responsibility that there is no morally relevant difference in Rachels' cases. In the cases envisioned by the AMA, however, an agent is held to be responsible for taking life by actively killing but is not held to be morally required to preserve life, and so not responsible for death, when removing the patient from extraordinary means (under conditions a–c above). I shall elaborate this latter point momentarily. My only conclusion thus far is the negative one that Rachels' arguments rest on weak foundations. His cases are not relevantly similar to euthanasia cases and do not support his apparent conclusion that the active/passive distinction is *always* morally irrelevant.

II

I wish first to consider an argument that I believe has powerful intuitive appeal and probably is widely accepted as stating the main reason for rejecting Rachels' views. I will maintain that this argument fails, and so leaves Rachels' contentions untouched.

I begin with an actual case, the celebrated Quinlan case.[6] Karen Quinlan was in a coma, and was on a mechanical respirator which artifi-

---

[6]As recorded in the Opinion of Judge Robert Muir Jr., Docket No. C-201-75 of the Superior Court of New Jersey, Chancery Division, Morris County (November 10, 1975).

cially sustained her vital processes and which her parents wished to cease. At least some physicians believed there was irrefutable evidence that biological death was imminent and the coma irreversible. This case, under this description, closely conforms to the passive cases envisioned by the AMA. During an interview the father, Mr. Quinlan, asserted that he did not wish to kill his daughter, but only to remove her from the machines in order to see whether she would live or would die a natural death.[7] Suppose he had said—to envision now a second and hypothetical, but parallel case—that he wished only to see her die painlessly and therefore wished that the doctor could induce death by an overdose of morphine. Most of us would think the second act, which involves active killing, morally unjustified in these circumstances, while many of us would think the first act morally justified. (This is not the place to consider whether in fact it is justified, and if so under what conditions.) What accounts for the apparent morally relevant difference?

I have considered these two cases together in order to follow Rachels' method of entertaining parallel cases where the only difference is that the one case involves killing and the other letting die. However, there is a further difference, which crops up in the euthanasia context. The difference rests in our judgments of medical fallibility and moral responsibility. Mr. Quinlan seems to think that, after all, the doctors might be wrong. There is a remote possibility that she might live without the aid of a machine. But whether or not the medical prediction of death turns out to be accurate, if she dies then no one is morally responsible for directly bringing about or causing her death, as they would be if they caused her death by killing her. Rachels finds explanations which appeal to causal conditions unsatisfactory; but perhaps this is only because he fails to see the nature of the causal link. To bring about her death is by that act to preempt the possibility of life. To "allow her to die" by removing artificial equipment is to allow for the possibility of wrong diagnosis or incorrect prediction and hence to absolve oneself of moral responsibility for the taking of life under false assumptions. There may, of course, be utterly no empirical possibility of recovery in some cases since recovery would violate a law of nature. However, judgments of empirical impossibility in medicine are notoriously problematic—the reason for emphasizing medical fallibility. And in all the hard cases we do not *know* that recovery is empirically impossible, even if good *evidence* is available.

The above reason for invoking the active/passive distinction can now be generalized: Active termination of life removes all possibility of life for the patient, while passively ceasing extraordinary means may not. This is not trivial since patients have survived in several celebrated cases where, in

---

[7]See Judge Muir's Opinion, p. 18—a slightly different statement, but on the subject.

knowledgeable physicians' judgments, there was "irrefutable" evidence that death was imminent.[8]

One may, of course, be entirely responsible and culpable for another's death either by killing him or by letting him die. In such cases, of which Rachels' are examples, there is no morally significant difference between killing and letting die precisely because whatever one does, omits, or refrains from doing does not absolve one of responsibility. Either active or passive involvement renders one responsible for the death of another, and both involvements are equally wrong for the same principled moral reason: it is (*prima facie*) morally wrong to bring about the death of an innocent person capable of living whenever the causal intervention or negligence is intentional. (I use causal terms here because causal involvement need not be active, as when by one's negligence one is nonetheless causally responsible.) But not all cases of killing and letting die fall under this same moral principle. One is sometimes culpable for killing, because morally responsible as the agent for death, as when one pulls the plug on a respirator sustaining a recovering patient (a murder). But one is sometimes not culpable for letting die because not morally responsible as agent, as when one pulls the plug on a respirator sustaining an irreversibly comatose and unrecoverable patient (a routine procedure, where one is *merely* causally responsible).[9] Different degrees and means of involvement assess different degrees of responsibility, and our assessments of culpability can become intricately complex. The only point which now concerns us, however, is that because different moral principles may govern very similar circumstances, we are sometimes morally culpable for killing but not for letting die. And to many people it will seem that in passive cases we are not morally responsible for causing death, though we are responsible in active cases.

This argument is powerfully attractive. Although I was once inclined to accept it in virtually the identical form just developed.[10] I now think that, despite its intuitive appeal, it cannot be correct. It is true that different degrees and means of involvement entail different degrees of responsibility, but it does not follow that we are *not* responsible and therefore are absolved of possible culpability in *any* case of intentionally allowing to die. We are responsible and *perhaps* culpable in either active or passive cases.

---

[8]This problem of the strength of evidence also emerged in the Quinlan trial, as physicians disagreed whether the evidence was "irrefutable." Such disagreement, when added to the problems of medical fallibility and causal responsibility just outlined, provides in the eyes of some one important argument against the *legalization* of active euthanasia, as perhaps the AMA would agree.

[9]Among the moral reasons why one is held to be responsible in the first sort of case and not responsible in the second sort are, I believe, the moral grounds for the active/passive distinction under discussion in this section.

[10]In *Social Ethics*, as cited in the permission note to this article.

Here Rachels' argument is entirely to the point: It is not primarily a question of greater or lesser responsibility by an active or a passive means that should determine culpability. Rather, the question of culpability is decided by the moral *justification* for choosing either a passive or an active means. What the argument in the previous paragraph overlooks is that one might be unjustified in using an active means or unjustified in using a passive means, and hence be culpable in the use of either; yet one might be justified in using an active means or justified in using a passive means, and hence not be culpable in using either. Fallibility might just as well be present in a judgment to use one means as in a judgment to use another. (A judgment to allow to die is just as subject to being based on *knowledge which is fallible* as a judgment to kill.) Moreover, in either case, it is a matter of what one knows and believes, and not a matter of a particular kind of causal connection or causal chain. If we kill the patient, then we are certainly causally responsible for his death. But, similarly, if we cease treatment, and the patient dies, the patient might have recovered if treatment had been continued. The patient might have been saved in either case, and hence there is no morally relevant difference between the two cases. It is, therefore, simply beside the point that "one is sometimes culpable for killing . . . but one is sometimes not culpable for letting die"—as the above argument concludes.

Accordingly, despite its great intuitive appeal and frequent mention, this argument from responsibility fails.

III

There may, however, be more compelling arguments against Rachels, and I wish now to provide what I believe is the most significant argument that can be adduced in defense of the active/passive distinction. I shall develop this argument by combining (1) so-called wedge or slippery slope arguments with (2) recent arguments in defense of rule utilitarianism. I shall explain each in turn and show how in combination they may be used to defend the active/passive distinction.

(1) *Wedge arguments* proceed as follows: if killing were allowed, even under the guise of a merciful extinction of life, a dangerous wedge would be introduced which places all "undesirable" or "unworthy" human life in a precarious condition. Proponents of wedge arguments believe the initial wedge places us on a slippery slope for at least one of two reasons: (i) It is said that our justifying principles leave us with no principled way to avoid the slide into saying that all sorts of killings would be justified under similar conditions. Here it is thought that once killing is allowed, a firm line between justified and unjustified killings cannot be securely drawn. It is thought best not to redraw the line in the first place, for redrawing it will

inevitably lead to a downhill slide. It is then often pointed out that as a matter of historical record this is precisely what has occurred in the darker regions of human history, including the Nazi era, where euthanasia began with the best intentions for horribly ill, non-Jewish Germans and gradually spread to anyone deemed an enemy of the people. (ii) Second, it is said that our basic principles against killing will be gradually eroded once some form of killing is legitimated. For example, it is said that permitting voluntary euthanasia will lead to permitting involuntary euthanasia, which will in turn lead to permitting euthanasia for those who are a nuisance to society (idiots, recidivist criminals, defective newborns, and the insane, e.g.). Gradually other principles which instill respect for human life will be eroded or abandoned in the process.

I am not inclined to accept the first reason (i).[11] If our justifying principles are themselves justified, then any action they warrant would be justified. Accordingly, I shall only be concerned with the second approach (ii).

(2) *Rule utilitarianism* is the position that a society ought to adopt a rule if its acceptance would have better consequences for the common good (greater social utility) than any comparable rule could have in that society. Any action is right if it conforms to a valid rule and wrong if it violates the rule. Sometimes it is said that alternative rules should be measured against one another, while it has also been suggested that whole moral *codes* (complete sets of rules) rather than individual rules should be compared. While I prefer the latter formulation (Brandt's), this internal dispute need not detain us here. The important point is that a particular rule or a particular code of rules is morally justified if and only if there is no other competing rule or moral code whose acceptance would have a higher utility value for society, and where a rule's acceptability is contingent upon the consequences which would result if the rule were made current.

Wedge arguments, when conjoined with rule utilitarian arguments, may be applied to euthanasia issues in the following way. We presently subscribe to a no-active-euthanasia rule (which the AMA suggests we retain). Imagine now that in our society we make current a restricted-active-euthanasia rule (as Rachels seems to urge). Which of these two moral rules would, if enacted, have the consequence of maximizing social utility? Clearly a restricted-active-euthanasia rule would have *some* utility value, as Rachels notes, since some intense and uncontrollable suffering would be eliminated. However, it may not have the highest utility value in the structure of our present code or in any imaginable code which could be made current, and therefore may not be a component in the

---

[11]An argument of this form, which I find unacceptable for reasons given below, is Arthur Dyck, "Beneficent Euthanasia and Benemortasia: Alternative Views of Mercy," in M. Kohl, ed., *Beneficent Euthanasia* (Buffalo, N.Y.: Prometheus Books, 1975), pp. 120f.

ideal code for our society. If wedge arguments raise any serious questions at all, as I think they do, they rest in this area of whether a code would be weakened or strengthened by the addition of active euthanasia principles. For the disutility of introducing legitimate killing into one's moral code (in the form of active euthanasia rules) may, in the long run, outweigh the utility of doing so, as a result of the eroding effect such a relaxation would have on rules in the code which demand respect for human life. If, for example, rules permitting active killing were introduced, it is not implausible to suppose that destroying defective newborns (a form of involuntary euthanasia) would become an accepted and common practice, that as population increases occur the aged will be even more neglectable and neglected than they now are, that capital punishment for a wide variety of crimes would be increasingly tempting, that some doctors would have appreciably reduced fears of actively injecting fatal doses whenever it seemed to them propitious to do so, and that laws of war against killing would erode in efficacy even beyond their already abysmal level.

A hundred such possible consequences might easily be imagined. But these few are sufficient to make the larger point that such rules permitting killing could lead to a general reduction of respect for human life. Rules against killing in a moral code are not *isolated* moral principles; they are pieces of a web of rules against killing which forms the code. The more threads one removes, the weaker the fabric becomes. And if, as I believe, moral principles against active killing have the deep and continuously civilizing effect of promoting respect for life, and if principles which allow passively letting die (as envisioned in the AMA statement) do not themselves cut against this effect, then this seems an important reason for the maintenance of the active/passive distinction. (By the logic of the above argument, passively letting die would also have to be prohibited if a rule permitting it had the serious adverse consequence of eroding acceptance of rules protective of respect for life. While this prospect seems to me improbable, I can hardly claim to have refuted those conservatives who would claim that even rules which sanction letting die place us on a precarious slippery slope.)

A troublesome problem, however, confronts my use of utilitarian and wedge arguments. Most all of us would agree that both killing and letting die are justified under some conditions. Killings in self-defense and in "just" wars are widely accepted as justified because the conditions excuse the killing. If society can withstand these exceptions to moral rules prohibiting killing, then why is it not plausible to suppose society can accept another excusing exception in the form of justified active euthanasia? This is an important and worthy objection, but not a decisive one. The defenseless and the dying are significantly different classes of persons from aggressors who attack individuals and/or nations. In the case of aggressors, one does not confront the question whether their lives are no longer *worth living*. Rather, we reach the judgment that the aggressors' morally blameworthy actions justify counteractions. But in the case of the dying and the otherwise ill, there is no morally blameworthy action to justify our own. Here we are required to accept the judgment that their lives are no longer *worth living* in order to believe that the termination of their lives is justified. It is the latter sort of judgment which is feared by those who take the wedge argument seriously. We do not now permit and never have permitted the taking of morally blameless lives. I think this is the key to understanding why recent cases of intentionally allowing the death of defective newborns (as in the now famous case at the Johns Hopkins Hospital) have generated such protracted controversy. Even if such newborns could not have led meaningful lives (a matter of some controversy), it is the wedged foot in the door which creates the most intense worries. For if we once take a decision to allow a restricted infanticide justification or any justification at all on grounds that a life is not meaningful or not worth living, we have qualified our moral rules against killing. That this qualification is a matter of the utmost seriousness needs no argument. I mention it here only to show why the wedge argument may have moral force even though we *already* allow some very different conditions to justify intentional killing.

There is one final utilitarian reason favoring the preservation of the active/passive distinction.[12] Suppose we distinguish the following two types of cases of wrongly diagnosed patients:

1. Patients wrongly diagnosed as hopeless, and who will survive even if a treatment *is* ceased (in order to allow a natural death).
2. Patients wrongly diagnosed as hopeless, and who will survive only if the treatment is *not ceased* (in order to allow a natural death).

If a social rule permitting only passive euthanasia were in effect, then doctors and families who "allowed death" would lose only patients in class 2, not those in class 1; whereas if active euthanasia were permitted, at least some patients in class 1 would be needlessly lost. Thus, the consequence of a no-active-euthanasia rule would be to save some lives which could not be saved if both forms of euthanasia were allowed. This reason is not a *decisive* reason for favoring a policy of passive euthanasia, since these classes (1 and 2) are likely to be very small and since there might be counterbalancing reasons (extreme pain, autonomous expression of the patient, etc.) in favor of active euthanasia. But certainly it is *a* reason favoring only passive euthanasia and one which is morally relevant and ought to be considered along with other moral reasons.

---

[12]I owe most of this argument to James Rachels, whose comments on an earlier draft of this paper led to several significant alterations.

IV

It may still be insisted that my case has not touched Rachels' leading claim, for I have not shown, as Rachels puts it, that it is "the bare difference between killing and letting die that makes the difference in these cases."[13] True, I have not shown this, and in my judgment it cannot be shown. But this concession does not require capitulation to Rachels' argument. I adduced a case which is at the center of our moral intuition that killing is morally different (in at least some cases) from letting die; and I then attempted to account for at least part of the grounds for this belief. The grounds turn out to be other than the *bare* difference, but nevertheless *make* the distinction morally relevant. The identical point can be made regarding the voluntary/involuntary distinction, as it is commonly applied to euthanasia. It is not the bare difference between voluntary euthanasia (i.e., euthanasia with patient consent) and involuntary euthanasia (i.e., without patient consent) that makes one justifiable and one not. Independent moral grounds based on, for example, respect for autonomy or beneficence, or perhaps justice will alone make the moral difference.

In order to illustrate this general claim, let us presume that it is sometimes justified to kill another person and sometimes justified to allow another to die. Suppose, for example, that one may kill in self-defense and may allow to die when a promise has been made to someone that he would be allowed to die. Here conditions of self-defense and promising justify actions. But suppose now that someone A promises in exactly similar circumstances to kill someone B at B's request, and also that someone C allows someone D to die in an act of self-defense. Surely A is obliged equally to kill or to let die if he promised; and surely C is permitted to let D die if it is a matter of defending C's life. If this analysis is correct, then it follows that killing is sometimes right, sometimes wrong, depending on the circumstances, and the same is true of letting die. It is the justifying reasons which make the difference whether an action is right, not merely the kind of action it is.

Now, *if* letting die led to disastrous conclusions but killing did not, then letting die but not killing would be wrong. Consider, for example, a possible world in which dying would be indefinitely prolongable even if all extraordinary therapy were removed and the patient were allowed to die. Suppose that it costs over one million dollars to let each patient die, that nurses consistently commit suicide from caring for those being "allowed to die," that physicians are constantly being successfully sued for malpractice for allowing death by cruel and wrongful means, and that hospitals are uncontrollably overcrowded and their wards filled with

[13]Rachels, p. 244, and reprinted above, p. 316.

communicable diseases which afflict only the dying. Now suppose further that killing in this possible world is quick, painless, and easily monitored. I submit that in this world we would believe that *killing is morally acceptable but that allowing to die is morally unacceptable*. The point of this example is again that it is the circumstances that make the difference, not the bare difference between killing and letting die.

It is, however, worth noticing that there is nothing in the AMA statement which says that the bare difference between killing and letting die itself and alone makes the difference in our differing moral assessments of rightness and wrongness. Rachels forces this interpretation on the statement. Some philosophers may have thought the bare difference makes the difference, but there is scant evidence that the AMA or any thoughtful ethicist *must* believe it in order to defend the relevance and importance of the active/passive distinction. When this conclusion is coupled with my earlier argument that from Rachels' paradigm cases it follows only that the active/passive distinction is sometimes, but not always, morally irrelevant, it would seem that his case against the AMA is rendered highly questionable.

V

There remains, however, the important question as to whether we *ought* to accept the distinction between active and passive euthanasia, now that we are clear about (at least one way of drawing) the moral grounds for its invocation. That is, should we employ the distinction in order to judge some acts of euthanasia justified and others not justified? Here, as the hesitant previous paragraph indicates, I am uncertain. This problem is a substantive moral issue—not merely a conceptual one—and would require at a minimum a lengthy assessment of wedge arguments and related utilitarian considerations. In important respects empirical questions are involved in this assessment. We should like to know, and yet have hardly any evidence to indicate, what the consequences would be for our society if we were to allow the use of active means to produce death. The best hope for making such an assessment has seemed to some to rest in analogies to suicide and capital punishment statutes. Here it may reasonably be asked whether recent liberalizations of laws limiting these forms of killing have served as the thin end of a wedge leading to a breakdown of principles protecting life or to widespread violations of moral principles. Nonetheless, such analogies do not seem to me promising, since they are still fairly remote from the pertinent issue of the consequences of allowing active humanitarian killing of one person by another.

It is interesting to notice the outcome of the Kamisar-Williams debate on euthanasia—which is almost exclusively cast by both writers in a consequential, utilitarian framework.[14] At one crucial point in the debate, where possible consequences of laws permitting euthanasia are under discussion, they exchange "perhaps" judgments:

> I [Williams] will return Kamisar the compliment and say: "Perhaps." We are certainly in an area where no solution is going to make things quite easy and happy for everybody, and all sorts of embarrassments may be conjectured. But these embarrassments are not avoided by keeping to the present law: we suffer from them already.[15]

Because of the grave difficulties which stand in the way of making accurate predictions about the impact of liberalized euthanasia laws—especially those that would permit active killing—it is not surprising that those who debate the subject would reach a point of exchanging such "perhaps" judgments. And that is why, so it seems to me, we are uncertain whether to perpetuate or to abandon the active/passive distinction in our moral thinking about euthanasia. I think we *do* perpetuate it in medicine, law, and ethics because we are still somewhat uncertain about the conditions under which *passive* euthanasia should be permitted by law (which is one form of social *rule*). We are unsure about what the consequences will be of the California "Natural Death Act" and all those similar acts passed by other states which have followed in its path. If no untoward results occur, and the balance of the results seems favorable, then we will perhaps be less concerned about further liberalizations of euthanasia laws. If untoward results do occur (on a widespread scale), then we would be most reluctant to accept further liberalizations and might even abolish natural death acts.

In short, I have argued in this section that euthanasia in its active and its passive forms presents us with a dilemma which can be developed by using powerful consequentialist arguments on each side, yet there is little clarity concerning the proper resolution of the dilemma precisely because of our uncertainty regarding proclaimed consequences.

[14]Williams bases his pro-euthanasia argument on the prevention of two consequences: (1) loss of liberty and (2) cruelty. Kamisar bases his anti-euthanasia position on three projected consequences of euthanasia laws: (1) mistaken diagnosis, (2) pressured decisions by seriously ill patients, and (3) the wedge of the laws will lead to legalized involuntary euthanasia. Kamisar admits that individual acts of euthanasia are sometimes justified. It is the rule that he opposes. He is thus clearly a rule-utilitarian, and I believe Williams is as well (cf. his views on children and the senile). Their assessments of wedge arguments are, however, radically different.

[15]Glanville Williams, "Mercy-Killing Legislation—A Rejoinder," *Minnesota Law Review* **43** (no. 1) (1958), p. 5.

I reach two conclusions at the end of these several arguments. First, I think Rachels is incorrect in arguing that the distinction between active and passive is (always) morally irrelevant. It may well be relevant, and for moral reasons—the reasons adduced in section III above. Second, I think nonetheless that Rachels may ultimately be shown correct in his contention that we ought to dispense with the active/passive distinction—for reasons adduced in IV–V. But if he is ultimately judged correct, it will be because we have come to see that some forms of active killing have generally acceptable social consequences, and not primarily because of the arguments he adduces in his paper—even though *something* may be said for each of these arguments. Of course, in one respect I have conceded a great deal to Rachels. The bare difference argument is vital to his position, and I have fully agreed to it. On the other hand, I do not see that the bare difference argument does play or need play a major role in our moral thinking—or in that of the AMA.

Defective Newborns and the Morality of Termination
Richard B. Brandt

The *legal* rights of a fetus are very different from those of a newborn. The fetus may be aborted, legally, for any reason or no reason up to twenty-four or twenty-eight weeks (U.S. Supreme Court, *Roe v. Wade*). But, at least in theory, immediately after birth an infant has all the legal rights of the adult, including the right to life.

The topic of this paper, however, is to identify the moral rights of the newborn, specifically whether *defective* newborns have a right to life. But it is simpler to talk, not about "rights to life," but about when or whether it is *morally right* either actively or passively (by withdrawal of life-support measures) to terminate defective newborns. It is also better because the conception of a right involves the notion of a sphere of autonomy—something is to be done or omitted, but only if the subject of the rights wants or consents—and this fact is apt to be confusing or oversimplifying. Surely what we want to know is whether termination is

From Marvin Kohl, ed., *Infanticide and the Value of Life* (Buffalo, N.Y.: Prometheus Books, 1978), pp. 46-60. Reprinted with the permission of Prometheus Books.

morally right or wrong, and nothing can turn on the semantics of the concept of a "right."[1]

What does one have to do in order to support some answer to these questions? One thing we can do is ask—and I think myself that the answer to this question is definitive for our purposes—whether rational or fully informed persons would, in view of the total consequences, support a moral code for a society in which they expected to live, with one, or another, provision on this matter. (I believe a fully rational person will at least normally have some degree of benevolence, or positive interest in the welfare or happiness of others; I shall not attempt to specify how much.) Since, however, I do not expect that everyone else will agree that answering this question would show what is morally right, I shall, for their benefit, also argue that certain moral principles on this matter are coherent with strong moral convictions of reflective people; or, to use Rawls's terminology, that a certain principle on the matter would belong to a system of moral principles in "reflective equilibrium."

Historically, many writers, including Pope Pius XI in *Casti Connubii* (1930), have affirmed an absolute prohibition against killing anyone who is neither guilty of a capital crime nor an unjust assailant threatening one's life (self-defense), except in case of "extreme necessity." Presumably the prohibition is intended to include withholding of food or liquid from a newborn, although strictly speaking this is only *failing* to do something, not actually *doing* something to bring about a death. (Would writers in this tradition demand, on moral grounds, that complicated and expensive surgery be undertaken to save a life? Such surgery is going beyond normal care, and in some cases beyond what earlier writers even conceived.) However the intentions of these writers may be, we should observe that historically their moral condemnation of all killing (except for the cases mentioned) derives from the Biblical injunction, "Thou shalt not kill," which, as it stands and without interpretation, may be taken to forbid suicide, killing of animals, perhaps even plants, and hence cannot be taken seriously.

Presumably a moral code that is coherent with our intuitions and that rational persons would support for their society would include some prohibition of killing, but it is another matter to identify the exact class to which such a prohibition is to apply. For one thing, I would doubt that killing one's self would be included—although one might be forbidden to kill one's self if that would work severe hardship on others, or conflict with the discharge of one's other moral obligations. And, possibly, defective newborns would *not* be included in the class. Further, a decision has

[1]Here I disagree with Michael Tooley, "Abortion and Infanticide," *Philosophy and Public Affairs* **2** (1972), pp. 37–65, esp. pp. 44–49.

to be made whether the prohibition of killing is *absolute* or only *prima facie*, meaning by "prima facie" that the duty not to kill might be outweighed by some other duty (or right) stronger in the circumstances, which could be fulfilled only by killing. In case this distinction is made, we would have to decide whether defective newborns fall within the scope of even a prima facie moral prohibition against killing. I shall, however, not attempt to make this fine distinction here, and shall simply inquire whether, everything considered, defective newborns—or some identifiable group of them—are excluded from the moral prohibition against killing.

THE PROSPECTIVE QUALITY
OF LIFE OF DEFECTIVE NEWBORNS

Suppose that killing a defective newborn, or allowing it to die, would not be an *injury*, but would rather be doing the infant a favor. In that case we should feel intuitively less opposed to termination of newborns, and presumably rational persons would be less inclined to support a moral code with a prohibition against such action. In that case we would feel rather as we do about a person's preventing a suicide attempt from being successful, in order that the person be elaborately tortured to death at a later stage. It is no favor to the prospective suicide to save his life; similarly, if the prospective life of defective newborns is bad we are doing them a favor to let them die.

It may be said that we have no way of knowing what the conscious experiences of defective children are like, and that we have no competence in any case to decide when or what kind of life is bad or not worth living. Further, it may be said that predictions about a defective newborn's prospects for the future are precarious, in view of possible further advances of medicine. It does seem, however, that here, as everywhere, the rational person will follow the evidence about the present or future facts. But there is a question how to decide whether a life is bad or not worth living.

In the case of *some* defective newborns, it seems clear that their prospective life is bad. Suppose, as sometimes happens, a child is hydrocephalic with an extremely low I.Q., is blind and deaf, has no control over its body, can only lie on its back all day and have all its needs taken care of by others, and even cries out with pain when it is touched or lifted. Infants born with spina bifida—and these number over two per one thousand births—are normally not quite so badly off, but are often nearly so.

But what criterion are we using if we say that such a life is bad? One criterion might be called a "happiness" criterion. If a person *likes* a moment of experience while he is having it, his life is so far good; if a person *dislikes* a moment of experience while he is having it, his life is so far bad. Based on such reactions, we might construct a "happiness curve" for a person, going up above the indifference axis when a moment of experience is liked—and how far above depending on how strongly it is liked—and dipping down below the line when a moment is disliked. Then this criterion would say that a life is worth living if there is a net balance of positive area under the curve over a lifetime, and that it is bad if there is a net balance of negative area. One might adopt some different criterion: for instance, one might say that a life is worth living if a person would *want* to live it over again given that, at the end, he could remember the whole of it with perfect vividness in some kind of grand intuitive awareness. Such a response to this hypothetical holistic intuition, however, would likely be affected by the state of the person's drives or moods at the time, and the conception strikes me as unconvincing, compared with the moment-by-moment reaction to what is going on. Let us, for the sake of the argument, adopt the happiness criterion.[2]

Is the prospective life of the seriously defective newborn, like the one described above, bad or good according to this criterion? One thing seems clear: that it is *less* good than is the prospective life of a normal infant. But is it bad?

We have to do some extrapolating from what we know. For instance, such a child will presumably suffer from severe sensory deprivation; he is simply not getting interesting stimuli. On the basis of laboratory data, it is plausible to think the child's experience is at best boring or uncomfortable. If the child's experience is painful, of course, its moments are, so far, on the negative side. One must suppose that such a child hardly suffers from disappointment, since it will not learn to expect anything exciting, beyond being fed and fondled, and these events will be regularly forthcoming. One might expect such a child to suffer from isolation and loneliness, but insofar as this is true, the object of dislike probably should be classified as just sensory deprivation; dislike of loneliness seems to depend on the

---

[2]Professor P. Foot has made interesting remarks on when a life is worth living. See her "Euthanasia," *Philosophy and Public Affairs* **6** (1977), 85–112, especially pp. 95–96. She suggests that a good life must "contain a minimum of basic goods," although not necessarily a favorable balance of good over evil elements. When does she think this minimum fails? For one thing, in extreme senility or severe brain damage. She also cites as examples of conditions for minimal goods that "a man is not driven to work far beyond his capacity; that he has the support of a family or community; that he can more or less satisfy his hunger; that he has hopes for the future; that he can lie down to rest at night." Overwhelming pain or nausea, or crippling depression, she says, also can make life not worth living. All of these, of course, except for cases of senility and brain damage, are factors fixing whether stretches of living are highly unpleasant.

If a person thinks that life is not good unless it realizes certain human potentialities, he will think life can be bad even if liked—and so far sets a higher standard than the happiness criterion. But Foot and such writers may say that even when life is not pleasant on balance, it can still be good if human potentialities are being realized or these basic minimal conditions are met; and in that sense they set a lower standard.

deprivation of past pleasures of human company. There are also some positive enjoyments: of eating, drinking, elimination, seeing the nurse coming with food, and so on. But the brief enjoyments can hardly balance the long stretches of boredom, discomfort, or even pain. On the whole, the lives of such children are bad according to the happiness criterion.

Naturally we cannot generalize about the cases of all "defective" newborns; there are all sorts of defects, and the cases I have described are about the worst. A child with spina bifida may, if he survives the numerous operations, I suppose, adjust to the frustrations of immobility; he may become accustomed to the embarrassments of no bladder or bowel control; he may have some intellectual enjoyments like playing chess; he will suffer from observing what others have but he cannot, such as sexual satisfactions, in addition to the pain of repeated surgery. How does it all balance out? Surely not as very good, but perhaps above the indifference level.

It may fairly be said, I think, that the lives of some defective newborns are destined to be bad on the whole, and it would be a favor to them if their lives were terminated. Contrariwise, the prospective lives of many defective newborns are modestly pleasant, and it would be some injury to them to be terminated, albeit the lives they will live are ones some of us would prefer not to live at all.

CONSENT

Let us now make a second suggestion, not this time that termination of a defective newborn would be doing him a favor, but this time that he *consents* to termination, in the sense of expressing a rational deliberated preference for this. In that case I suggest that intuitively we would be *more* favorably inclined to judge that it is right to let the defective die, and I suggest also that for that case rational persons would be more ready to support a moral code permitting termination. Notice that we think that if an ill person has signified what we think a rational and deliberated desire to die, we are morally better justified in withdrawing life-supporting measures than we otherwise would be.

The newborn, however, is incapable of expressing his preference (giving consent) at all, much less expressing a rational deliberated preference. There could in theory be court-appointed guardians or proxies, presumably disinterested parties, authorized to give such consent on his behalf; but even so this would not be *his* consent.

Nevertheless, there is a fact about the mental life of the newborn (defective or not) such that, if he could understand the fact, it seems he would not object—even rationally or after deliberation, if that were possible—to his life being terminated, or to his parents substituting another child in his place. This suggestion may seem absurd, but let us see. The explanation runs along the lines of an argument I once used to support the morality of abortion. I quote the paragraph in which this argument was introduced:[3]

> Suppose I were seriously ill, and were told that, for a sizeable fee, an operation to save "my life" could be performed, of the following sort: my brain would be removed to another body which could provide a normal life, but the unfortunate result of the operation would be that my memory and learned abilities would be wholly erased, and that the forming of memory brain traces must begin again from scratch, as in a newborn baby. Now, how large a fee would I be willing to pay for this operation, when the alternative is my peaceful demise? My own answer would be: None at all. I would take no interest in the continued existence of "myself" in that sense, and I would rather add the sizeable fee to the inheritance of my children. . . . I cannot see the point of forfeiting my children's inheritance in order to start off a person who is brand new except that he happens to enjoy the benefit of having my present brain, without the memory traces. It appears that some continuity of memory is a necessary condition for personal identity *in an important sense*.

My argument was that the position of a fetus, at the end of the first trimester, is essentially the same as that of the person contemplating this operation: he will consider that the baby born after six more months will not be *he* in any *important* and *motivating* sense (there will be no continuity of memory, and, indeed, maybe nothing to have been remembered), and the later existence of this baby, in a sense bodily continuous with his present body, would be a matter of indifference to him. So, I argued, nothing is being done to the fetus that he would object to having done if he understood the situation.

What do I think is necessary in order for the continuation of my body with its conscious experiences to be worthwhile? One thing is that it is able to remember the events I can now remember; another is that it takes some interest in the projects I am now planning and remembers them as my projects; another is that it recognizes my friends and had warm feelings for them, and so on. Reflection on these states of a future continuation of my body with its experiences is what makes the idea motivating. But such motivating reflection for a newborn is impossible: he has no memories that he wants recalled later; he has no plans to execute; he has no warm feelings for other persons. He has simply not had the length of life necessary for these to come about. Not only that: the conception of these things cannot be motivating because the concept of some state of affairs being motivating requires roughly a past experience in which similar states of affairs were satisfying, and he has not lived long enough for

[3]Richard B. Brandt, "The Morality of Abortion," in an earlier form in *The Monist* **56** (1972), 504–526, and in revised form in R.L. Perkins, ed., *Abortion: Pro and Con* (Cambridge, Mass.: Schenkman, 1974).

the requisite conditioning to have taken place. (The most one could say is that the image of warm milk in his mouth is attractive; he might answer affirmatively if it could be put to him whether he would be aversive to the idea of no more warm milk.) So we can say, not merely that the newborn does not want the continuation of himself as a subject of experiences (he has not the conceptual framework for this); he does not want *anything* that his own survival would promote. It is like the case of the operation: there is nothing I want that the survival of my brain with no memory would promote. Give the newborn as much *conceptual* framework as you like; the *wants* are not there, which could give significance to the continuance of his life.

The newborn, then, is bound to be *indifferent* to the idea of a continuation of the stream of his experiences, even if he clearly has the idea of that. It seems we can *know* this about him.

The truth of all this is still not for it to be the case that the newborn, defective or not, gives *consent* to, or expresses a preference for, the termination of his life. *Consent* is a performance, normally linguistic, but always requiring some conventional *sign*. A newborn, who has not yet learned how to signalize consent, cannot give consent. And it may be thought that this difference makes all the difference.

In order to see what difference it does make in this case, we should ask what makes adult consent morally important. Why is it that we think euthanasia can be practiced on an adult only if he gives his consent, at least his implied consent (e.g., by previous statements)? There seem to be two reasons. The first is that a person is more likely to be concerned with his own welfare, and to take steps to secure it, than are others, even his good friends. Giving an individual control over his own life, and not permitting others to take control except when he consents, is normally to promote his welfare. An individual may, of course, behave stupidly or shortsightedly, but we think that on the whole a person's welfare is best secured if decisions about it are in his hands; and it is best for society in the normal case (not for criminals, etc.) if persons' own lives are well-served. The second reason is the feeling of security a person can have, if he knows the major decisions about himself are in his own hands. When they are not, a person can easily, and in some cases very reasonably, suppose that other persons may well be able to do something to him that he would very much like them not to do. He does not have to worry about that if he knows they cannot do it without his consent.

Are things different with the newborn? At least he, like the fetus, is not yet able to suffer from insecurity; he cannot worry about what others may do to him. So the second reason for requiring consent cannot have any importance in his case. His situation is thus very unlike that of the senile adult, for an adult can worry about what others may do to him if they judge him senile. And this worry can well cast a shadow over a lot of life. But how about the first reason? Here matters are more complex. In the case of children, we think their own lives are better cared for if certain decisions are in the hands of others: the child may not want to visit the dentist, but the parents know that his best interests are served by going, and they make him go. The same for compulsory school attendance. And the same for the newborn. But there is another point: that society has an interest, at certain crucial points, that may not be served by doing just exactly what is for the lifelong interest of the newborn. There are huge costs that are relevant, in the case of the defective newborn. I shall go into that problem in a moment. It seems, then, that in the case of the newborn, *consent* cannot have the moral importance that it has in the case of adults.

On the other hand, then, the newborn will not *care* whether his life is terminated, even if he understands his situation perfectly; and, on the other hand, consent does not have the moral importance in his case that it has for adults. So, while it seems true that we would feel better about permitting termination of defective newborns if only they could give rational and deliberated consent and gave it, nevertheless when we bear the foregoing two points in mind, the absence of consent does not seem morally crucial in their case. We can understand why rational persons deciding which moral code to support for their society would not make the giving of consent a necessary condition for feeling free to terminate an infant's life when such action was morally indicated by the other features of the situation.

REPLACEMENT IN ORDER TO GET A BETTER LIFE

Let us now think of an example owing to Derek Parfit. Suppose a woman wants a child, but is told that if she conceives a child now it will be defective, whereas if she waits three months she will produce a normal child. Obviously we think it would be wrong for the mother not to delay. (If she delays, the child she will have is not the *same* child as the one she would have had if she had not delayed, but it will have a better life.) This is the sole reason why we think she should delay and have the later-born child.

Suppose, however, a woman conceives but discovers only three months later that the fetus will become a defective child, but that she can have a normal child if she has an abortion and tries again. Now this time there is still the same reason for having the abortion that there formerly was for the delay: that she will produce a child with a better life. Ought she not then to have the abortion? If the child's life is bad, he could well complain that he had been injured by deliberately being brought to term. Would he complain if he were aborted, in favor of the later normal child? Not if the argument of the preceding section is correct.

But now suppose the woman does not discover until after she gives birth that the child is seriously defective, but that she could conceive again and have a normal child. Are things really different, in the first few days? One might think that a benevolent person would want, in each of these cases, the substitution of a normal child for the defective one, of the better life for the worse one.

THE COST AND ITS RELEVANCE

It is agreed that the burden of care for a defective infant, say one born with spina bifida, is huge. The cost of surgery alone for an infant with spina bifida has been estimated to be around $275,000.[4] In many places this cost must be met by the family of the child, and there is the additional cost of care in an institution, if the child's condition does not permit care at home—and a very modest estimate of the monthly cost at present is $1,100. To meet even the surgical costs, not to mention monthly payments for continuing care, the lives of members of the family must be at a most spartan level for many years. The psychological effects of this, and equally, if not more so, of care provided at home, are far-reaching; they are apt to destroy the marriage and to cause psychological problems for the siblings. There is the on-going anxiety, the regular visits, the continuing presence of a caretaker if the child is in the home. In one way or another the continued existence of the child is apt to reduce dramatically the quality of life of the family as a whole.

It can be and has been argued that such costs, while real, are irrelevant to the moral problem of what should be done.[5] It is obvious, however, that rational persons, when deciding which moral code to support, would take these human costs into account. As indeed they should: the parents and siblings are also human beings with lives to live, and any sacrifices a given law or moral system might call on them to make must be taken into account in deciding between laws and moral codes. Everyone will feel sympathy for a helpless newborn; but everyone should also think, equally vividly, of all the others who will suffer and just how they will suffer—and, of course, as indicated above, of just what kind of life the

[4]See A.M. Shaw and I.A. Shaw, in S. Gorovitz, et al., *Moral Problems in Medicine* (Englewood Cliffs, N.J.: Prentice-Hall, 1976), pp. 335–341.

[5]See, for instance, Philippa Foot, "Euthanasia," esp. pp. 109–111. She writes: "So it is not for their sake but to avoid trouble to others that they are allowed to die. When brought out into the open this seems unacceptable; at least we do not easily accept the principle that adults who need special care should be counted too burdensome to be kept alive." I would think that "to avoid trouble to others" is hardly the terminology to describe the havoc that is apt to be produced. I agree that adults should not be allowed to die, or actively killed, without their consent, possibly except when they cannot give consent but are in great pain; but the reasons that justify different behavior in the two situations have appeared in the section, "Consent."

defective newborn will have in any case. There is a choice here between allowing a newborn to die (possibly a favor to it, and in any case not a serious loss), and imposing a very heavy burden on the family for many years to come.

Philosophers who think the cost to others is irrelevant to what should be done should reflect that we do not accept the general principle that lives should be saved at no matter what cost. For instance, ships are deliberately built with only a certain margin of safety; they could be built so that they would hardly sink in any storm, but to do so would be economically unfeasible. We do not think we should require a standard of safety for automobiles that goes beyond a certain point of expense and inconvenience; we are prepared to risk a few extra deaths. And how about the lives we are willing to lose in war, in order to assure a certain kind of economic order or democracy or free speech? Surely there is a point at which the loss of a life (or the abbreviation of a life) and the cost to others become comparable. Is it obvious that the continuation of a marginal kind of life for a child takes moral precedence over providing a college education for one or more of his siblings? Some comparisons will be hard to make, but continuing even a marginally pleasant life hardly has absolute priority.

DRAWING LINES

There are two questions which must be answered in any complete account of what is the morally right thing to do about defective newborns.

The first is: If a decision to terminate is made, how soon must it be made? Obviously it could not be postponed to the age of five, or of three, or even a year and a half. At those ages, all the reasons for insisting on consent are already cogent. And at those ages, the child will already care what happens to him. But ten days is tolerable. Doubtless advances in medicine will permit detection of serious prospective defects early in pregnancy, and this issue of how many days will not arise.

Second, the argument from the quality of the prospective life of the defective newborn requires that we decide which defects are so serious that the kind of life the defective child can have gives it no serious claim as compared with the social costs. This issue must be thought through, and some guidelines established, but I shall not attempt this here.

One might argue that, if the newborn cannot rationally care whether its life ends or not, the parents are free to dispose of a child irrespective of whether he is defective, if they simply do not want it. To this there are two replies. First, in practice there are others who want a child if the parents do not, and they can put it up for adoption. But second, the parents are *injuring* a child if they prevent it from having the good life it could have had. We do not in general accept the argument that a person is free to injure another, for no reason, even if he has that person's consent. In view of these facts, we may expect that rational, benevolent persons deciding which moral code to support would select one that required respect for the life of a normal child, but would permit the termination of the life of a seriously defective child.

ACTIVE AND PASSIVE PROCEDURES

There is a final question: that of a choice between withdrawal of life-supporting measures (such as feeding), and the active, painless taking of life. It seems obvious, however, that once the basic decision is made that an infant is not to receive the treatment necessary to sustain life beyond a few days, it is mere stupid cruelty to allow it to waste away gradually in a hospital bed—for the child to suffer, and for everyone involved also to suffer in watching the child suffer. If death is the outcome decided upon, it is far kinder for it to come quickly and painlessly.

SELECTED SUPPLEMENTAL READINGS

BEAUCHAMP, TOM L.,"The Moral Justification for Withholding Heroic Procedures," in *Who Decides?* ed., Nora Bell. Clifton, N.J.: The Humana Press, 1982.

BEAUCHAMP, TOM L. AND LEROY WALTERS, eds., *Contemporary Issues in Bioethics* (2nd ed.). Belmont, Calif.: Wadsworth, 1982, chap. 8.

BEAUCHAMP, TOM L. AND JAMES F. CHILDRESS, *Principles of Biomedical Ethics*. New York: Oxford University Press, 1979, chaps IV, VII.

BEAUCHAMP, TOM L. AND ARNOLD I. DAVIDSON, "The Definition of Euthanasia," *The Journal of Medicine and Philosophy* **4** (1979).

BEAUCHAMP, TOM L. AND SEYMOUR PERLIN, eds., *Ethical Issues in Death and Dying*. Englewood Cliffs, N.J.:Prentice-Hall, 1978.

BEHNKE, JOHN A. AND SISSELA BOK, *The Dilemma of Euthanasia*. Garden City, N.Y.: Doubleday Anchor Books, 1975.

BOK, SISSELA, "Personal Directions for Care at the End of Life," *New England Journal of Medicine* **295** (August 12, 1976).

CARSE, JAMES P. AND ARLENE B. DALLERY, eds., *Death and Society*. New York: Harcourt Brace Jovanovich, 1977.

CHILDRESS, JAMES F., "To Live or Let Die," in *Priorities in Biomedical Ethics*. Philadelphia, Pa.: The Westminster Press, 1981.

DOWNING, A.B., *Euthanasia and the Right to Die*. New York: The Humanities Press, 1970.

ENGELHARDT, H. TRISTRAM, JR., "Euthanasia and Children: The Injury of Continued Existence," *Journal of Pediatrics* **83** (1973).

FEINBERG, JOEL, "Voluntary Euthanasia and the Inalienable Right to Life," *Philosophy and Public Affairs* **7** (1978).

FLETCHER, GEORGE, "Prolonging Life," *Washington Law Review* **42** (1967), 999–1016.

FLETCHER, JOSEPH, "Ethics and Euthanasia," in *To Live and To Die: When, Why, and How*, ed., Robert H. Williams. New York: Springer-Verlag, 1973.

FOOT, PHILIPPA, "Euthanasia," *Philosophy and Public Affairs* **6** (Winter 1977).

GLOVER, JONATHAN, *Causing Death and Saving Lives*. Harmondsworth, England: Penguin Books, 1977.

HARE, R. M.: "Euthanasia: A Christian View," *Philosophic Exchange* **2** (Summer 1975).

KAMISAR, YALE, "Some Non-Religious Views Against Proposed 'Mercy-Killing' Legislation," *Minnesota Law Review* **42** (1958).

KLUGE, EIKE-HENNER W., *The Practice of Death*. New Haven, Conn.: Yale University Press, 1975.

KOHL, MARVIN, ed., *Beneficent Euthanasia*. Buffalo, N.Y.: Prometheus Books, 1975.

———, ed., *Infanticide and the Value of Life*. Buffalo, N.Y.: Prometheus Books, 1978.

———, *The Morality of Killing*. New York: Humanities Press, 1974.

LADD, JOHN, ed., *Ethical Issues Relating to Life and Death*. New York: Oxford University Press, 1979.

MAGUIRE, DANIEL C., *Death By Choice*. Garden City, N.Y.: Doubleday, 1974.

MAPPES, THOMAS A. AND JANE S. ZEMBATY, *Social Ethics: Morality and Social Policy* (2nd ed.). New York: McGraw-Hill, 1981.

MCCORMICK, RICHARD A., "To Save or Let Die," *Journal of the American Medical Association* **229** (July 8, 1974).

MASSACHUSETTS GENERAL HOSPITAL, CLINICAL CARE COMMITTEE, "Optimum Care for Hopelessly Ill Patients," *New England Journal of Medicine* **295** (August 12, 1976).

MENZEL, PAUL T., "Are Killing and Letting Die Morally Different in Medical Contexts?" *Journal of Medicine and Philosophy* **4** (1979).

RACHELS, JAMES, "Euthanasia," in *Matters of Life and Death*, ed. T. Regan. New York: Random House, 1980.

———, "Killing and Starving to Death," *Philosophy* **54** (April 1979).

RAMSEY, PAUL, *Ethics at the Edges of Life*, Part II. New Haven, Conn.: Yale University Press, 1978.

SHAW, ANTHONY, "Dilemmas of 'Informed Consent' in Children," *New England Journal of Medicine* **289** (October 25, 1973).

SINGER, PETER, *Practical Ethics*. New York: Cambridge University Press, 1979.

STRONG, CARSON, "Euthanasia: Is the Concept Really Nonevaluative?" *The Journal of Medicine and Philosophy* **5** (1980).

SUCKIEL, ELLEN K., "Death and Benefit in the Permanently Unconscious Patient: A Justification of Euthanasia," *The Journal of Medicine and Philosophy* **3** (1978).

TRAMMELL, RICHARD L., "The Presumption Against Taking Life," *The Journal of Medicine and Philosophy* **3** (1978).

VEATCH, ROBERT, *Death, Dying and the Biological Revolution*. New Haven, Conn.: Yale University Press, 1976.

WEIR, ROBERT F., ed., *Ethical Issues in Death and Dying*. New York: Columbia University Press, 1977.

WILLIAMS, GLANVILLE, " 'Mercy-Killing' Legislation—A Rejoinder," *Minnesota Law Review* **43** (1958).

———, "Euthanasia and Abortion," *University of Colorado Law Review* **38** (1966).

WILLIAMS, PETER, "The Right of Innocents to Be Killed," *Ethics* **87** (July 1977).
WOOZLEY, A.D., "Euthanasia and the Principle of Harm," *Philosophy and Public Policy*. Norfolk, Va.: Teagle and Little, 1977.

ENCYCLOPEDIA OF BIOETHICS ARTICLES

Acting and Refraining, Harold Moore
Aging and the Aged: Ethical Implications in Aging, Drew Christiansen
Death and Dying: Ethics: Systematic Perspective, Sissela Bok
Death and Dying: Ethics: Right to Refuse Treatment, Alexander M. Capron
Death and Dying: Ethics: Rights of the Terminally Ill, George J. Annas
Double Effect, William E. May
Infanticide, Michael Tooley
Life: Value of Life, Peter Singer
Life: Quality of Life, Warren T. Reich
Life Support Devices: Philosophical Perspective, A.G.M. van Melsen
Pain and Suffering: Philosophical Perspective, Jerome Shaffer
Paternalism, Tom L. Beauchamp
Person, A.G.M. van Melsen

chapter eleven

Research with Human Subjects

Informed Consent in Therapy and Experimentation

Alan Donagan

I. A CASE STUDY IN THE TRANSITION FROM COMMON RATIONAL MORAL KNOWLEDGE TO PHILOSOPHICAL

At Helsinki in 1964 the World Medical Association solemnly declared that, in using a new therapeutic measure in which clinical research is a secondary purpose, "if at all possible, consistent with patient psychology, the doctor should obtain the patient's freely given consent after the patient has been given a full explanation"; and that, in clinical research with no therapeutic purpose, nothing whatever may be done to a human being "without his full

From Alan Donagan, "Informed Consent in Therapy and Experimentation," *The Journal of Medicine and Philosophy* 2 no. 4 (1977). © 1977 by the Society for Health and Human Values. Reprinted by permission of *The Journal of Medicine and Philosophy* and the author.

My research has been supported by the John Simon Guggenheim Memorial Foundation, by a grant from the National Science Foundation to the Center for Advanced Study in the Behavioral Sciences, and by the University of Chicago, to all of whom I offer my gratitude. I desire to thank Gerald L. Perkoff, M.D., for advice on philosophical as well as on medical topics; and also James M. Gustafson, Brian Barry, Albert R. Jonsen, and Robert L. Simon. Two excellent anthologies were much used in preparing this paper, namely, Katz (1972) and Ladimer and Newman (1963), cited below.

consent, after he has been fully informed."[1] Not all physicians welcomed the Helsinki Declaration, although it was arrived at only after an extensive debate in the medical profession throughout the world, which sprang from disclosures before the U.S. Military Tribunal at Nuremberg of crimes committed upon human beings in the name of medical research. Of those who did not welcome it, some distrusted moral codes as such; others complained that the Helsinki formulations were unclear, and still others that they were impracticable and even hypocritical.

And yet, with little attention from the public, biomedical research was transformed in the decade that followed. In institutions engaged in such research, it is now standard practice that all experiments on human subjects be sanctioned by a supervisory committee charged, among other things, with seeing to it that nothing is done to such a subject without his informed consent. And, following a proposal of Henry K. Beecher,[2] a number of medical journals now refuse papers based on experimentation on human subjects if they do not supply adequate evidence of those subjects' informed consent.

This professional consensus emerged out of professional discussions, in which every point was thoroughly debated, and some acrimoniously. Its emergence is a vivid example of what Kant took to be the first and crucial stage in constructing a philosophy of morals, a stage which he described, with a pomposity I find endearing, as "the transition from common rational moral knowledge to philosophical."[3] Only a very arrogant philosopher, and probably a very silly one, would claim as a philosopher to instruct his fellows as to how they ought to conduct themselves. With the exception of Plato, all the great moral philosophers have taken their task to be to identify what is sound and coherent in the practical moral thinking that goes on around them, and to investigate its rational structure. As grammarians and logicians know to their sorrow, the structure of intellectual operations which even unsophisticated folk carry out with ease may be very complex, and its character will then be difficult to discern just because those operations are familiar and habitual. That, I think, is why only the greatest moral philosophers—an Aristotle, an Aquinas, a Kant—have been able to penetrate the familiarity of everyday thinking about right and wrong, and to disclose its deeper structure.

[1]Jay Katz, *Experimentation with Human Beings.* New York: Russell Sage Foundation, 1972, pp. 312–313.

[2]Henry K. Beecher, "Ethics and Clinical Research," *New England Journal of Medicine* **274** (1966), pp. 1354–1360. Reprinted in J. M. Humber and Robert F. Almeder, eds., *Biomedical Ethics and the Law* (New York: Plenum Press, 1976). Reference to the latter. Excerpted in Katz, pp. 307–310.

[3]Immanuel Kant, *Grundlegung zur Metaphysik der Sitten,* 2nd ed. (Riga: J. F. Hartknoch, 1786), p. 1.

From time to time, however, the process of social change confronts a society with situations of unforeseen kinds which call for a moral response, but to which the application of the moral principles held by that society is not evident. When this happens, given that those situations are not such as to expose a flaw in the society's fundamental moral principles, the application of those principles must become a matter of debate; and since *ex hypothesi* the issue debated will have a rational solution, a consensus will be reached when controversy has made clear what that solution is. In order to reach it, members of the society will have to articulate what their moral principles are, and to work out how the newly accepted solution may be derived from them. At the same time, they will become aware of the errors that hindered acceptance of that solution, whether they were defective formulations of principles, or inadequate interpretations, or invalid derivations. Hence they will themselves have made the transition from common rational moral knowledge to philosophical—even though the philosophy is at the stage Kant called "popular."[4]

Historical debates and resolutions of this kind—for example, that occurring over the legitimacy of usury as modern commerce developed, and that over the legitimacy of slavery—furnish academic philosophers with actual cases of popular moral philosophy they would do well to study. And because of its direct bearing on a number of issues in contemporary academic philosophy—most obviously, the controversy over utilitarianism—no such case of recent occurrence promises to be a more rewarding study than the acceptance by the medical profession of the requirement of informed consent.

No comprehensive history of the controversies that led to that acceptance is likely to be written; and for want of it, an outsider studying the evidence will miss much of historical and human significance. From one point of view, the debate was part of a process of self-regulation by which the medical profession forestalled the intrusion of public authority into certain of its activities. From another point of view, the latter phase of the debate, at least in the United States, can be regarded as an interchange in the medical profession on defensive strategy against a new kind of malpractice lawsuit. However, chronology shows that such interpretations are incomplete and superficial. That patients and experimental subjects not be acted on without their informed consent was demanded by a substantial body of physicians long before there were threats either from public authority or private litigants. Both prosecutors and tribunal at Nuremberg were guided throughout by medical advice. Even the Jewish Chronic Diseases Hospital Case of 1963–65, which appears to have been an unstated bone of contention in many professional exchanges in the late

[4]Kant, pp. 30–34.

sixties, would not have occurred but for the protests of physicians in charge of some of the patients involved.

The truth appears to be that, before the public at large thought of it at all, the problem of informed consent became a matter of controversy in the medical profession because of changes in the relations of physicians to patients, and of experimental medicine to clinical medicine, of which physicians naturally became conscious before the public. The contribution of laymen to defining some of the issues cannot be denied. But the doctrine of informed consent as we now have it is principally the achievement of the medical profession: lawyers and politicians entered the field late, and their contribution has been secondary. Philosophers, in good Hegelian fashion, for the most part arrived to take stock after the work had been done.

II. RELATED ISSUES

In philosophy of science, a historical example of scientific thinking is normally chosen for a case study only if what it exemplifies is judged scientifically sound. In the same way, if I had not judged philosophically sound the grounds on which the doctrine of informed consent came to be accepted, I should not have chosen the development of that doctrine for a case study in moral philosophy. This judgment, however, extends only to the core of the doctrine: to what it lays down about the consent of responsible adults to what is done to themselves. Outside that core, a number of related questions remain unsettled. Two should be mentioned.

The first is whether consent is required for therapy or experimentation carried out upon human beings who are not adults, or are not responsible—either briefly, or for a long time, or permanently. If consent is required for what is done to such persons, who is to give it? If parents, legal guardians, or near relatives, does their consent have the same range and force as that of a responsible adult to the same treatment or experiment carried out upon himself? In view of the extraordinary things some people have proved to be willing to consent to for others, in particular for their deformed or retarded children, it has been forcibly argued that nobody should have the right to consent to the performing of a non-therapeutic experiment upon another, and least of all, upon a child.[5]

The second is whether there are limits to what even a fully informed and responsible adult can allow a physician to do to him by way of therapy or experiment. As Pope Pius XII pointed out, in a much-quoted address, nobody can by his consent entitle another to do to him what he is not enti-

---

[5]Paul Ramsey, *The Patient as Person: Explorations in Medical Ethics* (New Haven, Conn.: Yale University Press, 1970), pp. 26–35.

tled to do to himself.[6] Most physicians would agree that in most circumstances suicide is wrong, and that therefore a responsible adult could not, by his informed consent, entitle a physician to carry out a lethal experiment on him in those circumstances. And yet, while nearly all physicians hold that there are other limitations as well upon what an informed, responsible adult's consent can entitle a therapist or an experimenter to do to him, there is much dispute as to what specifically they are.

Both these questions are very difficult, and occupy much of the discussion of consent that goes on today. But neither would arise at all unless it were regarded as settled that the informed consent of a responsible adult is necessary to any therapeutic or experimental procedure carried out upon him. The development of that doctrine is the sole case to be studied in what follows.

III. INFORMED CONSENT TO THERAPY

It has never been disputed that a necessary condition of the coming into existence of the relation between himself and his patient that is the source of a physician's professional responsibilities is that the patient have sought treatment from him, or that a sufficient condition of that relation's ceasing to exist is that the patient communicate to the physician his decision to terminate it. Except in emergencies, that a prospective patient asks for treatment does not suffice to make him a patient: physicians have always maintained that, as provided in the fifth section of the American Medical Association's *Principles of Medical Ethics*, "A physician may choose whom he will serve."[7] However, it has never been questioned that a patient's consent is necessary to his being a patient, and consequently that withdrawal of that consent terminates his being one.

Once a physician-patient relationship exists, what responsibilities to the patient does the physician incur by virtue of it? The Hippocratic oath, in its various forms,[8] lays down only one comprehensive responsibility,

---

[6]Pius XII, "Address to the First International Conference on the Histopathology of the Nervous System, September 14, 1952," *Acta Apostolicae Sedis* **44** (1952), p. 779. Translated in Irving Ladimer and Roger W. Newman, *Clinical Investigation in Medicine* (Boston: Law-Medicine Research Institute, Boston University, 1963), pp. 276–286.

[7]American Medical Association, *Opinions and Reports of the Judicial Council* (Chicago: American Medical Association, 1964), in Katz, pp. 313–314.

[8]The ancient text of the Hippocratic oath, in which, e.g., the physician forswears surgery, differs from later Christian versions of it (see Henry E. Sigerist, *A History of Medicine*. New York: Oxford University Press, 1961, 2: 301–304). Ludwig Edelstein (*The Hippocratic Oath*. Baltimore, Md.: The Johns Hopkins University Press, 1943) has established that its origin was Pythagorean. The heart of all versions of it, however, is that the physician is to act "in purity and holiness" solely for the benefit of the sick, and never to their harm.

which is formulated as follows in the version reproduced by Katz: "I will follow that system of regimen which, according to my ability and judgment, I consider for the benefit of my patients, and abstain from whatever is deleterious and mischievous."[9] Taken strictly, this binds the physician, as long as the physician-patient relationship endures, to treat his patients for their benefit, but according to what he, not they, judge that benefit to be, and to what he, not they, judge will most promote it.

When the bulk of his patients have little power, influence, or education, that is how a physician will tend to conduct himself toward them. But it is now a long time since a physician could claim that he ought so to treat his patients without being unintentionally comic.

Consider the following exchange in a case heard as late as 1961 (*Moore* v. *Webb*, 345 S.W. 2d, Mo. 1961). A patient had consulted a surgeon about a toothache. He was advised that extractions would be necessary, and he consented to that, but claimed at the same time to have insisted that they should be only partial. After x-ray examination, the surgeon decided that a complete extraction would be beneficial; and, without any further consultation, when the patient presented himself for the operation, extracted all his teeth. The patient sought to recover damages for an operation to which he had not consented. At the trial this passage occurred between surgeon and plaintiff's attorney:

> . . . I think you should strive to do for the patient what is the best thing over a long period of time for the patient. We tried to abide by that.
> Q: Isn't that up to the patient? A: No, I don't think it should be. If they go to a doctor they should discuss it. He should decide. . . .
> Q: Isn't this up to the patient? . . . If I want to keep these teeth, can't I do it? A: You don't know whether they are causing you trouble.
> Q: That is up to me, isn't it? A: Not if you came to see me it wouldn't be.[10]

That this dialogue seems to belong in the captions of a silent movie shows how out-of-date is the conception of the physician-patient relation it presents. But in what ways is it out of date?

In an influential paper published in 1956, the psychiatrists Thomas Szasz and Marc Hollender distinguished three basic models of the physician-patient relation, more than one of which may be combined in any actual specimen of it. The first, or "activity-passivity" model, they describe as "the oldest conceptual model," and characterize it as "based on the effect of one person on another in such a way and in such circumstances that the person acted upon is unable to contribute actively, or is considered inanimate." According to it, a patient resembles a helpless infant, and a physician an active parent. The second, or "guidance-

[9]Katz, p. 311.
[10]Katz, p. 649.

cooperation" model, they describe as underlying much of medical practice, and characterize it as one in which both patient and physician are active, but in which "the patient is expected to 'look up to' and to 'obey' his doctor" and is "neither to question nor to argue nor disagree with the orders he receives." The prototype of this model is the relation between "the parent and his (adolescent) child." The third, or "mutual participation" model, is characterized as "predicated on the postulate that equality among human beings is desirable," and as an "interaction" in which physician and patient "(1) have approximately equal power, (2) [are] mutually interdependent (i.e., need each other), and (3) engage in activities that will be in some ways satisfactory to both." Sometimes relations satisfying this model are "overcompensatory," but sometimes they are medically necessary, as for example in the treatment of most chronic illnesses, where "the patients' own experiences provide valuable and important clues for therapy" and the program of treatment "is principally carried out by the patient."[11]

Although profoundly suggestive, the Szasz-Hollender models partly obscure the change from which the informed consent requirement has grown by confounding two distinct generic physician-patient relations, which I shall call the treatment relation and the choice of course of treatment relation. For our purposes, it is the latter that counts.

The Szasz-Hollender models largely hold for the treatment relation: that is, the therapeutic relation between physician and patient as treatment is actually going on. This relation appears to have three specific kinds: (1) physician active and patient wholly passive, as in surgery under a general anaesthetic; (2) patient active as well as physician, but merely in following the physican's specific instructions; and (3) patient active as well as physician, and deciding many substantive questions of treatment for himself. By contrast, there seem to be only two specific kinds of choice of course of treatment relation: (1) physician chooses the patient's course of treatment until either terminates the physician-patient relation; and (2) physician proposes, patient decides. The Szasz-Hollender triad obscures the fact that each of the two kinds of choice of course of treatment relation is compatible with each of the three kinds of treatment relation. For example, a choice of course of treatment relation in which the physician chooses is perfectly compatible with a treatment relation in which the patient, a diabetic say, decides for himself many therapeutic questions. Likewise, a choice of course of treatment relation in which a patient, having rejected his physician's first recommendation, and, after inquiring about alternatives that are medically acceptable to his physician, chooses another, is perfectly compatible with his choosing a course of treatment in which he will

[11]Thomas S. Szasz and Marc H. Hollender, "A Contribution to the Philosophy of Medicine—The Basic Models of the Doctor-Patient Relationship," *Archives of Internal Medicine*, **97** (1956). Excerpts from pp. 585–587 in Katz, pp. 229–230.

be in the most passive of all treatment relations—surgery under a general anaesthetic.

There are, of course, cases in which there is no distinction between course of treatment and treatment, as when a patient agrees to have a flu shot. But there will be a distinction wherever a course of treatment is complex. Advancing a claim to decide on the course of treatment one is to undergo in no way encroaches upon the physician's authority over how that course of treatment is to be carried out.

The express requirement of informed consent to therapy, I suggest, is no more than the formal recognition of a change taking place in the predominant form of physician-patient relation: a change from a "physician decides" kind of choice of course of treatment relation to a "physician proposes, patient decides" kind. And physicians who exhibit the deepest understanding of the physician-patient relation have seen in this change a realization of something present in it all along. Consider the following statement by Otto E. Guttentag: "the *original* and, indeed, the basic justification for our profession [is that]...one human being is in distress, in need, crying for help; and another fellow human being is concerned and wants to assist him. The cry for help and the desire to render it precipitate the relationship. Here *both* the healing and the sick persons are subjects, fellow-companions, partners to conquer a common enemy who has overwhelmed one of them. Theirs is a relationship between two 'I's'...I have called it 'mutual obligation of equals.' "[12]

In the majority of the writings known to me in which the requirement of informed consent is accepted (I had almost said "all," but I have made no systematic count), that requirement is grounded upon one or another of three principles, which, although not identical, are nevertheless connected, namely: (1) that in nature as it is known to us, human beings have a dignity and worth that is unique; (2) the Kantian principle that a human being is never to be used merely as a means, but always at the same time as an end; and (3) a principle laid down in the Declaration of Independence, which, as we shall see, is far from merely political, that every human being is endowed with an inalienable right to life, liberty, and the pursuit of happiness. In many of those writings, as in Guttentag's paper, these principles are explicitly or implicitly acknowledged to have been transmitted, in Western societies, largely through the Judaeo-Christian religious tradition, in which it is held that, unlike the innocent beasts, man is "created in the image of God, and tempted by the devil."[13]

[12]Otto E. Guttentag, "The Problem of Experimentation on Human Beings: The Physician's Point of View," *Science* 117 (1953), pp. 206–210, in Ladimer and Newman, pp. 63–69. Excerpts in Katz, pp. 918–919.

[13]Guttentag, in Ladimer and Newman, p. 69.

Of course, despite their historical connection, the conception of man expressed in this doctrine is logically separable from any belief in God or the devil.

In an important and justly influential statement on the ethics of consent, Paul Ramsey has shown that the requirement of consent is connected with the fidelity human beings owe one another in their interactions: "The principle of an informed consent [he wrote] is a statement of the fidelity between the man who performs medical procedures and the man on whom they are performed. . . . Fidelity is between man and man in these procedures. Consent expresses or establishes this relationship, and the requirement of consent sustains it."[14] But connecting the requirement of consent with "the faithfulness that is normative for all the . . . moral bonds of life with life" is only the first stage in its justification: Ramsey correctly went on to derive faithfulness itself from the unique dignity of man: "A human being is more than a patient or experimental subject; he is a *personal* subject—every bit as much a man as the physician-experimenter."[15] And that, of course, returns us to the first of the three principles above.

Recognition of every human being as having a unique dignity as human, and as therefore being an end in every relation in which others may morally stand to him, entails that no human being may legitimately be interfered with in pursuing his conception of his happiness in whatever way seems best to him, provided that in doing so he does not himself violate human dignity. A man is not deprived of his right to life, liberty, and the pursuit of happiness by preventing him from taking away the lives and liberty of others, or interfering with their pursuit of happiness, even if that can only be done at the cost of his life or liberty. An inalienable right may be forfeited. Nor does one violate another's human dignity by forcibly preventing him from killing himself, or destroying his own capacity to lead a human life. But no human being has the right to impose on another his view of that other's happiness, or of how that other's happiness may best be promoted. Paul Ramsey has drawn the corollary for medical practice by adapting a saying of Lincoln: "No man is good enough to cure another without his consent."[16]

For this reason, no physician in the Western moral tradition has ever questioned that for a physician to lay hands on a patient's body (to "touch" him, in legal parlance) in any way to which that patient has not consented is wrong. Common lawyers call that wrong "assault and battery." The legal principle was stated in a celebrated opinion of Chief Judge Cardozo:

[14]Ramsey, p. 5.

[15]Ramsey, p. 5.

[16]Ramsey, p. 7.

"Every human being of adult years and sound mind has a right to determine what shall be done with his own body; and a surgeon who performs an operation without his patient's consent, commits an assault, for which he is liable in damages" (*Schloendorff* v. *New York Hospitals* 105 N.E. 92; N.Y. 1914). As Marcus L. Plante has put it, in a magisterial article, "It is the patient's prerogative to accept medical treatment or take his chances of living without it."[17]

Yet although physicians seem never to have disputed this important principle, as the case of *Moore* v. *Webb* discussed above shows, some of them were slow to grasp its implications. By merely consulting a physician, and not discontinuing treatment, a patient does not confer on that physician the right to administer whatever treatment he judges best. Before embarking on any course of treatment, a physician must secure his patient's consent to it; and he cannot secure consent unless he informs his patient, in words that patient can understand, of the nature and character of the course of treatment proposed. The most frequent complaints of patients in civil actions against physicians for battery have not been that treatment was administered without consent, or that their consent was obtained by outright misrepresentation, but rather that they were not informed of important parts of what would be done (e.g., that the patient was informed of what would be done to his prostate, but not that, in order to do it, his spermatic cords would be severed and tied off), or that they were informed in technical or ambiguous language they did not understand (e.g., that the patient was told that a mastectomy would be performed, but did not understand that mastectomy is the removal of a breast). It is now generally conceded that, if any such complaint is true in fact, the physician has committed a grave wrong. And a physician is simply not competent if he is unable to describe, in words intelligible to his patients, everything that could matter to them as patients about the character of any course of treatment he proposes.

Avoidance of battery, however, is not enough to satisfy the principle of consent. For, in deciding whether or not to consent to a proposed course of treatment, a patient will certainly want to take into account any hazards that may be collateral to administering the proposed treatment. But here a difficulty arises. Nobody questions that good medical practice may require a physician to be reticent in discussing a patient's condition with him, if telling the full truth may disturb the patient needlessly and perhaps jeopardize his recovery. Many physicians conceived this duty of reticence to extend to what they should tell certain patients, especially those liable to be very disturbed by it, of hazards collateral to treatments proposed. And when Plante wrote on the subject, medical and legal opin-

[17]Marcus L. Plante, "An Analysis of Informed Consent," *Fordham Law Review* **36** (1968), pp. 639–672. Excerpts in Katz, pp. 599–600.

ion were in agreement that what information about collateral hazards a physician is called upon to divulge to a patient is a matter of expert medical judgment.[18]

A very little reflection will show that, in a physician-patient relation in which the patient decides upon the course of treatment proposed by the physician, this agreed opinion was muddled. Having conceded that, except in emergencies, it is for a responsible adult patient to decide whether or not he is to receive any proposed course of treatment, it is inconsistent to allow that he may be refused information essential to forming an intelligent judgment on the question. Indeed, for a physician to assume the right to conceal a certain hazard is to make that hazard count for nothing in the patient's deliberations, and so in part to usurp the prerogative to decide. Unless a physician is prepared to maintain that his patient is no longer responsible, and the public is rightly becoming reluctant to accept a physician's word on that, the patient has a right to all the information he needs to make a judgment.

Nor is it for the physician to decide what that information is. It is true, and as far as I know undisputed, that only a medical expert is qualified to judge what benefits are to be hoped for from a proposed treatment, and their probability, and what evils are to be feared, and their probability. Having reached a scientific conclusion on these questions, he will then try to judge what values and disvalues his patient would reasonably assign to the respective probabilities that those hopes and those fears will be realized, and will recommend a course of treatment accordingly. However, the judgment he makes as to what values and disvalues a patient ought to assign to those probabilities is patently not an exercise of his medical expertise. The surgeon general is within his medical province in informing us that cigarette smoking imperils our health; but he would not be if he were to add that we ought to account that peril of more weight than satisfying our craving to smoke. Again, simplifying a set of cases that have been litigated: a physician is within his medical province in advising his patient that while a serious prostate ailment can be cured by a certain treatment with 90 percent probability, there is a 20 percent probability that a collateral result will be infertility or diminished sexual capacity; but it is as a man, and not as a medical expert, that he proceeds to judge that the high probability of the cure hoped for should outweigh the low probability of the collateral harm that is feared. It is for the patient, not for the physician, to decide such questions, although most patients give a good deal of weight to their physicians' advice.

It follows that, as a U.S. Appellate Court ruled in *Canterbury* v. *Spence* (464 F 2d 772, CA DC 1972): "The test for determining whether a particu-

---

[18]Plante, p. 656, and Don Harper Mills, "Whither Informed Consent?" *Journal of the American Medical Association* **229** (1974), p. 307.

lar peril may be divulged is its materiality to the patient's decision: all risks potentially affecting the decision must be unmasked."[19] What is material to a patient's decision depends upon what values and disvalues *he* assigns to the respective probabilities of various possible outcomes of a proposed course of treatment, and not on those his physician thinks ought to be assigned to them. For example, different patients will assign very different disvalues to slight chances of death or serious disability, and they have the right to act on those they assign.

As these complexities became apparent, even physicians who advocated the principle of informed consent began to speak of "the fallacy [of] ... uncritically accepting [informed consent] as an easily attainable goal, whereas it is often beyond our full grasp."[20] Those less favorable to the principle derided it as irksome, superfluous, and often gratuitously distressing,[21] and even as calculated to empty surgeons' consulting rooms.[22] Both reactions agree that the principle of informed consent cannot be a binding practical principle, but at best is an ideal to be approximated. To the extent that a principle is morally binding, it must be capable of being observed.

But can the principle of informed consent not be so formulated as to be capable of being observed? Is it not a logical development of the perfectly orthodox doctrine of the physician-patient relationship set out by Guttentag?

That an exact and applicable doctrine of informed consent is possible was soon demonstrated by the activities of courts in developing one. And so, in part from investigations of their problems with malpractice suits, physicians began to work out a practicable professional principle. Sober discussions such as those of Mills have largely established that there is "a line of reasonable disclosure ... that is consistent with good medical practice and that affords reasonable legal safety."[23] And this line is morally as well as legally obligatory. The principal difficulty discerned by Beecher in requiring informed consent is that the physician often does not know all the collateral risks incurred in undergoing a certain treatment. Experi-

[19]Quoted in Joseph E. Simonaitis, "More About Informed Consent, Part I," *Journal of the American Medical Association* **224** (1973), pp. 1831–1832; and Joseph E. Simonaitis, "More About Informed Consent, Part II," *Journal of the American Medical Association* **225** (1973), p. 91.

[20]Henry K. Beecher, "Some Fallacies and Errors in the Application of the Principle of Consent in Human Experimentation," *Clinical Pharmacology and Therapeutics* **3** (1962), p. 145.

[21]Preston J. Burnham, "Medical Experimentation in Humans," *Science* **152** (1966), pp. 448–450. Excerpts in Katz, pp. 658–659.

[22]William J. Irvin, "Now, Mrs. Blare, About the Complications ... ," *Medical Economics* **40** (1963), pp. 102–108. Excerpts in Katz, pp. 721–722, 929–930, 1040.

[23]Mills, p. 307; cf. Alan Meisel, "Informed Consent—the Rebuttal," *Journal of the American Medical Association* **234** (1975), p. 615; and Mills, "Informed Consent—the Rejoinder," *Journal of the American Medical Association* **234** (1975), p. 616.

menters are necessarily even more in the dark than therapists. Since physicians can only be required to do what they can do, the principle of informed consent cannot be interpreted as requiring them to provide all the information whatever that would be material to a patient's decision, but only all the information at the disposal of a competent practitioner, and any special knowledge they may have acquired themselves. They can also be required to inform their patients that, medicine being an inexact science, there is a small chance in any radical treatment of grave unforeseeable collateral effects, and that there may also be unforeseeable contingencies with harmful results.

In twenty years time it is predictable that cases such as *Canterbury* v. *Spence* will be perceived as no more than registering a logical development in medical practice arising from a distinction physicians had already drawn between their province as scientific practitioners and their province as medical advisers. It has, after all, been in no small part through the educative efforts of physicians that patients have been learning that they must accept ultimate responsibility for whatever courses of treatment they undergo, and that they cannot blame their physicians when risks they decide to take become realities.

A recently reported "clinicosociologic" conference perhaps allows us a glimpse of the view that will prevail in the future. The case was discussed of an eighty-six-year-old lady, who was able to communicate with her physicians and supply an accurate medical history, but who because of failures of memory had assigned legal responsibility for her affairs to a guardian. She was found to have an asymptomatic abdominal aortic aneurysm. The rupture of such an aneurysm is immediately fatal, if complete, and fatal within hours to days if partial. Often, however, it can be prevented surgically, by elective aneurysm replacement. The physician, after telephoning a surgeon, decided that the risks of such surgery were too great and recommended against it. His recommendation was discussed with the guardian and accepted, but not with the patient. Six months later the aneurysm partially ruptured, and, in the emergency room, a different surgeon discussed with her what should be done, making clear the risks of surgery, now very much greater. Despite those risks, she chose it. The guardian could not be reached. Thirty hours after surgery she died. Two remarks on the case by Dr. Gerald Perkoff are of great interest. On the initial decision not to operate, he said: "[I]t was a mistake not to have operated earlier when she was well. . . . Had this patient interacted personally with the surgeon at the time of her first visit, it clearly would have been preferable. . . . Either the internist or the surgeon, or both, should have insisted upon a consultation visit."[24] What matters here is less

---

[24]Philip E. Cryer, and John M. Kissane, eds., "Clinicosociologic Conference: Decisions regarding the Provision or Withholding of Therapy," *American Journal of Medicine* **61** (1976), p. 918.

Perkoff's disagreement with the original physician's recommendation than his insistence that the patient should have been given the opportunity to decide. And on the second, and fatal, decision to operate, he said: "[T]he question I asked myself . . . is 'Can a physician do other than treat a patient if the patient is completely informed and desires treatment?' The answer I gave was that there is no other choice but to treat such a patient."[25]

IV. INFORMED CONSENT TO EXPERIMENTATION

Therapeutic medicine is inescapably experimental; for, since no two patients are medically identical, even in a case in which prognosis after treatment is regarded as unproblematic, every physician ought to be alert should *this* one, after all, turn out to be exceptional. However, even when, with his informed consent, a highly risky treatment is administered to a patient, in therapeutic experimentation the end that determines whether or not that treatment is administered is the patient's good. That, incidentally, it may advance medical science, and so presumably benefit many human beings in the future, is a secondary and nondetermining consideration.

Medical science advanced rapidly in the past century because the haphazard experimentation inseparable from any intelligently administered medical treatment was supplemented by systematic experimentation, more or less well designed. Some of it was abhorrent. For example, valuable results on the transmission of venereal diseases were obtained by methods differing from the abominations punished at Nuremberg only in scale and in that the wretched subjects were procured by deceit rather than by force.[26] But such cases were a minority. The great nineteenth-century authority, Claude Bernard, both preached and practiced, as "the principle of medical morality," that one is "never to carry out on a human being an experiment that cannot but be injurious to him in some degree, even if the outcome could be of great interest to science, that is to say, the health of other human beings."[27] However, in Walter Reed's classic experimental investigation at Havana in 1900 of how yellow fever is transmitted, and in subsequent experiments by Richard P. Strong in the Philippines on plague and beriberi, it was held permissible to carry out procedures that

[25]Cryer and Kissane, p. 918.

[26]Vikenty Veressayev, *The Memoirs of a Physician*, trans. Simeon Linden (New York: Alfred A. Knopf, 1916), excerpts in Katz, pp. 284–291; R. J. V. Pulvertaft, "The Individual and the Group in Modern Medicine," *Lancet* 2 (1952), excerpts in Katz, pp. 291, 707, 825.

[27]Quoted in R. A. McCance, "The Practice of Experimental Medicine," *Proceedings of the Royal Society of Medicine* 44 (1950), pp. 189–194, in Ladimer and Newman, p. 72.

could be nothing but harmful, provided that the subjects were volunteers. In these experiments there was no question of carrying out any procedure known to be gravely harmful or lethal; but procedures were permitted that could not but have been harmful to some degree, and that could have been greatly harmful or lethal, and sometimes were.[28]

In this paper, it is assumed that a human being is entitled to volunteer the use of his body for at least some risky experiments (see Sec. II, above). Hence it will also be assumed that the genuine consent of human subjects to risky experiments for which they are entitled to volunteer is a sufficient condition of the moral permissibility of those experiments. But whether it is also a necessary condition has been questioned, in view of the magnitude of the benefits of mankind at large of the experiments of Reed, Strong, and others. Is it wrong to sacrifice the health of a few, or even their lives, for the sake of the lives and health of the many, both now and in the future?

At the Nuremberg trials, the defense recognized that if the voluntary consent of the human subjects to an experiment is essential to its legal permissibility, as the tribunal ultimately ruled that it is[29] then the case for the defendants was hopeless. And so it had no choice but to argue that such consent is not legally essential. The argument for this position by Dr. Robert Servatius, on behalf of Dr. Karl Brandt, although primarily legal, is of very great ethical interest.[30] Its cardinal points were three. (1) A state may demand a sacrifice from an individual on behalf of the community; and decisions as to what the interests of the community are, what those interests require, and how great a sacrifice may be demanded are all to be made by the state alone. (2) There are no pertinent valid distinctions to be drawn between conscripting somebody for military service, ordering somebody to drop an atomic bomb, and requiring somebody to submit to medical experimentation. (3) In the history of medicine, numerous experiments have been carried out on human beings without their informed consent; and "looking through the medical literature, one cannot escape the growing conviction that the word 'volunteer,' where it appears at all, is used only as a word of protection and camouflage."[31]

The most embarrassing of Servatius's three points, namely, 3, morally tended to support the prosecution. It is true that numerous experiments have been carried out by physicians on unconsenting human beings, but for most of the present century at least, they have been the

[28]Louis L. Lasagna, "Special Subjects in Human Experimentation," *Daedalus* (Spring 1969), pp. 449–452. Excerpt in Katz, p. 381.

[29]*Trials of War Criminals at the Nuernberg Military Tribunals Under Control Council Law*, No. 10, vols, 1-2, "The Medical Case," Nuernberg, October 1946–April 1949. Washington, D.C.: U.S. Government Printing Office, n.d., 2:181–182. (Cited as *Trials, Nuremberg.*)

[30]*Trials, Nuremberg*, 2:126–130.

[31]*Trials, Nuremberg*, 2:128

shame of medicine. And even if the word "volunteer" in the report of an experiment is for protection and camouflage, that only shows that camouflage was thought necessary—and why should it have been, unless it was acknowledged that to experiment on a human being without his consent is wrong? It should be added that Servatius seems to have been mistaken as to the facts. Although there are strong objections to some of the kinds of volunteers that have been used as subjects in the United States— for example, imprisoned or condemned criminals—there is also good evidence that most of them have genuinely been volunteers.[32]

Servatius's first two points, however, are in no way weakened by the failure of his third. Yet they are formulated in terms of a political theory that is anathema to those who uphold classical Western, that is nonstatist, political theories, and the conceptions of the human good that go with them. But it is plain that his first point would be unaffected as an argument against the requirement of consent had he spoken of a genuinely democratic society instead of *a* state, and of the institutions of a genuinely democratic society instead of *the* state. Genuinely democratic societies have been known to compel unwelcome actions in the name of social goods, although not always the same goods as those in the name of which undemocratic societies have acted.

A second adjustment that must be made in order fairly to appraise Servatius's arguments is to separate their appraisal from all the circumstances of the Nuremberg medical case not directly relevant to them. As I read the published volumes, most if not all the accused would justly have been condemned even had the necessity of consent not been affirmed by the tribunal, on the ground that the scientific incompetence of some of the experimental designs, and the nonmedical purposes of others, would have left no choice but to pronounce the experimenters guilty of gratuitous killing, mutilating, and other forms of injury.[33] There is every reason to suppose that, even if the first two points in Servatius's argument were to be accepted, modifying them according to a less obnoxious political theory, the number of sanctioned dangerous experiments would be comparatively few, as would the number of deaths and serious injuries caused by them.

Once they have been sanitized in this way, Servatius's two points are not shocking at all, academically at least: they are straightforward applications of a disputed but academically respectable doctrine, namely, utilitarianism in its generalized form, according to which what is right is defined as what is for the greatest *good* of the greatest number. (Its most familiar specific form is the hedonistic one of Bentham and Mill, in which good is identified with happiness.) Hence it is not surprising that, during the very

[32]Katz, pp. 1020–1026, 1028–1034.

[33]*Trials, Nuremberg*, 1:73–74; See also Leo Alexander, "Medical Science under Dictatorship," *New England Journal of Medicine* **241** (1949); excerpts from pp. 39–43 in Katz, p. 302.

period in which the organized medical profession was preparing to reaffirm at Helsinki the Nuremberg principle of informed consent, many individual physicians were concluding that the principle need not be observed in responsibly conducted scientific experimentation. What the Nuremberg tribunal really condemned, they appear to have thought, was not experimentation without informed consent, but only atrocious experimentation. Indeed, in 1962, in a passage endorsed by Beecher himself, Walter Modell wrote: "I . . . think that when society confers the degree of physician on a man it instructs him to experiment on his fellow. I think that when a patient goes to a physician for treatment, regardless of whether he consents to it, he is also unconsciously presenting himself for the purpose of experimentation."[34]

What happens when those who thus unconsciously present themselves for experimentation become conscious of it was demonstrated in the Jewish Chronic Diseases Hospital Case, which began less than two years after Modell wrote.[35] That case is particularly important, because the experiment involved was perfectly harmless and was from a scientific point of view admirably conducted. The facts of the case pertinent to the present study are as follows. In the summer of 1963, at the request of an outside cancer research institute, the medical director of the hospital agreed to permit physicians from the institute to inject into twenty-two patients suspensions of cells obtained from cultures of human cancer tissue, in order to determine the mechanism and rate of rejection of the injected material by debilitated but noncancerous subjects. It was asserted by the experimenters that spoken consent was obtained from the subjects, but it was not disputed that the subjects were not told that what was to be injected contained cancer cells. The reason given for this reticence was that, although the experiment was neither harmful nor hazardous, if the dread word "cancer" had been used the subjects would have been misled and unnecessarily distressed. Ultimately, the medical director of the hospital and the principal investigator were found by the Board of Regents of the University of the State of New York (which has jurisdiction over all licensed professions excluding that of law) to be guilty of fraud and deceit in the practice of medicine.

Much sympathy was rightly expressed for the physicians thus censured. For they had acted in good conscience, even if erroneously; and they had done nothing different in kind from what many others had done or advocated. And some sympathizers went further. Had the censured physicians not achieved a significant if modest scientific result, at the cost of no harm to anybody beyond a temporary mild discomfort? Why then

---

[34]Walter Modell, "Comment [on Beecher, 1962]," *Clinical Pharmacology and Therapeutics* **3** (1962), p. 146. Excerpt in Katz, p. 316.

[35]For documentation, see Katz, pp. 9–65.

should the attorney general for New York, in a memorandum to the
Board of Regents, have written as though he was addressing the Nuremberg tribunal.[36]

The answer emerges from what the defenders of experimentation
without informed consent wrote in the years that followed; for it became
evident that, if from excusing what was done in the Jewish Chronic
Diseases Hospital Case (which they seldom mentioned, although they cannot but have had it in mind) they were to pass on to justifying it, they
would have no option but to present a sanitized version of the defense
offered by Servatius at Nuremberg.

With exemplary courage, a number of them did so. The most
forthright was Walsh McDermott, in some "Opening Comments" that have
already outlived the 1967 Colloquium they introduced. He put forward a
democratic version of Servatius's first point in these words: "... as a
society we enforce the social good over the individual good across a whole
spectrum of nonmedical activities every day, and many of these activities
ultimately affect the health or the life of an individual. . . . [W]hen the
conflict is head on, when the group interest and the individual interest are
basically irreconcilable . . . we try to depersonalize the process by spreading
responsibility for decision throughout a framework of legal institutions."[37]
It should be noticed that McDermott acknowledged that "we" only "try to
depersonalize" this process, without noting that those societies that have
succeeded are unappealing as models.

He also enriched Servatius's second point with an additional example
of a head-on conflict between individual interest and social interest that is
resolved according to the latter, namely, "the decision to impose capital
punishment."[38] But, in declaring that situations in clinical medicine "in
which it clearly seems to be in the best interests of society that [certain
scientific] information be obtained . . . [which] can be obtained only from
studies on certain already unlucky individuals" belong to the same "hard
core" of cases as situations requiring military conscription or capital punishment, he did not substantially differ from Servatius.[39]

The same two points recur in papers by Guido Calabresi, Louis L.
Jaffe, and Louis Lasagna, which arose out of conferences arranged by the
American Academy of Arts and Sciences, and were published in *Daedalus*
for Spring 1969. Calabresi, indeed, furnished yet another example of
Servatius's second point: "Many activities are permitted, even though *sta-*

[36]Katz, pp. 44–48.

[37]Walsh McDermott, "Opening Comments to Colloquium: The Changing Mores of
Biomedical Research," *Annals of Internal Medicine* **67** (1967) (suppl. 7), p. 39. Excerpts in Katz,
pp. 926–927, 931.

[38]McDermott, p. 39.

[39]McDermott, p. 40.

tistically we know they will lose lives, since it costs too much to engage in these activities more safely, or to abstain from them altogether."[40] All three followed McDermott in concluding that, in the Helsinki Declaration, and in subsequent promulgations by such bodies as the U.S. Food and Drug Administration and the National Institutes of Health, our society either has mistaken the nature of its own morality, as evidenced by the practices it sanctions, or is hypocritical. Its error or hypocrisy ought to be corrected by repudiating the requirement of informed consent. But even when that correction has been made, the problem will remain of how nonvolunteer research subjects are to be obtained. At this point Jaffe assured his readers that his argument was not "the ominous prolegomenon to a program for conscripting human guinea pigs,"[41] and those who accept the utilitarian argument would probably do the same. Calabresi, for example, declared that right-minded scholars "ought to be devoting themselves to the development of a workable but not too obvious control system...."[42] Jaffe himself looked to developments in the common law. Lasagna appeared to imagine that all would be well if physicians and public alike would only embrace situation ethics.[43] None made any significant advance upon McDermott's ironical conclusion: "Obviously we cannot convene a constitutional convention of the Judaeo-Christian culture and add a few amendments to it. Yet, in a figurative sense, unless we can do something very much like that... the problem, at its roots, is unsolvable and we must continue to live with it."[44]

[40]Guido Calabresi, "Reflections on Medical Experimentation in Humans," *Daedalus* (Spring 1969), pp. 387–405. Reprinted in Paul A. Freund, ed., *Experimentation with Human Subjects* (New York: George Braziller, 1970).

[41]Louis L. Jaffe, "Law as a System of Control," *Daedalus* (Spring 1969), pp. 406–426. Reprinted in Freund; excerpts in Katz, pp. 721–722, 929–930, 1040.

[42]Calabresi, p. 405.

[43]That there can be such a thing as "situation ethics" as opposed to "rule ethics" is a gross error, which has a common ancestry with the discredited educational fallacy that there is such a thing as "teaching children" as opposed to "teaching subjects." Any rational system of moral rules has to do with how human beings ought to act in different situations, and, when from a moral point of view situations differ relevantly, it must treat them differently. But this in no way entails that there are not kinds of action that are wrong in all situations, e.g., murder—accurately defined to exclude such justifiable forms of homicide as self-defense. The contention that experimenting on a responsible adult human being without his consent is wrong in all situations entails neither that all situations should be treated in the same way nor that there are no situations in which it is permissible to experiment on a human being without his consent—e.g., certain kinds of situations, not discussed in this paper, in which responsibility is impaired. While conceding too much to doctrines of situation ethics fashionable at the time, John Fletcher ["Human Experimentation: Ethics in the Consent Situation," *Law and Contemporary Problems* **32** (1967), pp. 620–649] indirectly brings out how little doubt "situational" approaches throw on the requirement of informed consent. See also Ramsey (n. 5), and, for a devastating general criticism of situation ethics, his *Deeds and Rules in Christian Ethics* (New York: Scribner's, 1967).

[44]McDermott, p. 41; cf. McDermott, "Comment on [Jaffe], 'Law as a system of Control'," in Freund, *Experimentation with Human Subjects*. Excerpts in Katz, pp. 926–927, 931.

It is regrettable that these distinguished physicians and lawyers should have assumed that generalized utilitarianism is the only moral position pertinent to examining the cases which, according to their second point, are of the same kind as the "hard core" ones in medical experimentation. It is true by definition that, from the point of view of generalized utilitarianism, the only thing that counts in settling any moral question is what would be for the greatest good of the greatest number. But there are other moral positions, among them the Judaeo-Christian one, according to which a variety of nonutilitarian considerations may count.

Setting aside Servatius's case of dropping an atomic bomb on a city, on the ground that it is dubious whether that is permissible on either utilitarian or Judaeo-Christian grounds, let us consider the cases offered by Servatius, McDermott, and Calabresi. In the Judaeo-Christian moral tradition, it is held permissible for a civil society to attach penal sanctions to its laws, in extreme cases even the sanction of death, without ceasing to treat the persons so punished as ends; for when laws themselves have a moral sanction, to punish those who break them in itself treats them as genuinely responsible for their deeds. Punishment is not inflicted primarily for deterrence or reformation, but as what the criminal deserves. Again, in compelling citizens to serve in a just war on threat of punishment, a civil society only compels them to uphold a good common to them all, and not primarily the good of others. The very concept of a common good has fallen into disrepute partly because it has become confounded with the idea of the good of the many as opposed to that of the few. Even though the Judaeo-Christian tradition applauds a sacrifice by one man for his fellows, it utterly denies the right of his fellows, no matter how many, to compel that sacrifice.[45] Finally, while certain kinds of laxity in safety regulations are morally objectionable, for example, allowing a machine tended by human beings to be used when it is only a question of time when it will blow up, other kinds are not, for example, allowing the use of a machine that would be dangerous in the hands of an unskilled operator. Laxities of the latter kind, even when it is statistically predictable that some injuries will result, and not necessarily to the negligent operator, do not sacrifice the few to the many: they merely allow, without compelling, many to risk being among the few. Hence, from a Judaeo-Christian point of view, securing nonvolunteer subjects for medical research is *not* an action of the same kind as conscripting for military service, imposing capital punishment, or tolerating certain kinds of risky activities: they have nonutilitarian justifications, it does not.

And so we come to the first point. If a piece of medical research would be for the greatest good of the greatest number, then according to generalized utilitarianism, nonvolunteer subjects may be procured for it

[45]Ramsey, *The Patient as Person*, pp. 28, 107–108.

by one or other of the only two possible methods: lawful compulsion as in the Nuremberg case, or deception as in the Jewish Chronic Diseases Hospital case. Is this justification of those methods acceptable?

The consensus reached by the organized medical profession is that it is not acceptable. And, in a case study such as this, that is the principal thing to be said. Among physicians, "there is essentially no valid argument about the basic principle that informed consent—or whatever may be its legal equivalent in a specialized situation—is a prerequisite for human experimentation."[46] They recognize that they have neither legal nor moral authority to compel nonvolunteers to be experimental subjects; and the great majority of them would repudiate, as unprofessional, any suggestion that they experiment on conscripts provided by the state. And most of them now agree that it is equally inadmissible to procure experimental subjects by deception, whether by misrepresentation or by withholding information those subjects would consider material.

It is not disputed that observing the requirement of informed consent may delay otherwise desirable scientific progress. But David D. Rutstein's doctrine is now widely accepted that "ethical constraints that prohibit certain human experiments are similar in their effects as are scientific constraints on the design of experiments."[47] To use his example, in research on infectious hepatitis, it is a scientific constraint that no laboratory animal has been found that is susceptible to hepatitis, in which the large quantities of the virus needed for vaccine manufacture can be grown, and it is an ethical constraint that "it is not ethical to use human subjects for the growth of a virus for any purpose."[48]

Herrman L. Blumgart has succinctly formulated the accepted reason why the requirement of informed consent must be satisfied, and it is the familiar Judaeo-Christian one: "To use a person for an experiment without his consent is untenable; the advance of science may be retarded, but more important values are at stake."[49] Pre-eminent among those values is respecting the autonomy of potential experimental subjects. The decision whether or not they are to participate can only be theirs. Admittedly, invading their autonomy may be good for science and good for most people. But, in Beecher's words, "a particularly pernicious myth is the one that depends on the view that ends justify means. A study is ethical or not at its inception. It does not become ethical merely because it turned up

---

[46]Geoffrey Edsall, "A Positive Approach to the Problem of Human Experimentation," *Daedalus* (Spring 1969), pp. 463–479. Excerpt in Katz, p. 559.

[47]David D. Rutstein, "The Ethical Design of Human Experiments," *Daedalus* (Spring 1969), pp. 523–541. Excerpts in Katz, pp. 906–907.

[48]Rutstein, p. 529.

[49]Herrman L. Blumgart, "The Medical Framework for Viewing the Problem of Human Experimentation," *Daedalus* (Spring 1969), pp. 248–274.

valuable data. Sometimes such a view is rationalized by the investigator as having produced the most good for the most people. This is blatant statism. Whoever gave the investigator the god-like right to choose martyrs?"[50] He might have added that those who fancy they are playing God are nearly always possessed by devils.

V. RETROSPECT

The history has been outlined of two cases in which the medical profession confronted a conflict between a supposed moral constraint on professional practice and the attainment of two of its supposed ends—the health of each patient, and the health of the community at large. In both, the issue was between conceptions of moral duty, that on the one side being based on unconditional respect for persons as ends, each of those on the other alleging a requirement that a certain producible good be maximized: in the first, an individual good; in the second, a universal or "utilitarian" one. For both of the latter "consequentialist" positions appeal was made to ends that have important places in the practice of medicine. Hence both were perceived at once to have serious claims to acceptance, and were ably defended.

The history of how the conflict between the anticonsequentialist position and its consequentialist rivals was resolved is of the greatest interest to moral philosophy. From the beginning, physicians were forced to consider what is implicit in the traditional—and imperfectly understood—relation between physician and patient on which medical morality ultimately depends, and to investigate whether what on the surface seem plainly to be ultimate ends of medicine—in therapy, the health of the individual patient, and in experimentation, the health of the community at large— can justify weakening the commitment to respect for human beings that was more and more seen to underlie the traditional physician-patient relation. The result, as we have seen, was the reaffirmation of the less obvious position. The doctrine was repudiated that admittedly good consequences can justify attaining them by means in which the respect owed to human beings as such is violated. And in the process, the "common moral knowledge" implicit in the best traditional medical practice was consciously formulated as a general truth. There was a transition from common moral knowledge to knowledge of the kind Kant called "philosophical."

As Kant recognized, any such transition raises further philosophical problems. Having identified the ethical principles that are the foundation of a certain part of our common moral knowledge, we must go on to inves-

---

[50]Henry K. Beecher, "Consent in Clinical Experimentation: Myth and Reality," *Journal of the American Medical Association* **195** (1966), pp. 34–35. Excerpts in Katz, pp. 583, 638.

tigate the nature of those principles and how they are justified—to construct what he called a "metaphysic of morals," that is, a philosophical theory of morality.

And a further problem can be discerned. The moral principle implicit in the traditional conception of the physician-patient relationship rests on the conception of all human beings as autonomous ends in themselves, whose existence is beyond price. But do the theoretical medical sciences regard human beings in that way? Do they not rather lead to the concept of man which William James called "medical materialism"? If so, can these two points of view be reconciled? Or is medicine afflicted with multiple personality? But that is for another study.

Proxy Consent
H. Tristram Engelhardt, Jr.

One of the most contested issues concerning experimentation involving human subjects is the role of proxy consent. If consent functions as a way of respecting the freedom of individuals by gaining their leave in order to use them in research, then proxy consent in the case of children is suspect, although this could not be the case where competent individuals have indeed enacted a power of attorney in order to convey to others the right to make decisions on their behalf while they are incapacitated.

A number of individuals have, on the basis of respect for persons, argued against the practice of proxy consent in the case of the participation of incompetents in experimentation. Paul Ramsey, for example, would allow proxy consent only in cases where such consent is made on behalf of the manifest good of the individual concerned—for example, a parent consenting to therapeutic experimentation, with the prime intention of choosing the form of therapy most likely to be of use to the child. To quote Ramsey:

> From consent as a canon of loyalty in medical practice it follows that children, who cannot give a mature and informed consent, or adult incompetents, should not be made the subjects of medical experimentation unless, other remedies having failed to relieve their grave illness, it is reasonable to believe that the administration of a drug as yet untested or insufficiently tested on human beings, or the performance of an untried operation, may further the *patient's own recovery.* . . . The consent-requirement means: "Never

"Proxy Consent," by H. Tristram Engelhardt, Jr. is reprinted here with the permission of the author.

submit children to medical investigation not related to their own treatment, except in face of epidemic conditions endangering also each individual child."[1]

Ramsey's objection is based on the contention that to make a child subject to an experiment involving any risk or discomfort is to use that child as a means merely, rather than acknowledging it with the respect due to persons.

In short, Ramsey's argument is that one should treat all humans the same, and, since one treats adult persons with respect due to free agents, one should do the same with respect to infants. He puts this very strongly, "[children] can be harmfully used, or they can simply be used with no harm. Both the degradation of the body's fortress and being treated as a means only are human violations."[2] This position would exclude children from any nontherapeutic research, except passive observation involving no touching or other intrusion. Ramsey's position evidently is meant to apply to all humans who might be incapacitated, and precluded from giving free and informed consent.

The preponderance of those engaged in biomedical and behavioral research appears to accept more readily the practice of using infants and other incompetents as research subjects. Although the Nuremberg Code omits mention of the use of incompetents, provision for this is explicitly made in the Declaration of Helsinki: "If he is legally incompetent the consent of the legal guardian should be obtained."[3] Curran and Beecher must be counted in this group. They have argued for allowing research involving immature children (those under 14 years of age) when there is no discernible risk: "Not to allow such studies would greatly hamper important nutritional, psychological, and educational studies in children, as well as studies of inborn errors of metabolism and genetic defects."[4] That is, there are special issues raised concerning the physiological and psychological responses of children and the mentally ill that can only be answered by research involving these populations.

Moreover, standard treatment for adults, tried for the first time in special populations (e.g., children) constitutes an *experiment*. As Leon Eisenberg points out, "There is a non-trivial risk whenever a drug is given for the first time to a child. Further, the more potent the drug in treating the condition at which it is directed, the greater the risk of undesired side

[1]Paul Ramsey, *The Patient as Person: Explorations in Medical Ethics* (New Haven, Conn.: Yale University Press, 1970), pp. 11f,16.

[2]Paul Ramsey, "The Ethics of a Cottage Industry in an Age of Community and Research Medicine," *New England Journal of Medicine* **284** (April 1, 1971), p. 704.

[3]Declaration of Helsinki, III, 3a, p. 103.

[4]William J. Curran and Henry K. Beecher, "Experimentation in Children," *Journal of the American Medical Association*, **210** (October 6, 1969), p. 83.

effects."[5] Such experimentation is particularly troublesome when, as in the case of the rubella vaccine, its prime intention is not to prevent disease in the children vaccinated (but rather in fetuses in the case of rubella vaccine). To encompass experimentation such as the trial of the rubella vaccine, one would not only have to allow intrusive experimentation on incompetent populations redounding to the benefit of that population (i.e., aiding in the development of treatment of childhood diseases or mental illnesses), but one would also have to include research that cannot be done in other populations (e.g., use of rubella vaccine in pediatric-age populations would always be, at the time of its first introduction, experimental—and insofar as the major goal would be to prevent fetal defects, it would to that extent not be for the benefit of the population of children). In order to have a rubric to encompass all such experimentation on children and other incompetents, one would need a rule somewhat similar to that forwarded by the AMA, that

> ... minors or mentally incompetent persons may be used as subjects only if:
> (1) the nature of the investigation is such that mentally competent adults would not be suitable subjects; (2) consent, in writing, is given by a legally authorized representative of the subject under circumstances in which an informed and prudent adult would reasonably be expected to volunteer himself or his child as a subject.[6]

One would, in short, have to have a rule which sanctioned experimentation on incompetents, when that experimentation was nontherapeutic and involved very minimal risks and discomforts.

There have been several attempts to resolve the problem of the use in research of incompetents and, in particular, children. Suggestions have been made of a procedural sort, namely, that one should move progressively into younger age groups, thus avoiding any very unexpected reactions in the introduction of new drugs.[7] On the other hand, Richard McCormick has attempted to give a solution in principle. He wishes to justify those experiments involving children "that are scientifically well-designed (and therefore offer hope of genuine benefit), that cannot succeed unless children are used ... [and] that contain no discernible risk or undue discomfort for the child."[8] McCormick's position thus contrasts with Paul Ramsey's, for McCormick would allow subjecting children to

---

[5]Leon Eisenberg, *Experiments and Research with Humans: Values in Conflict* (Washington, D.C.: National Academy of Sciences, 1975), p. 97.

[6]American Medical Association, *Opinions and Reports of the Judicial Council*. Chicago: American Medical Association, 1971, p.12.

[7]Alexander Capron, "Legal Considerations Affecting Clinical Pharmacological Studies in Children," *Clinical Research* **21** (February 1973), pp. 141–150.

[8]Richard A. McCormick, "Proxy Consent in the Experimental Situation," *Perspectives in Biology and Medicine* **18** (August 1974), 14.

discomfort. McCormick justifies such use—that is, subjection to discomfort—of the child on the basis of what the child *ought* to wish to do.

> To share in the general effort and burden of health maintenance and disease control is part of our flourishing and growth as humans. To the extent that it is good for all of us to share this burden, we all *ought* to do so. And to the extent that we *ought* to do so, it is a reasonable construction or presumption of our wishes to say that we would do so . . . sharing in the common burden of progress in medicine constitutes an individual good for us all *up to a point.*[9]

It is in this fashion that McCormick justifies extensive experimentation and research upon children, which is morally foreclosed according to Ramsey's account.

Both Paul Ramsey and Richard McCormick frame their arguments as if one had to consider the will or wishes of incompetents. Yet, it is precisely because incompetents have no will, in the sense of a moral will, that they are incompetent; they cannot choose. There is, thus, no contradiction between the AMA's statement that minors and mentally incompetent persons can be used in research on the basis of proxy consent, and the assertion that "no person may be used as a subject against his will."[10] One does not violate the will of a baby as one brings it kicking and screaming to a harmless pin prick as its sole contribution to a hematologist's study of small infants. There is no one's will or freedom to violate. Infants, though often willful, have no free will, and are not the object of respect in the sense that adults are. Thus, one respects the right of a Werner Forsmann to catheterize his own heart[11] at unknown and, perhaps, considerable risk, while one does not accept the free consent of a normal 3-year-old child to similarly volunteer itself. Proxy consent does not exist to respect the child as a moral agent, but rather to safeguard its best interests.

If proxy consent is not seen as a safeguard against the violation of an infant's wishes (on the grounds that it is not a free agent as normal adults are), but rather as a means to protect its best interests, it follows that experimentation that does not involve an increase of risk over that of the usual ambience in which it lives, or any significant discomfort, should be allowed. One is not violating anyone's moral integrity. The point is rather to preserve the physical and psychological integrity of the child. Experiments that do not set at risk the physical or psychological integrity of the child, or other incompetents, should be, *prima facie*, allowable.

---

[9]McCormick, p. 12f

[10]*Opinions and Reports of the Judicial Council*, p. 12. My arguments have involved children not capable of free choice—not older children who are and constitute a different and more complex problem. Children and other incompetents should be involved in all such decisions insofar as they are able.

[11]*Nobel Lectures, Physiology or Medicine, 1942–1962* (Amsterdam: Elsevier, 1964), p. 511.

McCormick's point can then be reformulated, not in terms of what the child ought to wish, but in terms of what minor increase in risks should reasonably be borne by all of us as members of a society that has chosen to pursue certain goals, including the improvement of health care.[12] This final issue is too complex for the scope of this essay. The broadest notion that can be addressed here is that nearly all societies recognize a certain minimal level of risk as a social obligation to which one may be said to have implicitly consented by one's presence. Of course if they were competent, the children might protest, even to the point of demanding exit from the society. But insofar as they are not, they are not bearers of *freedom*, and need not be respected. They are, however, bearers of *interests*, and therefore must be cared for. Thus, again, in conclusion, proxy consent functions not as a way of respecting incompetents as moral agents, but as a way of protecting their best interests. Therefore, experiments that would not act against their interests, by exposing them to physical or social psychological risks greater than those in the usual environment are, *prima facie*, proper. Experiments involving very minimal risks (nearly that of the subject's ambience) and minor discomfort, may be justifiable in terms of an appeal to the minimal duties that each of us owe to our society. In the second case, there will surely be no clear lines drawn. One would hope that such lines will be drawn by prudent persons. But the absence of black-and-white distinctions should not cause one to retreat into the darkness, rather than to attempt to draw reasonable lines in the twilight.

[12]An important critique of this position is given by Professor Hans Jonas, "Philosophical Reflections on Experimenting with Human Subjects," *Daedalus* **98** (Spring 1969), esp. pp. 229f.

Consent to Medical Research on Children

Carl Wellman

It is widely believed, at least it is often said, that it is morally wrong to subject any human being to medical research without his or her free informed consent. Precisely why this is, or even might be, wrong remains something of a mystery because most of the rapidly growing literature dealing with consent in medical ethics is more concerned with the application of this

From Carl Wellman, "Consent to Medical Research on Children," *Archives for Philosophy of Law and Social Philosophy* 12, pp. 85–105; a paper from the sixth conference of Amintaphil, March 10–12, 1978. Reprinted by permission of the author.

requirement to problematic cases than with its theoretical justification. As long as the general principle that consent to medical research is morally necessary remains virtually unquestioned, it may be imagined that any inquiry into its justification would be an idle exercise in theoretical speculation. I suggest, on the contrary, that we would have a much better understanding of when and how the principle of consent applies in practice if we had a better grasp of the reasons that lie behind that principle in the first place.

I. THE RELEVANCE OF CONSENT

The central question is this: WHY is it morally wrong to conduct medical research without the consent of the human subject? Too few moral philosophers confront this question directly, and those that do have not managed to answer it adequately. Without making any attempt at a complete review of the literature, let me confess my doubts about the usual explanations of the moral relevance of consent to medical research.

The obvious act-utilitarian explanation is that it is morally wrong to subject human beings to medical research without their consent because medical research without consent is always less useful than comparable medical research with consent. Where medical research requires the active cooperation of the subject, perhaps to answer questions truthfully or to take drugs regularly, it is easy to imagine that the consent of the subject helps to ensure the utility of the research. But when drugs are simply injected into a passive patient, for example, it is hard to see why the absence of consent renders the results of the experiment less valid or valuable. Often the process of obtaining consent even seems harmful by causing the subject unnecessary anxiety or by actually distorting the results of the research. In short, the positive correlation between the consent of the subject and the utility of the research in each and every case is very dubious indeed.

Let us pretend that the vaccines we now have to protect humans from polio and measles were initially developed in part by experiments upon children who were given no opportunity to consent to the research. Surely the tremendous value of the results of this research would amply justify it on act-utilitarian grounds. What could possibly be wrong with subjecting children to such useful experiments with or without their consent? The morally sensitive person is, I suppose, indignant at the risk to which these children were, let us pretend, exposed. But risk would appear to be completely irrelevant on act-utilitarianism. Suppose that I play my own variation of Russian Roulette. I insert one round of ammunition into my six shooter, spin the cylinder, aim at someone who is not looking, and pull the trigger. If he and I are unlucky, I have acted wrongly because my act has dreadfully harmful consequences. But if we are lucky and no harm is actually done, then act-utilitarianism cannot condemn my act as morally wrong. Presumably one reason that much medical research requires the consent of the subject is that it exposes the subject to serious risk. Just because act-utilitarianism cannot deal adequately with the moral relevance of risk, it cannot readily explain the moral necessity for consent to medical research.

One of the advantages of rule-utilitarianism is that it can explain why it is morally wrong to treat anyone in a dangerous manner even when no actual harm results. A rule prohibiting dangerous conduct, at least where the level of risk is considerable and the value of lucky instances of the conduct is modest, would be useful in the long run because it would prevent the actual harm of unlucky instances at the expense of relatively little value lost. Still, rule-utilitarianism has difficulties of its own when it tries to explain the utility of any rule requiring the consent of the subject to medical research.

One difficulty is that genuine consent seems to be an impractical ideal. Saying "I consent" does not constitute a genuine act of giving consent if the speaker is uttering the demanded formula under constraint or in ignorance of the nature of the research to which he is to be subjected. The personal relationship between researcher and potential subject, especially if they also stand in the relation of physician to patient, is typically such as to impose considerable pressure upon the potential subject to consent to the research. This is even more true if the potential subject belongs to one of the dependent groups like children or prisoners. Again, the potential subject almost always lacks the medical training really to understand the information provided so that being fully informed means in practice being totally confused more often than fully enlightened. Studies have also shown that in most instances the subjects of research have psychological blocks that prevent them from truly appreciating the risks and discomforts to which they may be exposing themselves, especially in therapeutic research. It may well be that it is impossible to achieve fully free informed consent. But what can be the use of a rule requiring the impossible?

One might, of course, require consent, even though it might never in practice be ideally free and informed. But many argue that the practice of obtaining consent is a useless ritual because it provides no real protection to the potential subject. Since the potential subject lacks the medical knowledge to distinguish real risks from imaginary ones, he is almost as likely to consent to dangerous research as to innocuous experiments. It is even alleged that a zealous researcher can always obtain consent when he wants it by presenting his research in a favorable light. The only reliable protection for the subjects of medical research seems to be the conscience of the researcher, perhaps supervised by a review board of equally competent colleagues. What is the utility of a rule requiring in addition the *pro forma* consent of the subject?

A very different perspective is provided by the ethics of love. Any act of subjecting another human being to medical research without his or her consent may be construed as an unloving act. But it is far from clear just how the moral imperative "Love Thy Neighbor" calls for obtaining the consent of the subject. If one takes the love of a parent for his or her child as one's model, love seems to require acts of caring for the beloved, of contributing to its welfare and protecting it from harm, rather than constantly asking the child's consent to one's caring acts. If one takes the love of God as one's model, it might seem that the loving researcher would be prepared to sacrifice a few subjects for the well-being of all mankind. After all, God did give his only begotten son for the sins of the world.

A more promising route for a theological ethics to take is an appeal to the sacredness of man. It is immoral to sacrifice any individual human, even for the welfare of mankind, because each human being is sacred to God. But what does it mean to say that each human is sacred? If it means that each human is consecrated to the use of God, much as a temple or cemetery is sacred, then a researcher can plausibly claim that using a human being as a subject in medical research designed to promote the welfare of God's human creatures is using that subject in God's work. And if consent is required in the pursuit of the researcher's vocation, then one might more appropriately ask the consent of God, to whom the human is consecrated, than that of the subject. On the other hand, if "sacred" means worthy of reverence, as God and everything divine is sacred, then it is one more theological mystery how asking the consent of the potential subject expresses reverence. Perhaps all that reverence for the subject requires is that one proceed with the research, with or without consent, in a spirit of awe and respect for this human image of God. I do to not deny that reverence requires consent; I only complain that the link between the two is not explained.

A very similar theory was advanced by Kant in the second formulation of his categorical imperative. Certainly the most popular, and probably the most plausible, explanation of why the consent of the subject to medical research is morally necessary is that to subject any person to medical research without consent is to treat this person as a mere means and to fail to respect his or her practical rationality. On this very abstract level, this explanation is tempting. But the more fully one inquires into the details of this explanation, the more one wonders precisely why it is that to fail to obtain consent is to treat the subject of research as a mere means.

One version of the Kantian explanation holds that to perform medical research on any human being without consent is to treat the subject as a mere means because the subject is merely acted on, like a thing, but is not an actor in the research, like a second person. When the subject gives consent, however, he or she becomes by this act a partner in a cooperative research enterprise. Noble as this transformation from passive object to cooperative agent sounds, I remain sceptical. Even after consent, the subject of medical research is typically acted on rather than an actor in the research. The subject does not do anything in any morally significant sense, for example, when the researcher injects a drug into his body and observes the results. To be sure, if the researcher hands the subject some pills and the subject pops them into his mouth and swallows them, then he has taken an active part in the research. But if all that a Kantian ethics requires is that the subject of research be an actor in the research project, then as long as one takes pills or performs some other act, the additional act of giving consent would seem to be entirely unnecessary. A truly Kantian explanation must probe more deeply than the distinction between being acted on and being actor in research.

Another, and more profound, version of the Kantian explanation appeals to the notion of the autonomy of the rational moral agent. Every human being possesses practical reason and, thus, the capacity for autonomous choice. Only if the subject of medical research consents to the research is his or her autonomy respected because only if he or she has consented is he or she subjected to the research by his or her own free choice. Brushing aside obscurities in the notion of autonomy, this explanation proves too much. If the autonomy of the human subject requires consent to medical research in this way, why does it not equally and for the same reason require consent to every other sort of treatment as well? This implies that it is wrong to give my friend a surprise birthday party without first obtaining his or her consent and that it is morally wrong for a medical researcher to ask a potential subject for his or her consent without first asking for his or her consent to be asked for his or her consent. Surely this is a *reductio ad absurdum.* What is needed here is some sort of explanation of why it is that certain kinds of actions upon others, such as medical research, are wrong without their consent while other kinds of actions upon others, such as asking for their consent, do not morally require their prior consent.

My hypothesis is that consent is morally necessary precisely when one's mode of conduct threatens or invades one or more ethical rights of some second party. This hypothesis receives some confirmation from a sampling of a few paradigm cases of kinds of act that cry out for the consent of the party affected by them—reading someone's mail, using someone's property, postponing repayment of a debt, using someone's name as a reference, releasing or publishing confidential information about someone. These kinds of action are prima facie morally wrong in the absence of consent just because they invade important ethical rights of others, such as the right to privacy or the right to the exclusive use of one's property.

I suggest that similarly the consent of the human subject is morally required for medical research because medical research typically threatens fundamental ethical rights of the subject. All research by its very nature involves the collection and storing of information about the subject; therefore, where this information is potentially damaging to the individual, research invades his right to privacy. Many of the procedures used in medical research, such as taking case histories, or taking blood samples or trying out chemotherapy, range from mildly discomforting to downright painful. These disturbing intrusions into the life of the subject invade his right to privacy in another way. Whenever significant medical risk is involved, experimentation threatens the subject's moral right to personal security, in extreme cases even his right to life. The subject's moral right to truth is at stake whenever research requires or allows the deception of the subject, sometimes an essential condition for the reliability of the data. Nontherapeutic research uses the subject as a means of acquiring scientific knowledge without offering any medical benefit to the subject; accordingly it threatens his moral right to freedom from exploitation. By applying an unproved and uncertain treatment to a patient in need of medical care, therapeutic research can invade the patient's moral right to the best medical care his physician can provide. It is because medical research threatens or invades these and other moral rights of the subject that it is morally wrong unless that subject has given his or her consent to it.

But if medical research really does invade the moral rights of the subject in these various ways, how can the consent of the subject make it morally permissible? Why do not the very same rights that make such research morally wrong if conducted without consent continue to make it morally wrong even after consent? The answer is that the subject's act of giving consent constitutes an act of waiving his or her relevant ethical claim-rights against the researcher. Each ethical claim right is a system of ethical autonomy with respect to one or more core claims.[1] This implies that the possessor of the right has various sorts of freedom and control over these core claims, usually including the ethical power to waive these claims and thereby to suspend or cancel their correlative duties. Thus, by his act of giving consent to the medical research, the potential subject relieves the researcher of his or her prior moral duties to refrain from treating the subject in certain ways. With these duties removed, medical research becomes, in the absence of other wrong-making characteristics, morally permissible.

The suggestion that the consent of the subject is required for medical research because of the moral rights of the subject is not news, of course,

---

[1]Carl Wellman, "A New Conception of Human Rights," in *Human Rights*, ed. E. Kamenka and A.E-S. Tay (London: Edward Arnold, 1978).

but the way in which consent and rights are related has usually been misconstrued. It is often said that the moral point of obtaining consent is to protect the subject from risk to life or limb or health and in this way to secure his moral right to personal security or to bodily integrity. But when a human being consents to medical research, fully informed of the medical risks involved, the human subject is *not* protected from risk. The point of obtaining consent is not to prevent the subject from being exposed to medical risk, but to legitimize the researcher's actions that impose that risk. Again, when a subject gives his consent to having highly personal or potentially damaging information about himself collected, stored and even published in some form, his consent does not prevent his privacy from being invaded; it simply keeps the researcher's invasion of his privacy from being morally wrong. The moral relevance of free informed consent is recognized only when consent is construed as an act of waiving one or more moral rights that otherwise stand in the way of medical research.

It is usually asserted, and I agree, that the subject who has once given free informed consent remains free to withdraw his or her consent at any time as the research progresses. This is easily explained on my hypothesis. Since waiving a right is not identical with renouncing or divesting oneself of the right, the subject retains his or her moral claim-rights against the researcher and can reclaim them at any moment. This rules out any contractarian explanation of the relevance of consent to medical research. Versions of the social contract theory, especially as they bear on issues of social justice, are very much in the air these days. They might suggest that in giving consent the potential subject is contracting with the researcher to permit the researcher to subject him to specified research procedures. That this is not so can be seen from the fact that the subject is not bound by his consent as he would be bound by any contract; he may withdraw his consent at any time and cease to permit the researcher to subject him to further medical research. This means that the moral relevance of consent to medical research is quite different from the relevance that the social contract theory ascribes to consent as the ground of political obligation.

II. CONSENT
AS AN ETHICAL POWER

I have suggested that we interpret consent to medical research as the subject's act of waiving his or her relevant moral rights against the researcher. To speak of "waiving one's rights," however, is to speak the idiom of the law, for it is in the province of legal claim-rights that the concept of waiving one's rights has its home. And in legal theory, the act of waiving a right is standardly taken to be one instance of exercising a legal power. This suggests that consent to medical research ought analogously to be interpreted in ethical theory as one instance of the exercise of an ethical power. But we look in vain in the language of utilitarianism, of Kantianism and of theological ethics for any terminology in which to express this analogy. Let us, therefore, inquire whether any such analogy exists and, if it does, whether it is theoretically illuminating.

A *legal power* is the legal capacity to perform some act that has specific legal consequences and that is normally performed in order to bring about some such consequences. Typical examples of legal powers are one party's legal power to contract with some second party who has made him an offer, the owner's legal power of giving his property to another, a citizen's legal power of renouncing his or her citizenship, a single person's legal power of marrying someone of the opposite sex, a clergyman's legal power of performing the marriage ceremony, and the creditor's legal power of waiving his legal claim to repayment....

I suggest that by analogy we introduce into ethical theory the concept of an ethical power. An ethical power is the ethical ability to perform some act that has specific ethical consequences and that is normally performed in order to bring about some such consequences. A paradigm case is the ethical power to make a promise. One usually, but not always, exercises this ethical power by saying, in the appropriate circumstances and with a straight face, "I promise to do such and so." The ethical consequence is that the speaker is then morally obligated, at least prima facie, to do such and so. This is an ethical consequence because moral obligations are ethical, and this is a consequence in the sense that the statement that one has in fact said "I promise to do such and so" logically implies (in some way still being debated among moral philosophers) the statement that one ought to do such and so. But this consequence follows only on the presupposition that the speaker was, at the time of uttering those fateful words, ethically competent to make that promise. What is required ethically is not the linguistic ability to use the words "I promise..." correctly or the physical capacity to utter those noises, but possession of the ethical qualifications for promising. To be ethically capable of promising one must understand the nature of the act one is promising to perform, have the moral maturity to understand what it is to commit oneself to future action, not be coerced into saying "I promise...," etc. This ethical capacity to promise is an ethical power in the strict sense because one normally says "I promise..." in order to bind oneself morally to a certain action....

What, if anything, have we gained by this digression? Does it really matter that the concept of an ethical power is lacking from traditional ethical theory? Let me begin by confessing openly that there is one respect in which this conception is of no help whatsoever. One cannot explain *how* the act of giving consent to medical research cancels certain of the researcher's duties to the subject by saying "consenting is an exercise of the ethical power of cancelling duties" any more than one can explain how opium puts one to sleep by referring to its dormative powers. Again, I do not imagine for a moment that the ethical problems concerning exactly how or why the fact that someone said "I promise..." implies that the speaker now has an obligation to do what he said he would do are solved by noting that saying "I promise..." is exercising one's ethical power of imposing obligations upon oneself. If the concept of an ethical power is illuminating for ethical theory, it must be in other ways.

The concept of an ethical power is an essentially dynamic concept; it is the concept of a capacity to *act* in a way that *changes* the ethical situation, perhaps by creating or cancelling obligations. Accordingly, any ethical theory that lacks this concept, and the derivative concept of an ethical liability, tends to neglect the dynamic aspects of ethics. Traditional ethical theory has focussed upon the static side of ethics because it has concerned itself primarily with what *is* right or wrong, good or bad. The concepts of value and obligation do not in themselves call our attention to the ways in which values and obligations can be and are changed through human action. Ways of acting in order to create or extinguish moral duties become the direct subject of theoretical attention only when one introduces some such concept as that of an ethical power....

The concept of an ethical power points in two directions, forward to possible ethical consequences and backward to the competence in which it is grounded. It is my authorization from my wife that makes me competent to give away her cat. This is, however, only one very special case of an ethical power. There are many kinds of ethical power. The power to make a promise differs from the power to release someone from a promise. The power to impose obligations upon some second party by issuing orders to him or her differs from the power to cancel certain duties of another toward oneself by consenting to being treated in some manner, a manner that would otherwise be *prima facie* wrong. Each sort of ethical power will have its own sort of competence, a set of qualifications that may be similar in some ways and different in some ways from other sorts of ethical competence. The systematic study of the various sorts of competence has been missing because traditional ethical theory has lacked the concept of an ethical power. One tiny corner of this area has, to be sure, been intensively studied. There is a large body of literature dealing with moral responsibility, with the competence to perform an action for which one may properly be held morally responsible. But this is only one very special sort of ethical competence. The introduction of the concept of an ethical power opens up the entire field of ethical competence for theoretical investigation.

In our attempt to understand the moral relevance of consent to medical research, we discovered that the difficulties that traditional ethical theories have had in explaining why consent is morally necessary stem in part from a serious inadequacy in the vocabulary and conceptual apparatus of traditional ethics. My hypothesis that in giving consent the potential subject of research is waiving one or more of his moral claim-rights against the researcher has led to the concept of an ethical power. I have given a partial analysis of this concept and suggested ways in which the addition of this concept to ethics will considerably increase the potential explanatory power of ethical theory.

III. THE CONSENT
OF THE CHILD

Now let us turn from theoretical explanation to practical application. Can my hypothesis provide any helpful guidance when applied to the moral justifiability of medical research upon children? Research on children promises to be a crucial test case just because it appears to be recalcitrant to my hypothesis. The obvious difficulties are that it is most uncertain what moral rights, if any, children possess and that there are grave doubts about the capacity of children, especially young children, to give consent to medical research.

General doubts about the practicability of fully free and informed consent become intensified in the special case of children. To be sure, even a young child may be able to say "I consent" or to sign his or her name on a consent form, but his childish act may not constitute genuine consent. It might not be fully free because children are so highly vulnerable and so completely dependent upon those who care for them that they may be coerced in subtle and indirect ways into doing what they think their parents or other adults wish. It might not be fully informed because the child lacks the background knowledge to interpret the bare facts presented to him or her and has not yet developed the capacity of reason sufficiently to appreciate fully their relevance to the decision at hand. . . .

Is the consent of the child subject morally necessary in the sense that it is morally wrong to perform medical research on the child without his or her consent? If the child possesses the moral rights to privacy, personal security, life, freedom from deception, freedom from exploitation, and the best medical care his or her physician can provide—all rights threatened by typical medical research—then it is morally wrong to subject the child to research without his or her consent. Well, then, is a child capable of possessing such moral rights? The answer depends as much upon one's conception of a moral right as upon the nature of a child. I conceive of a moral right as a system of ethical autonomy, a complex structure of ethical claims, liberties, powers and immunities.[2] On this conception, only

[2]Wellman, pp. 52–55.

an autonomous being can possess rights. Since an ethical liberty is a liberty of doing some specified action and an ethical power is a power of bringing about some specific ethical consequence by one's action, only a being capable of moral action can meaningfully be said to possess either an ethical liberty or an ethical power. And since liberties and powers are essential elements in every moral right, only an autonomous moral agent may properly be said to possess a moral right. Given plausible assumptions about the nature of young children, it follows that infants have no moral rights at all and that children acquire rights only gradually as they develop their moral maturity and achieve the status of autonomous moral agents. Since pretty much the same mental capacities are required to choose rationally and to give free informed consent, the capacity to possess moral rights develops hand in hand with the capacity to waive the gradually acquired rights. Hence, I propose as a general rule that the consent of the child subject to medical research is morally necessary whenever and to the degree that the child is capable of giving that consent. Where the child really is incapable of consent, but let us not be too quick to presume such incapacity, his or her consent to medical research is not necessary. The reason consent is not then necessary, however, is not the child's incapacity to give it but the parallel incapacity to possess the moral rights that would be waived were consent possible.

Since growth in moral autonomy is a very gradual process, it will not be possible to draw any sharp lines between the age of moral immaturity and the age of consent. I suggest that in all doubtful cases the conscientious researcher ought to obtain the consent of the child, imperfect as that consent might be. It is better to err on the side of respecting the child as a moral agent for two reasons. To the extent that the child has already achieved the status of a moral agent, its moral autonomy requires that its rights be respected. Also, treating a child as though it were fully responsible is an essential part of the process by which it achieves moral maturity, and refusing to treat a child as an equal retards the growth of practical reason and self-respect in the child.

So much for the moral necessity of obtaining the consent of the child. Is the consent of a child subjected to medical research sufficient to justify that research morally? The reply is in the negative, and for three reasons. First, probably there are some moral rights that are unwaivable. The traditional belief in inalienable rights is as venerable as it is obscure. One sense in which a right might be inalienable is that its possessor lacks the ethical power to waive it. I believe that a human being does have some ethical rights that he cannot waive, probably the right to freedom from torture and possibly the right not to be killed. Second, there are many wrongmaking characteristics that are independent of rights. It is surely wrong to inflict unnecessary suffering upon an animal even though animals lack the capacity to possess any right to freedom from torture. Accordingly, even when the relevant rights of a human subject to medical research have been waived, there may well be other considerations that make the research morally wrong, for example that it is so poorly designed that it is incapable of producing significant results. Third, medical research may be morally wrong because it threatens or invades the rights of persons other than the subject. A case in point is medical research upon a child when the parents have not given their consent.

IV. THE CONSENT
OF THE PARENT

It is usually maintained, quite correctly, that medical research on a child is morally wrong unless the parents have given their free informed consent. Can the moral necessity of parental consent also be explained on the hypothesis that the act of consent is an act of waiving some moral right or rights that would otherwise be violated by the research? I believe that it can.

Parental consent might be interpreted as proxy consent. Perhaps in giving their consent the parents are acting for the child in waiving the child's moral rights to privacy, personal security, etc. This explanation should not be rejected out of hand. Parents often do seem to act for their child. They open savings accounts in their child's name, take out insurance for their child (not to be confused with taking out insurance *on* their child), and make promises on behalf of their child. Especially when the child is too young to be capable of giving free informed consent himself or herself, it is plausible to hold that the parents can and do act for their child.

Still, this popular interpretation of parental consent is beset with serious difficulties. (1) One must explain what it is that authorizes the parents to act for their child. My banker or real estate agent can act for me only because I have authorized him to do so, but presumably a child incapable of giving consent is equally incapable of authorizing its parents to act for it in waiving its moral rights. I do not assume that the only possible ground for the moral authority of the parents to act for their child is an authorization from their child, but I do insist that until some other valid ground is specified, the allegation that the parents are, ethically speaking, acting for their child is entirely groundless. (2) The difficulty goes deeper than this. What could it *mean* to say that the parent acts for the child? Expressions like "acts for" or "acts on behalf of" are ambiguous. Sometimes they mean that one party acts as agent of the other party, that the act of the former is to be taken as the act of the latter; at other times they mean that the former acts for the sake of or in the interest of the latter. It is easy enough to understand how the parent can act for the sake of or in the interest of the child, but then it is acting as caretaker and not as proxy. It is hard to see what sense could be attached to the assertion that the parent acts as agent of or in place of the child when it has been conceded that the child is incapable of acting for itself. If it does not make any sense to speak of "the action of x," then it cannot make any more sense to say that some action of y is "a substitute for the action of x." Only of two moral agents does it make sense to say that the act of one replaces the act of the other. (3) This interpretation fails to explain precisely what needs explaining, why it is that parental consent is morally necessary, for proxy consent must surely be nearly always unnecessary. If the child has achieved moral maturity, then there is no need of proxy consent simply because the child is quite capable of consenting for himself or herself. If the child has not yet become an autonomous person, then there is no need for consent at all because the child has not yet acquired moral rights that need to be waived by any act of consent. (4) This interpretation also threatens to make the consent of the child, where it is possible, redundant. If the parent really is acting as proxy for the child, then the consent of the parent *is* the consent of the child, just as my broker's act of buying ten shares of stock in my name constitutes my purchase of that stock. My worry about redundancy is not so much that as philosophers we do violence to Ockham's razor as that as moralists we might justify violations of the moral rights of the child. Parental consent should not be allowed to function as a disguised coercion of the child. This implies that parental consent should not be interpreted so that it makes the free informed consent of the child, where possible, unnecessary.

Fortunately there is a very different and more adequate interpretation of parental consent to medical research that arises from an understanding of the parent's duties to the child. Normally, the parent has a moral duty to care for the child. This includes at least the duty to see to it that the child's basic human needs for food, shelter, clothing, personality development, education and protection of life and health are satisfied. But the parent cannot fulfill this duty to care for the child if friends, neighbors, strangers or just busybodies are free to interfere with his or her activities of raising and providing for the child. Thus by something like the Kantian principle that ought implies can, the parent's duty to care for the child implies an ethical claim-right of the parent against others that they not interfere with the parental activity of caring for the child. But medical research on the child does often, and perhaps inevitably, interfere with this activity. It invades the privacy of the child-parent relationship, involves the child in activities that may preclude others the parent would choose to have the child engage in, and may even expose the health of the child to risk. Therefore, medical research upon the child is morally wrong unless the parents of the child consent to it and thereby waive their claim-right to freedom from interference with their care of the child. Thus, in giving their consent, the parents are not acting as proxies for their child and waiving their child's moral claim-rights against the researcher; they are acting for themselves and waiving their own rights.

Is the consent of one parent sufficient to waive these parental rights to freedom from interference with their activity of caring for their child? Well, in families where there is only one parent with any moral duty to care for the child, clearly only one parent needs to consent to the research on that child. Even in families with two responsible parents, the consent of one parent can count as consent of both provided that the other parent has authorized him or her to act for her or him with respect to the child. An analogous, if somewhat trivial, case is that in which either my wife or I accept an invitation to dinner on behalf of both of us. Since we both regard consultation on such matters as an unnecessary and undesirable bother, we have an understanding with each other that we each have the ethical power to accept any social invitation issued to us as a couple. Similarly, in families in which husband and wife cooperate and have an understanding that each will back the other up, the act of one parent counts morally, barring any exceptional circumstances, as the act of both. Here proxy consent does play a role; but it is the consent of one parent for both rather than the consent of parent for child.

There has been considerable debate as to the limits of the morally justifiable exercise of the parental ethical power of consenting to medical research on the child. Several moral philosophers have argued that the parental duty to protect the life and health of the child rules out any parental consent to nontherapeutic research upon the child where there is any significant medical risk at all. (Note the need to clarify the sense of "rules out." Is it alleged that any parental act that purports to give consent would be ethically null and void *or* that although it would have its usual ethical consequences, it would be morally wrong? Here is one illustration of the need for distinguishing between an ethical power and an ethical liberty, for it is not clear which is being denied in this case.) There is also the problem of whether it is ethically possible and morally proper for a parent to consent to an experimental therapy for the sake of research when there is available an established therapeutic procedure that could be used to treat the child.

Debate continues to focus on two guiding principles. (1) The parent can properly consent to medical research upon the child involving medical risk to that child only if such medical risk is outweighed by expected medical benefit to the child. This principle strikes me as unduly restrictive. Granting for the moment that in acting *as parent* the parent ought to consider only the interests of the child and that among the duties of parental care the duty of protecting the child is most stringent, why must medical risk always be outweighed by medical benefit? It would seem as though occasionally some other interest of the child might serve to justify a modest medical risk. Moreover, I might wish to retract what I initially granted. I am very dubious that the parental duty to protect the child from danger does always take precedence over the parent's other duties of caring for the child. It is not in the child's best interests to be over-protective, and sometimes the duty to help the child develop his or her personality or the duty to educate the child may morally dictate exposing the child to some risk to life or limb or health. Finally, even acting *as parent* the parent may well appeal to considerations other than the interests of the child. The child-parent relationship is one that exists within the family; to stand in the relation of parent to child is to occupy two roles in the institution of the family. If it happens that the family consists of only one parent and one child, they still constitute a family. Therefore, in acting as a parent the parent might well consider family interests that need not be identical with any interests of the child.

A less restrictive principle is that (2) the parent may consent to any medical research on the child to which the child would consent if the child were fully rational and capable of free informed consent. Since altruistic action can be rationally justified and the child, if rational, would sometimes choose to engage in such action, the parent may expose the child to medical risk whenever the proposed research upon the child is rationally justified. The trouble with this principle is that it is of the wrong sort. It would be an appropriate principle to govern parental consent if parental consent were interpreted as proxy consent. But since in giving his or her consent the parent is waiving his or her own rights and not the relevant rights of the child, there is no reason why the parental decision to give or withhold consent should be governed by what the child would decide if the child were an autonomous rational agent. The parental decision should be guided by what it is rational for the parent himself or herself as parent to decide.

Accordingly I propose a different principle to limit parental consent to medical research on the child. (3) The parent may consent only to medical research that will not interfere seriously with the parental activity of caring for the child and that promises benefits to mankind that more than offset any risk to the subject. Since the moral relevance of parental consent to medical research arises from the parental duty to care for the child, it is appropriate to ground the limits to morally justifiable consent upon that same duty. Still, this limitation might well permit consent to some non-therapeutic research involving significant risk, for this research might not seriously interfere with the parental activity of raising the child. The compatibility, or lack of it, between the conduct of the research and the parental activity of caring for the child will depend upon the detailed nature of the research and the parent's plans for this period in the child's life.

V. CONCLUSION

A central presupposition of contemporary medical ethics is that it is morally wrong to subject any human being to medical research without the person's free informed consent. I have argued that traditional ethical theories have to date been unable to explain the moral relevance of consent to medical research and have proposed the hypothesis that in giving consent the subject is waiving certain moral claim-rights against the researcher. This led to the suggestion that the explanatory power of ethical theory would be increased by the addition of the concept of an ethical power to its conceptual apparatus. Finally, I have applied my hypothesis to several moral problems that arise with respect to the consent of parent and child to medical research on children.

Where do we go from here? On to the theory of rights and, at the same time, back to more fundamental ethical theory. My hypothesis will be illuminating in practice and justified in theory only if we can define more precisely the moral rights at stake in medical research and identify the grounds of such moral rights. Presumably these grounds will be found in some sort of utilitarian or Kantian or theological ethics. But I predict that only an ethical theory that takes account of ethical powers and immunities can provide adequate grounds for ethical rights. Such an enriched ethical theory will be better able to give an adequate explanation of the exercise of our various ethical powers, including the act of giving consent to medical research.

SELECTED SUPPLEMENTARY READINGS

AMERICAN PSYCHOLOGICAL ASSOCIATION, AD HOC COMMITTEE ON ETHICAL STANDARDS IN PSYCHOLOGICAL RESEARCH, *Ethical Principles in the Conduct of Research with Human Participants.* Washington, D.C.: American Psychological Association, 1973.

ANNAS, GEORGE, et al., *Informed Consent to Human Experimentation.* Cambridge, Mass.: Ballinger, 1977.

BARBER, BERNARD, et al., *Research on Human Subjects: Problems of Social Control in Medical Experimentation.* New York: Russell Sage Foundation, 1973.

———, *Informed Consent in Medical Therapy and Research.* New Brunswick, N.J.: Rutgers University Press, 1980.

BEAUCHAMP, TOM L., AND JAMES F. CHILDRESS, *Principles of Biomedical Ethics.* New York: Oxford University Press, 1979, chaps. III–V and Appendices.

BEAUCHAMP, TOM L., et al., *Ethical Issues in Social Science Research.* Baltimore, Md.: The Johns Hopkins University Press, 1982.

BEAUCHAMP, TOM L. AND LEROY WALTERS, eds., *Contemporary Issues in Bioethics* (2nd ed.). Belmont, Calif.: Wadsworth, 1982.

BEECHER, HENRY K., *Research and the Individual: Human Studies.* Boston: Little, Brown, 1970.

BLACKSTONE, WILLIAM T., "The American Psychological Association Code of Ethics for Research Involving Human Participants: An Appraisal," *Southern Journal of Philosophy* **13** (Winter 1975).

BYAR, DAVID P., "Randomized Clinical Trials: Perspectives on Some Recent Ideas," *New England Journal of Medicine* **295** (July 8, 1976).

CAMPBELL, A.G.M., "Infants, Children, and Informed Consent," *British Medical Journal* **3** (August 3, 1974).

CAPRON, ALEXANDER M., "Informed Consent in Catastrophic Disease Research and Treatment," *University of Pennsylvania Law Review* **123** (December 1974).

CHILDRESS, JAMES F., "Compensating Injured Research Subjects: The Moral Argument," *Hastings Center Report* **6** (December 1976).

———, *Priorities in Biomedical Ethics*. Philadelphia, Pa.: Westminster Press, 1981, chap. 3.

FOST, NORMAN C., "A Surrogate System for Informed Consent," *Journal of the American Medical Association* **233** (August 18, 1975).

FREUND, PAUL, ed., *Experimentation with Human Subjects*. New York: George Braziller, 1970.

FRIED, CHARLES, *Medical Experimentation: Personal Integrity and Social Policy*. New York: American Elsevier, 1974.

GRAY, BRADFORD H., *Human Subjects in Medical Experimentation*. New York: John Wiley, 1975.

KATZ, JAY, WITH ALEXANDER M. CAPRON AND ELEANOR SWIFT GLASS, *Experimentation with Human Beings*. New York: Russell Sage Foundation, 1972.

MCCORMICK, RICHARD A., "Proxy Consent in the Experimentation Situation," *Perspectives in Biology and Medicine* **18** (Autumn 1974).

———, "Experimentation in Children: Sharing in Sociality," *Hastings Center Report* **6** (December 1976).

———, "Experimental Subjects: Who Should They Be?" *Journal of the American Medical Association* **235** (May 17, 1976).

NATIONAL COMMISSION FOR THE PROTECTION OF HUMAN SUBJECTS OF BIOMEDICAL AND BEHAVIORAL RESEARCH, *Report and Recommendations: Research on the Fetus*. DHEW Publication No. (OS) 76–127 (1976). *Appendix to Report and Recommendations: Research on the Fetus*. DHEW Publication No. (OS) 76–128 (1976).

———, *Report and Recommendations: Research Involving Prisoners*. DHEW Publication No. (OS) 76–131 (1976). *Appendix to Report and Recommendations: Research Involving Prisoners*. DHEW Publication No. (OS) 76–132 (1976).

———, *Report and Recommendations: Psychosurgery*. DHEW Publication No. (OS) 77–0001 (1977). *Appendix to Report and Recommendations: Psychosurgery*. DHEW Publication No. (OS) 77–0002 (1977).

———, *Disclosure of Research Information Under the Freedom of Information Act*. DHEW Publication No. (OS) 77–0003 (1977).

———, *Report and Recommendations: Research Involving Children*. DHEW Publication No. (OS) 77–0004 (1977). *Appendix to Report and Recommendations: Research Involving Children*. DHEW Publication No. (OS) 77–0005 (1977).

———, *Report and Recommendations: Research Involving Those Institutionalized as Mentally Infirm*. DHEW Publication No. (OS) 78–0006 (1978). *Appendix to Report and Recommendations: Research Involving Those Institutionalized as Mentally Infirm*. DHEW Publication No. (OS) 78–0007. (1978).

———, *Report and Recommendations: Institutional Review Boards*. DHEW Publication No. (OS) 78–0008 (1978). *Appendix to Report and Recommendations: Institutional Review Boards*. DHEW Publication No. (OS) 78–0009 (1978).

————, *Report and Recommendations: Ethical Guidelines For the Delivery of Health Services by DHEW.* DHEW Publication No. (OS) 78–0010 (1978). *Appendix to Report and Recommendations: Ethical Guidelines for the Delivery of Health Services by DHEW.* DHEW Publication No. (OS) 78–0011 (1978).

————, *The Belmont Report: Ethical Guidelines for the Protection of Human Subjects of Research.* DHEW Publication No. (OS) 78–0012 (1978). *Appendices A and B to The Belmont Report: Ethical Guidelines for the Protection of Human Subjects of Research.* DHEW Publication Nos. (OS) 78–0013–14 (1978).

RAMSEY, PAUL, "The Enforcement of Morals: Nontherapeutic Research on Children," *Hastings Center Report* **6** (August 1976).

————, "Children as Research Subjects: A Reply," *Hastings Center Report* **7** (April 1977).

ROBERTSON, JOHN A., "Compensating Injured Research Subjects: The Law," *Hastings Center Report* **6** (December 1976).

ROBISON, WADE L. AND MICHAEL PRITCHARD, eds., *Medical Responsibility.* Clifton, N.J.: The Humana Press, 1979.

VEATCH, ROBERT M., *Case Studies in Medical Ethics.* Cambridge, Mass.: Harvard University Press, 1977, chap. 11.

WALTERS, LEROY, "Some Ethical Issues in Research Involving Human Subjects," *Perspectives in Biology and Medicine* **20** (Winter 1977).

Encyclopedia of Bioethics
Articles

Behavioral Research, Herbert C. Kelman
Biomedical Research, Robert J. Levine
Human Experimentation: History, Gert H. Brieger
Human Experimentation: Basic Issues, Alexander M. Capron
Human Experimentation: Philosophical Aspects, Charles Fried
Human Experimentation: Social and Professional Control, Mark S. Frankel
Informed Consent in Human Research: Social Aspects, Bradford H. Gray
Informed Consent in Human Research: Ethical and Legal Aspects, Karen Lebacqz and Robert J. Levine

chapter twelve

Animal Rights
and Animal Research

All Animals Are Equal

Peter Singer

In recent years a number of oppressed groups have campaigned vigorously for equality. The classic instance is the Black Liberation movement, which demands an end to the prejudice and discrimination that has made blacks second-class citizens. The immediate appeal of the black liberation movement and its initial, if limited, success made it a model for other oppressed groups to follow. We became familiar with liberation movements for Spanish-Americans, gay people, and a variety of other minorities. When a majority group—women—began their campaign, some thought we had come to the end of the road. Discrimination on the basis of sex, it has been said, is the last universally accepted form of discrimination, practiced without secrecy or pretense even in those liberal circles that have long prided themselves on their freedom from prejudice against racial minorities.

From Peter Singer, "All Animals Are Equal," *Philosophic Exchange* 2, no. 1 (1974). Reprinted by permission of the author. This article is reprinted unabridged.

Passages of this article appeared in a review of *Animals, Men and Morals*, ed. S. and R. Godlovitch and J. Harris (London: Gollancz and Taplinger, (1972) in *The New York Review of Books* (April 5, 1973). The whole direction of my thinking on this subject I owe to talks with a number of friends in Oxford in 1970–71, especially Richard Keshen, Stanley Godlovitch, and, above all, Roslind Godlovitch.

One should always be wary of talking of "the last remaining form of discrimination." If we have learned anything from the liberation movements, we should have learned how difficult it is to be aware of latent prejudice in our attitudes to particular groups until this prejudice is forcefully pointed out.

A liberation movement demands an expansion of our moral horizons and an extension or reinterpretation of the basic moral principle of equality. Practices that were previously regarded as natural and inevitable come to be seen as the result of an unjustifiable prejudice. Who can say with confidence that all his or her attitudes and practices are beyond criticism? If we wish to avoid being numbered among the oppressors, we must be prepared to rethink even our most fundamental attitudes. We need to consider them from the point of view of those most disadvantaged by our attitudes, and the practices that follow from these attitudes. If we can make this unaccustomed mental switch we may discover a pattern in our attitudes and practices that consistently operate so as to benefit one group—usually the one to which we ourselves belong—at the expense of another. In this way we may come to see that there is a case for a new liberation movement. My aim is to advocate that we make this mental switch in respect of our attitudes and practices towards a very large group of beings: members of species other than our own—or, as we popularly though misleadingly call them, animals. In other words, I am urging that we extend to other species the basic principle of equality that most of us recognize should be extended to all members of our own species.

All this may sound a little farfetched, more like a parody of other liberation movements than a serious objective. In fact, in the past the idea of "The Rights of Animals" really has been used to parody the case for women's rights. When Mary Wollstonecroft, a forerunner of later feminists, published her *Vindication of the Rights of Women* in 1792, her ideas were widely regarded as absurd, and they were satirized in an anonymous publication entitled *A Vindication of the Rights of Brutes.* The author of this satire (actually Thomas Taylor, a distinguished Cambridge philosopher) tried to refute Wollstonecroft's reasonings by showing that they could be carried one stage further. If sound when applied to women, why should the arguments not be applied to dogs, cats and horses? They seemed to hold equally well for these "brutes"; yet to hold that brutes had rights was manifestly absurd; therefore the reasoning by which this conclusion had been reached must be unsound, and if unsound when applied to brutes, it must also be unsound when applied to women, since the very same arguments had been used in each case.

One way in which we might reply to this argument is by saying that the case for equality between men and women cannot validly be extended to nonhuman animals. Women have a right to vote, for instance, because they are just as capable of making rational decisions as men are; dogs, on the other hand, are incapable of understanding the significance of voting, so they cannot have the right to vote. There are many other obvious ways in which men and women resemble each other closely, while humans and other animals differ greatly. So, it might be said, men and women are similar beings, and should have equal rights, while humans and nonhumans are different and should not have equal rights.

The thought behind this reply to Taylor's analogy is correct up to a point, but it does not go far enough. There *are* important differences between humans and other animals, and these differences must give rise to *some* differences in the rights that each have. Recognizing this obvious fact, however, is no barrier to the case for extending the basic principle of equality to nonhuman animals. The differences that exist between men and women are equally undeniable, and the supporters of Women's Liberation are aware that these differences may give rise to different rights. Many feminists hold that women have the right to an abortion on request. It does not follow that since these same people are campaigning for equality between men and women they must support the right of men to have abortions too. Since a man cannot have an abortion, it is meaningless to talk of his right to have one. Since a pig can't vote, it is meaningless to talk of its right to vote. There is no reason why either Women's Liberation or Animal Liberation should get involved in such nonsense. The extension of the basic principle of equality from one group to another does not imply that we must treat both groups in exactly the same way, or grant exactly the same rights to both groups. Whether we should do so will depend on the nature of the members of the two groups. The basic principle of equality, I shall argue, is equality of consideration; and equal consideration for different beings may lead to different treatment and different rights.

So there is a different way of replying to Taylor's attempt to parody Wollstonecroft's arguments, a way which does not deny the differences between humans and nonhumans, but goes more deeply into the question of equality, and concludes by finding nothing absurd in the idea that the basic principle of equality applies to so-called "brutes." I believe that we reach this conclusion if we examine the basis on which our opposition to discrimination on grounds of race or sex ultimately rests. We will then see that we would be on shaky ground if we were to demand equality for blacks, women, and other groups of oppressed humans, while denying equal consideration to nonhumans.

When we say that all human beings, whatever their race, creed or sex, are equal, what is it that we are asserting? Those who wish to defend a hierarchical, inegalitarian society have often pointed out that by whatever test we choose, it simply is not true that all humans are equal. Like it or not, we must face the fact that humans come in different shapes and sizes;

they come with differing moral capacities, differing intellectual abilities, differing amounts of benevolent feeling and sensitivity to the needs of others, differing abilities to communicate effectively, and differing capacities to experience pleasure and pain. In short, if the demand for equality were based on the actual equality of all human beings, we would have to stop demanding equality. It would be an unjustifiable demand.

Still, one might cling to the view that the demand for equality among human beings is based on the actual equality of the different races and sexes. Although humans differ as individuals in various ways, there are no differences between the races and sexes *as such*. From the mere fact that a person is black, or a woman, we cannot infer anything else about that person. This, it may be said, is what is wrong with racism and sexism. The white racist claims that whites are superior to blacks, but this is false—although there are differences between individuals, some blacks are superior to some whites in all of the capabilities and abilities that could conceivably be relevant. The opponent of sexism would say the same: A person's sex is no guide to his or her abilities, and this is why it is unjustifiable to discriminate on the basis of sex.

This is a possible line of objection to racial and sexual discrimination. It is not, however, the way that someone really concerned about equality would choose, because taking this line could, in some circumstances, force one to accept a most inegalitarian society. The fact that humans differ as individuals, rather than as races or sexes, is a valid reply to someone who defends a hierarchical society like, say, South Africa, in which all whites are superior in status to all blacks. The existence of individual variations that cut across the lines of race or sex, however, provides us with no defense at all against a more sophisticated opponent of equality, one who proposes that, say, the interests of all those with intelligence quotients below 100 be given less consideration than the interests of those with ratings above 100. Would a hierarchical society of this sort really be so much better than one based on race or sex? I think not. But if we tie the moral principle of equality to the factual equality of the different races or sexes, taken as a whole, our opposition to racism and sexism does not provide us with any basis for objecting to this kind of inegalitarianism.

There is a second important reason why we ought not to base our opposition to racism and sexism on any kind of factual equality, even the limited kind which asserts that variations in capacities and abilities are spread evenly between the different races and sexes: We can have no absolute guarantee that these abilities and capacities really are distributed evenly, without regard to race or sex, among human beings. So far as actual abilities are concerned, there do seem to be certain measurable differences between both races and sexes. These differences do not, of course, appear in each case, but only when averages are taken. More important still, we do not yet know how much of these differences is really due to the different genetic endowments of the various races and sexes, and how much is due to environmental differences that are the result of past and continuing discrimination. Perhaps all of the important differences will eventually prove to be environmental rather than genetic. Anyone opposed to racism and sexism will certainly hope that this will be so, for it will make the task of ending discrimination a lot easier; nevertheless it would be dangerous to rest the case against racism and sexism on the belief that all significant differences are environmental in origin. The opponent of, say, racism who takes this line will be unable to avoid conceding that if differences in ability did after all prove to have some genetic connection with race, racism would in some way be defensible.

It would be folly for the opponent of racism to stake his whole case on a dogmatic commitment to one particular outcome of a difficult scientific issue which is still a long way from being settled. While attempts to prove that differences in certain selected abilities between races and sexes are primarily genetic in origin have certainly not been conclusive, the same must be said of attempts to prove that these differences are largely the result of environment. At this stage of the investigation we cannot be certain which view is correct, however much we may hope it is the latter.

Fortunately, there is no need to pin the case for equality to one particular outcome of this scientific investigation. The appropriate response to those who claim to have found evidence of genetically-based differences in ability between the races or sexes is not to stick to the belief that the genetic explanation must be wrong, whatever evidence to the contrary may turn up: Instead we should make it quite clear that the claim to equality does not depend on intelligence, moral capacity, physical strength, or similar matters of fact. Equality is a moral ideal, not a simple assertion of fact. There is no logically compelling reason for assuming that a factual difference in ability between two people justifies any difference in the amount of consideration we give to satisfying their needs and interests. The principle of the equality of human beings is not a description of an alleged actual equality among humans: It is a prescription of how we should treat humans.

Jeremy Bentham incorporated the essential basis of moral equality into his utilitarian system of ethics in the formula: "Each to count for one and none for more than one." In other words, the interests of every being affected by an action are to be taken into account and given the same weight as the like interests of any other being. A later utilitarian, Henry Sidgwick, put the point in this way: "The good of any one individual is of no more importance, from the point of view (if I may say so) of the Universe, than the good of any other."[1] More recently, the leading figures in contemporary moral philosophy have shown a great deal of agreement

[1]*The Methods of Ethics* (7th Ed.), p. 382.

in specifying as a fundamental presupposition of their moral theories some similar requirement which operates so as to give everyone's interests equal consideration—although they cannot agree on how this requirement is best formulated.[2]

It is an implication of this principle of equality that our concern for others ought not to depend on what they are like, or what abilities they possess—although precisely what this concern requires us to do may vary according to the characteristics of those affected by what we do. It is on this basis that the case against racism and the case against sexism must both ultimately rest; and it is in accordance with this principle that speciesism is also to be condemned. If possessing a higher degree of intelligence does not entitle one human to use another for his own ends, how can it entitle humans to exploit nonhumans?

Many philosophers have proposed the principle of equal consideration of interests, in some form or other, as a basic moral principle; but, as we shall see in more detail shortly, not many of them have recognized that this principle applies to members of other species as well as to our own. Bentham was one of the few who did realize this. In a forward-looking passage, written at a time when black slaves in the British dominions were still being treated much as we now treat nonhuman animals, Bentham wrote:

> The day *may* come when the rest of the animal creation may acquire those rights which never could have been witholden from them but by the hand of tyranny. The French have already discovered that the blackness of the skin is no reason why a human being should be abandoned without redress to the caprice of a tormentor. It may one day come to be recognised that the number of the legs, the villosity of the skin, or the termination of the *os sacrum*, are reasons equally insufficient for abandoning a sensitive being to the same fate. What else is it that should trace the insuperable line? Is it the faculty of reason, or perhaps the faculty of discourse? But a full-grown horse or dog is beyond comparison a more rational, as well as a more conversable animal, than an infant of a day, or a week, or even a month, old. But suppose they were otherwise, what would it avail? The question is not, Can they reason? nor Can they *talk?* but, *Can they suffer?*[3]

In this passage Bentham points to the capacity for suffering as the vital characteristic that gives a being the right to equal consideration. The capacity for suffering—or more strictly, for suffering and/or enjoyment or happiness—is not just another characteristic like the capacity for language, or for higher mathematics. Bentham is not saying that those who try to mark "the insuperable line" that determines whether the interests of a

---

[2]For example, R. M. Hare, *Freedom and Reason* (Oxford, 1963) and J. Rawls, *A Theory of Justice* (Harvard, 1972); for a brief account of the essential agreement on this issue between these and other positions, see R. M. Hare, "Rules of War and Moral Reasoning," *Philosophy and Public Affairs*, vol. I, no. 2 (1972).

[3]*Introduction to the Principles of Morals and Legislation*, Chap. XVII.

being should be considered happen to have selected the wrong characteristic. The capacity for suffering and enjoying things is a prerequisite
for having interests at all, a condition that must be satisfied before we can
speak of interests in any meaningful way. It would be nonsense to say that
it was not in the interests of a stone to be kicked along the road by a school-
boy. A stone does not have interests because it cannot suffer. Nothing that
we can do to it could possibly make any difference to its welfare. A mouse,
on the other hand, does have an interest in not being tormented, because
it will suffer if it is.

If a being suffers, there can be no moral justification for refusing to
take that suffering into consideration. No matter what the nature of the
being, the principle of equality requires that its suffering be counted
equally with the like suffering—in so far as rough comparisons can be
made—of any other being. If a being is not capable of suffering, or of
experiencing enjoyment or happiness, there is nothing to be taken into
account. This is why the limit of sentience (using the term as a convenient,
if not strictly accurate, shorthand for the capacity to suffer or experience
enjoyment or happiness) is the only defensible boundary of concern for
the interests of others. To mark this boundary by some characteristic like
intelligence or rationality would be to mark it in an arbitrary way. Why not
choose some other characteristic, like skin color?

The racist violates the principle of equality by giving greater weight
to the interests of members of his own race, when there is a clash between
their interests and the interests of those of another race. Similarly the
speciesist allows the interests of his own species to override the greater
interests of members of other species.[4] The pattern is the same in each
case. Most human beings are speciesists. I shall now very briefly describe
some of the practices that show this.

For the great majority of human beings, especially in urban, industri-
alized societies, the most direct form of contact with members of other
species is at mealtimes: We eat them. In doing so we treat them purely as
means to our ends. We regard their life and well-being as subordinate to
our taste for a particular kind of dish. I say "taste" deliberately—this is
purely a matter of pleasing our palate. There can be no defense of eating
flesh in terms of satisfying nutritional needs, since it has been established
beyond doubt that we could satisfy our need for protein and other essential nutrients far more efficiently with a diet that replaced animal flesh by
soy beans, or products derived from soy beans, and other high protein
vegetable products.[5]

[4]I owe the term "speciesism" to Dr. Richard Ryder.

[5]In order to produce 1 lb. of protein in the form of beef or veal, we must feed 21 lbs.
of protein to the animal. Other forms of livestock are slightly less inefficient, but the average
ratio in the U.S. is still 1:8. It has been estimated that the amount of protein lost to humans in
this way is equivalent to 90% of the annual world protein deficit. For a brief account, see
Frances Moore Lappe, *Diet for a Small Planet* (Friends of The Earth/Ballantine, New York
1971), pp. 4–11.

It is not merely the act of killing that indicates what we are ready to do to other species in order to gratify our tastes. The suffering we inflict on the animals while they are alive is perhaps an even clearer indication of our speciesism than the fact that we are prepared to kill them.[6] In order to have meat on the table at a price that people can afford, our society tolerates methods of meat production that confine sentient animals in cramped, unsuitable conditions for the entire durations of their lives. Animals are treated like machines that convert fodder into flesh, and any innovation that results in a higher "conversion ratio" is liable to be adopted. As one authority on the subject has said, "cruelty is acknowledged only when profitability ceases."[7] So hens are crowded four or five to a cage with a floor area of twenty inches by eighteen inches, or around the size of a single page of the *New York Times*. The cages have wire floors, since this reduces cleaning costs, though wire is unsuitable for the hens' feet; the floors slope, since this makes the eggs roll down for easy collection, although this makes it difficult for the hens to rest comfortably. In these conditions all the birds' natural instincts are thwarted: They cannot stretch their wings fully, walk freely, dust-bathe, scratch the ground, or build a nest. Although they have never known other conditions, observers have noticed that the birds vainly try to perform these actions. Frustrated at their inability to do so, they often develop what farmers call "vices," and peck each other to death. To prevent this, the beaks of young birds are often cut off.

This kind of treatment is not limited to poultry. Pigs are now also being reared in cages inside sheds. These animals are comparable to dogs in intelligence, and need a varied, stimulating environment if they are not to suffer from stress and boredom. Anyone who kept a dog in the way in which pigs are frequently kept would be liable to prosecution, in England at least, but because our interest in exploiting pigs is greater than our interest in exploiting dogs, we object to cruelty to dogs while consuming the produce of cruelty to pigs. Of the other animals, the condition of veal calves is perhaps worst of all, since these animals are so closely confined that they cannot even turn around or get up and lie down freely. In this way they do not develop unpalatable muscle. They are also made anemic

---

[6] Although one might think that killing a being is obviously the ultimate wrong one can do to it, I think that the infliction of suffering is a clearer indication of speciesism because it might be argued that at least part of what is wrong with killing a human is that most humans are conscious of their existence over time, and have desires and purposes that extend into the future—see, for instance, M. Tooley, "Abortion and Infanticide," *Philosophy and Public Affairs*, vol. 2, no. 1 (1972). Of course, if one took this view one would have to hold—as Tooley does—that killing a human infant or mental defective is not in itself wrong, and is less serious than killing certain higher mammals that probably do have a sense of their own existence over time.

[7] Ruth Harrison, *Animal Machines* (London: Stuart, 1964). This book provides an eye-opening account of intensive farming methods for those unfamiliar with the subject.

and kept short of roughage, to keep their flesh pale, since white veal fetches a higher price; as a result, they develop a craving for iron and roughage, and have been observed to gnaw wood off the sides of their stalls, and lick greedily at any rusty hinge that is within reach.

Since, as I have said, none of these practices cater to anything more than our pleasures of taste, our practice of rearing and killing other animals in order to eat them is a clear instance of the sacrifice of the most important interests of other beings in order to satisfy trivial interests of our own. To avoid speciesism we must stop this practice, and each of us has a moral obligation to cease supporting the practice. Our custom is all the support that the meat industry needs. The decision to cease giving it that support may be difficult, but it is no more difficult than it would have been for a white Southerner to go against the traditions of his society and free his slaves; if we do not change our dietary habits, how can we censure those slaveholders who would not change their own way of living?

The same form of discrimination may be observed in the widespread practice of experimenting on other species in order to see if certain substances are safe for human beings, or to test some psychological theory about the effect of severe punishment on learning, or to try out various new compounds just in case something turns up. People sometimes think that all this experimentation is for vital medical purposes, and so will reduce suffering overall. This comfortable belief is very wide of the mark. Drug companies test new shampoos and cosmetics that they are intending to put on the market by dropping them into the eyes of rabbits, held open by metal clips, in order to observe what damage results. Food additives, like artificial colorings and preservatives, are tested by what is known as the "LD_{50}"—a test designed to find the level of consumption at which 50% of a group of animals will die. In the process, nearly all of the animals are made very sick before some finally die, and others pull through. If the substance is relatively harmless, as it often is, huge doses have to be force-fed to the animals, until in some cases sheer volume or concentration of the substance causes death.

Much of this pointless cruelty goes on in the universities. In many areas of science, nonhuman animals are regarded as an item of laboratory equipment, to be used and expended as desired. In psychology laboratories experimenters devise endless variations and repetitions of experiments that were of little value in the first place. To quote just one example, from the experimenter's own account in a psychology journal: At the University of Pennsylvania, Perrin S. Cohen hung six dogs in hammocks with electrodes taped to their hind feet. Electric shock of varying intensity was then administered through the electrodes. If the dog learned to press its head against a panel on the left, the shock was turned off, but otherwise it remained on indefinitely. Three of the dogs, however, were required to wait periods varying from 2 to 7 seconds while being shocked before making the response that turned off the current. If they failed to wait, they received further shocks. Each dog was given from 26 to 46 "sessions" in the hammock, each session consisting of 80 "trials" or shocks, administered at intervals of one minute. The experimenter reported that the dogs, who were unable to move in the hammock, barked or bobbed their heads when the current was applied. The reported findings of the experiment were that there was a delay in the dogs' responses that increased proportionately to the time the dogs were required to endure the shock, but a gradual increase in the intensity of the shock had no systematic effect in the timing of the response. The experiment was funded by the National Institutes of Health, and the United States Public Health Service.[8]

In this example, and countless cases like it, the possible benefits to mankind are either nonexistent or fantastically remote, while the certain losses to members of other species are very real. This is, again, a clear indication of speciesism.

In the past, argument about vivisection has often missed the point, because it has been put in absolutist terms: Would the abolitionist be prepared to let thousands die if they could be saved by experimenting on a single animal? The way to reply to this purely hypothetical question is to pose another: Would the experimenter be prepared to perform his experiment on an orphaned human infant, if that were the only way to save many lives? (I say "orphan" to avoid the complication of parental feelings, although in doing so I am being overfair to the experimenter, since the nonhuman subjects of experiments are not orphans.) If the experimenter is not prepared to use an orphaned human infant, then his readiness to use nonhumans is simple discrimination, since adult apes, cats, mice and other mammals are more aware of what is happening to them, more self-directing and, so far as we can tell, at least as sensitive to pain, as any human infant. There seems to be no relevant characteristic that human infants possess that adult mammals do not have to the same or a higher degree. (Someone might try to argue that what makes it wrong to experiment on a human infant is that the infant will, in time and if left alone, develop into more than the nonhuman, but one would then, to be consistent, have to oppose abortion, since the fetus has the same potential as the infant—indeed, even contraception and abstinence might be wrong on this ground, since the egg and sperm, considered jointly, also have the same potential. In any case, this argument still gives us no reason for selecting a nonhuman, rather than a human with severe and irreversible brain damage, as the subject for our experiments.)

[8]*Journal of the Experimental Analysis of Behavior*, vol. 13, no. 1 (1970). Any recent volume of this journal, or of other journals in the field, like the *Journal of Comparative and Physiological Psychology*, will contain reports of equally cruel and trivial experiments. For a fuller account, see Richard Ryder, "Experiments on Animals," in *Animals, Men and Morals*.

The experimenter, then, shows a bias in favor of his own species whenever he carries out an experiment on a nonhuman for a purpose that he would not think justified him in using a human being at an equal or lower level of sentience, awareness, or ability to be self-directing. No one familiar with the kind of results yielded by most experiments on animals can have the slightest doubt that if this bias were eliminated the number of experiments performed would be a minute fraction of the number performed today.

Experimenting on animals, and eating their flesh, are perhaps the two major forms of speciesism in our society. By comparison, the third and last form of speciesism is so minor as to be insignificant, but it is perhaps of some special interest to those for whom this paper was written. I am referring to speciesism in contemporary philosophy.

Philosophy ought to question the basic assumptions of the age. Thinking through, critically and carefully, what most people take for granted is, I believe, the chief task of philosophy, and it is this task that makes philosophy a worthwhile activity. Regrettably, philosophy does not always live up to its historic role. Philosophers are human beings and they are subject to all the preconceptions of the society to which they belong. Sometimes they succeed in breaking free of the prevailing ideology; more often they become its most sophisticated defenders. So, in this case, philosophy as practiced in the universities today does not challenge anyone's preconceptions about our relations with other species. By their writings, those philosophers who tackle problems that touch upon the issue reveal that they make the same unquestioned assumptions as most other humans, and what they say tends to confirm the reader in his or her comfortable speciesist habits.

I could illustrate this claim by referring to the writings of philosophers in various fields—for instance, the attempts that have been made by those interested in rights to draw the boundary of the sphere of rights so that it runs parallel to the biological boundaries of the species *homo sapiens*, including infants and even mental defectives, but excluding those other beings of equal or greater capacity who are so useful to us at mealtimes and in our laboratories. I think it would be a more appropriate conclusion to this paper, however, if I concentrated on the problem with which we have been centrally concerned, the problem of equality.

It is significant that the problem of equality, in moral and political philosophy, is invariably formulated in terms of human equality. The effect of this is that the question of the equality of other animals does not confront the philosopher, or student, as an issue in itself—and this is already an indication of the failure of philosophy to challenge accepted beliefs. Still, philosophers have found it difficult to discuss the issue of human equality without raising, in a paragraph or two, the question of the status of other animals. The reason for this, which should be apparent from what I have said already, is that if humans are to be regarded as equal to one another, we need some sense of "equal" that does not require any actual, descriptive equality of capacities, talents or other qualities. If equality is to be related to any actual characteristics of humans, these characteristics must be some lowest common denominator, pitched so low that no human lacks them—but then the philosopher comes up against the catch that any such set of characteristics which covers *all* humans will not be possessed *only* by humans. In other words, it turns out that in the only sense in which we can truly say, as an assertion of fact, that all humans are equal, at least some members of other species are also equal—equal, that is, to each other and to humans. If, on the other hand, we regard the statement "All humans are equal" in some nonfactual way, perhaps as a prescription, then, as I have already argued, it is even more difficult to exclude nonhumans from the sphere of equality.

This result is not what the egalitarian philosopher originally intended to assert. Instead of accepting the radical outcome to which their own reasonings naturally point, however, most philosophers try to reconcile their beliefs in human equality and animal inequality by arguments that can only be described as devious.

As a first example, I take William Frankena's well-known article "The Concept of Social Justice".[9] Frankena opposes the idea of basing justice on merit, because he sees that this could lead to highly inegalitarian results. Instead he proposes the principle that:

> ... all men are to be treated as equals, not because they are equal, in any respect but simply because they are human. They are human because they have emotions and desires, and are able to think, and hence are capable of enjoying a good life in a sense in which other animals are not.

But what is this capacity to enjoy the good life which all humans have, but no other animals? Other animals have emotions and desires, and appear to be capable of enjoying a good life. We may doubt that they can think—although the behavior of some apes, dolphins, and even dogs suggests that some of them can—but what is the relevance of thinking? Frankena goes on to admit that by "the good life" he means "not so much the morally good life as the happy or satisfactory life", so thought would appear to be unnecessary for enjoying the good life; in fact to emphasize the need for thought would make difficulties for the egalitarian since only some people are capable of leading intellectually satisfying lives, or morally good lives. This makes it difficult to see what Frankena's principle of equality has to do with simply being *human*. Surely every sentient being

[9]In R. Brandt (ed.), *Social Justice* (Englewood Cliffs, N.J.: Prentice-Hall, 1962); the passage quoted appears on p. 19.

is capable of leading a life that is happier or less miserable than some alternative life, and hence has a claim to be taken into account. In this respect the distinction between humans and nonhumans is not a sharp division, but rather a continuum along which we move gradually, and with overlaps between the species, from simple capacities for enjoyment and satisfaction, or pain and suffering, to more complex ones.

Faced with a situation in which they see a need for some basis for the moral gulf that is commonly thought to separate humans and animals, but can find no concrete difference that will do the job without undermining the equality of humans, philosophers tend to waffle. They resort to high-sounding phrases like "the intrinsic dignity of the human individual";[10] they talk of the "intrinsic worth of all men" as if men (humans?) had some worth that other beings did not,[11] or they say that humans, and only humans, are "ends in themselves", while "everything other than a person can only have value for a person."[12]

This idea of a distinctive human dignity and worth has a long history; it can be traced back directly to the Renaissance humanists, for instance to Pico della Mirandola's *Oration on the Dignity of Man*. Pico and other humanists based their estimate of human dignity on the idea that man possessed the central, pivotal position in the "Great Chain of Being" that led from the lowliest form of matter to God Himself; this view of the universe, in turn, goes back to both classical and Judeo-Christian doctrines. Contemporary philosophers have cast off these metaphysical and religous shackles and freely invoke the dignity of mankind without needing to justify the idea at all. Why should we not attribute "intrinsic dignity" or "intrinsic worth" to ourselves? Fellow humans are unlikely to reject the accolades we so generously bestow on them, and those to whom we deny the honor are unable to object. Indeed, when one thinks only of humans, it can be very liberal, very progressive, to talk of the dignity of all human beings. In so doing, we implicitly condemn slavery, racism, and other violations of human rights. We admit that we ourselves are in some fundamental sense on a par with the poorest, most ignorant members of our own species. It is only when we think of humans as no more than a small subgroup of all the beings that inhabit our planet that we may realize that in elevating our own species we are at the same time lowering the relative status of all other species.

The truth is that the appeal to the intrinsic dignity of human beings appears to solve the egalitarian's problems only as long as it goes unchallenged. Once we ask *why* it should be that all humans—including infants,

---

[10]Frankena, p. 23.

[11]H. A. Bedau, "Egalitarianism and the Idea of Equality," in *Nomos IX: Equality*, ed. J. R. Pennock and J. W. Chapman (New York: Lieber-Atherton, 1967).

[12]G. Vlastos, "Justice and Equality," in Brandt, *Social Justice*, p. 48.

mental defectives, psychopaths, Hitler, Stalin and the rest—have some kind of dignity or worth that no elephant, pig or chimpanzee can ever achieve, we see that this question is as difficult to answer as our original request for some relevant fact that justifies the inequality of humans and other animals. In fact, these two questions are really one: Talk of intrinsic dignity or moral worth only takes the problem back one step, because any satisfactory defense of the claim that all and only humans have intrinsic dignity would need to refer to some relevant capacities or characteristics that all and only humans possess. Philosophers frequently introduce ideas of dignity, respect and worth at the point at which other reasons appear to be lacking, but this is hardly good enough. Fine phrases are the last resource of those who have run out of arguments.

In case there are those who still think it may be possible to find some relevant characteristic that distinguishes all humans from all members of other species, I shall refer again, before I conclude, to the existence of some humans who quite clearly are below the level of awareness, self-consciousness, intelligence, and sentience, of many nonhumans. I am thinking of humans with severe and irreparable brain damage, and also of infant humans. To avoid the complication of the relevance of a being's potential, however, I shall henceforth concentrate on permanently retarded human beings.

Philosophers who set out to find a characteristic that will distinguish humans from other animals rarely take the course of abandoning these groups of humans by lumping them in with the other animals. It is easy to see why they do not. To take this line without rethinking our attitudes to other animals would entail that we have the right to perform painful experiments on retarded humans for trivial reasons; similarly it would follow that we had the right to rear and kill these humans for food. To most philosophers these consequences are as unacceptable as the view that we should stop treating nonhumans in this way.

Of course, when discussing the problem of equality it is possible to ignore the problem of mental defectives, or brush it aside as if somehow insignificant.[13] This is the easiest way out. What else remains? My final example of speciesism in contemporary philosophy has been selected to show what happens when a writer is prepared to face the question of human equality and animal inequality without ignoring the existence of mental defectives, and without resorting to obscurantist mumbo-jumbo. Stanley Benn's clear and honest article "Egalitarianism and Equal Consideration of Interests"[14] fits this description.

Benn, after noting the usual "evident human inequalities" argues,

---

[13]E.g. Bernard Williams, "The Idea of Equality," in *Philosophy, Politics and Society* (second series), eds. P. Laslett and W. Runciman (Blackwell, Oxford, 1962), p. 118; J. Rawls, *A Theory of Justice*, pp. 509–10.

[14]*Nomos IX: Equality*; the passages quoted are on pp. 62ff.

correctly I think, for equality of consideration as the only possible basis for egalitarianism. Yet Benn, like other writers, is thinking only of "equal consideration of human interests." Benn is quite open in his defence of this restriction of equal considerations:

> ... not to possess human shape *is* a disqualifying condition. However faithful or intelligent a dog may be, it would be a monstrous sentimentality to attribute to him interests that could be weighed in an equal balance with those of human beings ... if, for instance, one had to decide between feeding a hungry baby or a hungry dog, anyone who chose the dog would generally be reckoned morally defective, unable to recognize a fundamental inequality of claims.
>
> This is what distinguishes our attitude to animals from our attitude to imbeciles. It would be odd to say that we ought to respect equally the dignity or personality of the imbecile and of the rational man ... but there is nothing odd about saying that we should respect their interests equally, that is, that we should give to the interests of each the same serious consideration as claims to considerations necessary for some standard of well-being that we can recognize and endorse.

Benn's statement of the basis of the consideration we should have for imbeciles seems to me correct, but why should there be any fundamental inequality of claims between a dog and a human imbecile? Benn sees that if equal consideration depended on rationality, no reason could be given against using imbeciles for research purposes, as we now use dogs and guinea pigs. This will not do: "But of course we do distinguish imbeciles from animals in this regard," he says. That the common distinction is justifiable is something Benn does not question; his problem is how it is to be justified. The answer he gives is this:

> ... we respect the interests of men and give them priority over dogs not *insofar* as they are rational, but because rationality is the human norm. We say it is *unfair* to exploit the deficiencies of the imbecile who falls short of the norm, just as it would be unfair and not just ordinarily dishonest, to steal from a blind man. If we do not think in this way about dogs, it is because we do not see the irrationality of the dog as a deficiency or a handicap, but as normal for the species. The characteristics, therefore, that distinguish the normal man from the normal dog make it intelligible for us to talk of other men having interests and capacities, and therefore claims, of precisely the same kind as we make on our own behalf. But although these characteristics may provide the point of the distinction between men and other species, they are not in fact the qualifying conditions for membership, or the distinguishing criteria of the class of morally considerable persons; and this is precisely because a man does not become a member of a different species, with its own standards of normality, by reason of not possessing these characteristics.

The final sentence of this passage gives the argument away. An imbecile, Benn concedes, may have no characteristics superior to those of a dog; nevertheless this does not make the imbecile a member of "a different species" as the dog is. *Therefore* it would be "unfair" to use the imbecile for medical research as we use the dog. But why? That the imbecile is not rational is just the way things have worked out, and the same is true of the dog—neither is any more responsible for their mental level. If it is unfair to take advantage of an isolated defect, why is it fair to take advantage of a more general limitation? I find it hard to see anything in this argument except a defence of preferring the interests of members of our own species because they are members of our own species. To those who think there might be more to it, I suggest the following mental exercise. Assume that it has been proven that there is a difference in the average, or normal, intelligence quotient for two different races, say whites and blacks. Then substitute the term "white" for every occurrence of "men" and "black" for every occurrence of "dog" in the passage quoted, and substitute "high IQ" for "rationality" and when Benn talks of "imbeciles" replace this term by "dumb whites"—that is, whites who fall well below the normal white IQ score. Finally, change "species" to "race." Now reread the passage. It has become a defence of a rigid, no-exceptions division between whites and blacks, based on IQ scores, *notwithstanding an admitted overlap* between whites and blacks in this respect. The revised passage is, of course, outrageous, and this is not only because we have made fictitious assumptions in our substitutions. The point is that in the original passage Benn was defending a rigid division in the amount of consideration due to members of different species, despite admitted cases of overlap. If the original did not, at first reading, strike us as being as outrageous as the revised version does, this is largely because although we are not racists ourselves, most of us are speciesists. Like the other authors' articles, Benn's stands as a warning of the ease with which the best minds can fall victim to a prevailing ideology.

The Case Against Animals

R.G. Frey

WHAT HAS SENTIENCY TO DO WITH THE POSSESSION OF RIGHTS?

Can at least some moral rights be extended from human beings to animals? Plainly, this question presupposes that human beings *have* moral rights, and on a different occasion I should try to show—what many utilitarians and others have long argued—that a powerful case can be brought

This essay is a compilation of two articles by R.G. Frey. The first, "The Case Against Animals," appeared in *Animal Rights: A Symposium*, eds. David Paterson and Richard D. Ryder (London: Centaur Press, 1979); the second, "Animal Rights," appeared in *Analysis* 37 (June 1977), 186–89. Permission for reprinting has been given by the publishers (Centaur and Basil Blackwell) and by the author and the Royal Society for the Prevention of Cruelty to Animals.

I am grateful to the editor and to my colleagues H.M. Robinson and P. Helm for comments and suggestions.

against the truth of this presupposition. Perhaps this case could be made to collapse; but the history of ethics teaches us that it is by no means an easy thing to show that human beings do have moral rights, and I know of no argument to this effect that commands general assent among philosophers. If human beings do not have moral rights, then the question of their extension from humans to animals simply does not arise; there is, so to speak, nothing to extend. And if there is nothing to extend, then arguments for animals' rights which turn upon such an extension are accordingly vitiated.

On this occasion, however, I want to turn to one of the means by which it is thought the extension in question can be carried out, namely, sentiency. If human beings have (certain) moral rights because they are sentient, then many animals, because they, too, are sentient, also possess (these) moral rights. So runs the extension, and it represents a powerful current in much recent thinking on the subject of animal rights. I am myself, however, inclined to think that sentiency has nothing to do with who does and who does not have rights, so that I obviously am at odds with a good many animal rightists, for whom sentiency is, if not the guarantor of, then at least the main hope for the inclusion of animals within the class of right-holders. This whole matter, of course, is a very complex one, and time allows for only a few general remarks at best; so I shall confine myself to bringing out and briefly enlarging upon a little-discussed assumption—an assumption about what has value—which seems to me to lie at the very basis of a sentiency criterion for the possession of rights.

The term "sentient" means "having the power of sense-perception", and nearly all animal rightists go on to include under the term the "capacity to experience pain."[1] We must not, however, get things in reverse: the higher animals are not sentient because they can have experiences of pain; rather, they can have experiences of pain because they are sentient proper, i.e., because they have the power of sense-perception. No creature which lacks the power of sense-perception can experience pain; indeed, in the appropriate sense, it cannot have experiences at all. Since almost no one today denies that at least the higher animals can, because they are sentient-proper, experience pain, it follows on this usage that they are sentient; and if we presume the truth of a sentiency criterion for the possession of rights, it follows that they have rights.

To this basic account of sentiency, one or two animal rightists want to make the odd addition. Joel Feinberg, for example, wants to include under the term "sentience" the various elements which make up a conative life, such as wishes and desires, which he thinks the higher animals have.[2]

[1]See, for example, Andrew Linzey, *Animal Rights* (London: S.C.M. Press, 1976), chap. 3.

[2]Joel Feinberg, "The Rights of Animals and Unborn Generations," in *Philosophy and Environmental Crisis*, ed. William T. Blackstone (Athens, Ga.: University of Georgia Press, 1974), pp. 49–51.

Now I think what is common to all of these items included under the term "sentience"—to sense-perceptions, pains and the elements of a conative life—is, roughly speaking, that they either are or presuppose experiences, and experiences, clearly, are phenomena that are *had* by creatures. Creatures which have or can have experiences are sentient and are generally labelled "beings"; creatures which cannot have experiences are not sentient and are not generally labelled "beings" but "things." Notice two points. First, a being is not sentient because it has or can have this or that *kind* of experiences—as if having experiences of this or that kind *constituted* sentiency—but rather because it has or can have experiences *per se.*[3] Second, the question of whether a being who has or can have experiences *prefers* some kinds of experiences to others, e.g. pleasurable to painful ones, is a secondary affair; for only if the creature has or can have experiences in the first place do questions of its preferring some kinds of experiences to others arise.[4] On the sentiency criterion, then, I think it is ultimately the fact that human beings and the higher animals have experiences which is used to distinguish them from everything else and is the fundamental basis of the claim that they are the possessors of moral rights. Thus, it is because rivers do not and/or cannot have experiences, not because they do not and/or cannot have experiences of a particular kind and because they do not and/or cannot prefer one kind of experiences to another, that they are not sentient beings. And, lacking sentiency, rivers have no rights.

It is ironic that this result of the application of a sentiency criterion, in part in order to combat speciesism, is itself blatantly speciesist in character. For, to put the matter rather pompously, it condemns the whole of non-sentient creation, including the lower animals, at best to a much inferior moral status or, as we shall see, at worst possibly to a status completely beyond the moral pale. In essence, non-sentient creation is "simply there" for sentient creation to do with as it sees fit. Animal rightists have objected to the Christian view of man as having dominion over the rest of creation;[5] but the only revolution they effect by means of a sentiency criterion is to give man and the higher animals dominion over the rest of creation. The criterion, then, does not eliminate speciesism; on the contrary, it broadens the category of those who can practise it, or, in the case of the higher

---

[3]My point here may be put in the form of an example. Suppose an operation were performed on a rabbit as a result of which, *ex hypothesi*, though the rabbit could no longer feel pleasure and pain, its other experiences remained unaffected: would not the rabbit nevertheless remain a sentient being? For it still eats, sleeps, hops about, etc.

[4]I disagree, therefore, with Mary Anne Warren's account of sentiency in this respect; see her article "Do Potential People have Moral Rights?" *Canadian Journal of Philosophy* **7** (1977), 283–286.

[5]See, for example, Peter Singer, *Animal Liberation* (London: Jonathan Cape, 1976), chap. 5; and Linzey, chap. 2.

animals, who can have it practised on their behalf. If one is going to complain about speciesism in the first place, why go on to practise it by means of a sentiency criterion?

But the matter goes deeper than this. For, lacking sentiency, the things which make up non-sentient creation lack not only moral rights but also what I shall call moral standing.[6] By this, I mean that, in the absence of sentiency, they are not themselves the bearers or repositories of value in their own right; they have, in other words, no value in themselves. Feinberg, for example, is emphatic about this:

> A mere thing, however valuable to others, has no good of its own. The explanation of that fact, I suspect, consists in the fact that mere things have no conative life.... Interests must be compounded somehow out of conations; hence mere things have no interests. *A fortiori*, they have no interests to be protected by legal or moral rules. Without interests a creature can have no "good" of its own, the achievement of which can be its due. Mere things are not *loci* of value in their own right, but rather their value consists entirely in their being objects of other beings' interests.[7]

Non-sentient creation, in short, lacks even moral standing, since the things which comprise it lack a good of their own and are not *loci* of value in their own right. Sentient creation, therefore, is favoured, and whatever value non-sentient creation has lies in its usefulness or instrumental value to sentient creation, a speciesist but convenient conclusion, in view of the havoc we wreak upon non-sentient creation.

Now if the beings which comprise sentient creation are *loci* of value in their own right, then what is it about these beings that makes them *loci* of value? Clearly, on the sentiency criterion, it is their allegedly distinguishing feature, viz., their sentiency, their conative lives. And what is it that underlies and is presupposed by their sentiency, their conative lives? It is, as I have remarked, the having of experiences. Accordingly, if I am right, what appears to be at the very basis of a sentiency criterion, in the sense that this is what at bottom it involves, is the view that having experiences is valuable in its own right. It is just because the things which comprise non-sentient creation do not and/or cannot have experiences that they are not *loci* of value in their own right and are beyond the moral pale, whereas it is just because the beings which comprise sentient creation do and/or can have experiences that they have moral standing and so are in a position to possess moral rights.

---

[6]I coin this phrase as the moral analogue to the legal notion of "legal standing," but all I mean is that it is "possessed of value in itself" in this context.

[7]Feinberg, p. 50. Feinberg's position here is this: mere things are not *loci* of value in their own right because they lack interests, and they lack interests because they lack a conative life, which, as we saw earlier, Feinberg includes under "sentience"; ultimately, then, it is because mere things lack sentiency that they have no "good" of their own and are not *loci* of value in their own right.

What, then, is the support for the view that having experiences is valuable in its own right? The fact is that I have been able to find none in the writings of animal rightists;[8] the truth is, I think, that they *implicitly* assume that having experiences is valuable in its own right. Indeed, I think they have to assume this; for unless one argues or assumes that having experiences is valuable in its own right and suffices to confer moral standing upon creatures who have or are capable of having experiences, what reason has one for thinking that sentiency is a criterion for the possession of *moral* rights at all? Put differently, why are stones (a) not *loci* of value in their own right and (b) completely lacking in moral rights? It makes no sense to say, e.g., that it is because they lack this or that kind of experiences; for the whole point of stones, rivers, valleys, etc., is that they lack any and all kinds of experiences whatever. They are not sentient because they lack this or that kind of experience but rather because they lack experiences altogether; and it is this fact, I am suggesting, which on a sentiency criterion places them beyond the moral pale, that is, beyond the realm of those things, as Feinberg would have it, which have a good the achievement of which can be their due.

Thus, if I am correct, then the implicit assumption that having experiences is valuable in its own right lies at the very basis of a sentiency criterion and is used to confer moral standing and moral rights upon one part of creation and to refuse them to another. Quite simply, an assumption of this magnitude and importance requires argument in its support: it is by no means obviously true, nor can I see any immediate reason to give way in the face of it. For if asked to name those things one regarded as intrinsically valuable, I think many would reply that, *if anything* is intrinsically valuable (in order by this formulation to leave open the possibility that nothing is), then such things as deep and lasting friendship in the fullest of senses and the development of one's talents are. What I strongly suspect is that virtually no one would cite having experiences per se as among the class of the intrinsically valuable.

ANIMAL RIGHTS

[Another argument] consists in using the cases of babies and the severely mentally-enfeebled to force the inclusion of animals within the class of right-holders. Those who use the argument proceed this way: they first cite the many and various criteria by which philosophers and others have tried to show why human beings possess rights but animals do not, and then claim of each and every one of these criteria that it would exclude babies and the severely mentally-enfeebled as right-holders; since we all agree that babies and the severely mentally-enfeebled do have

---

[8]This is not surprising, of course, once one comes to realize the status of the view as an *implicit* assumption, as I go on to note.

rights, each and every one of the criteria must be rejected as a criterion for the possession of rights. The form of the argument, then, is as follows:

1. Each and every criterion for the possession of rights that excludes animals from the class of right-holders also excludes babies and the severely mentally-enfeebled from the class of right-holders;
2. Babies and the severely mentally-enfeebled, however, do have rights and so fall within the class of right-holders;
3. Therefore, each and every one of these animal-excluding criteria must be rejected as a criterion for the possession of rights.

Obviously, this argument is essentially negative and indirect, in that it does not aim so much to establish directly the positive thesis that animals have rights as to establish the negative thesis that animal-excluding criteria for the possession of rights will not do, since they exclude as well babies and the severely mentally-enfeebled. (Of course, the implication of the negative thesis is that, if we go on to adopt a criterion for the possession of rights that *includes* babies and the severely mentally-enfeebled within the class of right-holders, then it will include animals within the class of right-holders.) Thus, for example, rationality as a criterion must be discarded, for otherwise we obtain a singularly objectionable result:

> If we accord moral rights on the basis of rationality, what of the status of newly born children, "low grade" mental patients, "intellectual cabbages" and so on? Logically, accepting this criterion, they must have no, or diminished, moral rights.[9]

Instances of this argument abound, and by means of it possession of rationality or of a language, the recognition and discharge of moral obligations, the possession of a culture, the acceptance of and participation within societal and communal relationships, the possession of interests (where this connotes that something S is in one's interest, that one cares or exhibits concern about S, and perhaps that one is prepared to do something about and even to think that one ought to do something about S), etc., are all rejected as criteria for the possession of rights.

I want to suggest that the present argument does not work. It hinges upon premise (2), that is, upon treating the cases of babies and the severely mentally-enfeebled as open and shut so far as the possession of rights is concerned. Premise (2), however, is not obvious and requires defence; but the best defences of it, *if they stand at all*, specifically exclude animals from the class of right-holders. Therefore, either premise (2) cannot be defended or else premise (1)—that every animal-excluding criterion for the possession of rights also excludes babies and the severely mentally-enfeebled—is false; either way, this important argument for animal rights fails.

[9]Linzey, p. 24.

Is it so very clear that babies and the severely mentally-enfeebled do have rights—do have rights, that is, without the addition of *further arguments* which themselves exclude animals as right-holders?

For example, consider again the rationality requirement:

Only beings which are rational possess rights.

Given a suitably restrictive analysis of rationality, babies and the severely mentally-enfeebled will be excluded from the class of rational beings and so from the class of right-holders; on this requirement, they simply have no rights. Since, upon the same analysis of rationality, animals also are not rational, it follows that they have no rights either.

Now there are three arguments by which one might try to include babies and the severely mentally-enfeebled within the class of right-holders and so to defend premise (2); each in turn, however, specifically excludes Fido from this class.

(1) One might try to include the baby by means of the *potentiality argument*: the baby is potentially rational. Of course, the baby is not at present rational, and if actual rationality is insisted upon, then the baby has no rights. On the other hand, the potentiality argument does separate the case of the baby from that of Fido, who is not conceded even potential rationality.

(2) One might try to include the severely mentally-enfeebled by means of the *similarity argument*: in all other respects except rationality and perhaps certain mental accomplishments, the severely mentally-enfeebled betray strong similarities to other members of our species, and it would and does offend our species horribly to deprive such similar creatures of rights. If this argument is rejected, on the ground that rationality is the requirement for possessing rights and other similarities are beside the point, then the severely mentally-enfeebled do not have rights. On the other hand, the similarity argument does separate the severely mentally-enfeebled from Fido, who does not bear anything like (even) sufficient physical similarities to ourselves to warrant similar inclusion.

Animal liberationists, of course, will also object to the similarity argument on the ground that it smacks strongly of speciesism. For it does enshrine, if not advocate, active discrimination against other species in favour of our own.

(3) One might try to include both babies and the severely mentally-enfeebled by means of the *religious argument*: babies and the severely mentally-enfeebled possess immortal souls. If this argument is rejected, on the ground that, even if they possess immortal souls, beings must also possess rationality in order to have rights, or on the ground that there is no good evidence for the existence of such souls, then neither babies nor the severely mentally-enfeebled possess rights. On the other hand, the religious argument does separate both from Fido, who is not conceded an immortal soul by the argument's proponents.

The upshot is this. Unless one of these three arguments is accepted, we have no basis upon which to differentiate the cases of babies and the severely mentally-enfeebled from that of animals; and if all three of the arguments *are rejected*, and there are serious objections to each, then it follows on the requirement under consideration that babies, the severely mentally-enfeebled and animals are alike in not being right-holders. In other words, the best defences of premise (2) collapse, with the result that the premise cannot sustain the weight put upon it. If, however, one of these three arguments *is accepted*, so that babies and the severely mentally-enfeebled are held to fall within the class of right-holders, then we find that that argument itself specifically *excludes* animals from the class of right-holders. In other words, premise (1) is false, since not every animal-excluding criterion for the possession of rights excludes babies and the severely mentally-enfeebled.

For these reasons, then, I conclude that either premise (2) cannot be defended or else premise (1) is simply false, so that, in either case, this most important argument in behalf of animal rights fails.

SELECTED SUPPLEMENTARY READINGS

BEAUCHAMP, TOM L., AND LEROY WALTERS, eds., *Contemporary Issues in Bioethics* (2nd ed.). Belmont, Calif.: Wadsworth, 1982, chap. 12.

BECKER, EARNEST, "Toward the Merger of Animal and Human Studies," *Philosophy of the Social Sciences* **4** (June-September 1974).

CLARK, STEPHEN R. L., "Animal Wrongs," *Analysis* **38** (June 1978).

———, "the Rights of Wild Things," *Inquiry* **22** (1979).

FEINBERG, JOEL, "The Rights of Animals and Unborn Generations," in *Philosophy and Environmental Crisis*, ed. William Blackstone. Athens, Ga.: University of Georgia Press, 1974.

———, "Human Duties and Animal Rights," in *On the Fifth Day*, eds. R.K. Morris and M.W. Fox. Washington, D.C.: Acropolis Press, 1978.

FOX, MICHAEL, " 'Animal Liberation': A Critique," *Ethics* **88** (January 1978).

———, "Animal Suffering and Rights," *Ethics* **88** (January 1978).

FREY, R.G., "Animal Rights," *Analysis* **37** (June 1977).

———, "Interests and Animal Rights," *Philosophical Quarterly* **27** (July 1977).

———, *Interests and Rights: The Case Against Animals*. Oxford, England: Clarendon Press, 1980.

GRENE, MARJORIE, "People and Other Animals," *Philosophical Forum* **3** (Winter 1972).

Inquiry **22** (Summer 1979). Special issue on animals.

JAMIESON, DALE, AND TOM REGAN, "Animal Rights: A Reply to Frey," *Analysis* **38** (January 1978).

LEVIN, MICHAEL, "Animal Rights Evaluated," *Humanist* **37** (July-August 1977).

LOCKWOOD, MICHAEL, "Singer on Killing and the Preference for Life," *Inquiry* **22** (1979).

MCCLOSKEY, H.J., "Moral Rights and Animals," *Inquiry* **22** (1978).

MARGOLIS, JOSEPH, "Animals Have No Rights and are not the Equal of Humans," *Philosophic Exchange* **1** (Summer 1974).

MIDGLEY, MARY, *Beast and Man*. Ithaca, N.Y.: Cornell University Press, 1979.

MORRIS, RICHARD KNOWLES, AND MICHAEL W. FOX, eds., *On the Fifth Day: Animal Rights and Human Ethics.* Washington, D.C.: Acropolis Press, 1978.

NARVESON, JAN, "Animal Rights," *Canadian Journal of Philosophy* **7** (March 1977).

NELSON, LEONARD, "Duties to Animals," in his *System of Ethics.* New Haven, Conn.: Yale University Press, 1956.

PASSMORE, JOHN, "The Treatment of Animals," *Journal of the History of Ideas* **36** (April-June 1975).

PATERSON, D.A., AND RICHARD RYDER, eds., *Animal Rights: A Symposium.* London: Centaur Press, 1979.

REGAN, TOM, "The Moral Basis of Vegetarianism," *Canadian Journal of Philosophy* **5** (1975).

———, "McCloskey on Why Animals Cannot Have Rights," *Philosophical Quarterly* **26** (July 1976).

———, "Feinberg on What Sorts of Beings Can Have Rights," *Southern Journal of Philosophy* (Winter 1976).

———, "Narveson on Egoism and the Rights of Animals," *Canadian Journal of Philosophy* **7** (March 1977).

———, "Frey on Interests and Animal Rights," *Philosophical Quarterly* **27** (October 1977).

———, "Fox's Critique of Animal Liberation," *Ethics* **88** (January 1978).

———, "An Examination and Defense of One Argument Concerning Animal Rights," *Inquiry* **22** (1979).

———, "Utilitarianism, Vegetarianism, and Animal Rights," *Philosophy and Public Affairs* **9** (1980).

REGAN, TOM, AND PETER SINGER, eds., *Animal Rights and Human Obligations.* Englewood Cliffs, N.J.: Prentice-Hall, 1976.

RYDER, RICHARD, *Victims of Science.* London: Davis-Poynter, 1975.

SINGER, PETER, "Animal Liberation," *New York Review of Books* **20** (April 5, 1973). [A review of *Animals, Men, and Morals*, eds. Godlovitch and Harris. New York: Grove Press, 1973].

———, "All Animals Are Equal," *Philosophic Exchange* **1** (Summer 1974).

———, *Animal Liberation.* New York: Random House, 1975.

———, "A Reply to Professor Levin's 'Animal Rights Evaluated'," *The Humanist* **37** (July-August 1977).

———, "The Fable of the Fox and the Unliberated Animals," *Ethics* **88** (January 1978).

———, "Animals and the Value of Life," in *Matters of Life and Death*, ed. Tom Regan. New York: Random House, 1980.

———, *Practical Ethics.* New York: Cambridge University Press, 1979.

———, "Utilitarianism and Vegetarianism," *Philosophy and Public Affairs* **9** (1980).

SPRIGGE, T.L.S., "Metaphysics, Physicalism, and Animal Rights," *Inquiry* **22** (1979).

STEINBOCK, BONNIE, "Speciesism and the Idea of Equality," *Philosophy* **53** (April 1978).

SUMNER, L.W., "A Matter of Life and Death," *Nous* (May 1976).

WATSON, RICHARD A., "Self-Consciousness and the Rights of Non-Human Animals and Nature," *Environmental Ethics* **1** (Summer 1979).

Encyclopedia Of Bioethics
Articles

Animal Experimentation: Historical Aspects, Richard D. French
Animal Experimentation: Philosophical Perspective, Peter Singer
Biomedical Research, Robert J. Levine